The Lion at Dawn

CAMPAIGNS & COMMANDERS

GREGORY J. W. URWIN, SERIES EDITOR

CAMPAIGNS AND COMMANDERS

GENERAL EDITOR

Gregory J. W. Urwin, *Temple University, Philadelphia, Pennsylvania*

ADVISORY BOARD

Lawrence E. Babits, *Greenville, North Carolina*
James C. Bradford, *Texas A&M University, College Station*
David M. Glantz, *Carlisle, Pennsylvania*
Jerome A. Greene, *Denver, Colorado*
Victor Davis Hanson, *Hoover Institution of Stanford University, Stanford*
Herman Hattaway, *Leawood, Kansas*
J. A. Houlding, *Rückersdorf, Germany*
Eugenia C. Kiesling, *U.S. Military Academy, West Point, New York*
Timothy K. Nenninger, *National Archives, Washington, D.C.*
Frederick C. Schneid, *High Point University*
Timothy J. Stapleton, *University of Calgary*

The Lion at Dawn

Forging British Strategy in the Age
of the French Revolution, 1783–1797

Nathaniel Jarrett

University of Oklahoma Press : Norman

This book is published with the generous assistance of the McCasland Foundation, Duncan, Oklahoma.

Library of Congress Cataloging-in-Publication Data

Names: Jarrett, Nathaniel, author.
Title: The lion at dawn : forging British strategy in the age of the French Revolution, 1783–1797 / Nathaniel Jarrett.
Description: Norman : University of Oklahoma Press, [2022] | Series: C&C = Campaigns and commanders | Includes bibliographical references and index. | Summary: "How Prime Minister William Pitt the Younger and his ministers forged British diplomatic and military strategy through the tumultuous years of war and rivalry from 1783 to 1797, shedding new light on the emergence of modern Britain, its empire, and early efforts to create a stable and peaceful international system"—Provided by publisher.
Identifiers: LCCN 2022015088 | ISBN 978-0-8061-9071-6 (hardcover) ISBN 978-0-8061-9392-2 (paper)
Subjects: LCSH: Pitt, William, 1759–1806. | National security—Great Britain. | Great Britain—Foreign relations—1760–1820. | Great Britain—Military policy. | Great Britain—History, Military—18th century. | Great Britain—Politics and government—1760–1820. | France—History—Revolution, 1789–1799—Foreign public opinion, British. | BISAC: HISTORY / Wars & Conflicts / Napoleonic Wars | HISTORY / Modern / 18th Century
Classification: LCC DA505 .J37 2022 | DDC 941.07/3—dc23/eng/20220610
LC record available at https://lccn.loc.gov/2022015088

The Lion at Dawn: Forging British Strategy in the Age of the French Revolution, 1783–1797 is Volume 75 in the Campaigns and Commanders series.

The paper in this book meets the guidelines for permanence and durability of the Committee on Production Guidelines for Book Longevity of the Council on Library Resources, Inc. ∞

Copyright © 2022 by the University of Oklahoma Press, Norman, Publishing Division of the University. Paperback published 2024. Manufactured in the U.S.A.

All rights reserved. No part of this publication may be reproduced, stored in a retrieval system, or transmitted, in any form or by any means, electronic, mechanical, photocopying, recording, or otherwise—except as permitted under Section 107 or 108 of the United States Copyright Act—without the prior written permission of the University of Oklahoma Press. To request permission to reproduce selections from this book, write to Permissions, University of Oklahoma Press, 2800 Venture Drive, Norman OK 73069, or email rights.oupress@ou.edu.

In loving memory of Jewell E. Jarrett

Contents

List of Maps	ix
Acknowledgments	xi
Introduction	1
1. Britain's Return to Europe, 1783–1787	13
2. The Triple Alliance, 1788–1790	37
3. Overreach at Ochakov, 1791	60
4. Principled Neutrality and Political Recovery, 1792	74
5. Between Revolution and Partition, 1793	92
6. Counterrevolution and Collective Security, 1793	120
7. The Prussian Bond, 1794	136
8. Division and Defeat, 1794	162
9. The Peace of Basel and the New Triple Alliance, 1795	191
10. War and Peace, 1796–1797	213
Conclusion: Successors and Success, 1798–1815	238
Abbreviations	251
Notes	253
Bibliography	301
Index	315

Maps

The Dutch Crisis, 1787	35
The Hertzberg Plan, 1788	55
British plans for 1793	101
Operations of 1793	116
British plans for 1794	146
Operations of 1794	159
British plans for 1795	203
Operations of 1795	207

Acknowledgments

My wonderful family naturally belongs at the top of my acknowledgements. My wife, Kambria, has shown me infinite patience and love as I have labored at this project, and my greatest joy in completing this publication is to finally be able to honor her sacrifices. My sons, James and Daniel, have been diligent in reminding me to take breaks and play. My parents deserve special thanks as they instilled in me a love of learning and tirelessly supported me and equipped me with the tools to succeed in my academic endeavors. My father, Michael Jarrett, shared with me his enjoyment of history and has been a valuable sounding board for my projects. My mother, Victoria Jarrett, cultivated in me a love of writing, generously assists me through copyediting, and gives me endless encouragement. My thanks also go out to my brother, Matthew Jarrett, and to Kambria's parents, TJ and Nancy Rosengarth, for the support they have given me as I worked on this project.

Frederick Schneid is responsible for converting my casual interest in history into a real passion during his classes at High Point University. He showed me what it meant to be a historian, both as a researcher and as an educator, and he has continued to support me as both mentor and friend as I moved on to graduate school and the professional world beyond.

Michael Leggiere deserves tremendous credit for his guidance and mentorship of myself and many others. He has always challenged me to pursue the highest standards of excellence, and I will be forever grateful for his investment in me. Aside from being an excellent educator and mentor, Leggiere is also a tireless advocate for his students and for the field of military history, which I admire and appreciate.

Marilyn Morris, Guy Chet, Nancy Stockdale, and Michael Greig provided excellent insight and feedback throughout my graduate school career and this project. I also received generous support from the Department of History at the University of North Texas (UNT) under the direction of Richard McCaslin.

The Military History Center at UNT as well as the Toulouse Graduate School and the College of Arts and Sciences all contributed essential financial support that made the research for this project possible. I must also thank the Masséna Society both for providing a welcoming community of Napoleonic scholars as well as for providing financial support for graduate students like myself to do research and then present our findings at international conferences. Once funded, my research trips benefitted from very kind and helpful individuals at various archives, including, but certainly not limited to, Julie Ash at the National Archives of the United Kingdom, Lynn Bruce at the National Records of Scotland, and Terese Austin and Jayne Ptolemy at the William L. Clements Library.

My colleagues in graduate school deserve my thanks as well for the discussion, ideas, encouragement, and laughter that helped to shape this work. Jordan Hayworth blazed a trail one year ahead of me in going from High Point University to UNT, and he consistently set the bar very high at every step of the way. Nevertheless, he was always generous with his time and thoughts as we spent hours trading ideas and insights on the War of the First Coalition. Casey Baker has been an excellent friend throughout our graduate careers and beyond, from keeping each other sane during our first journey to the National Archives of the United Kingdom to our unending dialogue about British strategy in the War of the First Coalition. I am grateful as well to Andrew Tzavaras, Jonathan Abel, Chad Tomaselli, Eric Smith, Hailey Stewart, Kyle Hatzinger, Michelle Findlater, Michael Stout, Sarah Jameson, and Chris Menking, all of whom have been wonderful companions. From beyond UNT, I am thankful for the encouragement and advice I received from Huw Davies, Kenneth Johnson, Kevin McCranie, Mark Gerges, and Alexander Mikaberidze.

I extend my thanks as well to my colleagues at Wesleyan Christian Academy. The fine administrative team has facilitated my continued professional growth, and my fellow faculty members have encouraged and supported me as I have completed this project. My students have also been wonderful, bringing me joy and laughter daily.

It is with sorrow that I must offer my gratitude to Donald Horward posthumously. Until his death on 31 October 2021, Dr. Horward devoted his life to advancing scholarship on the Napoleonic Era. He directed more than one hundred graduate students, including my own mentor, Michael Leggiere. Donald Horward welcomed me into the wonderful family of Napoleonic scholars he had helped create, and I count myself very fortunate to be part of his tradition.

To others not mentioned, know that I am grateful for you as well and that I recognize that this project would have been impossible without such generous support from so many.

Introduction

On 1 February 1793, the National Convention of revolutionary France declared war on Great Britain and the Netherlands, adding them to France's list of enemies in the War of the First Coalition, which already included Austria and Prussia. Although British prime minister William Pitt the Younger had famously predicted fifteen years of peace just one year earlier, the French declaration of war initiated nearly a quarter century of war between Britain and France, with only one brief, thirteen-month respite. Britain entered the war amid both a nadir in British diplomacy and internal political divisions over the direction of British foreign policy.

After becoming prime minister in 1783 in the aftermath of the American War of Independence, Pitt pursued financial and naval reform to recover British strength and proposed cautious interventionism to end Britain's diplomatic isolation in Europe. He hoped to create a collective security system based on the principles of the territorial status quo, trade agreements, neutral rights, and the resolution of diplomatic disputes through mediation—armed mediation if necessary. While his domestic measures largely succeeded, Pitt's foreign policy suffered from a paucity of like-minded allies, contradictions between traditional hostility to France, and emergent concerns about growing Russian power, the limited ability to project power on the Continent, and the even more limited will of Parliament to support interventionism. These challenges continued to plague Britain's wartime diplomacy and military strategy, leading to failure in the War of the First Coalition and leaving the British fighting alone after the Treaty of Campo Formio secured peace between France and London's last Continental ally, Austria, on 18 October 1797. While Pitt's collective security vision served as the basis for future coalitions, culminating in the multilateral Quadruple Alliance and Vienna Congress System, which Robert Stewart, Viscount Castlereagh, constructed between 1813 and 1815, that dream proved to be beyond Pitt's reach in the 1780s and 1790s.

In examining Pitt's foreign policy from 1783 to 1797, in this book I consider a question of continuity or change that can be divided into two elements. First, did Pitt's administration adhere to the Continental or blue-water school of British strategic thought? Second, in either case, did Pitt oversee the development of policies primarily in emulation of past precedents or did he conceive new approaches? While acknowledging the complexities within these dichotomies, I argue that Pitt developed and pursued a grand strategy that sought British security through a novel Eurocentric collective security system that prefigured the Vienna settlement of 1815.

Both of these questions have a rich tradition of historiographical dialogue involving historians of both the eighteenth and nineteenth centuries. Brendan Simms provides one of the most extensive and direct treatments of the question of a European or colonial focus in eighteenth-century British foreign policy. In *Three Victories and a Defeat*, Simms describes the recurring conflict between Tory blue-water visions for British strategy and the Whig emphasis on the Protestant interest or balance of power in Europe. He blames the Tory ascendancy in the wake of the Seven Years War for Britain's isolation in Europe and resulting defeat in the American War of Independence. Simms ends by noting the younger Pitt's interest in restoring a more natural European focus to British foreign policy in order to regain security through agency on the Continent.[1]

Simms's work offers a counterpoint to a larger historiographical trend in the late-twentieth century that emphasizes the Atlantic world and global connections in eighteenth-century British foreign policy. While this trend usefully highlights hitherto minimized or ignored contacts and exchanges, it also carries with it the danger of distorting the relative priority that contemporaries placed on global versus European connections. The question of whether European or colonial affairs enjoyed primacy in shaping British foreign policy in the eighteenth century remains a vibrant historiographical debate.[2] Both views have several advocates, while others, like Jeremy Black, have emphasized that eighteenth-century British statesmen contested Britain's appropriate strategic focus just as much as historians have.[3]

Pitt's personal approach to this dilemma also continues to be the subject of considerable debate. Beginning with John W. Fortescue's 1906 condemnation of Pitt's alleged preference for maritime strategy at the expense of Europe, some historians interpret the younger Pitt's policies as a continuation of his father's blue-water strategy.[4] As with the trend for the broad scope of the eighteenth century, this interpretation has shifted recently toward an appreciation for Pitt's European concerns.[5] Here, too, Jeremy Black champions the prevalence of debate, contradiction, and either balance or paradox in Pitt's handling of European and imperial concerns.[6] Pitt's biographers tend to support Black's approach while suggesting that Pitt's personal views generally leaned toward a focus on Europe.[7] Throughout this book, I support this trend by arguing that the prime minister consistently subordinated colonial and maritime concerns to European objectives.

Regarding the question of whether Pitt's foreign policy in the 1780s and 1790s emulated past precedents or looked to forge new paths, the majority of the literature describes Pitt as more of a relic than a prophet in his foreign policy. The dominant narrative remains that of a Second Hundred Years War spanning from the 1688 Glorious Revolution to the final defeat of Napoleon in 1815. In this context, those historians that view Pitt as a proponent of a bluewater strategy tend to argue that he sought primarily to replicate his father's colonial conquests while outsourcing the European war to Continental allies through subsidies.[8] In his work on the Caribbean campaigns during the French Revolutionary Wars, Michael Duffy argues that Pitt viewed the War of the First Coalition as a renewal of the Anglo-French maritime contest that had characterized the American War of Independence.[9] For historians that instead emphasize the European dimension of Pitt's foreign policy, his attempts to create a multilateral alliance system in Europe become echoes of the Grand Alliances against Louis XIV.[10] Scholars have preferred to treat the Anglo-French alliance of 1716–31 and the rapprochement of the 1780s as aberrations rather than true contradictions to the Second Hundred Years War paradigm.[11] Within this framework, the outbreak of the Revolutionary and Napoleonic Wars attains a false sense of inevitability, which minimizes Pitt's willingness to break with such traditional foreign policy forms in pursuit of his objectives.

In his influential study of the European state system from 1763 to 1848, Paul Schroeder also presents Pitt's policies as largely belonging to the past, specifically to the eighteenth-century balance of power system that the Revolutionary and Napoleonic Wars swept away. He defines the balance of power as a system governed by the following informal rules: "compensations; indemnities; alliances as instruments for accruing power and capability; *raison d'état*; honor and prestige; Europe as a family of states; and finally, the principle or goal of balance of power itself."[12] Schroeder indicates that Pitt sought to employ these rules to continue Britain's competition with France for hegemony overseas and in western Europe, an idea supported by others like Charles Esdaile.[13] Despite this, Schroeder does acknowledge that Pitt's attempt to create a collective security system from 1788 to 1791 represented a new idea rather than simply nostalgia for the Grand Alliances in the early decades of the eighteenth century.[14]

Jeremy Black largely echoes Schroeder's analysis in *British Foreign Policy in an Age of Revolutions, 1783–1793*, but the scope of the book prevents him from carrying his analysis of those policies further into the War of the First

Coalition.[15] In a study of Pitt's administration, Michael Duffy also suggests that Pitt charted a new course in foreign policy, primarily in his conception of a collective security system to preserve British interests and prevent wars in Europe. He makes note of two previous attempts of a similar project: Earl James Stanhope's creation of the Quadruple Alliance of Britain, France, Austria, and the United Provinces in 1718 to contain Spanish aggression and Thomas Pelham-Holles's, First Duke of Newcastle, effort to revive that alliance without France between 1748 and 1755 to protect the balance of power.[16] However, this comparison is approximate as the former case represented a temporary arrangement and the latter targeted only France as the power to be restrained.[17] As Duffy observes, Pitt's collective security scheme, in contrast to the earlier alliance plans, proposed to welcome all states in a permanent system to prevent aggression from any power.[18] In this book, I corroborate and expand on Duffy's interpretation to demonstrate that Pitt brought fresh ideas to British foreign policy and preferred principles to precedents in his management of diplomacy.

Works that focus on the Napoleonic Era as the foundation for nineteenth-century European history also tend to portray Pitt as more forward than backward thinking. Apart from Schroeder, these works generally present Pitt as the founding father of the Quadruple Alliance and Congress System that Castlereagh forged during the Sixth Coalition and Congress of Vienna from 1813 to 1815. However, they typically ascribe these ideas specifically to the plans for organizing the Third Coalition in 1805 or even the Second Coalition in 1798. As such, the idea for a multilateral alliance and a congress system to secure the peace of Europe is viewed as a reaction to the overwhelming threat of revolutionary France.[19] In contrast, in *The Younger Pitt*, Michael Duffy draws the line of continuity for this scheme back to Pitt's collective security plans that preceded the French Revolutionary Wars. That assertion receives cursory attention as befits a minor component of a concise text that covers a large topic. Here, I expand on that interpretation, drawing the line of continuity clearly and explicitly from Pitt's rise to power in 1783 through the conclusion of the War of the First Coalition in 1797, thereby connecting it to the established continuum from 1798 to 1815.[20]

British foreign policy is generally not the product of one man alone, and analyzing Pitt's foreign policy requires one to consider the contributions of others in shaping his ideas. Pitt entered office at the age of twenty-four with only two years of political experience. While he served briefly as chancellor of the exchequer in the ministry of William Petty, Second Earl of Shelburne, in 1782, Pitt lacked the reputation and connections of a more seasoned politician. Pitt's formidable intellect partly compensated for his lack of administrative experience. His interest in science, mathematics, and economics endowed him with enthusiasm for matters of finance and efficiency. These passions and his talent for translation and memorization produced an attention to detail that served him well in his efforts as secretary of the treasury to reform British finances.[21] Nevertheless, Pitt recognized clearly that these skills could scarcely offset his inexperience with the subtleties of politics and diplomacy; therefore, he relied on dialogue with friends and colleagues to refine his views and execute his projects.[22]

Pitt found little agreement within the government and diplomatic corps regarding the states that Britain should view as allies or adversaries. Many held to a traditional blue-water strategy, which made Russia in combination with either Austria or Prussia appear as natural allies to provide a counter to Britain's permanent commercial and colonial rival, France. However, some found the increasingly aggressive behavior of the eastern powers more threatening and urged rapprochement with France and Spain to curtail the rising threat of Russia in particular. Pitt sympathized with both points of view and struggled to develop a coherent foreign policy to reconcile them.[23]

As Pitt held his position primarily at the king's pleasure, he necessarily consulted the views of King George III on foreign policy. George III remained politically influential and diplomatically active. During his first two decades on the throne, he presented himself as a patriot king, emphasizing his English identity in contrast to the strong Hanoverian influence that had characterized his predecessors. In the realm of foreign policy, this meant prioritizing British maritime and colonial interests over supposedly Hanoverian concerns on the European continent. Nevertheless, George III did maintain a strong, if quiet, Continental perspective, ever mindful of Hanover's position without losing sight of Britain's own interests in Europe. Like many in Britain, the shock of losing the thirteen American colonies prompted the king to reevaluate the direction of British foreign policy. Although open to novel measures like a rapprochement with France, he often urged caution to avoid unnecessary commitments or wars, countering the more hawkish views of some diplomats and Cabinet ministers.[24]

The presence of a strong Whig opposition in Parliament led by Charles James Fox also constrained Pitt's latitude in foreign policy. The Foxite Whigs tended to favor a blue-water approach to foreign policy. They were always ready to criticize Pitt for what they viewed as unnatural Continental commitments or for timidity in promoting Britain's maritime and imperial interests. Pitt's dearth of political connections meant that his first administration was constructed to maximize its ability to withstand the Whigs in Parliament rather than to achieve unity or efficiency. Owing to this lack of cohesion, that Cabinet initially proved an ineffective organ of policy. Lord Chancellor Edward Thurlow, First Baron Thurlow, and Lord President Charles Pratt, First Earl Camden, offered considered insights on foreign policy when consulted, but they neither approached the subject with enthusiasm nor actively pushed a particular agenda. Of this initial Cabinet, only Master-General of the Ordnance Charles Lennox, Third Duke of Richmond, and Foreign Secretary Francis Osborne, Marquess of Carmarthen—both outspoken in their hatred of France—contributed actively to Pitt's foreign policy.[25]

Although Pitt remained distant from the other members of the Cabinet, he consulted close associates in more junior positions and relied on advice from various British diplomats such as Joseph Ewart, Sir James Harris, and William Eden. Ewart and Harris generally reinforced the Francophobia exhibited by Richmond and Carmarthen while Eden advocated a rapprochement with France that more closely matched the inclinations of Pitt and George III. The two primary junior officials that Pitt consulted were Henry Dundas, a friend from Parliament who served as treasurer of the navy, and Pitt's cousin, William Wyndham, First Baron Grenville, who received appointment as paymaster of the forces. Pitt became intimate friends with both men between his first arrival in Parliament in 1781 and his acceptance of office in 1783. He later elevated both to Cabinet positions, raising their rank to match the importance he placed on them. The contribution of Dundas and Grenville remained limited during Pitt's first years in office while they occupied lower posts, but their influence grew after Pitt promoted them. During the War of the First Coalition, Dundas served first as home secretary and later as secretary of state for war, and Grenville headed the Foreign Office.[26]

The close relationship between these three men has caused historians to describe them as a triumvirate. Beyond formal Cabinet meetings, Pitt regularly shared drinks and dinners with either or both men, over which they often discussed government business. In 1791, Eden, who had become Baron Auckland, observed of Pitt and Grenville that "whatever is written to the one may be considered as written to the other."[27] In 1794, Pitt himself commented that "every act of [Dundas is] as much mine as his."[28] This intimate communication between these three men proved beneficial for facilitating the business of government, yet it can become maddening to a scholar to repeatedly find letters referencing conversations and meetings without further explanation. This somewhat artificially constrains historical analysis to correspondence and official papers regarding the policies that resulted from these informal gatherings and prevents a full understanding of the debates and dialogue that occurred privately over drinks late at night.[29]

Despite the close friendship they both enjoyed with Pitt, Dundas and Grenville brought very different skills, personal attributes, and political views to Pitt's government. Dundas was a socially and politically savvy individual who had already adroitly navigated politics in London for nearly a decade by the time Pitt took office, and he had advanced to the top of the Scottish legal system in the decade preceding his entrance into politics. While little is known of their first meetings, Dundas apparently developed an admiration for Pitt's intelligence, talent, and integrity after the latter gained a seat in Parliament in 1781. No great leader himself and perceiving Pitt to be the best hope of rallying opposition to the more radical Whigs, Dundas was instrumental in orchestrating the formation of Pitt's first ministry and defending it in the House of Commons during its shaky early days. Dundas continued to serve as Pitt's primary social and political networking asset throughout the latter's term as prime minister. Dundas's home (and disposition) at Wimbledon proved better for entertaining than Pitt's abode at Downing Street, so the Scotsman frequently held important social gatherings there with Pitt often staying the night in a designated room. These social gatherings included Pitt's first meeting with one of the scholars he respected most: Adam Smith.[30]

Dundas's official role evolved as years passed, but he consistently advocated for the interests of his native Scotland and the strengthening and reforming of British India; he also generally promoted blue-water foreign policy and strategy. Dundas based his political clout largely on the influence he wielded in Scotland through family and professional connections, which received a significant boost when George III awarded him the position of Keeper of the Privy Seal of Scotland for life in 1782. Even apart from his other qualities, Dundas's ability to manage Scotland therefore made him indispensable to Pitt's government. He was also instrumental in crafting Pitt's India Reform Bill that passed in 1784 and created a Board of Control for the East India Company. Both Dundas and Grenville sat on this board, and Dundas became its president. When Dundas became home secretary in 1791, colonial affairs fell under his purview, combining with his Indian responsibilities to give him a more imperial outlook on British foreign affairs. This outlook colored his inclinations when he shifted from home secretary to secretary of state for war in 1794.[31]

Grenville was an opposite of Dundas in many ways. Like Pitt, he was born in 1759, making them both seventeen years younger than Dundas with correspondingly less experience in politics. In contrast to Dundas's gregarious nature, Grenville had a cold and aloof bearing that made him a poor manager of people by his own admission.[32] While Dundas rose to political prominence through a legal career and did most of his political maneuvering in the House of Commons, Grenville was born and raised as a cosmopolitan aristocrat, ultimately advocating for the government in the House of Lords. Grenville joined Pitt's first administration initially in the junior role of paymaster of the forces, but he earned his place in the Cabinet by serving the prime minister as a trusted agent and foreign policy consultant throughout the 1780s. He generally advocated for a more Continental orientation of British foreign policy and strategy, though always with great caution and pragmatism.[33]

Grenville will feature more prominently in this study because of its focus on European diplomacy and foreign policy in which Grenville played an official and well-documented role. This focus is not, however, intended to downplay the importance of Dundas either as a member of the Cabinet or as a friend of Pitt. Dundas remained in Pitt's inner circle throughout the period in consideration here, but, as his influence on foreign policy was more informal and his position and interest inclined him toward greater attention to the colonies and domestic affairs, opportunities for highlighting his views herein are fewer than those for observing Grenville's.[34] Rather than trying to parse out primacy of influence between Dundas and Grenville over Pitt, I view Pitt as a leader in his own right with his own ideals that he pursued while still seeking out and learning from the wisdom and opinions of his trusted friends and colleagues. Although historians have made much of the influences on Pitt, particularly Dundas and Grenville, it is noteworthy that none of these individuals were ever completely satisfied with the direction of British foreign policy, especially during the War of the First Coalition. Dundas almost always lamented the diversion of resources from the colonies to the Continent while the pragmatic Grenville expressed frustration with Pitt's inclination toward idealism in Continental diplomacy. Both men went so far as to offer their resignations in moments of extreme disagreement during the war. Notably, neither of them actually left the administration in these instances despite Pitt enforcing his wishes over their protests. Thus, while it is safe to assume that Dundas and Grenville had input on virtually every measure that the government took during Pitt's first administration, it is equally true that the final decisions rested with Pitt. Although he certainly did not develop it in a vacuum, the policy of seeking British security in Europe through a collective security system designed to protect neutral states and the territorial status quo against all aggressive powers belongs primarily to Pitt.[35]

These principles represented a rejection of the Tory policies of Pitt's immediate predecessors. The traditional Tory blue-water view eschewed entanglements in Europe in favor of a strict focus on commerce, naval supremacy, and colonial growth. This view held ascendancy from William Pitt the Elder's rise to leadership in 1757, during the Seven Years War, through the American War of Independence. The elder Pitt demonstrated this focus on Britain's maritime empire through the unprecedented commitment of British resources to the colonial conflict. In addition, the equally unprecedented decision to retain extensive colonial conquests rather than trade them for European concessions bore witness to the primacy of colonial interests in Tory foreign policy. This imperial focus and comparative disregard for the states of continental Europe ultimately contributed to Britain's isolation and defeat in the American War of Independence.[36]

British failure in that conflict led to a partial revival of the older, traditionally Whig view that subordinated commercial, colonial, and naval concerns to interventionism in Europe on behalf of the balance of power for the sake of British security. Beginning with the Glorious Revolution of 1688, the predominantly Whig administrations of the early eighteenth century took a keen interest in Continental affairs. They sought allies to oppose the expansionism of Bourbon France and Spain and to protect the Protestant Succession of the Glorious Revolution from a Bourbon-backed Jacobite threat. The security and independence of the United Provinces and Hanover formed a consistent theme of British foreign policy during this period of Whig ascendancy. Parliamentary opposition often challenged these concerns as illegitimate and arising from foreign Dutch or Hanoverian concerns. This perception contributed to the unpopularity of Continental alliances and wars, which British public opinion compared unfavorably with the clearer British interests that colonial conflicts served. The elder Pitt had capitalized on this sentiment to rise to power in 1757 as the popular champion of British maritime interests against the royal distortion of British foreign policy toward Hanover.[37]

Both the notion of European politics taking precedence in British foreign policy over colonial concerns and the idea of securing Britain's European interests through a robust alliance system had ample precedent in the eighteenth century. However, Pitt's approach to these principles differed significantly from those of his predecessors. Pitt engaged with Europe to promote and protect Britain's own commercial and strategic interests rather than to safeguard Hanover, distract France, or defend the Protestant Succession from a Jacobite threat. He sought a broad alliance system not as a means of furthering Britain's competition with its traditional Bourbon rivals but rather to preserve the peace of Europe, strengthening Britain's strategic position and commerce through collective security.

Pitt departed from the tradition of viewing France as the permanent enemy and correspondingly assuming Russia and Austria or Prussia to be natural friends, rendering the narrative of a Second Hundred Years War as a descriptor of Anglo-French relations in the eighteenth century problematic. He sought productive commercial relationships with Continental states and the preservation of peace and the status quo to facilitate that commerce and prevent the emergence of a hostile bloc of naval powers capable of directly threatening

Great Britain. Thus, Pitt pursued cooperation with other states favoring the status quo but opposed aggressive and expansionist states. During his first decade in office, Pitt pressed for rapprochement with France and even sided with Versailles to oppose Austrian and Russian aggrandizement. His foreign policy leaned in this direction until the French declaration of war in 1793. Despite the irruption of an Anglo-French war, Pitt harbored no desire to destroy Britain's old rival. Instead, his goal remained the same as before the war: the creation of a stable European diplomatic system to provide security to all members and to eliminate aggressive wars through either mediation or force. This objective drove Pitt's efforts to build a coalition during the war and shaped his response to both the Revolution and the counterrevolution in France.

Pitt's quest for British security and prosperity through collective security in Europe touches on themes and questions that resonate throughout British history, enduring to the present and likely remaining relevant for the foreseeable future. Castlereagh carried the torch of Pitt's European security vision, engaging actively with the Congress System established in 1815 until he extinguished it along with his own life on 12 August 1822. Like Pitt, Castlereagh had championed a European orientation for British foreign policy against significant popular and political opposition from those who adhered to the blue-water view of British interests. Over the course of the nineteenth century after Castlereagh, Britain's foreign policy focus shifted away from continental Europe in favor of the Great Game in Asia and the related Eastern Question.

Nevertheless, throughout both the nineteenth and early twentieth centuries, the British found themselves repeatedly and reluctantly forced to engage with European wars and crises. Even at its peak, Britain's maritime empire proved insufficient to guarantee British security without strong European allies. In the aftermath of the Second World War, some Britons thought again as Pitt did in the 1780s that British security required participation in a European collective security system. Winston Churchill articulated this view in his famous Zurich speech on 19 September 1946, proposing "to re-create the European family, or as much of it as we can, and provide it with a structure under which it can dwell in peace, in safety, and in freedom. We must build a kind of United States of Europe."[38] From that time to the present, the United Kingdom has participated in several multinational cooperative arrangements, including the United Nations, the North Atlantic Treaty Organization, and the European Union. The efficacy and advisability of these organizations and the merits of Britain's ties to Europe have always occasioned a vibrant debate just as Pitt's European policies did. The continued vitality of this debate has been most recently demonstrated by a referendum on 23 June 2016 in which a narrow majority of the British electorate voted in favor of "Brexit," that is, removing the United Kingdom from the European Union. The subsequent efforts to separate Britain politically and economically from Europe have been difficult, complex, and contentious, and so the debate over pursuing British interests through inclusion or insularity continues.

I have relied on extensive archival documents to support my assertions about Pitt's foreign policy and chart the precise course of the continuity of thought from Pitt's appointment to the treasury office in 1783 through the end of the War of the First Coalition on the European continent. In particular, the diplomatic papers in the Foreign Office division of the National Archives of the United Kingdom at Kew provide the most useful insight into the implementation of British foreign policy. Papers from the Home Office and War Office divisions describe the operations of the British military to support Pitt's foreign policy commitments. Diverse collections of private papers from the National Archives and the British Library provide insight into the personal relationships upon which Pitt relied to build political support for his policies. The National Library of Scotland and the National Records of Scotland furnish this study with additional private and public correspondence primarily from Pitt's war secretary and confidant, Henry Dundas. Last, the William L. Clements Library at the University of Michigan in Ann Arbor contains collections of private papers from both Pitt and Dundas, thereby filling some gaps in the official records. Analysis of these documents demonstrates that the principles underpinning Pitt's European collective security goals shaped his approach to both foreign policy in peace and strategy in war from 1783 to 1797.

Numerous collections of published primary sources supplement the archival documents. Many descendants of the British ministers and diplomats of the Revolutionary and Napoleonic Era gathered and published collections of diaries and correspondence. Among them, the published correspondence of Grenville and of prominent diplomats like Malmesbury and Eden illustrate the dialogue between the British government and the agents that shaped British diplomacy.[39] Published collections of correspondence from French, Austrian, Dutch, and Russian agents provide a broader perspective for the critical evaluation of British accounts and impressions.[40]

I owe a heavy historiographical debt to the works of many historians who have previously studied this period. John Ehrman's definitive three-volume biography of Pitt provides the most comprehensive narrative of this period of British history and serves as a valuable starting point for any research on the Younger Pitt.[41] Jeremy Black's analysis of British foreign policy during Pitt's first decade in office proved extremely useful for guiding research on the period of 1783 to 1793.⁴² Finally, the works of Michael Duffy, especially his unpublished 1971 dissertation on Anglo-Austrian relations during the French Revolutionary Wars, provide both an excellent guide to archival sources and valuable insight into British strategic thinking in the 1780s and 1790s.⁴³ I aim to build on the foundation laid by these and other eminent predecessors to improve our understanding of the role Pitt played in reshaping the European state system during the revolutionary era.

CHAPTER 1

Britain's Return to Europe, 1783–1787

On 3 September 1783, delegates from Great Britain signed formal peace treaties with France, Spain, and the United States to end the American War of Independence. The war left Britain politically divided, economically drained, militarily exhausted, and diplomatically isolated. During the political upheaval that followed, George III ultimately appointed William Pitt the Younger to lead the government as first lord of the treasury on 19 December 1783. Taking charge in an atmosphere of tremendous anxiety, Pitt strove to restore Britain to a position of prominence within the European state system. To achieve this goal, he pursued fiscal and naval reform while seeking allies on the European continent to end Britain's dangerous isolation.[1]

Despite the importance he placed on ending British isolation, Pitt initially approached foreign policy with caution and hesitancy for several reasons. First, he placed a higher priority on the success and continuation of his domestic reforms than on obtaining a Continental ally. Thus, while he sought allies, he remained averse to any partnership that could lead to war and thus interrupt his reform programs. In addition, he refused to seek allies from a position of weakness. Pitt understood that obtaining an alliance for the purpose of securing another power's protection while Britain appeared weak would diminish rather than increase British influence in Europe. Instead, he sought to entice other powers to court Britain as an alliance partner, which would allow him to negotiate from a position of strength and ensure that the resultant treaty served British interests. However, to make Britain an attractive partner, Pitt needed time to restore British strength and credibility.

To revive British finances, Pitt worked in three interrelated directions: trade, domestic economic growth, and credit. Both he and Dundas were admirers of Adam Smith and advocated for breaking monopolies, expanding markets, and promoting free trade.² In commerce, the Pitt ministry pursued new trade opportunities to compensate for the expected decrease in trade with the now-independent North American colonies. This initiative led to several new commercial treaties with other European powers and prompted Pitt to take an active interest in tapping the economic potential of eastern Europe. To improve government revenue domestically, Pitt followed the guiding principle of efficiency with a holistic approach. He cut costs, reducing military establishments and pensions as well as auditing government spending to eliminate expenditure on redundant or unnecessary positions. Pitt also raised revenue by adjusting taxation to minimize its negative impact on commerce. He reduced commercial duties to encourage taxable, legitimate commerce and escalated enforcement of these duties to further discourage smuggling. Although this lowered the duties, it raised government revenue by increasing compliance and consumption. He applied a similar approach to taxation, utilizing mostly indirect taxes and focusing on increasing efficiency and accountability. These fiscal reforms represented a continuation of the same movement to rationalize the empire's financial structure that had precipitated the American war.³

For Pitt, these financial reforms served primarily to facilitate the restoration of the two main pillars of British power: the national credit and the Royal Navy. In this regard, he found rare agreement with the Whig opposition leader, Charles James Fox. In a minor debate over the merits of a bill to refinance the debts of the navy and ordnance departments, Fox condemned the plan as a breach of faith with creditors. According to the record of the debate: "He asked what it was that had given us distinction amongst the other powers of Europe? Was it not the purity and reputation of our credit? It was this that had conciliated confidence from every quarter and furnished us with those resources which were the foundations of our distinction and of our grandeur." In response, "Pitt agreed with the right hon. gentleman precisely in his ideas respecting the public credit. He differed, however, from him in the application of his reasoning to the present point."⁴ While Pitt and Fox often disagreed on the methodology of maintaining Britain's credit, both accepted the importance of good credit for British military power and influence in Europe.

Rescuing the teetering national credit required Pitt to reduce the staggering national debt of £213,000,000 from Britain's recent wars. In 1786, he proposed to direct £1,000,000 annually from the surplus he expected from his other reforms into a sinking fund dedicated to redeeming government bonds. That redemption would reduce the government's annual interest payments to creditors—the largest single expense in the budget. The money thus saved on interest payments would be added to the annual sinking fund payment, accelerating the rate of debt redemption each year. His plan worked, and, by 1

February 1793, the sinking fund had eliminated £10,242,100 of British debt and boosted confidence in British credit.[5]

George III approved of Pitt's plan of financial reform to restore Britain's diplomatic weight. On 30 March 1786, the day after Pitt proposed his sinking fund to Parliament, the king wrote:

> Considering Mr. Pitt has had the unpleasant office of providing for the expenses incurred by the last war, it is but just he should have the full merit he deserves of having the public know and feel that he has now proposed a measure that will render the nation again respectable if she has the sense to remain quiet some years and not, by wanting to take a shewy [sic] part in the transactions of Europe, again become the dupe of other powers and from ideas of greatness draw herself into lasting distress. The old English saying is applicable to our situation: England must cut her coat according to her cloth.[6]

Like Pitt, the king drew a clear connection between Britain's financial strength and its diplomatic influence. He did not urge British isolation from European politics but rather cautious engagement to ensure that Britain's resources covered its commitments and that any such commitment genuinely served British interests.

Regarding the navy, Pitt recognized the need for the same attention that he lavished on financial matters. Naval setbacks during the American war had exposed the limits of Britain's control of the sea. Most notably, local French naval superiority had allowed the pivotal Franco-American victory at Yorktown. More broadly, Bourbon and Dutch fleets around the world stretched the Royal Navy to its limits. Beyond the shores of Virginia, the Royal Navy had failed to prevent Spain's conquest of Minorca and proved unable to guarantee the safety of the home islands from a French invasion. To regain British naval supremacy, Pitt initiated a parliamentary inquiry into the state of the navy, obtained between £2,000,000 and £3,000,000 from Parliament each year for the construction of ships and port defenses, and reduced corruption in the navy's command structure.[7]

Economic and naval vitality served the overriding objectives of increasing Britain's appeal as an ally and facilitating Pitt's efforts to end diplomatic isolation. Heavy-handed British diplomacy at the conclusion of the Seven Years War had alienated most of the Continental powers, leaving Britain isolated in the American War of Independence. That isolation, more than any form of weakness, had crippled Britain during the American war. The absence of a Continental ally to threaten France directly had allowed the French to focus all their resources on the naval war to decisive effect. While Britain stood alone in 1783, France secured alliances with Spain, Austria, and the United Provinces, and an Austro-Russian alliance even brought Russia into the network. As indicated by the American war, this string of alliances posed a serious military threat to Britain and seemed poised to dominate Europe with no regard to British interests or security concerns. As such, Pitt's foreign policy continued the efforts of his immediate predecessors to overturn the apparent French hegemony in Europe.[8]

Russia's annexation of the Crimea on 19 April 1783 in violation of prior treaties with the Ottoman Empire created the first crisis that provided a potential opening for Britain to reconnect with the Continent and disrupt the French alliance network. The increase of Russian power at the expense of the Ottoman Empire, a traditional French ally, created tension between Versailles and St. Petersburg. French efforts to rally opposition to Russian expansion exposed fractures in the French alliance network, which had seemed so formidable from the British perspective. Although allied with France, Joseph II of Austria placed greater value on his connection with Russia and so supported the aggressive policies of Catherine II. Thus, the Crimean Crisis pitted the Bourbon powers of western Europe against the Austro-Russian alliance of eastern Europe.[9] The British government could reasonably hope to disrupt the potentially hostile bloc and win allies by offering support to either side. However, the timing of the crisis and a lack of consensus within the British government prevented the realization of its diplomatic potential.[10]

As Russian intervention in the Crimea began in 1782, the task of managing Britain's response straddled the conclusion of the American war and passed through two other ministries before becoming Pitt's problem. Even as Britain and France negotiated to end their maritime conflict, the prime minister at the time, William Petty, Second Earl of Shelburne, entertained proposals from French foreign minister Charles Gravier, comte de Vergennes, for an Anglo-French concert to resist this Russian threat to the balance of power. Shelburne hoped successful peace negotiations would lead to an Anglo-French alliance to mediate the affairs of Europe. To the chagrin of both Shelburne and Vergennes, Shelburne's successors paid little heed to French appeals for a concerted response to Russia's aggression in the Crimea.[11]

In April 1783, the unpopularity of the peace treaties that ended the American war led to the collapse of the Shelburne ministry. This included both Henry Dundas and William Pitt, who occupied junior roles. Shelburne and Dundas conspired to spare George III the necessity of turning to Fox's radical Whigs by assembling a new ministry around the young and untarnished character of Pitt. This came to naught when Pitt declined for fear of not being able to obtain majorities in Parliament to sustain his administration in power. Thus, George III reluctantly turned to the only group capable of forming a government: an awkward coalition of Foxites and a group of Tories led by Frederick North, Second Earl of Guilford.[12]

Although Fox was the dominant personality of this coalition, he was forced to concede the post of first lord of the treasury, traditionally the position associated with the role of prime minister, to North to maintain their fragile alliance. Instead, Fox assumed the role of a very active foreign secretary, from which he provided the de facto leadership of the coalition government.[13] Unlike Shelburne, he expressed more interest in using the Crimean Crisis to separate Russia, Austria, or both from their French connection than in joining France to defend the balance of power in eastern Europe.[14] Fox hoped to exploit the Crimean Crisis to forge a connection with Russia as a foundation for a broader alliance system that included Prussia. He observed to the British envoy to France on 12 September 1783: "The present circumstances must furnish us with some opportunity of forming a league to balance the Family Compact, and ... I am very happy to find that every one of the present ministers agree with me in this respect. Some have their partialities to the [Holy Roman] Emperor, as ... I have to the King of Prussia."[15] From Fox's perspective, French diplomatic ascendancy in Europe represented a more pressing threat to Britain than Russian expansion in the Black Sea region.

George III agreed that Russian projects were not yet so threatening as to require a unified Anglo-French response. However, the king found Catherine's expansionism distasteful and cautioned Fox against committing Britain to support her efforts, believing in "the propriety of being civil to both [the Austrian and Russian] courts and lying by till we really see by the events which must occur in a few months what line we ought to pursue. By being too anxious, we may do wrong, and the critical situation of Russia must soon oblige her to court us."[16] Like Fox, George wished to secure allies for Britain and diminish the threat of France's diplomatic network. However, the king no more wanted to involve Britain in a war against France over the Balkans on Russia's behalf than he wanted to join France in fighting a Balkan war against Russia to support the Ottoman Empire. Instead, George preferred to wait for Russia's anticipated need for an ally to counter the French to force Catherine to appeal to Britain. Such an appeal would allow Britain to negotiate from a position of strength and reenter Continental politics as a powerful mediator rather than a junior partner in a Russian or French alliance.[17]

In December, George coordinated the Parliamentary defeat of Fox's bill to reorganize the British East India Company and used the occasion to exchange the Fox–North ministry for one more palatable to him under Pitt's leadership.[18] Once again, Dundas served as the primary political instrument, alongside the king himself, for orchestrating the formation of Pitt's first ministry, this time with Pitt's full concurrence.[19] With Pitt in power, Carmarthen became foreign secretary and assumed the management of the British response to the Crimean Crisis. At Pitt's insistence, Carmarthen adopted the care and caution that George had recommended to Fox, agreeing to use Britain's limited influence at Constantinople to urge a peaceful resolution but refusing to consider a formal guarantee of any resulting treaty. Meanwhile, Carmarthen communicated openly about the matter with the Russian ambassador, preserving the possibility of closer Anglo-Russian relations.[20]

The crisis ended on 8 January 1784 with Turkish acceptance, at French urging, of the Second Convention of Aynali Kavak, which legitimized the Russian annexation. The combination of caution and changing leadership in 1783 prevented Britain from either incurring unwanted commitments or benefitting from the crisis. Carmarthen refused the French suggestion that the British join them to guarantee the convention unless the Russians requested it, and St. Petersburg saw no need to seek such a guarantee from a weakened and seemingly politically unstable Britain.[21]

Despite the Franco-Russian tension, the Crimean Crisis resulted in no change to the diplomatic alignments of Europe. Thus, Carmarthen continued Fox's efforts to counterbalance the dangerous French alliance bloc with a British equivalent. Carmarthen wrote that he and Pitt agreed on this objective yet also on "the necessity of avoiding, if possible, the entering into any engagements likely to embroil us in a new war."[22] Immediately following the formation of the Pitt administration, Sir James Harris, a supporter of Fox, wrote: "To recover our weight on the continent by judicious alliances is the general wish of every man the least acquainted with the interests of this country."[23] While most in Britain agreed on the ends, British statesmen disagreed on the best means of achieving Britain's foreign policy goals. These disagreements animated parliamentary debates and even divided the Pitt ministry. While Carmarthen's journal indicates consensus between himself and Pitt, his correspondence in the following months suggests that Carmarthen chafed at Pitt's caution.[24]

A new event in northern Europe in the summer of 1784 provided the occasion for this foreign policy debate and exposed the differences between the prime minister and foreign secretary. On 6 July 1784, Carmarthen reported to George III that France had concluded a treaty with Sweden, ceding its West Indian island of St. Barthélemy to Stockholm in return for gaining Gothenburg as a French naval base in the Baltic.[25] The British cared little if France bargained away an island to Sweden, but a French naval base in the Baltic posed a serious commercial and military threat. Carmarthen sought to use this intelligence as a tool to enlist Russia and Denmark in an anti-French alliance system. However, the king maintained his theme of caution:

This is certainly not a pleasing measure to us, but I do not see that Russia will otherwise feel herself hurt at it than as she seems to dislike her neighbors entering into treaties with any powers but her. Perhaps if we are too forward in conveying this intelligence, she may lay it rather to the account of our wishing to treat with her than to any other motive, and her coldness does not incline me to exceed the bounds of civility. Besides, till I see this country in a situation more respectable as to army, navy, and finances, I cannot think anything that may draw us into troubled waters either safe or rational.[26]

Pitt expressed hope that the incident would lay the foundation for a more cooperative relationship with Denmark and Russia, but he echoed George's mistrust of Russia, insisting that any joint action "be so conducted so as not to commit us too far."[27]

On 9 June 1784, Carmarthen protested this inactivity strongly. He urged Pitt to end British isolation, outlining possible partners for an alliance system to promote British interests in Europe on the assumption of mutual Anglo-French hostility. Contrary to Fox's preference for Prussia, Carmarthen viewed an alliance with Russia and Austria as most desirable yet unlikely on account of Austria's connection with France and Russia's recent coldness toward Britain. Regarding possible alternatives, he considered a vague Prussian proposal for a quadruple alliance of Britain, Prussia, Russia, and Denmark.[28] In that letter and in another on 23 June, Carmarthen anxiously urged haste in ending British isolation by forging a connection wherever possible.[29] The foreign secretary feared the possibility of the French pressing the diplomatic advantages they gained in the American war to deliver another blow to the shaken British Empire. He prioritized ending diplomatic isolation above Britain's own internal recovery.

The following day, Pitt declared his agreement with Carmarthen's ideas in principle but insisted unequivocally on proceeding with extreme caution to avoid being drawn into a Continental conflict that did not serve British interests.[30] Pitt approved of the suggestion of approaching Denmark but also insisted that no such measure should commit Britain to a Baltic war should one erupt. He recommended playing on the general expectation that Britain would act only to oppose French expansion by inducing Russia and Denmark to court Britain as a counter to France. Notably, Pitt acknowledged the assumption from both Carmarthen and the Russian court that Britain and France would remain enemies yet did not echo this sentiment himself.[31] While Pitt agreed with Carmarthen's desire to end Britain's isolation, he adhered to the king's policy of engaging with Europe from a position of strength rather than undertaking commitments contrary to British interests out of desperation. He wrote to a friend on 8 August 1785, "Let peace continue for five years, and we shall again look any power in Europe in the face."[32]

Carmarthen remained undaunted and wrote a letter to Pitt on 28 September 1784, again urging decisive action. He declared that the circumstances favored the creation of "that system in Europe which can alone secure to this country a prospect of remaining unmolested by France." He claimed that this alliance system "which had so long been in contemplation" would not only "secure the tranquility of the north," it would also protect the general balance of power from French aggression. Carmarthen projected that a triple alliance of Britain, Russia, and Denmark would be relatively easy to forge if only Pitt and the king would consent to try. Betraying his frustrations, Carmarthen lamented, "I think a very small exertion of our former spirit would now be of infinite service."[33]

Carmarthen viewed the rise of the eastern powers in general, and Russia in particular, not as a new expansionist threat to the balance of power but as a source of new opportunities to rally allies against Bourbon ambitions in Europe. Tentative overtures to Russia and Denmark consistent with Pitt's caution yielded no result. Unconvinced of Britain's political stability or its willingness to act, Catherine II saw little value in a British alliance. The Danes took their lead from St. Petersburg, refusing to move closer to Britain without Russia. Despite Carmarthen's urging, little came of the Gothenburg affair.[34]

Pitt agreed with Carmarthen's pursuit of a multilateral alliance system but wanted to forge Continental connections only if he could do so without disrupting his financial and naval recovery programs. An alliance with Prussia or Russia might embroil Britain in an unwanted war in eastern Europe as readily as it might forestall war in western Europe. As noted, Pitt sought to avoid an alliance that might compromise British interests. France's alliance with Austria, which threatened French connections with Sweden, Poland, and the Ottoman Empire by way of Austria's alliance with Russia, provided a glaring example of such faulty calculations.[35]

After the failure of these indecisive efforts to gain an alliance with Russia, similarly isolated Prussia stood as Britain's most probable European ally capable of cooperation in both western and eastern Europe. In September 1785, Carmarthen had instructed special envoy Lord Charles Cornwallis to initiate an exchange of views with Frederick II in the hopes of laying the foundations for a future alliance if the response proved favorable.

> Your Lordship will not fail to observe that in the present situation of affairs, it is our wish rather to listen to what may be proposed by His Prussian Majesty than to make any direct proposal on our part. Former transactions have convinced this court of the great caution necessary to be observed in every branch of political intrigue, and therefore it behooves us more than ever . . . to proceed with that degree of caution and circumspection as will neither engage us too deeply on the one hand, nor, on the other, prevent that Prince from listening to

any proposals of a more direct tendency towards friendship and alliance should future circumstances oblige us to wish for such a connection.[36]

These instructions illustrate the duality of policy formed by the divided Cabinet, encompassing Pitt's caution and Carmarthen's impatience to forge some alliance as well as, perhaps, the foreign secretary's personal preference for Austria.[37]

Frederick hesitated to return to the British alliance that had proved less than satisfactory to him during the Seven Years War for fear of again finding himself in an unwanted conflict with France. In response to Cornwallis's mission, the aging monarch offered a bleak perspective on the European balance of power. He portrayed the string of alliances connecting Spain to France, France to Austria, and Austria to Russia together with the Franco-Dutch connection as a solid bloc arrayed against mutually isolated Britain and Prussia. Frederick expressed concern that the fleets of these states outnumbered the British navy, and he balked at the possibility of an Anglo-Prussian alliance, fearing that such an alliance might draw a preemptive strike.[38]

While Frederick refused to join the British in creating a new diplomatic system, the revival of Britain's older connection with Austria appeared to benefit from circumstances in 1784 and 1785. An Austro-Dutch dispute over navigation rights on the Scheldt River and indemnities placed Austria at odds with France, providing a potential opening for British diplomacy.[39] Joseph II wished to lift Dutch restrictions on the navigation of the Scheldt to increase Austria's commercial revenue from the region. On 4 May 1784, he used technical Dutch violations of existing treaties from the wars of Louis XIV as a pretext to demand a total revision of the arrangements between the Austrian Netherlands and the United Provinces. He presented the Dutch an ultimatum on 23 August, which they rejected. Thereafter, both parties sought support from their mutual French ally while mobilizing for a potential war.[40]

The French response favored the Dutch, placing more importance on keeping The Hague aligned with Versailles than on supporting Joseph's efforts to maximize the value of his provinces. Finding that he could not increase Belgium's value without sacrificing his French alliance, Joseph attempted to trade the Austrian Netherlands for more agreeable territory. He sought to execute the long-standing Habsburg project in which the Wittelsbachs would cede Bavaria to Austria and receive the Austrian Netherlands as compensation.[41] Joseph revived the idea in November 1784, seeking support for the measure from Louis XVI in return for Austrian acceptance of French mediation of the Scheldt dispute. After some deliberation, Versailles replied that it could not support the exchange without Prussian consent. Unwilling to seek Prussian support, which might include concessions to Berlin, Joseph dropped the matter.[42]

Although the Austrians and French considered the matter to be concluded, the British learned of it only indirectly, prompting suspicions of an ongoing Franco-Austrian plot to divide Germany and the Low Countries between them. The Scheldt Crisis clearly involved essential British geopolitical interests in the Low Countries, but the appropriate course forward remained unclear. The division between Versailles and Vienna appeared to offer Pitt and Carmarthen the chance "of separating . . . the House of Austria from France" if they offered Austria support for the opening of the Scheldt or the exchange.[43] Such a course could lead to better relations with Russia as well but also alienate the Prussians and the Dutch. Conversely, Dutch and Prussian opposition to Austrian schemes created a similar opportunity to exploit the affair to overcome Frederick's scruples toward a British alliance and potentially separate the Dutch from France. However, a course of action favoring the Dutch and the Prussians would offend Austria and render a Russian alliance even more remote.

The prevalence of rumor instead of official information on the Scheldt Crisis in British diplomatic circles alongside a sense of urgency created an atmosphere of alarm.[44] From his vantage point at The Hague, Harris wrote: "I never in my life felt so deeply interested in the concerns of Europe as at this present instant. I have, perhaps, expressed this sentiment too strongly in my official letters by this post, but I am so impressed with the idea that this is the last favorable moment England will have to resume its proper place amongst the European powers that my zeal and anxiety get the better of every other consideration."[45] He urged a sympathetic Carmarthen to choose quickly between taking the Austrian or Prussian side of the matter, warning that Joseph's projects posed a long-term threat to the balance of power and, thus, British security. Harris advised that "a strong, explicit, and friendly declaration nearly to the effect I have taken the liberty to mention in my enclosure A, would lead us to that certainty we have long wanted and force the Emperor to either return to his former connections with us or to pronounce that he gives them up forever."[46]

The "enclosure A" to which Harris referred offered a thorough and perceptive analysis of the balance of power and Britain's position within it. In this enclosure, Harris identified the Peace of Westphalia as the governing point of reference for the balance of power, yet he declared that it was no longer effective as such despite the constant reference to it in European diplomatic transactions. Harris further claimed that "the revolution in the relative strength of many of the great powers which took place immediately after that period" as well as the rise of Russia rendered the principles of the Westphalian balance obsolete. In this "new order of things," Harris predicted that "a new system seems at length on the eve of working itself out." With regard to the impact of these observations on Britain, he declared that soon, "England will be called upon to take, once more, a share in the concerns of the continent, and . . . the line of conduct she holds at this important conjuncture will decide whether she is again to become a leading power . . . or whether she is to remain exposed to all the dangers of an isolated system."[47]

The Peace of Westphalia to which Harris referred encompassed the treaties that ended the Thirty Years War in 1648. The Thirty Years War marked the culmination of the religious and dynastic wars that had characterized Europe since the Reformation began, pitting the Habsburg bid for dynastic dominance and confessional uniformity against Bourbon France and several Protestant powers in and out of the Holy Roman Empire. With the French and Protestant victory, the resulting multilateral peace established a consensus on territorial boundaries and rejected the notion of universal monarchy and confessional uniformity. As Harris observed, this peace established the idea of a balance of power rather than hegemony as the default and desired condition of Europe. These principles received an update in 1713–15 in the peace of Utrecht that ended the War of the Spanish Succession. That war and the other wars of French king Louis XIV that preceded it represented a Bourbon bid for hegemony in Europe, capitalizing on their successes earlier in the seventeenth century. An alliance led by the British, the Dutch, and the Austrians contained this expansion of French power, and the resulting peace of Utrecht reinforced the established rejection of universal monarchy. This settlement included several specific restrictions on French power while also formally articulating the notion of a balance of power for the purpose of preserving peace. While these peace settlements succeeded in generally stabilizing the balance of power in western and central Europe, they did not account for the subsequent growth of the powerful Prussian and Russian monarchies in eastern Europe. As Harris articulated, the rise of these eastern powers and the partition diplomacy they increasingly practiced posed an existential threat to the balance of power as previously understood in western Europe.[48]

Having enumerated the problems with the balance of power, Harris turned to the more specific question of the crisis at hand. He argued that the British response should depend on that of France. If France opposed Austria, he suggested that Britain needed only to "hold a neutral language, to give the belligerent powers time to weary and exhaust themselves while she takes leisure to recover her own vigor and not appear at all till she can stand forth in a way to give that turn to the contest which may be the most consistent with her interest." However, Harris suggested that if France acquiesced to Joseph's proposals, Britain should intervene to modify the arrangement by preserving in the Low Countries a barrier to protect both the Netherlands and the Holy Roman Empire from France. He concluded, "If the Emperor subscribes to this proposal, the old system is preserved under another shape, and it is so manifestly advantageous to him that, if he declines it, there cannot be the smallest doubt that his principles are inimical to a degree against England and that, in conjunction with his two powerful allies, he meditates views of ambition, which if not opposed in time will overset the liberties of all Europe."[49] Harris fundamentally feared the growth of Joseph's more predatory vision of the balance of power and pleaded for British action to save the outdated seventeenth-century balance and adapt it to the changed circumstances. Despite Harris's urging, the fog through which the British viewed events limited the possibility of taking informed and effective measures and rendered Pitt more cautious than Harris.[50]

While uncertainty froze the British ministers, George III took action that aligned with Harris's advice.[51] Joseph's initiatives aroused strong opposition from the Dutch and many German princes, including George. He considered the Belgium-Bavaria exchange contrary to both British and Hanoverian interests. For Britain, a weak, independent ruler would replace a strong Austrian barrier to French expansion into the strategically and economically vital Low Countries. For Hanover, Joseph's action represented a gross abrogation of the traditional rights of the German princes and an expansion of Austrian power within the Holy Roman Empire, a concern shared by Frederick II. The Prussian king warmed to the British, encouraging more open communication between London and Berlin, but he remained hesitant to take the relationship further. Hanover provided an alternate means of establishing a connection within the structure of the Holy Roman Empire without committing to larger entangling alliances. Amid some confusion regarding the status of the exchange project, George decided to oppose it in his capacity as Elector of Hanover by forming a *Fürstenbund* with the rulers Prussia and Saxony on 23 July 1785.[52]

Joseph and Catherine viewed the league as needless and inflammatory, given the abandonment of the project months earlier.[53] The displeasure of the imperial powers dashed any immediate hopes of enlisting either as Britain's principal Continental ally. In addition, the anticipated rupture between Austria and France over the Scheldt Crisis never occurred, and the Fürstenbund failed to provide the basis for an Anglo-Prussian alliance.[54] The affair also reinforced the perception that Anglo-French hostility made less sense in the context of the rising acquisitiveness of the eastern powers. The affair ended with Austrian acceptance of French mediation, which averted the exchange and protected Dutch rights over the Scheldt, achieving precisely the result that George III sought in joining the Fürstenbund. This broadly beneficial outcome, from a British perspective, was marred by the conclusion of a formal, permanent Franco-Dutch alliance and Britain's own failure to gain an ally.[55]

In response to this result, the Duke of Richmond wrote a lengthy memorandum for the Cabinet that proposed solutions to British isolation in general and the Franco-Dutch connection more specifically. Like Carmarthen and Harris, Richmond assumed a permanent Anglo-French rivalry. In his view, all other foreign policy considerations remained secondary to defending British interests from French aggression and containing French power in Europe. He proposed using British connections in the Netherlands to influence the Dutch to propose British accession to the Franco-Dutch alliance. Richmond postulated that the French would refuse such a proposal, thus exposing their offensive and hostile intent toward Britain. This refusal would theoretically strengthen the efforts of the pro-British party at The Hague to convince the Dutch to withdraw from the alliance. Richmond gave little consideration to the possibility that France might accept the proposal, noting: "But to say the truth, the rivalry of the command of the sea must ever, I fear, make England and France enemies and prevent any permanent alliance subsisting between them."[56]

Unable to consider rapprochement with France seriously, Richmond's proposal for breaking the Franco-Dutch alliance took on a desperate air as he prophetically considered the alliance's consequences for Britain and summarized the dangers of isolation. He identified the lack of Continental allies and the resources of the thirteen colonies as the key distinctions between Britain's strategic position in 1785 and its situation in the wars of the early eighteenth century. While he disclaimed any understanding of whether the loss of the colonies truly weakened British commerce, he identified the absence of American manpower from the British navy as the most serious detriment for British military strength. Richmond then presented a vision of Europe even gloomier than that which Frederick II articulated to Cornwallis. He observed that the French network of alliances neutralized not only the great powers of Europe but also all the secondary powers, including states like Morocco and Algiers by virtue of their treaties with Spain. Richmond then extrapolated the ramifications of this isolation for British national security, speculating that France, supported by its allies, would overpower Britain in the Caribbean, the East Indies, and even in the English Channel. He claimed that French naval success in these areas would lead to an invasion of Ireland followed by an invasion of Britain itself. He summarized his assessment with drama: "Under such circumstances what are we to look for but utter ruin!"[57]

In this context, Richmond identified Austria as the most valuable state for Britain to detach from the French system and into an alliance with Britain to keep the French preoccupied in Europe and limit Versailles's freedom to pursue an aggressive maritime and colonial policy. Thus, he bitterly lamented George's decision to join the Fürstenbund and alienate Joseph II. In Richmond's view, the Belgium-Bavaria exchange could have strengthened Austria significantly while posing little threat to Britain or Hanover, and British support for the measure could have induced Austria to trade its French alliance for one with Britain. He even suggested that "if all Germany was swallowed up by the House of Austria, would she not become a most tremendous rival to France and of course a most useful friend to England?"[58]

Richmond expressed little but contempt for Prussia, before finally expounding on the importance of Russia to Britain's strategic situation.

> Russia in every point of view is the most beneficial ally that Great Britain can have. Russia is an immense and growing market for all our manufactures, and in return supplies us with the most essential articles for our navy and particularly the hemp, pitch, and timber which we can get from no other country. Russia has men to raise armies if necessary for our assistance, and a powerful navy that will greatly tell for or against us. The views of Russia in Europe, Asia, or Turkey cannot be prejudicial to us, and her assistance may be of the greatest importance.[59]

Viewing the Bourbon family compact as a permanent foe and Russia and Austria as natural allies, Richmond's views remained firmly rooted in the bluewater traditions of the earlier eighteenth century.

Although Richmond penned his memorandum at Pitt's request, the latter soon demonstrated a greater willingness than Richmond to break with traditional rivalries to improve Britain's position in Europe. Richmond's memorandum indicates that he had made a casual remark to Pitt or Carmarthen about asking to join the Franco-Dutch alliance and that Pitt had subsequently requested that he explain his idea more fully for the Cabinet to consider. Considering that Pitt subsequently pursued rapprochement with France, it is possible that he saw such a proposal not as a ruse to break up the French bloc but as a serious option to remedy Britain's strategic dilemmas. In July 1786, British and Spanish diplomats signed a convention resolving several disputes over commerce and colonial possessions in Central America.[60] Two months later, Pitt took a step toward an Anglo-French rapprochement with the Eden Treaty, a commercial treaty between the two powers designed to lift restrictions on trade and travel between the two countries. Although these two treaties hardly amounted to friendly relations with the Bourbon monarchies, they reduced commercial and colonial friction.[61]

These commercial negotiations emerged partially as a fulfillment of Britain's obligations to the treaties that had ended the American War of Independence. They also reflected Pitt's desire to improve Britain's diplomatic and commercial position throughout Europe through trade treaties. Pitt's ministry had avoided commercial negotiations while its mistrust of France and the threat of a

European war remained high in 1784.⁶² However, by 1785, the French lost patience and began levying punitive duties on British commerce, prompting the British Cabinet to commence serious negotiations for the required commercial treaty.⁶³

Pitt exercised the same caution in these negotiations as he displayed in his earlier foreign policy ventures. He resisted French pressure to conclude a treaty quickly and to commit to broad principles as a basis for future, more specific arrangements. Instead, he insisted, despite Eden's complaints, on a detailed treaty that left little to interpretation and clearly served British interests.⁶⁴ He noted, "In every point of view it is essential that before the conclusion, everything should be fully and distinctly understood."⁶⁵

In the eighteenth century, such demands often characterized the diplomacy of a party seeking to avoid a concrete commitment or to delay a distasteful obligation, an interpretation bolstered by earlier British reluctance regarding these treaties. However, Pitt's correspondence reveals that his insistence on precision was not a delaying tactic but rather a necessity born of tensions between the two states and the certain political contentiousness of any such treaty. Pitt wrote to Carmarthen of the need to "show M. de Vergennes that we are really in earnest to forward the negotiation."⁶⁶ To Eden, he promised, "No time shall be lost unnecessarily."⁶⁷

Far from wishing to delay or undermine the negotiations, Pitt became increasingly open to an Anglo-French rapprochement. In his regular reports, Eden relayed to Pitt the apparent sincerity of the French desire for friendly relations. In particular, Eden recorded an unusually transparent conversation with the French controller-general of finances, Charles Alexandre de Calonne, regarding the debts of France and Britain and the means of financing them.⁶⁸ In response, Pitt mused:

> M. de Calonne seems to have been so communicative as to make one almost suspect he had some particular object in giving an impression which is at the first view unfavorable to his own country. But if the account he gave you is just, it seems that they will after some time begin to have the means of extricating themselves quicker than we can hope to do. But their embarrassment must, I think, be sufficient in the interval to secure at least for a time a sincere disposition to peace.⁶⁹

Carmarthen proved less willing to relinquish his suspicions, doubtfully commenting to Eden, "*If* France can ever be sincere, I have no doubt of your abilities bringing the great object of your mission to a favorable as well as speedy conclusion."⁷⁰

Pitt's insistence on detail paid dividends when he defended the treaty to a more skeptical Parliament in February 1787. Beginning with the address of thanks to the king in the House of Commons, debate immediately turned to the question of whether France and Britain could be partners or whether they must always be rivals. Fox described at length France's history (from an Anglocentric perspective) of pursuing universal monarchy in Europe. He then mocked the idea that France had sincerely become, like Britain, a power favoring the status quo and existing balance in Europe, an idea that historiographical consensus now generally supports.[71]

Three weeks later, in the formal debate over the treaty, Pitt forcefully argued against Fox and the widespread Francophobe prejudice he represented: "Considering the treaty in its political view, [I] should not hesitate to contend against the too-frequently advanced doctrine that France was, and must be, the unalterable enemy of Britain. [My] mind revolted from that position as monstrous and impossible. To suppose that any nation could be unalterably the enemy of another was weak and childish. It had neither its foundation in the experience of nations nor in the history of man."[72] Pitt acknowledged the traditional enmity between the two countries but argued that the treaty promised to strengthen Britain economically without demanding blind trust of France. He nevertheless asserted that he did trust France in this instance. Ultimately, Pitt sought to improve Britain's international position commercially, militarily, and diplomatically, and he cared more for efficacy than tradition in his efforts to do so.[73]

While the Eden Treaty passed in Parliament, concurrent negotiations for a renewal of an Anglo-Russian commercial agreement collapsed, and Catherine II instead concluded an advantageous trade treaty with the French. This accentuated the chilling of relations between Britain and Russia but also underscored the persistence of the Anglo-French rivalry in relations with third parties despite their partial rapprochement. In addition, the Franco-Russian treaty highlighted the conflict between France's traditional connection to the Ottoman Empire and its more novel efforts to establish good relations with Russia. The termination of the Anglo-Russian commercial agreement also prompted Pitt to search for an alternate source of the grain and naval supplies hitherto supplied by St. Petersburg.[74]

In another nontraditional move, Pitt sought this alternative in hapless Poland, which possessed the theoretical capacity to replace Russia as the primary supplier of Britain's naval stores and was a major source of grain as well. However, several difficulties obstructed any British hopes of adopting Poland as a trade partner. Polish exports traveled out of the country primarily along either the Vistula River into the Baltic or the Dnieper River into the Black Sea, but the Poles did not have complete control over these rivers. To the south, Russia controlled the mouth of the Dnieper at Kherson. To the north, the Poles controlled the port of Danzig that connected the Vistula to the Baltic. However, Prussia's share of the First Partition of Poland included approximately one hundred miles of the river between the Polish cities of Danzig and Thorn. Both Prussia and Russia crippled Polish trade through exorbitant transit duties along the Vistula and Dnieper.[75]

The Polish government lacked the power to improve its commercial situation. According to British intelligence, the combined Polish and Lithuanian military establishments at the start of 1783 numbered no more than 20,000 men by the most generous estimates, paling in comparison to the armies of its neighbors. In addition, the infamous *liberum veto* of the noble assembly, the *Sejm*, rendered the government too weak to strengthen or reform itself. Compounding these hurdles, any reform effort was suppressed by Russia's considerable influence in Warsaw. Owing to this weakness, Poland's neighbors ignored its pleas and demands without fear of retribution. Thus, the development of Anglo-Polish trade would require the British government to undertake more active interventionism to obtain Russian or Prussian concessions.[76]

A series of upheavals in European politics in 1787 provided the occasion for Carmarthen, Harris, and Ewart to push Pitt toward more ambitious policies in both eastern and western Europe. In the west, tensions between Dutch Stadtholder William V, Prince of Orange, and the anti-Orangist, republican Patriot party erupted into civil war.[77] This created a crisis in a country of vital importance to British interests both in Europe and overseas. Throughout the eighteenth century, the preservation of British influence in the Netherlands loomed large in British foreign policy. Three factors necessitated close Anglo-Dutch relations. First, its geographical position made it the ideal launching point for an invasion of England. In addition, Britain derived tremendous economic benefit from trade with and through the Low Countries. Finally, the substantial Dutch fleet and extensive Dutch colonial possessions in the Indian Ocean and Southeast Asia held the potential either to secure or threaten the British position in India. The loss of the American colonies dramatically increased the importance of India in British colonial policy, which correspondingly enhanced the importance of the Dutch in British foreign policy.[78]

In the east and farther from traditional British interests, unresolved tensions between Russia and the Ottoman Empire over Georgia and the Crimea led to a Turkish declaration of war, pitting the armies of the Austro-Russian alliance against Turkish forces in the Balkans.[79] With the two imperial courts thus engaged in a Balkan war, Britain gained greater room to maneuver in western Europe. To support a more interventionist policy, Carmarthen more aggressively sought a European ally with similar views and a powerful army. In this endeavor, the timing also seemed favorable. The death of Frederick II on 17 August 1786 left the Prussian throne in the hands of the untested Frederick

William II. He, like the British, saw in the Dutch Crisis and the Balkan war an opportunity to reassert Prussian interests in European affairs and to end Berlin's own dangerous isolation.[80]

The conflict between the Orangists and the Patriots had emerged during the American War of Independence as the war became a focal point for conflicting Dutch political ideologies. Those with republican sympathies supported the Americans and the French, while the supporters of the Orangist stadtholderate favored the British cause. Conflict within the Netherlands continued after the war ended, as did Anglo-French competition for influence over the United Provinces. The British sought to gain a Dutch alliance by backing the Orangist regime while the French supported the more republican Patriot party. This led to a standoff between London and Versailles after both refused to concede the immense strategic value of the Netherlands. Yet, in the context of commercial rapprochement, neither desired war.[81]

Sir James Harris represented Britain at The Hague, and the task of turning the Dutch civil conflict to British benefit fell to him. Before his dismissal, Fox had appointed Harris to The Hague. Although Harris remained a supporter of Fox, Pitt confirmed the appointment, eager to capitalize on Harris's two decades of diplomatic experience at Madrid, Berlin, and St. Petersburg. Like Fox, Harris hoped for an alliance between Britain and Prussia rather than Austria, a stance that put him at odds with Carmarthen. Harris also shared Fox's Francophobia instead of Pitt's diplomatic flexibility. While this predilection colored all of Harris's correspondence, it perfectly suited his mission to undermine French influence in the United Provinces and draw that country into the British sphere.[82] Recognizing the strategic value of the Netherlands and the importance of breaking British isolation by regaining The Hague as an ally, Harris observed that "the honor, the welfare, nay, the very existence of England as a great power appears to be deeply concerned in the upshot of the present crisis."[83]

After arriving at The Hague in 1784, Harris sought to use the means available to him as British minister plenipotentiary to rally the Orangists into a cohesive party to restore the Stadtholder to full power and expel French influence. However, his instructions from Whitehall prevented him from offering the Orangists any concrete assurances of British support. While Carmarthen urged Harris to separate the Dutch from France through political machinations, he also cautioned against compromising Britain's recovery with commitments that might lead to war with France. "Yet even the attainment of this object must not be purchased at the expense of having to support at all events the enfeebled and impoverished remains of a distressed and divided country."[84] Harris struggled to make progress between 1784 and 1786, having neither commitment from Pitt to take decisive action nor an organized Orangist party to support in the Netherlands.[85]

Given that William V's wife, Princess Wilhelmina, was the niece of Frederick II (and sister of future Prussian king Frederick William II), Harris hoped in vain to gain the support of Prussian influence in favor of the Orangist cause. However, Frederick refused to chart a course that might lead to war with France and potentially Austria and Russia as well. The aging warrior king had challenged that alliance before at great cost and preferred to end his days in peace rather than another existential struggle. Thus, Prussian influence promoted inaction and conciliation with France, undermining rather than aiding Harris's mission.[86] Armed with French support and Prussian quiescence, the Patriot party steadily eroded the power of the stadtholderate, weakening William V, as Harris thought, with the eventual intent of converting the Netherlands into a true democratic republic. Successful French resolution of the Scheldt Crisis yielded the Franco-Dutch alliance of 1785, entrenching the Patriot party and, with it, French influence in the United Provinces. William V, fearing for the safety of his family, left The Hague and took his family to Het Loo palace in the loyalist province of Gelderland. These circumstances reduced Harris's access to the royal family and pushed him to the margins of Dutch court politics despite his best efforts. Harris's letters during this period describe his desperate and fruitless efforts to combat French influence and his constant frustrations with both the meekness of his Orangist friends and the limited support he received from the Cabinet.[87]

Despite his frustrations, Harris demonstrated some sympathy for the caution dictated from Whitehall. In another letter to Ewart, he addressed the question of whether Britain should pursue an Austrian or Prussian alliance to support its Continental interests. Regarding the Cabinet's hesitance to pursue either too eagerly, Harris observed:

> Many motives . . . justify this system of delay. Our future safety as well as future consequence depend on our not committing ourselves imprudently to the Continent. . . . England is not in a situation to want allies, and warm as I am in wishing to see her once more topping her part on the Continent, yet I had rather wait for the moment . . . when, instead of seeking connections, her alliance shall be sought for. This seems to me to be the system adopted by the present Cabinet, and it incontestably is a wise one.[88]

Although generally an advocate of a Prussian connection, Harris's experience at The Hague with disagreeable Prussian ministers and policies eventually brought him to appreciate the caution mandated from London.

In May 1786, Harris's fortunes shifted when he met the Orangist pensionary of the province of Zeeland, Laurens Pieter van de Spiegel. Unlike Harris, who relied on spies and an unreliable network of "friends," Spiegel possessed an extensive network of connections within the government. While Harris had necessarily trodden lightly to avoid the appearance of British meddling in Dutch politics, Spiegel took more overt and proactive measures to promote the Orangist cause without the stigma of foreign interference.[89]

Spiegel initially offered to force a crisis by having Zealand secede from the United Provinces on the grounds that the Patriots had violated the Dutch constitution. With Carmarthen's full support, Harris rejected this as likely to lead to war, which Pitt still sought to avoid. Spiegel prophetically argued that France was unprepared for war and would not fight to retain its position in the Netherlands, but he also offered an alternative course.[90] He proposed to rally William V to take a more decisive role in opposing the Patriots and promoting the Orangist and constitutional cause, something Harris as a foreigner had failed to achieve in two years. Harris noted, "The cooperation between [Spiegel] and myself is to be carefully concealed from the Prince (at least for a time), as he is of so suspicious a turn, and so jealous of being governed, that it is probable the umbrage he would take at this circumstance would make him blind to all the advantages he might derive from the measure." Despite his annoyance with the Prince of Orange, Harris expressed confidence in the pensionary: "I have only to add that my hopes on this occasion are buoyed up by those of [Spiegel]. My deference to his opinion is not slightly founded. He is the only man the Patriots dread—the only one the other side universally acknowledge as superior to them all."[91] If he succeeded, Spiegel proposed that George III issue a statement in support of the Stadtholder in the hope that the promise of foreign support would embolden the typically timid Orangists throughout the country. Spiegel succeeded in spurring the Stadtholder to action, and, on 5 July 1786, Harris delivered a memorial from the king supporting the Stadtholder. These moves escalated the simmering tensions rapidly to the point of open breach and armed conflict between the Stadtholder's troops and the Patriot Free Corps in September.[92]

The rupture in the Netherlands corresponded with a change of Prussian policy following the death of Frederick II in August 1786. The new king, Frederick William II, remained wary of plunging Prussia into a disastrous war but also took much more interest in the future and the welfare of his sister and her husband, the Princess and Prince of Orange. He dispatched Count Johann Eustach von Görtz to the Netherlands to negotiate a peaceful resolution to the crisis with the French ambassador while also coordinating his efforts with Harris. Harris commented to Carmarthen, "To say the truth, Görtz bears himself so fairly, and what he does so perfectly coincides with what he says, that if he does deceive, he employs a species of deception the Devil has hitherto reserved for his own use."[93]

On Carmarthen's advice, Harris wrote to Pitt directly, urging him to support the Stadtholder more openly and to end his refusal to commit Britain to a course that might lead to war.[94] Hitherto, Pitt had left the conduct of diplomacy largely to the traditional channel of correspondence between diplomats and the foreign secretary and simply ensured that Carmarthen's dispatches possessed appropriate restraint. Harris's direct contact brought Pitt closer to the action.[95] Pitt responded quickly to Harris's requests for money to support the Orangist cause. In May, he allowed Harris to return to London to discuss the situation in greater detail. Although Pitt and George III remained determined to avoid open war, Harris and Carmarthen not only increased Pitt's interest in the Dutch Crisis but also drew him deeper into the conduct of foreign policy.[96]

In an effort to expand British influence without committing his country to war, Harris tried without success to persuade the Orangists to formally request British mediation, a measure more palatable to Pitt's views. An opportunity to realize this idea arose when the Patriot party proposed to formally request French mediation of the crisis in hopes of forcing France to take a more open and active role on their behalf. Harris urged the Orangist party "to say they are not averse to the mediation of France, provided other great powers should be also called upon to act as mediators, and if they should be pressed to declare whom they mean by these powers, to name the three great monarchies which (besides France) surround the Republic—England, the Emperor, and Prussia." To support this measure and strengthen the resolve of the Orangists within the government, Princess Wilhelmina resolved to return to The Hague, traveling through the province of Holland, which remained largely controlled by the Patriot Free Corps.[97]

Wilhelmina's journey to The Hague furnished the first of two events that overcame the inertia surrounding the Dutch Crisis. On 28 June 1787, a Patriot Free Corps arrested the princess and detained her in a farmhouse, refusing to allow her to proceed to The Hague on orders from the Patriot military leadership.[98] Although they allowed her to return to Het Loo on 30 June, both the fact and manner of her detainment and the obstruction of her journey represented a major insult to the House of Orange. This incensed Frederick William who protested and mobilized troops to demand satisfaction.[99] Frederick William remained full of bluster but hesitant to act until the outbreak of the Russo-Turkish war on 19 August 1787 alleviated his fears of Austrian or Russian intervention.[100]

Meanwhile, financial crisis and ministerial division paralyzed France as Pitt gained confidence and unity within his own administration.[101] Pitt increasingly took personal responsibility for directing British foreign policy over the course of the summer of 1787. He drafted instructions to Harris, Ewart, and Eden; persuaded the king to support a strong stand on the Dutch Crisis; and built consensus within the Cabinet. Pitt's personal leadership manifested in his decision to dispatch Grenville, increasingly one of his closest confidants, to The Hague.[102] There, Grenville served as Pitt's personal agent to corroborate Harris's accounts and to support the ambassador's efforts. The confirmation that the Cabinet received from Grenville's mission led to an agreement to support Prussian military intervention in the United Provinces. In addition, Pitt took measures to mobilize the British army and Royal Navy and to raise troops from German princes to lend force to Anglo-Prussian cooperation. This preparation dispelled post-1783 Continental perceptions of Britain as a weak, passive, and declining power.[103]

Thus confident of British support, Austrian preoccupation, and French weakness, Frederick William issued an ultimatum demanding satisfaction from the Patriots for the insult to his sister. After the ultimatum expired without a positive response, he ordered Prussian troops to enter the United Provinces on 13 September. Patriot resistance evaporated in the face of the Prussian army, and William V regained effective control of the country before the end of the month. A secret Anglo-Prussian convention signed on 2 October outlined the terms for settling the Dutch Crisis and bound both powers to uphold the results of the intervention. The Dutch government accepted this on 10 October, and the convention was published on 20 October.[104]

To complete the success, London and Berlin only needed to secure formal French acceptance of the fait accompli. Based on Eden's reports, Pitt feared that the French might consider their prestige too far committed to allow the Patriots to fall without a fight, but he asserted his willingness to accept war rather than compromise the results of the Prussian action. Pitt's direct involvement in the execution of foreign policy lent British diplomacy a decisiveness it had lacked. Although willing to take the plunge into war if necessary, Pitt still wanted to avoid armed conflict if possible and dispatched Grenville again to Paris to work with Eden to help the French extricate themselves as honorably as possible.[105] Ultimately, Grenville's mission coupled with Britain's show of strength, Prussia's decisive campaign, and France's financial woes helped persuade Versailles to concede. The French formally accepted Prussian intervention in the United Provinces on 27 October 1787.[106]

While British success in the Dutch Crisis owed much to favorable if unpredictable circumstances, it also represented Pitt's leadership and synthesis of the multiple foreign policy views within the government. Pitt adopted the determination of Harris and Carmarthen to act decisively to detach the United Provinces from France even at the risk of war. However, he did not totally

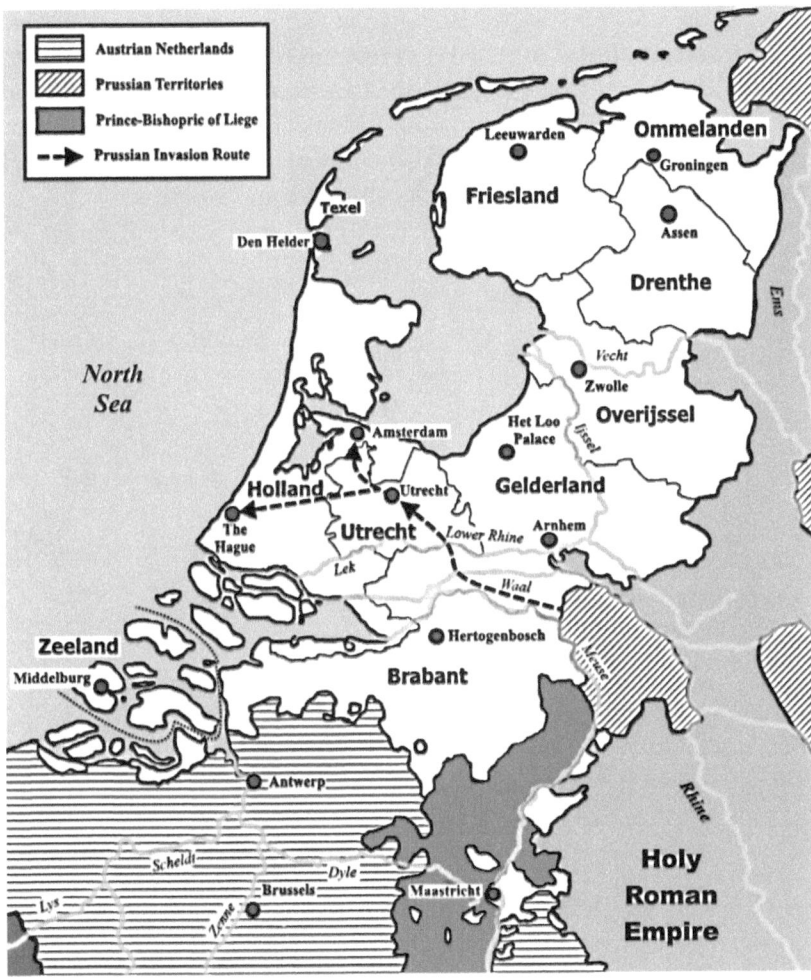

The Dutch Crisis, 1787

abandon the pursuit of rapprochement with France. Eden advocated Anglo-French friendship from his embassy, while in the Cabinet Thurlow cautioned against letting fears about French colonial ambitions dictate Britain's European policies. Pitt accepted Harris's and Ewart's advice to close ranks with Prussia to reach an accord on the Dutch Crisis. Nevertheless, he remained initially hesitant to convert that partnership into a more permanent alliance, reflecting the preference of Richmond and Carmarthen to regain an Austrian alliance rather than depend on an unknown Prussian monarch. Pitt's hesitance to hazard war by making extensive commitments demonstrated the influence of George III and the king's man in the Cabinet, Thurlow, as well as his own inclinations as a financial reformer. Nevertheless, after he became convinced of the necessity, Pitt successfully led the Cabinet to recommend more active measures to support the Prussians and persuaded the king to endorse them. Emboldened by his success, Pitt sought to develop his foothold in the Low Countries into a more comprehensive system designed to secure peace for Britain not through timid isolation but through a confident collective security system.[107]

CHAPTER 2

THE TRIPLE ALLIANCE, 1788–1790

Although disastrous for France, the Dutch Crisis of 1787 provided Britain with its first major diplomatic success in nearly a quarter century, and it brought Pitt his first personal triumph in foreign policy. Spain had hesitated to support a weakened France against a strong Britain, and Austrian ambivalence toward the French position in the United Provinces and preoccupation with a Turkish war effectively ended the strained Franco-Austrian entente. Freed from the fear of Franco-Austrian unity, Frederick William II adopted a more adventurous foreign policy that initially brought Britain, Prussia, and the newly restored Orangist regime of the United Provinces closer together.[1]

Diplomatic success allowed Pitt to end British isolation, but it also required him to define the parameters of Britain's renewed engagement with Europe. This led to the formation of a triple alliance between Britain, Prussia, and the United Provinces. Pitt intended for this to serve as the foundation for a broader, multilateral collective security system based on the principles of the territorial status quo, trade agreements, neutral rights, and the resolution of diplomatic disputes through mediation—armed mediation if necessary. He viewed such a system as the best means of extending British influence in Europe and protecting Britain from the dangers of isolation. These intentions and the accompanying system took shape fitfully in 1788 and 1789. Although the Anglo-Prussian relationship faced many disagreements and divisions of purpose, the Triple Alliance would succeed in achieving Pitt's initial foreign policy goals of restoring British strength and influence in Europe and disrupting the potentially hostile opposing bloc.

In theory, recent success empowered the British to seek an alliance with almost any state in Europe as long as the king, the Cabinet, and Parliament could accept the corresponding commitments. However, national security concerns, traditional rivalries, and diplomatic momentum pushed the British toward a triple alliance with the United Provinces and Prussia and away from rapprochement with France, Russia, or Austria. France remained Britain's chief potential rival due to its proximity and capacity to challenge the Royal Navy when supported by the Dutch and Spanish fleets. As for Russia, British politicians were just beginning to view St. Petersburg as a rival in the 1780s. It had been a traditional friend and trading partner, but Catherine II adopted a course that steadily alienated the British. The growth of the Russian navy during the eighteenth century attracted British attention, and the First Partition of Poland had so disgusted George III that he considered an alliance with France to overturn it.[2] Catherine's League of Armed Neutrality in 1780 caused the British tremendous alarm as it represented a Russian attempt to dictate maritime law contrary to British interests. These developments and the lapse of the traditional Anglo-Russian trade arrangement in 1786 caused Pitt to view Russia as unfriendly if not outright hostile. Austria under Joseph II also posed a concern as an aggressive power in Germany, but British politicians viewed Vienna's alliances with France and Russia and its aggressive trajectory as temporary and unnatural. The British government opposed Joseph's ambitious schemes from concern about their ramifications for French or Russian power more than out of apprehension about the threat of Austria in its own right.[3]

Although Pitt and Carmarthen ultimately parlayed success in the Dutch Crisis into alliances with Prussia and the United Provinces, such results were hardly the inevitable result of the temporary partnership of these states. Two years earlier, the Fürstenbund affair had involved similar circumstantial collaboration yet yielded no realignment. To gain an alliance, Britain needed Continental partners convinced of the value of a British connection. Securing an alliance also required a Cabinet willing to undertake the risks associated with Continental commitments. The negotiations of 1787–88 that produced the Triple Alliance benefited from better dispositions than those that had existed in 1785, both in potential allies and in British ministers.

The British guarantee of the Dutch settlement provided logical groundwork for an Anglo-Dutch alliance, which the restored government of William V eagerly solicited.[4] Within the Cabinet, only Lord Chancellor Thurlow opposed the Dutch alliance. Writing to Lord Privy Seal Granville Leveson-Gower, First Marquess of Stafford, Thurlow explained:

> Defense is our single object, and that is supposed to be pretty much in our own power. . . . I had rather not contract a defensive alliance with Holland for this short reason, that we do not want their defense, at least so probably or in such a degree as they may want ours. Nor can they give it, if they would, in the same extent, nor would they if they could. We [know too well] what sort of ally they always prove when we want them.[5]

Thurlow's opposition to the Dutch alliance arose from his preference for isolationism reminiscent of the decade preceding the American Revolution. However, the lord chancellor also observed, "My own opinions I don't recommend to much notice; because they are against every other opinion in the Cabinet; ... and because the steps we have lately taken drive them still further out of doors."[6] These comments suggest that Pitt's growing interest in proactive interventionism had drawn the majority of the Cabinet into favoring such policies.

Despite his personal opposition to Continental alliances, Thurlow conceded, "At the same time, there are many very solid considerations on the other side. Maintaining the point we have gained seems to render such an alliance requisite."[7] Based on this consideration, Harris began negotiating toward an Anglo-Dutch alliance with the Cabinet's approval as soon as news of French quiescence reached The Hague at the end of October. Harris conducted his negotiations primarily with his Dutch counterpart during the crisis, Laurens Pieter van de Spiegel, whom William V had elevated to the position of Grand Pensionary, a post approximately equivalent to that of prime minister in Britain. The two quickly reached agreement on most points except for the arrangements concerning both states' East Indian possessions. By April, Harris had persuaded the Cabinet to allow separate negotiations for the European alliance and for the treaty pertaining to Asian colonies and commerce. He feared that disputes over Asia might overturn the fragile British ascendancy at The Hague and undermine the treaty. Thus, on 15 April 1788, Harris obtained Dutch agreement to an alliance with Britain, guaranteeing the results of the recent crisis as well as each country's territorial integrity.[8]

That the Cabinet approved the separation of the European and colonial treaties with the Dutch to expedite the former reflects the emerging pattern of the Pitt administration's determination to avoid subordinating Britain's European interests to its global concerns. Colonial concerns certainly remained significant in British relations with its Continental neighbors, but they formed components of a broader foreign policy focus on Europe. This trend received official expression in negotiations with Prussia regarding the timeline of withdrawing the Prussian troops that had intervened in the United Provinces as well as the options for replacing them. Carmarthen rejected a Prussian request to facilitate the withdrawal of Prussian troops by transferring into Dutch service the Hessians that George III had contracted to support the Prussian intervention. Carmarthen explained "that it is the King's intention to keep a respectable force in readiness in order to be prepared for any emergency and to support the continental influence of Great Britain." Ewart noted that "both the King of Prussia and his ministers ... seem particularly pleased" with this reasoning despite the rejection of their request.[9]

Anglo-Prussian cooperation in the Dutch Crisis made an alliance between the two courts a natural extension of the Anglo-Dutch alliance. Such an arrangement had been in consideration even before the formal Anglo-Prussian agreement to intervene in the Dutch Crisis. On 27 September 1787, Ewart forwarded to Carmarthen the Dutch and Prussian expectations of a triple alliance of the three states.[10] On 12 October he relayed another, more specific Prussian proposal for Britain and Prussia to make separate arrangements with the Dutch based on their differing interests in the Netherlands. He also wrote that the Prussian foreign secretary, Count Ewald Friedrich von Hertzberg, expected that an Anglo-Prussian alliance formed afterward would bind those separate arrangements together. Notably, Hertzberg also expressed a preference for separate arrangements to avoid causing "alarm and jealousy among the other powers."[11] Starting in October 1787, each of Ewart's dispatches mentioned Hertzberg's desire to forge a triple alliance with Britain and the United Provinces.

Despite these eager proposals, the British remained noncommittal. Although Carmarthen received Ewart's letter of 27 September by 3 October and the letter of 12 October by the end of that month, he did not acknowledge the Prussian alliance proposal until responding on 2 December. In that letter, he echoed Hertzberg's concern that the formation of a triple alliance might offend the other powers and drive them into hostile connections. He agreed that separate arrangements would mitigate this danger and better facilitate future efforts to enlist other states into the new alliance system. Carmarthen embraced Hertzberg's latter proposal that Britain and Prussia should conclude separate alliances with the Dutch and suggested that they simply turn their secret convention of 2 October 1787 into a public guarantee of the Dutch settlement.[12]

This hesitancy to create a triple alliance immediately arose primarily from the stated fear of inspiring a counteralliance system. The British received reports from Berlin and St. Petersburg of a French attempt to forge their own triple alliance with Austria and Russia. Thurlow alluded to this in his own arguments against both the Dutch and Prussian alliances, complaining that these alliances would "plunge" Britain into unnecessary conflicts in Europe. He argued that the proposed Anglo-Prussian connection would preclude the revival of a more desirable Anglo-Austrian alliance. He predicted that the offense that Britain had given to France in the Dutch Crisis combined with the negative impact of the alliance on Austria would prompt those two powers to establish their own triple alliance with Russia. He warned that this would "bring Prussia and ourselves also to the condition of 1756" when a similar Anglo-Prussian arrangement had aggravated Austria and its allies and contributed to the outbreak of the Seven Years War.[13]

Carmarthen urged British diplomats to take this threat seriously and forward any information they could find relative to it. Nonetheless, the foreign secretary personally doubted that the three potentially hostile powers could reach a suitable agreement or coordinate their resources effectively. Revealing confidence hitherto lacking in British foreign policy under Pitt's leadership, he articulated his opinion that Britain and Prussia were well positioned geographically to coordinate a defense against hostile powers if necessary. He also asserted optimistically that "much additional force might be collected among the different powers of Europe to oppose such a confederacy." He named Sweden, Denmark, and Spain as potential allies and added that the smaller states of Germany and the Mediterranean might also support Britain and Prussia against the more aggressive alignment of France, Austria, and Russia.[14] This dispatch demonstrates a significant expansion of the leading ministers' vision for British foreign policy from their initially cautious goals of 1783.[15]

As indicated in Carmarthen's dispatch, British goals began to expand from simply securing the United Provinces and disrupting the alliance network of France, Spain, and the two imperial courts to countering that network directly with a larger collective security system. The idea of widening the alliance was not unique to the British. Ewart relayed to Carmarthen: "I understand the king of Prussia and his Cabinet dwell much on the expediency of contracting the closest engagement with His Majesty in order to consolidate the reciprocity of the connection of England and this country with the United Provinces to provide for their mutual security against the future attempts of France and to lay the foundation of the Northern Alliance, which His Prussian Majesty has so much at heart."[16] Ewart's subsequent messages often reported a Prussian desire to recruit Russia into such an alliance system. Additionally, the Swedish ambassador, Gustav Adam von Nolcken, approached Carmarthen on 23 December 1787 with a proposal from Gustav III. Carmarthen explained to Ewart that "the proposal is nothing less than the forming a quintuple alliance between Great Britain, Prussia, Sweden, Denmark, and Holland with a view to establish a permanent system of security to each of the contracting parties."[17]

The desire to widen the alliance furnished additional motivation for delaying the Prussian alliance until further negotiations might bring other states into the system. Beyond its greater strength, a wider alliance system held appeal as a means of restraining Prussia if Frederick William II proved more aggressive than the Cabinet wanted. Ewart's reports through the winter and into the spring of 1788 indicated an ambitious and acquisitive direction for Prussian foreign policy. On 22 December 1787, he sent Carmarthen the first report of what would become known as the Hertzberg Plan, named for the Prussian foreign secretary who conceived it. Ewart reported that the Prussians expressed a desire to bring an end to the Russo-Turkish War through armed mediation favoring Russia. They hoped to persuade the Ottomans to make concessions to Russia in return for all remaining Ottoman lands being guaranteed. Regarding Austrian compensation, Ewart wrote, "Should the Emperor in this case insist on making some acquisitions of importance, I have reason to suspect that this Court would expect to have an Equivalent on the side of Poland."[18]

Carmarthen avoided the question of mediation and concessions until finally acknowledging the Hertzberg Plan in April 1788 for the purpose of explicitly deferring all discussion of it. He acknowledged the logic that any increase in Austrian strength would represent a relative decline in Prussian strength as an ally for Britain, but he maintained that the moment was premature for taking any decisive measures against that possibility. He expressed doubts as to whether the Austrians and Russians would be militarily capable of making major conquests and "whether France has so far abandoned her former politics as to acquiesce in and favor such an arrangement."[19] This evasion allowed Anglo-Prussian negotiations to continue ultimately to the conclusion of the alliance much as the omission of colonial affairs from the Dutch treaty facilitated its completion. However, it only thinly concealed the underlying difference of purpose between the two courts.

While Hertzberg hoped to use a connection with the maritime powers to increase Prussia's weight in the competitive balance of power relative to Austria and Russia, Carmarthen asserted a more cooperative perspective that "the great object which we have in view is the continuance of peace as far as that is not inconsistent with our essential interests."[20] Harris articulated more clearly the reasons for Britain to oppose a scheme like the Hertzberg Plan: "I do not in my own mind like an accommodation that is to depend on the reciprocal aggrandizement of the belligerent powers and that of one of the mediating ones; it is establishing a principle of depredation, which upends all system and will I think stand in the way of that we are inclined to adopt."[21] The Hertzberg Plan rested on a predatory view of the balance of power that encouraged the partition of weaker, neutral states under the threat of war to preserve the competitive balance among the great powers. In contrast, the emerging British vision for a collective security system sought to maintain the balance through preservation of the territorial status quo, multilateral mediation of disputes, protection of weaker states, and the promotion of commerce. In the example of Poland, the Hertzberg Plan called for British assistance in orchestrating a partition to satisfy the jealousies of the eastern powers with vague hopes of bringing Russia into the new system. However, the British viewed Poland as a potential commercial partner and ally to integrate into the new system with a view to restraining all three of the eastern powers.[22]

Although Thurlow bemoaned the likelihood of a Prussian alliance embroiling Britain in wars in western Europe, eastern European issues dominated the attention of the Allies from the conception of the alliance to its collapse.[23] During the spring of 1788, the Russo-Turkish War animated Anglo-Prussian alliance discussions more than apprehensions about France. On 15 March, Ewart conveyed a Prussian proposal to use a guarantee of the Ottoman Empire as the basis for a larger alliance system. Echoing some of Carmarthen's optimism about the general diplomatic situation, Hertzberg argued that Spain, Sweden, Sardinia, and other Mediterranean states would likely embrace this system "to the great disparagement of the influence and political consideration of both France and Austria."[24] Carmarthen offered cautious agreement to this plan with subtle distinctions:

> It seems difficult, as I have already stated, to speak with precision respecting the Porte, under the present circumstances, but there seems the greatest reason to suppose that there will be a favorable opening for the joint mediation of His Majesty and the King of Prussia and possibly, if a peace were to be made under their influence, a subsequent guarantee of the dominions of the Porte might make a part of the proposed system and the Porte itself be included in the general defensive alliance.[25]

Both London and Berlin viewed Austrian and Russian aggrandizement at the expense of the Turks as a threat to the balance of power and hoped to mediate an end to the conflict to preserve the Ottoman Empire and mitigate this threat. However, the Prussian proposal emphasized undercutting the influence of France and Austria and only offered to guarantee the remaining territory of the Ottoman Empire. In contrast, the British response focused on strengthening the collective security system by including a guaranteed Ottoman Empire as an alliance partner.

In addition, both the Prussian and the Swedish alliance proposals revolved around the eastern European question of whether the prospective partners should view Russia as an ally to win or an enemy to restrain. The Swedish quintuple alliance proposal from December 1787 met with an initially positive reception in London. However, British and Prussian ministers determined after some probing that Gustav primarily hoped to strengthen Sweden against Russia and had thus far resisted Anglo-Prussian suggestions to include Russia in the system. Ewart reported from Berlin on 10 January 1788, "I perceive the decided opinion of this court is that, at all events, the basis of the Northern System should first be laid by engagements between England, Prussia, and Russia, to which they think the other powers proposed would then readily accede."²⁶ This Prussian perspective disregarded Swedish hopes for an alliance against Russia, instead anticipating that fear would compel the Swedes to accede to an alliance that included Russia, Prussia, and Britain.

In the spring of 1788, both the British and Prussian cabinets hoped to pull Russia away from Austria to become a partner, though their differences regarding the best means of achieving this end nearly soured the alliance negotiations.²⁷ Hertzberg expressed his opinion that "nothing would tend so effectually to induce other powers to accede to the system as the knowledge of so solid a foundation being laid."²⁸ This view had a British advocate in James Harris, who wrote to Carmarthen on 29 January 1788:

> The moment England, Prussia, and the Republic are allied, Russia will be very glad to become a fourth contracting party; that while the union is in suspense, she will waver between the two great parties in Europe and endeavor to keep her consequence by coquetting both sides.... Vanity and a thirst for fame being the Empress's ruling passion, she will always lean towards the strongest side, and the solid and formidable mass the three powers I mentioned above would form if intimately connected would be one to which I am sure she would be eager to join the instant a favorable opportunity was held out to her to escape from the arms of the Emperor.... For these reasons, I am clearly for closing immediately with Prussia—I think we could govern that court now, and if that is once ascertained I will be responsible for governing [the Dutch].²⁹

Harris's confidence of being able to "govern" Prussia willfully ignored the inconsistency and factionalism evident in Ewart's reports of the court of Frederick William during and after the Dutch Crisis. Similarly, his appraisal of Russian views reflected more of a projection of his own hopes than a realistic assessment of Catherine's attitudes.

The British Cabinet shared neither Hertzberg's confidence nor Harris's arrogance. On 2 April, Carmarthen explained to Ewart the Cabinet's belief in the necessity of delaying the alliance to avoid or mitigate its negative impact on relations with other states, particularly Russia. "It seems to be by no means the interest of either this country or Prussia to bring forward any measure which would have the effect of driving the Empress into more direct and open engagements with the court of Versailles."³⁰ On 14 May, Carmarthen reiterated this view in response to renewed Prussian pressure to conclude the alliance quickly. Although gradually relenting to this pressure for fear of driving the Prussians away with repeated refusals, Carmarthen still pleaded for delay: "A short time may possibly give an opportunity of comprehending more powers in the original formation of the alliance so as to give it at once that solidity and extent which the intrigues of other courts might render more difficult afterwards."[31] Unlike Harris and Hertzberg, the British Cabinet expected Catherine II to (correctly) view the new Anglo-Prussian system as a direct threat to Russia's dominance in eastern Europe. British ministers doubted the possibility of winning Russia over to the new system unless they could make it appear both strong enough to compete with a triple alliance of France, Austria, and Russia and diverse enough to diminish the impression of it being explicitly hostile in intent.

Parliamentary considerations also induced the Cabinet to favor delay. In his dispatch of 14 May, Carmarthen explained to Ewart that "the pressure of business in both Houses of Parliament at this period of the session has made it impossible for His Majesty's servants to give as full and early an attention as they wished to the many important considerations which are connected with the subject of the proposals you have transmitted."[32] Although in part a delaying tactic, Carmarthen did not lie when he complained of "the pressure of business in both Houses of Parliament." During the summer of 1788, both Lords and Commons rumbled with vigorous debates pertaining to the impeachment of Warren Hastings, the regulation of the slave trade, and the budget for 1788.[33] In addition to the distraction the debates caused, British administrations preferred to conduct contentious foreign policy business during parliamentary recesses. Pitt's ministry had followed this trend, managing the Fürstenbund Crisis, the Eden Treaty, and the Dutch Crisis almost entirely between parliamentary sessions. This allowed the Cabinet to present these diplomatic initiatives to Parliament as completed achievements rather than subjects for debate. Aside from complicating the decision process, parliamentary debate on diplomatic matters undermined the secrecy essential in controlling the impressions made on other states in the course of any negotiations. Pitt and Carmarthen hoped to avoid making their hopes and fears regarding the potential Prussian treaty the subject of parliamentary debate. To achieve this, they needed to extend negotiations through the conclusion of the parliamentary session in July.[34]

Through May and June, Prussian pressure for an alliance increased, and British objections diminished. The Russo-Turkish War remained indecisive, and no triple alliance of France, Austria, and Russia emerged to threaten the Anglo-Prussian entente. Ewart reported that British delays threatened to revive a French party at Berlin, and the approaching end of the parliamentary session removed an obstacle to more extensive alliance negotiations. Although British resistance to forming an alliance diminished, Anglophobe members of the Prussian court advocated articles in propositions for a treaty of alliance sure to draw objections from London. They proposed to bind Britain to aid Prussia in any Continental war while absolving Prussia of any responsibility to aid Britain in the event of a maritime conflict. Such propositions naturally drew British objections and accentuated Frederick William's frustration with British delays.[35]

To combat the Prussian king's irritations and circumvent the resurgent Francophile faction at the Prussian court, the British took advantage of Frederick William's planned trip to Het Loo to visit his sister in mid-June. The Cabinet authorized James Harris to negotiate a provisional treaty directly with the king if the opportunity arose during his visit to the Dutch royal residence. In addition, George III wrote to the Princess of Orange to apprise her of this and seek her assistance in facilitating such negotiations.[36]

Harris received his mission during a visit to England and hurried back to reach The Hague by 9 June. There he communicated with his usual Dutch contacts to gather information pertaining to Frederick William's visit. He ascertained that "the king of Prussia was dissatisfied with the delay, full of doubts and suspicions, and that there was a powerful party at Berlin who were employing every means to fix them on his mind and to indispose him against any connection with England." Harris then traveled to Het Loo on 10 June to communicate with the Princess of Orange, who confirmed what he had learned. After receiving the letter from George III, Wilhelmina pledged to support Harris's mission in any way she could. For his part, Harris resolved to eliminate the complicated details of the negotiation and regain Frederick William's confidence by refocusing on the core principles of the Anglo-Prussian cooperation.[37]

Frederick William II arrived at Het Loo on 11 June. The festivities attending the king's arrival prevented Harris from having an audience with him until the following morning. After considering Harris's proposal, Frederick William decided "that he thought it preferable to conclude the provisional alliance with the act of guarantee for Holland directly, and, in the meantime, to sound and consult with other powers on the general and more extensive alliance." Thus, with the Prussian king's approval, Harris and the Prussian minister to the United Provinces drafted and signed the Provisional Treaty of Loo on 13 June 1788. On 15 June, Harris reported that "in return, [Frederick William] only required that we should immediately consent to open a negotiation for the main treaty at Berlin; and I confess, my Lord, I am particularly anxious that this should be complied with."[38] Harris also emphasized his belief that hesitance to conclude the alliance with Prussia would drive Berlin, and The Hague with it, into the arms of France, leaving Britain "reduced to the same isolated situation we stood in some time ago, with the additional aggravation of having awakened the resentment and jealousy of our vindictive, implacable, and powerful enemies."[39]

In compliance with the agreement between Harris and Frederick William, Ewart began negotiating with Hertzberg at Berlin to convert the provisional alliance into a definitive alliance. On 14 July, Carmarthen forwarded to Ewart the British ratification of the provisional treaty along with instructions to bring the negotiations to a conclusion.[40] The primary remaining point of debate between Ewart and Hertzberg concerned the question of whether colonial or maritime conflict constituted a *casus foederis* for the alliance. Ultimately, Ewart persuaded the Prussians to accept that it did and sign the definitive treaty on 13 August.[41]

The treaties that the Dutch concluded with the British and Prussians on 15 April 1788 together with the Anglo-Prussian treaty of 15 June established what became known as the Triple Alliance.[42] Rather than a single treaty, three similar bilateral treaties bound the three states together. The Anglo-Dutch alliance provided for mutual defense of both European and colonial territory as well as a guarantee of the Dutch constitution and the hereditary position of Stadtholder to the House of Orange. The treaty also stipulated specific obligations in terms of the men and ships each state should provide the other in the event of war, and it included the promise of a future agreement pertaining to commerce and an exchange of territory in India.[43]

The Prussian treaties with Britain and the United Provinces followed a similar pattern with the exception of relieving Prussia of any obligation to send troops overseas. The public articles of the Anglo-Prussian treaty referenced previous engagements between the two courts to diminish the novelty of the alliance. Additionally, the treaty publicly affirmed both British and Prussian determination to defend the settlement of the Dutch Crisis by force and stipulated the amount of aid each could require of the other.[44] Significantly, the secret articles went farther than this simple guarantee. Reflecting the broadening vision of British ministers as well as a similar Prussian desire to aggregate strength, the third secret article announced that "the purpose of the treaty . . . is to contribute as much as possible to the general tranquility of Europe. The other powers of Europe (and specifically those of the North) whose interest may be similar to those of the high contracting parties shall be invited to accede to it." The preceding article pledged both states to coordinate "on all issues that may affect their particular connection as well as the general system of Europe" and specified mediation of the Russo-Turkish War as a first goal. Thus, haltingly, the British and Prussian ministers laid the foundation for a new alliance system on which both placed great hopes.[45] Emphasizing the goal of expanding the alliance, diplomatic correspondence commonly referred to this network in the ensuing years as "the federative system," "the system of the Allies," or even as a "coalition."[46]

From the start, the Triple Alliance faced difficulties arising from the differences between British and Prussian goals. Frederick William viewed the alliance as a tool for increasing Prussia's weight in the balance of power. He sought to use this added weight for intimidation or, if necessary, war to wrest concessions from Russia, Austria, or France for any gains they might make in Europe. In contrast, the British preferred to use the defensive alliance for, at most, armed mediation to restrain Russian, French, or Austrian expansionism and maintain the status quo. The existing political and territorial arrangement of Europe offered Britain prosperity and security. Pursuant to the lessons of the American War of Independence, Pitt's administration sought to prevent the unification of the Continent against Britain. This required the preservation of the existing balance of power that kept the German powers strong enough to resist both French and Russian domination but not strong enough to dominate central Europe themselves. Pitt intended to maintain the status quo by protecting intermediary states like the United Provinces, Poland, Sweden, the Ottoman Empire, and the smaller members of the Holy Roman Empire.[47]

Preserving this balance required unprecedented British engagement in eastern Europe, which posed serious challenges for Pitt's administration. Russian hostility toward Britain made the promotion of British interests in eastern Europe dependent on cooperation with Sweden, Poland, and the Ottoman Empire. The traditional alliances between France and these three states complicated such cooperation. Consequently, opposition to Russian expansion required a rapprochement with France, or at least France's allies, while the traditional Anglo-French rivalry encouraged cooperation with Russia. Pitt charted a course that required containing both the newer Russian expansionism and the historical French threat. A collective security system based on the Triple Alliance offered the best chance of achieving this objective, extending British influence in Europe and preserving the balance of power.[48]

The first test for the Triple Alliance emerged even before the conclusion of the Anglo-Prussian treaty. Russia's war with the Ottoman Empire enticed the impatient Gustav III to declare war on Catherine II on 6 July 1788. He hoped to consolidate his hold on Swedish Finland and drive a wedge between Russia and Denmark-Norway.[49] London and Berlin had hoped to enlist both Gustav and Catherine into their alliance system, but the Swedish declaration of war rendered this impossible. Both courts anticipated Sweden's defeat and feared the prospect of Russian aggrandizement in Scandinavia alongside similar success in the Balkans. Consequently, the two powers sought to mitigate the upheaval by pressuring Denmark to remain neutral. Placing greater importance on their Russian connection than the requests of the Triple Alliance, the Danes honored their alliance with Russia, declaring war on Sweden in August and invading with 10,000 men.[50]

In the effort to restrain Denmark and salvage Sweden, events outpaced communication. Ewart and the British envoy extraordinary at Copenhagen,

Hugh Elliot, threatened the Danes with a joint Anglo-Prussian attack without explicit approval from London. George III and his man in the Cabinet, Thurlow, objected to what they viewed as an unnecessary risk of war, and the king suggested approaching France for support in mediating the Baltic war. Despite these complaints, the Cabinet generally supported its ministers abroad. Pitt promised to honor the king's wish to sound out the French and to avoid war if at all possible, but he also supported Carmarthen's defense of Elliot's and Ewart's actions as within the bounds of their instructions. Ultimately, the Allies achieved partial success by neutralizing Denmark, but Catherine refused to accept Triple Alliance mediation and perpetuated the war that Gustav started.[51]

Despite British diplomatic involvement in the war in the Baltic and the conclusion of the alliance with Prussia, domestic concerns overshadowed foreign affairs when Parliament reconvened on 20 November 1788. Two weeks before the opening of Parliament, George III became incapacitated by an illness that eighteenth-century physicians interpreted as the onset of insanity. With the king's recovery uncertain, Fox and the Whigs pressed for a regency under George, the Prince of Wales. The administration battled with the Whigs in Parliament for the votes of independent Members of Parliament on the question of a regency. Owing to the prince's friendship with Fox, such a regency would almost certainly precipitate a change of ministry from Pitt to Fox, a prospect that rendered British foreign policy uncertain.[52]

Expectations of political change combined with the king's inability to approve measures or correspond with other monarchs brought British diplomacy almost to a halt. Efforts to enlist other powers like Spain to support Triple Alliance mediation in the Baltic and Balkan wars faltered as the future of the Triple Alliance appeared uncertain. Similarly, Catherine's anticipation of a more Russophile Foxite ministry encouraged her to rebuff Triple Alliance mediation offers. The tsarina placed such great hope in this political shift in Britain that she instructed her envoy in London, Count Semyon Vorontsov, to begin discussing foreign policy with the Whig leaders, Fox and the Duke of Portland.[53]

Joseph II also used the occasion to claim his right as emperor to approve or reject any measures to establish a regency for Hanover. While Parliament debated the regency question in Britain, George, Prince of Wales, defied Joseph, asserting himself as regent of Hanover with support from Britain's new ally, Prussia, and the rest of the Fürstenbund as well. King George's recovery in February 1789 ended the Regency Crisis in favor of the Pitt ministry and forestalled any changes in the direction of British foreign policy. Although the crisis temporarily undermined British diplomacy, the nascent network that the king and his ministers had constructed proved strong enough to endure the disruption. The Pitt ministry's success in this regard underscored the value of the Triple

Alliance and the importance of maintaining and strengthening a cooperative European collective security system.[54]

In 1789, fresh crises in both eastern and western Europe offered opportunities to extend the influence of the Triple Alliance but also highlighted divisions among its partners. While financial crisis expanded into revolution in France, all three partners of the Triple Alliance took much greater interest in an emerging revolution in the neighboring Austrian Netherlands.[55] In response to demands from Joseph II for a new constitution and a regular subsidy, the Belgians rebelled, declared independence from Austria, and defeated an Austrian army in late October 1789. Additionally, Joseph's aggressive centralizing reforms raised the threat of rebellion in Hungary. With France reduced to impotence by financial and political upheaval, Joseph attempted to solve his problems by reviving the "old system" of Austro-British cooperation. However, the opportunity for Anglo-Austrian rapprochement had passed with the conclusion of the Anglo-Prussian alliance, and George III remained angry about Joseph's behavior during the Regency Crisis. Joseph received the reply that the British would adhere to their alliance system and only act together with their Prussian ally.[56]

British insistence on coordinating with Prussia any response to the upheavals in Austria's territories maintained apparent solidarity within the Triple Alliance, but it also brought to the fore the differences between the British and Prussian conceptions of the new alliance system. Frederick William hoped to capitalize on the unrest within the Austrian territories to pressure Austria and Russia to accept the plan for mediation and territorial redistribution that Hertzberg had proposed to Ewart in December 1787. Thus, Berlin advocated supporting the Belgian revolutionaries and creating an independent principality under Triple Alliance protection to weaken Joseph and make him more receptive to Prussian mediation. To Pitt's administration, the Belgian question of 1789 posed no fewer difficulties than had the Belgian question in 1784–85. From a British perspective, both possible outcomes—Austrian or rebel victory—promised to undermine British interests in the Low Countries by reducing the traditional barriers to French influence over the United Provinces. The assertion of Austrian authority would strengthen Austria in the region and thus make the Dutch more vulnerable to the Austro-French alliance, while an independent Belgium would pose a negligible obstacle to French influence or military power. Pitt and Carmarthen, who became Duke of Leeds in March 1789, instructed British envoys to abstain from any interference in the crisis and only support the restoration of the status quo in Belgium: the ancient constitution that preserved weak Austrian authority.[57]

This position strained the Anglo-Prussian alliance as Hertzberg and Frederick William saw Austrian distress as the perfect opportunity to make gains at their rival's expense. Toward this end, Prussian diplomats attempted to stitch together their own separate and more aggressive diplomatic system encompassing Sweden, Poland, and the Ottoman Empire. All indications pointed to Frederick William's intention to attack Austria in the spring of 1790. Meanwhile Pitt and Leeds returned friendly responses to Austrian proposals for British accession to the Austro-Russian alliance and British mediation of Austria's Belgian difficulties. While the British refused to engage in either measure without their Prussian ally, they expressed eagerness for a rapprochement with Austria and hoped for the eventual accession of Austria to the Triple Alliance. The additional option furnished by this approach emboldened Pitt and Leeds to take a firm stand to restrain Berlin's aggressive plans, thus preventing Prussian intervention in the Austrian Netherlands throughout 1789 and 1790.[58]

Despite the caution that Leeds urged in his dispatches and Pitt's resistance to the aggressive Prussian designs, British ministers studied the Belgian situation with as much interest as their Prussian counterparts in the hope of finding some way to turn the affair into an advantage. The Belgian revolution of 1789 provided a preview of Pitt's resolution to subordinate questions of political ideology or even temporary strategic advantages to his diplomatic principles. The Cabinet considered ideas for using the revolution in the Austrian Netherlands to strengthen the Triple Alliance either by adding an independent Belgium to the alliance or by gaining Austrian accession by supporting the Austrian response. While neither of these outcomes was the result, the affair induced discussion about the relationship between revolutionary principles and foreign policy. Apparent connections between the French and Belgian revolutionaries and exiled Dutch Patriots suggested that political revolutions might provide foundations for diplomatic realignments and alterations to the map of Europe. Additionally, Pitt refused to consider the Belgian cause at all unless the Belgian Republic agreed to recognize the binding legality of existing international treaties. The British envoy at The Hague at this time, Alleyne Fitzherbert, noted that "the great object seems to be to oblige this new Republic to recognize the more important articles of subsisting treaties and to enroll, as it were, that recognition amongst the fundamental points of their constitution."[59] While willing to consider alterations to the map of Europe, Pitt refused to accept changes that simply repudiated the legal basis of the European state system. The cautious British response to the Belgian revolution demonstrated reluctance to trust revolutionary movements in questions of foreign policy. This distrust kept the British from supporting the Belgians while Austria recovered and ultimately suppressed the uprising by 1791.[60]

On the other side of Europe, the division of Russian resources between two wars loosened Catherine's grip on Polish politics. On 6 October 1788, the

Polish Sejm exercised its right to form a confederation, thereby eliminating the infamous liberum veto and attaining the ability to pass proposals by a simple majority. The Sejm then voted to demand that Catherine withdraw all Russian troops from Polish territory and started negotiations with the British, Prussian, and Swedish ambassadors for alliances. Both the British and Prussian governments took a keen interest in the fate of Poland, and the success or failure of the Triple Alliance as the foundation for a collective security system soon became intertwined with the Polish question.[61]

The British Cabinet responded to the changes in Poland in November 1788 by sending Daniel Hailes to replace Charles Whitworth as the British minister plenipotentiary at Warsaw with instructions to bring Poland into the Triple Alliance system. While the Poles first sought Prussian assistance for pragmatic reasons, they distrusted Berlin, fearing that eventual peace between Russia and the Ottoman Empire might lead to a Russo-Prussian partition agreement. On 8 February 1789, Hailes wrote to Carmarthen to report the great interest of the Poles in cultivating a close relationship with Britain. His Polish correspondents emphasized the commercial advantage of this relationship after forming the confederation Sejm, which they referred to as a revolution. He also relayed "that it is hoped, should an alliance take place between Prussia and [Poland], that England, a country on which they place their chief dependence, will not be backward in acceding to it." Hailes viewed Polish claims about the miraculous impact of their revolution on their military and commercial capabilities with skepticism. He advised that Poland's value as an ally "must be regulated by [the policies] of the power on whom it depends for support," be that Prussia or Russia. Correspondingly, he recommended that any Anglo-Polish connection must rest on the foundation of a Prusso-Polish understanding, advising his Polish colleagues accordingly.[62]

Concurrently, the British consul at Memel, James Durno, traveled to London and delivered a detailed report on the same issues. His report highlighted the immense potential of Poland as both a commercial and military partner but echoed Hailes's assessment of the difficulties. Durno's report outlined three advantages of seeking effective connections with Poland based on the support of Prussia:

> Firstly, to open in the Prussian sea ports a second market for such naval stores as we have hitherto been almost wholly dependent for on Russia. Secondly, to gain two new markets for our products and manufactures . . . in Prussia and in Poland; and through these, an indirect passage for them even into the heart of Russia. Thirdly, to secure the permanency of these advantages, by removing the danger, with which we are at present threatened, of the Russians transferring a great part of their own and of the Polish trade from the Baltic to the Black Sea.[63]

The danger to which Durno referred arose from Russian military success and the conquest of the region of Bessarabia, encompassing the fortress of Ochakov and the mouth of the Dniester River. These Russian advances threatened to eliminate the only avenue for Anglo-Polish trade not under either Russian or Prussian control. To avert this threat and maximize Anglo-Polish commerce through both the Baltic Sea and the Black Sea, Durno suggested that the Cabinet "make, firstly, the restitution of Ochakov and of all Bessarabia, the retention of which would command the navigation of the two great rivers Bug and Dniester, if not even of the Black Sea itself; and secondly, the renunciation of the free navigation of the Black Sea and passage of the Dardanelles . . . articles, sine qua non of the ensuing peace between the Russians and the Turks."[64] He expressed the prescient concern that the Prussians may not accept the long-term mutual commercial benefits of this arrangement as a substitute for territorial gains. Thus, he advised moving quickly while Prussian good will remained relatively strong and the Polish government eagerly pursued connections with the Triple Alliance.[65]

Efforts to bring Poland into the Triple Alliance foundered on the commercial disagreement between Britain and Prussia that Durno predicted. This was not simply an example of Britain acting as a nation of shopkeepers; rather, the dispute reflected divergent British and Prussian goals for Poland as a member of the alliance. The British hoped to use trade with Poland through Danzig and the Vistula to enrich and strengthen that country to the point of being a suitable replacement for Russia both economically and militarily. In contrast, Berlin sought to displace Russia as the dominant influence at Warsaw, extracting economic and military resources from Poland as a client state rather than as a partner. Owing to geographic limitations, the British necessarily refused to negotiate a separate arrangement with Poland without Prussian consent. Instead, British ministers insisted on standing by their more valuable Prussian ally, basing any Anglo-Polish connection on a Prusso-Polish understanding.[66]

On 26 March 1789, Hailes reported that Polish requests to renegotiate commercial arrangements with Prussia had received favorable but vague responses.[67] Nevertheless, the Polish government remained suspicious and placed greater reliance on British influence to force the Prussians to relax their stranglehold on commerce along the Vistula. Hailes informed his government of an offer for a direct Anglo-Polish connection on 27 March. The Poles suggested ceding to Britain their ports on the coast of Samogitia (Lithuania) as a means of establishing more direct contact and circumventing Prussian restrictions on Polish trade. Hailes doubted that such a measure would be effective or worth the cost to Britain. Instead, he argued for compromising with Prussia on the terms for Polish trade in the Baltic while cultivating Anglo-Polish trade through the

Black Sea by way of the Dniester, which flowed through only Polish and Turkish territory.[68]

Hailes went on, writing in cipher, to express concerns that if the Prussians learned of any such efforts to circumvent their interests in Polish trade, any hope of sincere Prusso-Polish cooperation would be dashed. Regarding the practicability of the project, Hailes suggested that the proposed cession could theoretically provide a closer connection between Britain and Poland but only with the support of the whole Sejm. He cautioned that the entrenched Prussian and Russian parties in the Sejm would work to frustrate British commercial projects in Poland. Countering this would require the formation and support of a comparable British party in the Sejm and even formally taking Poland under British protection. Hailes noted that the Poles clearly hoped to gain such British protection through the proposed cession and commercial arrangements. However, he questioned "how far we ought to engage for their independence and how far the benefits of a free trade with this country may compensate the difficulty of maintaining our influence in Poland and the danger arising from the protection of a sort of new colonies."[69] Fundamentally, Poland and Britain could do little for each other independent of Prussia because of Prussian control of the Vistula. Therefore, Hailes recommended that the Poles cultivate a good relationship with Prussia, and he advised his government to proceed cautiously in Polish affairs for fear of alienating Prussia or incurring unrealistic obligations to defend Polish independence.[70]

As negotiations between Poland and the Triple Alliance continued, the crisis in eastern Europe expanded. The tide of the Austro-Russian war with the Ottoman Empire shifted in favor the Russians in 1789 after they conquered the fortress of Ochakov near the mouth of the Dniester in December 1788. In addition, victories over Swedish forces in Finland and domestic unrest in Sweden threatened to allow the Russians to advance in that quarter as well. Meanwhile, Austria appeared to be on the brink of collapse with revolution in Belgium, simmering resentment in Hungary, and food riots in Vienna. Austrian weakness provided a tempting target to the hawkish members of the Prussian court including Hertzberg, who pressed with increasing insistence his ambitious plan for territorial rearrangement.[71]

The Hertzberg Plan called for armed mediation of the Russo-Turkish War to impose one of two choices on Vienna and St. Petersburg. Either they must accept the status quo ante bellum or provide Prussia compensation for any gains made at the expense of the Ottoman Empire. Specifically, Hertzberg called for Austria to balance any new acquisitions by returning Galicia (the Austrian portion of the First Partition) to Poland. Poland would then cede the cities of Danzig and Thorn together with surrounding territory to Prussia as Berlin's

The Hertzberg Plan, 1788

compensation for the Austrian and Russian gains. This cession constituted the primary objective of Hertzberg's foreign policy, and he sought it consistently by any means necessary. Although not explicitly stated, the ascendancy of Prussian over Russian influence in Warsaw would provide an additional advantage for Prussia. More interested in this influence than explicit commitment, the Prussian delegation at Warsaw prolonged the concurrent Prusso-Polish alliance negotiations to the chagrin of the Poles.[72]

Prussian efforts to restore the status quo through mediation received no objections from Whitehall. However, interest in Poland as a commercial and geopolitical alternative to Russia made Hertzberg's suggested territorial rearrangements unacceptable. Hertzberg and Frederick William eagerly anticipated Austrian and Russian rejection of the status quo. They instead expected the imperial courts to either cede territory to Prussia through negotiation or, by their rejection, provide an opportunity for Prussian armies to take advantage of their relatively weak and distracted condition.[73]

Unwilling to see Poland diminished by either Russian or Prussian aggrandizement, Pitt sought to secure the status quo as the basis for peace. British resistance to Russian expansion stemmed from growing commercial and geopolitical interest in Poland and desire to bring Warsaw into the Triple Alliance system as a strong partner. Russia's projected annexation of the Ochakov district threatened to place the Dniester River under Russian control, which posed two problems for the British vision for Poland. First, Russian territorial gains would prompt Prussian agitation for territorial concessions from Poland, making Berlin even less amenable to commercial negotiations designed to make Poland an effective ally. Second, as mentioned in Durno's report on 23 February 1789, Russia could use control of the Dniester to redirect Polish and Russian trade from the Baltic to the Black Sea under Russian rather than Polish or Turkish control. This second problem seriously threatened British policy toward Poland and Polish candidacy as a member of the Triple Alliance. Per Hailes's recommendation, Pitt chose to avoid antagonizing Prussia on the question of Polish trade through the Baltic based on the expectation of conducting Anglo-Polish commerce through the Black Sea. If Russian conquests eliminated this potential, little hope would remain of developing a productive relationship with Poland or even of upholding the principle of neutral rights and saving Poland from a second partition.[74]

Unlike Hertzberg, Pitt envisioned the Triple Alliance as a provision for the mutual security of its members and as a tool for arbitrating the conflicts of Europe to the benefit of its members, not as a mechanism for conquest. If it could save Sweden, Poland, and the Ottoman Empire from Russia, such a feat would cement the ascendancy of this British system over the competing predatory system of Russia, Austria, and France that Pitt had faced since 1783. Pitt increasingly recognized that Versailles fit poorly into a system that actively sought the destruction of France's old allies in eastern Europe. He went so far as to act on the king's belief that France might serve as a natural ally in efforts to contain Russia and attempted to recruit France into this British-led system. In 1789, Pitt asked the French to add their support to efforts to end the eastern wars on the basis of the status quo ante bellum. However, with the onset of the French Revolution, the French lacked the political and financial stability to consider any intervention in eastern Europe.[75]

Without French help, Pitt had to rely on Prussia as his primary partner in mediating an agreeable end to the war in the Balkans. British, Dutch, and Prussian ambassadors endeavored to coordinate this effort with Sweden, Poland, and the Ottoman Empire while pressing Catherine and Joseph to end hostilities without conquest. Triple Alliance overtures to Sweden and the Ottoman Empire remained limited as Pitt and Leeds refused to bind Britain to countries already at war. Only Poland offered the prospect of directly adding to the strength of Triple Alliance.

In Poland, the Anglo-Prussian cooperation that had restored the Orangists in the Netherlands already seemed to be deteriorating by the beginning of 1790. On 6 January, Hailes reported to Leeds that the Prussian envoy had politely asked him not to attend the Prusso-Polish alliance negotiations despite an open invitation from the Poles, who only reluctantly accepted his exclusion. He commented, "Your Grace will observe in what I have here mentioned a fresh and strong proof of the diffidence of this government in respect to Prussia, and of its wish to be supported and advised by Great Britain." That the Prussians named the cities of Danzig and Thorn as their price for granting commercial concession to the Poles during the very negotiations from which Hailes had been excluded appeared to justify Polish suspicions.[76]

While the outcomes of the crises in eastern and western Europe remained uncertain in 1790, an Anglo-Spanish standoff over colonial claims on the northwestern coast of North America provided the only unqualified success for Pitt's Triple Alliance system. Overlapping Anglo-Spanish claims in the Nootka Sound area of the northwestern Pacific coast of North America led to the capture of British whalers by Spanish authorities. Spanish action prompted widespread demands for satisfaction from the British. News of the incident reached London in January at the start of the parliamentary session, but both the British and Spanish proceeded cautiously while awaiting further information. The proprietor of the British outpost at Nootka Sound, which the Spanish claimed, arrived in London with a more extensive report of the apparently unwarranted Spanish aggression. Though not a disinterested source, this report prompted Pitt to demand satisfaction from the Spanish. After receiving a lukewarm response from the Spanish, the administration requested support for naval mobilization from Parliament before the end of the session in June and then proceeded with negotiations afterward.[77]

Pitt earnestly wished to avoid war, but he also recognized that public outrage at Spanish action required him to obtain some sort of satisfaction. If he achieved neither war nor settlement before the start of the next session of Parliament on 25 November 1790, Pitt knew the Whig opposition would present the ministry as incapable of defending essential British colonial interests. This concern substantially informed the government's approach to what became known as the Nootka Sound Crisis. Negotiations proceeded inconclusively at Madrid until Leeds, unwilling to bring an undecided matter before Parliament, dispatched an ultimatum on 28 October 1790.[78]

As tensions between Britain and Spain escalated in the Nootka Sound Crisis, both sought the support of allies. At the request of British diplomats, Berlin and The Hague expressed their support, readying themselves for a possible confrontation with Spain. Spanish overtures to the other major and minor powers of Europe returned no result. Only France offered Madrid any real hope of support. However, debate in the National Assembly over the question of materially backing Spain precipitated a broader discussion on the means of conducting French foreign policy. Ultimately, the National Assembly revoked the king's right to declare war without legislative approval. This political change mired the Spanish request for assistance in revolutionary politics, dramatically reducing the likelihood of French involvement. Facing a British-led alliance with no ally of their own, the Spanish capitulated, offering a compromise favoring British views, which Pitt accepted.[79] As with the Dutch Crisis, opposition criticism to the government's management of the Nootka Sound Crisis failed to overturn impressions of the affair as a triumph. In the debate over the king's speech at the opening of the session on 14 December 1790, the government defeated the opposition, 247 to 123.[80]

With regard to the European balance of power, the Nootka Sound Crisis produced two distinct results. First, it endowed Britain and the Triple Alliance with the appearance of strength, banishing any perceptions of continued British weakness after the American War of Independence. Second, it revealed that the Revolution had significantly reduced French assertiveness in foreign policy.

The Nootka Sound Crisis provided another opportunity to consider the implications of political revolution in the arena of foreign policy. The French decision to transfer control of foreign policy from the king to the legislature ensured that diplomatic questions became both politicized and public. This change and the accompanying hesitation to support Spain suggested that legislative control of foreign policy could potentially make France more diplomatically cautious. More explicitly, the National Assembly renounced wars of conquest on 22 May 1790. Revolutionary France seemed to favor Continental peace and maintenance of the status quo.[81] In broad terms, this made French foreign policy objectives compatible with Pitt's collective security vision. Thus, Pitt tentatively viewed the Revolution as favorable to British interests. However, the subsequent attempt by the National Assembly to negotiate a Franco-Spanish treaty against Britain foreshadowed the more aggressive republican nationalism of 1792 and 1793.[82]

The Nootka Sound Crisis also highlighted the foreign policy focus and intentions of the Pitt ministry. Between Pitt's naval reforms and reconstruction and the support of the Dutch fleet, British naval assets outnumbered those of Spain. In addition, Pitt's financial reforms and political success allowed his ministry to embark on a potential global conflict with confidence. If Pitt had sought to expand Britain's overseas empire at the expense of the Bourbon powers, he could not have wished for a better opportunity. However, his handling of the crisis indicated that he continued to place greater importance on strengthening Britain's position within Europe than on further colonial acquisitions. In the final settlement over the Nootka Sound Crisis, the Spanish offered a compromise in response to the British ultimatum of 28 October 1790. This refusal to comply fully with the ultimatum could have furnished a *casus bellum* had Pitt wanted war. Instead, he accepted this compromise to return his focus to the complex problems that the Triple Alliance system faced in eastern Europe. The colonial confrontation with Spain created an unwanted distraction from the more important contest with Russia over influence in central and eastern Europe.[83]

While the Triple Alliance continued to face many questions and difficulties as the British government struggled to grow it into an effective collective security system, Spanish capitulation in the Nootka Sound Crisis marked a distinct zenith for his foreign policy. The string of alliances that had threatened Britain from 1781 to 1787 was in shambles. Poor Austrian military performances in the Balkans and unrest throughout the Habsburg territories weakened Vienna's alliances with both Russia and France, and France's concurrent slide into revolution appeared to nullify its ability to support either Spain or Austria. Anglo-Prussian intervention in the Dutch civil war had separated the United Provinces from that opposing bloc as well, eventually leading to the formation of the Triple Alliance. By 1790, France's old allies, Sweden, Poland, and the Ottoman Empire, looked to this Triple Alliance for protection, and Austria and Russia began to solicit Triple Alliance mediation. Successful arbitration of the wars in the Baltic and the Balkans offered the prospect of gaining several new members for the Triple Alliance system and establishing it as the dominant power bloc in Europe.

CHAPTER 3

Overreach at Ochakov, 1791

The confidence Pitt gained from the successful resolution of the 1787 Dutch Crisis and the 1790 Nootka Sound Crisis contributed to a disastrous miscalculation that destroyed his diplomatic system the following year in the Ochakov Crisis. Despite an apparent trajectory of success, British collective security plans suffered from lack of agreement among the Allies, contradictions between traditional hostility to France and emergent opposition to Russian expansion, Britain's limited ability to project power on the Continent, and the limited will of Parliament and the British people to support such interventionism. These factors converged during the Ochakov Crisis of 1791, in which the efforts of the Triple Alliance to mediate an end to the Russo-Turkish War failed, leading to a collapse of the alliance. Although forced to reconsider its foreign policy, Pitt's administration remained dedicated to the Dutch alliance as well as the principles of collective security but distanced Britain from the increasingly predatory system of the eastern powers.

In 1790, successive Russian and Austrian victories against the Turks raised the possibility of a peace being concluded without Triple Alliance mediation. Both London and Berlin feared that a Russo-Austrian victory would irreparably damage the balance of power in eastern Europe, so their measures to secure peace through arbitration gained greater urgency. The Prussians tabled their remaining difficulties with the Poles regarding tariffs and territorial exchanges and, in March 1790, Polish and Prussian negotiators concluded a bilateral defensive alliance, which their respective governments ratified in April. The conclusion of a Prusso-Turkish alliance in June further strengthened the hands of the mediating powers. Just as Prussian diplomacy achieved the foundations for a war to chastise Austrian and Russian aggression, the bellicose Joseph II died in February 1790.[1]

Joseph's successor, Leopold II, immediately took conciliatory measures in both domestic and foreign policy to salvage the Habsburg monarchy from its precarious situation. The British envoy to Vienna, Sir Robert Murray Keith, relayed to the Duke of Leeds that Leopold enjoyed a reputation for "love of economy, good order, and justice." He added that the Austrians "believe him averse to war and hope that his first endeavor will be the restoration of the general tranquility."[2] Most notably, he eliminated Austrian objections to Prussian participation in the efforts of the Triple Alliance to mediate an end to the war with the Ottoman Empire. This resulted in the July 1790 Convention of Reichenbach, which secured Austrian acceptance of the status quo as the basis for peace with the Turks and eliminated Berlin's case for war by establishing the principle of Prussian compensation for any Austrian gains. In return, the Triple Alliance agreed to support the restoration of Habsburg rule in Belgium. Following the Convention of Reichenbach, Austrian and Turkish envoys met with Triple Alliance mediators at Sistovo to begin the lengthy process of negotiating a formal peace. While Austrian compliance seemingly brought the Allies closer to mediating an acceptable Russo-Turkish peace, Gustav III's decision to make a separate peace with Russia in August relieved some of the pressure on Catherine II, reducing her need to negotiate with the Turks.[3]

The success of the Triple Alliance proved fleeting when it tried to press its advantage in mediating an end to the Belgian Revolution. The British, Dutch, and Prussians urged both Leopold and the Belgians to negotiate under Triple Alliance mediation. Freed from the war in the Balkans and already beginning to restore stability in the other Austrian dominions, Leopold took a firmer stance, rejecting their offer and issuing an ultimatum to the rebels. The Belgians refused to accept Leopold's terms until after the ultimatum's expiration. No longer interested in a negotiated settlement, Leopold authorized troops to enter Belgium on 24 November 1790. Within one week, Habsburg forces gained effective control of the region. Despite his choice to dispel the rebels by force, Leopold reinstated the ancient rights and privileges that Belgium enjoyed prior to Joseph's reforms, thereby easing the restoration of order. The Triple Alliance attempted to maintain at least the pretense of mediation by concluding The Hague Convention on 10 December 1790 to guarantee the new arrangement in the Austrian Netherlands, but Leopold refused to ratify the convention. The Triple Alliance reluctantly accepted the Austrian action, which ended the crisis in the Low Countries with a solution amenable to British interests if not on British terms.[4]

Despite Leopold's relatively conciliatory attitude, Catherine continued to reject Triple Alliance mediation. Separate peace with Sweden and military success against the Turks removed any Russian need for outside arbitration based on the status quo ante bellum. Catherine sought peace but insisted on retaining the spoils of victory. This brought Anglo-Prussian disagreements on the nature of the Triple Alliance to the fore. The Prussians remained open to the prospect of Russian conquests along the Black Sea coast on the condition that Prussia received compensation in the form of Polish territory. In contrast, British resistance to Russian expansion stemmed from growing British commercial and geopolitical interest in expanding their nascent collective security system to eastern Europe in general and Poland in particular.[5]

Ochakov, a dated fortress on the northwest coast of the Black Sea, became the focal point of negotiations between the Russians, Ottomans, and the Triple Alliance. Catherine refused to return the fortress on the grounds that it threatened Russian security in the region. That past Ottoman offensives into Russian territory commenced from the fortress lent credence to her claim. The Russian ambassador in London, Vorontsov, endeavored unsuccessfully to persuade Pitt and Leeds that Russian acquisition of this territory between the prewar border and the Dniester River represented only a superficial change that promised enduring peace. This argument failed to impress Leeds, and he reiterated Allied insistence on the status quo ante bellum.[6] Russia's projected conquest of Ochakov and Bessarabia threatened to bring the Dnieper, Bug, and Dniester Rivers—and thus much of Polish trade—under Russian control. Pitt and Leeds viewed Russia's acquisition of Ochakov as an unacceptable extension of Russian power both over the Poles and into the Balkans.[7]

By the end of December 1790, negotiations reached an impasse, and Pitt learned from his diplomats that the German powers doubted British willingness to take action in response to Russian intransigence.[8] In Berlin, this doubt reanimated the critics of the British alliance at the Prussian court and threatened to unravel the Triple Alliance. In response, Leeds dispatched a series of overtures on 8 January 1791 to obtain the support or approval of Poland, Spain, Austria, and the Scandinavian countries for Triple Alliance intervention against Russia through the Baltic and Black Seas. These overtures not only demonstrated activity to those skeptical of British determination but also provided time for naval armaments and continued negotiations with Russia while waiting for responses.[9]

At Vienna, that dispatch formed part of an ongoing effort to wrest Leopold from his Russian alliance and gain his backing or at least a promise of neutrality in any ensuing conflict between Catherine and the Triple Alliance. Before Leeds's dispatch reached Vienna, Leopold himself suggested to the British envoy extraordinary to Austria, Thomas Bruce, Earl of Elgin, a defensive alliance of Britain, Prussia, Austria, and Russia that included a mutual guarantee of territory. He argued that such an arrangement "would establish peace on the most solid basis and effectually put it out of the reach of intrigue, of ambition, or of private interest . . . to throw Europe into a state of war." Leopold attributed this idea to his concern about the rise of what he called *"Les Principes Français"* and the efforts of the revolutionaries to spread those principles throughout Europe.[10]

Leeds responded positively but cautiously on 4 February, explaining the British objective of creating a collective security system. He declined to treat the suggestion as a formal offer, insisting that the moment was not right for such a measure and that Britain would only address a proposal of that nature jointly with its existing allies. Nevertheless, he asserted the Cabinet's desire "to establish and maintain in concert with the principal powers of Europe and particularly with the court of Vienna a pacific and defensive system which may not only prevent any occasion of misunderstanding among those powers but may enable them to act with effect for the preservation of the general peace of Europe."[11] Despite apparent agreement, this Anglo-Austrian exchange failed to alter the diplomatic situation. Pitt and Leeds refused to consider bringing Russia into the alliance until Catherine made peace with the Ottoman Empire, and Leopold remained too suspicious of Prussia to abandon his Russian ally to join an existing Anglo-Prussian system.

By March, Leeds had received ambivalent responses to most of his 8 January dispatches. Even the Dutch expressed reluctance to become involved in the affair despite their obligations to the Triple Alliance. Leeds's query found its best reception in Warsaw. The Polish government continued to express interest in forming a commercial treaty and defensive alliance with Britain. Although pleased with this response, the Cabinet sought to add Poland to the Triple Alliance rather than contract a bilateral Anglo-Polish alliance, which still required Prussian cooperation. In his dispatch to the British envoy extraordinary at Warsaw, Daniel Hailes, Leeds wrote, "There is nothing which would be more agreeable to His Majesty than to establish both a political and commercial connection with that country and that more particular proposals would be made . . . if it should appear that there is a reciprocal disposition in Poland to such a system in which Prussia must necessarily form a material part." With total disregard for Polish national pride and dignity, Leeds urged the Poles to accept Prussian demands to cede Danzig. He coldly argued that Prussian control of the Vistula upriver from the city already gave Berlin de facto control of it, meaning that the Poles would lose nothing of consequence through that concession.[12]

Despite the ostensible Prusso-Polish defensive alliance, the two powers remained unable to reach agreement on the question of territory and Polish trade through Baltic ports, which included Danzig since Polish goods had to cross Prussian territory to reach that city. These disputes forestalled any Polish accession to the Triple Alliance. The Poles sought to loosen Prussia's stranglehold on Baltic trade strictly through an exchange of commercial privileges and concessions. In contrast, Berlin demanded the cession of Danzig, if not Thorn as well, in return for allowing Polish commerce to pass through its Baltic ports with fewer restrictions.¹³

Following the January dispatches, Hailes pressed the Poles to come to terms with Prussia with increasing urgency. He preached the virtues of Polish independence secured through a close connection with the Triple Alliance but observed with growing concern the impatience and apparent indifference of the Prussian representatives. In February, Hailes speculated that this shift in Prussian attitude toward Poland arose from plans to partition the country with Russia rather than deal with the uncooperative Sejm. For its part, the confederation Sejm formed in 1788 had declared the territories of Poland inalienable and refused to violate this principle.¹⁴ In a last attempt to avoid the cession of Danzig, on 2 March 1791 the Poles proposed preliminary articles for an Anglo-Polish alliance not including Prussia. Hailes dutifully forwarded these to London but remained committed to the collective security system that relied on Prussian diplomatic and military support. He informed the Polish ministers that they "must enter into the system proposed completely and cordially or not at all."¹⁵

Frederick William II lost patience with British and Polish delays, and, on 11 March 1791, he demanded that the British join him in sending an ultimatum of armed mediation to St. Petersburg. Although willing to accept Russian gains if Prussia made equivalent acquisitions, Frederick William feared that the opportunity to profit from the situation was rapidly slipping away. If Catherine acquired Ochakov in a separate peace with the Porte without Triple Alliance mediation, Prussia would gain nothing. This Prussian demand brought matters to a head in London before projects to enlist Poland and other states into the Triple Alliance could bear fruit. On 22 March, the Cabinet resolved to join Prussia in a bilateral effort to force Catherine to make peace.¹⁶ They agreed to dispatch fleets to the Baltic and Black Seas and issue a final ultimatum to Catherine demanding that she accept the status quo ante bellum. Pitt drafted the ultimatum on 25 March, and a royal proclamation the same day offered bounties to recruit both seamen and landsmen.¹⁷

On 27 March, Leeds dispatched the ultimatum to Berlin for review and approval from the Prussian ministers. The note declared the intention of the Allies to arm and, if necessary, use force to induce Catherine to make peace on the basis of the status quo. More specifically, the British pledged to send a fleet into the Baltic to destroy the Russian fleet and ports there and subsequently to coordinate with a Prussian army marching into Livonia. The Cabinet pledged another fleet for the Black Sea to assist the Turkish fleet and armies. Finally, Leeds wrote to the British envoy at Berlin, urging him to "cultivate as far as possible the good disposition toward the allies which appears to subsist both in Poland and Turkey and ... to induce those two powers to accede to our system by becoming parties to a defensive alliance with this country, Prussia, and Holland." Leeds argued that "this measure would not only make the whole system still more respectable than it is at present but would be the surest method of contributing both to the prosperity and tranquility of those two countries in particular."[18] The expansion of the collective security system represented both the ends and the means of the British achieving success in the Ochakov Crisis.

In an accompanying letter of the same date, Leeds reiterated that "we have no object of ambition or aggrandizement in view . . . the end of our interference should be clearly and precisely ascertained, so that . . . no misconception may arise between the allies respecting the terms on which . . . a pacification may be afterwards acceded to." He then suggested that Britain and Prussia issue another declaration pledging to make peace as soon as Russia accepted the status quo. Leeds offered the additional provision:

> In case the course of events should make it proper for the allies by mutual consent to insist on terms beyond the status quo, they will not . . . look to any acquisition for themselves, but to procuring a still greater degree of security for the Porte on the Black Sea. It is likewise necessary with a view to secure the future friendship of Poland and to effect the great object of extending and consolidating the general system of our defensive alliance . . . to make a commercial treaty with Poland granting a free trade or moderate duties subject at most to no other restrictions than the three conditions required by Prussia whenever the cession of Danzig is agreed to by Poland.[19]

Although reluctant to go to war without a larger consensus of European powers, Pitt and Leeds were willing to risk hostilities as long as the war remained focused on building and preserving partnerships with Poland and the Ottoman Empire as part of the collective security system.

On 28 March 1791, Pitt delivered to the Commons a royal request to fund further naval armaments. He asserted the necessity of naval augmentation to support forcefully the hitherto unsuccessful diplomatic efforts to contain Russian ambitions. Less convincing was his insistence that the requested naval armament would further British interests and assist in establishing an equitable peace in Europe. Fox offered a brief counterpoint, claiming that the ministry provided insufficient information to warrant parliamentary support and declaring that the issue would be challenged as a matter of confidence in the king's ministers.[20]

Between 28 March and 16 April, the debate over naval armaments expanded into a comprehensive struggle for control not only of British foreign policy but the government itself. Beginning with the parliamentary debates over the king's speech on 29 March 1791, Pitt's ministry faced an eroding base of support in both Houses. The Russian ambassador, Vorontsov, played a major role in this political showdown. Vorontsov reportedly declared to Leeds:

> Since I see that the ministry is so blind as to persist—under the pretext of preserving Ochakov for the Turks, which should be of indifference to England—in an unjust war harmful to both countries, it is my duty to stop the damage. You doubtless have a majority of the two houses, but I know this country well enough to know that the ministry and parliament together can govern only with the support of the earls and the independent and propertied people. I declare to you ... that I will take all possible steps to inform the nation of your projects, which are so contrary to its interests. And I have too high a regard for the good sense of the English to abandon hope that the general outcry of the country will force you to abandon your unjust enterprise.[21]

According to Vorontsov, this bold declaration left the duke speechless. After exhausting all efforts to persuade Leeds to moderate Britain's anti-Russian policies, Vorontsov turned to the Whig opposition, the Russia Company lobby, and the newspapers. He supplied arguments against British intervention to members of the opposition and used connections he had developed during the Regency Crisis to sway supporters of the ministry into the opposition camp. The Whigs insisted that the ministry provide more information on how the failed negotiations necessitated the armament, and they questioned the wisdom of the anti-Russian policy in general.[22]

Speakers favoring the government responded vaguely as the Cabinet refused to allow full disclosure of their intentions. They faced an impossible situation. Complete transparency promised to undermine both the effort to intimidate Catherine and the strength of the Triple Alliance. Ultimately, Pitt wanted to threaten Russia into submission without going to war. His desire to avert war until absolutely unavoidable is evident in the edits to Leeds's initial draft of the ultimatum that Pitt either made himself or endorsed. Where Leeds had initially written, "active and effectual interference on the part of the Allies is now judged indispensably necessary," Pit reworded this to say, "it seems expedient that further preparations should be made without delay in case an active interference should be necessary." Where Leeds wrote that the British would send a fleet to the Black Sea, Pitt modified this to say that they would be "prepared in case it should become advisable to send such a fleet." These modifications could be in either Pitt's or Grenville's handwriting, but the fact that the final dispatch included the edits reflects Pitt's approval if not his authorship.[23]

In addition, Pitt needed to back Prussia to preserve the Triple Alliance, but his insistence on the status quo served to restrain more than support Frederick William's ambitions. He sought a settlement that would lay the groundwork for including the former belligerents in the collective security system. This required a peace to be based on the status quo to preserve Poland and the Ottoman Empire as viable alliance partners. A peace based on Ottoman territorial concessions and a partition of Poland would weaken both states and destroy their faith in the Triple Alliance. More broadly, it would undermine the British claim that the Triple Alliance sought peace through collective security rather than the aggrandizement of its members. This set British interests squarely against the Prussian goal of gaining Polish territory and maintaining Poland as a weak client state as a concession for accepting Russian gains in the Balkans.[24]

Pitt limited the explanation of the Cabinet's position in the Parliamentary debates because of the impossibility of presenting this complex policy in a positive or compelling manner. The ministry's tight-lipped stance also led to confusion and uncertainty in the pro-government newspapers and the ascendancy of opposition arguments in that sphere as well. As the debates deteriorated, Thurlow complained to Leeds about "our being gagged in the debates" and argued "that it would be better to come forward in both Houses in respect to the measures we were pursuing in our present discussion with Russia."[25]

The most thorough explanation to Parliament came from Pitt himself in the Commons on 29 March. He argued that since Parliament had approved the Triple Alliance, it should also approve temporary expenses aimed at preventing a disruption of the balance of power that would make the Triple Alliance relatively weaker and thus less effective for providing security. He further explained:

> It had once been a prevailing opinion in this country that Great Britain, from the peculiar advantage of her local situation, might maintain her rank and her consequence separate and unconnected with foreign powers, but from the moment that opinion was abandoned and we had connected ourselves with other powers, there could be no doubt but that we were under the necessity of watching the progress of events in Europe and taking measures to prevent the intent and purpose of those connections from being defeated.[26]

Pitt then argued that any reduction of the Ottoman Empire would have a correspondingly negative impact on Prussia's weight in the balance of power by either explicitly or implicitly strengthening Austria and Russia, thereby rendering Prussia a less effective ally for Britain.[27] Fox and several other opposition speakers objected that as Prussia had not been attacked, Britain need not go to war on its behalf. They further rejected Pitt's emphasis on the importance of preserving the existing balance of power. Instead, they advocated a view of Russia as a natural ally in the perpetual British rivalry with the Bourbon powers.[28]

Attempting to clarify his position, Pitt reiterated the aims of his foreign policy since the Dutch Crisis of 1787: "At that time we had no alliance on the continent, and it was deemed necessary for the security of our interests that we should be connected with some great land power who should at any time be able to check the attempts which others might make at a dangerous aggrandizement."[29] He argued that while Britain was not bound to intervene by its defensive alliance with Prussia, the same objectives and right of pursuing essential national interests justified intervention against Russia. He reiterated the danger that Russian aggrandizement posed to Prussia before describing his collective security vision.

> The end of this alliance was to give by their union such strength and authority as to be able at all times to compel other powers to abandon schemes of ambition and conquest which might endanger the general tranquility. To succeed in this, it was indispensably necessary that the alliance should be kept sufficient to its object and each party be in a condition to fulfill its part to the stipulations. What security then was there that Prussia could be so circumstanced if a powerful and ambitious neighbor were suffered to establish herself upon her very frontiers? What safety was there for Poland? What safety for Denmark or what for Sweden when Prussia shall be no longer in a condition to assist them? The safety of all Europe might afterwards be endangered should the same aspiring views continue to be entertained. Was it then to be said that we had no concern in the terms of pacification between Russia and the Porte? Many articles, the materials of manufacture, we received from Russia, but, of these articles, many could be obtained from other countries—from Poland for instance—and therefore we had a commercial interest in cultivating a trade with Poland and preventing Russia from obtaining such a decided command of the articles we wanted as to give or withhold them at her pleasure.[30]

Pitt still avoided full disclosure of his complex efforts to restrain both Prussia and Russia simultaneously, but his arguments explained with reasonable clarity his larger goals. Although the ministry managed to win the Parliamentary votes on the matter, their margin of victory shrank daily. The opposition remained unsatisfied with Pitt's broad vision, and even those that shared his views questioned whether the current circumstances warranted a war.[31]

The tense Parliamentary debates proved particularly damaging because they mirrored divisions within the Cabinet itself. Pitt had been slowly transforming the Cabinet from one composed out of political expediency to one composed of his own friends and confidants, yet the process remained incomplete as Pitt, Thurlow, Leeds, Camden, Richmond, and Granville Leveson-Gower, First Marquess of Stafford, all remained from the original Cabinet of 1784. Only two notable changes reflected the nascent transformation. First, Grenville replaced Thomas Townshend, First Viscount Sydney, as home secretary and replaced Leeds as leader of the House of Lords. Second, John Pitt, Second Earl of Chatham and the prime minister's older brother, replaced Richard Howe, First Earl Howe, as First Lord of the Admiralty. In addition, Pitt's friendship with Henry Dundas had grown to the point that Pitt consulted him as often as he did the Cabinet members on the government's business. As many of its members realized, the Cabinet had begun to lack cohesion, and Leeds complained of a sort of shadow Cabinet of Pitt, Grenville, and Dundas who "were daily closeted together for hours at a time."[32]

While the Cabinet generally agreed on the decision to mediate the Russo-Turkish War and press Catherine to accept the status quo ante bellum, they, like the government's supporters in Parliament, disagreed on the propriety of going to war over the matter. Grenville had consistently opposed the decision to risk war since the formation of the Triple Alliance, and while Dundas supported Pitt, he had no enthusiasm for that line of policy as his interest lay more in colonial ventures.[33] Richmond and Stafford expressed similar reservations though less consistently. They found substantial support from the ambassador to the United Provinces, William Eden, now First Baron Auckland, who constantly wrote to Pitt to present arguments against the armament in the form of Dutch reluctance to support the war and intelligence reports that diminished the economic and strategic value of the Ochakov district.[34]

In contrast, Thurlow, Leeds, and Chatham all advocated pressing the point with Russia even if it meant war. They received support from Ewart, who returned to London during the debates, but he wielded less influence than the ministry's former leading diplomat, Malmesbury. Malmesbury had sided with Fox and the Prince of Wales against Pitt and George III in the Regency Crisis, and so the king, after his recovery, refused to allow Malmesbury to remain in the diplomatic service. Malmesbury's energy and influence had played a significant role in rallying the ministry to decisive action during the Dutch Crisis, and his absence in 1791 left interventionist policies without a comparable advocate.[35]

On 12 April, the opposition presented a comprehensive attack on Pitt's foreign policy in eight resolutions. The government won the resulting division of Parliament but only by what Pitt viewed as an unacceptably narrow margin. Confronted with a crumbling situation in Parliament and a divided Cabinet, Pitt concluded that persistence would likely lead to the collapse of his ministry and its replacement by a government led by Fox. He believed this change in government would lead to a complete reversal of his foreign policy and the destruction of the Triple Alliance, which he saw as imperative to maintain British security and influence in Europe. Consequently, Pitt tasked Grenville with drafting new instructions for his diplomats beginning on 15 April.³⁶ Pitt best explained the change of policy in further instructions to Ewart dated 24 May:

> The obvious effect of our persisting would have been to risk the existence of the present Government, and with it the whole of our system both at home and abroad.... The overthrow of our system here, at the same time that it hazarded driving the Government at home into a state of absolute confusion, must have shaken the whole of our system abroad. It is not difficult to foresee what must have been the consequence to Prussia of a change effected by an opposition to the very measures taken in concert with that Court and resting on the avowed ground of our present system of alliance. On these considerations it is that we have felt the necessity of changing our plan and endeavoring to find the best expedient we can for terminating the business without extremities.³⁷

These instructions repudiated the former ultimatum and recommended an appearance of firmness alongside willingness to compromise.

Leeds refused to sign these instructions, which represented a complete reversal of his policies, so he tendered his resignation. Leeds's role as foreign secretary had become increasingly uncomfortable as Pitt took a more active role in directing foreign policy himself during and after the Dutch Crisis. This shift, combined with the loss of Malmesbury and the rise of Grenville to the Cabinet, rendered Leeds's position tenuous. Consequently, Pitt's decision to replace Leeds with Grenville as foreign secretary surprised no one. Nor did the corresponding decision to fill the post of home secretary that Grenville vacated with Dundas.³⁸ Having filled these two key positions with individuals with whom he enjoyed much greater trust and working relations, Pitt generally ceased interfering directly in the affairs of those offices. While he had used Grenville as a personal diplomatic agent to circumvent Leeds, he used no such circuitous arrangement during Grenville's tenure and had no need to do so.³⁹

Immediately, Grenville sought to contain and repair the diplomatic damage wrought by the political failure of the Ochakov Crisis. In April, Ewart returned to Berlin to salvage Prussian confidence in the value of a British alliance. Grenville also dispatched a special envoy unaffiliated with the Ochakov affair, William Fawkener, to St. Petersburg to attempt to repair Anglo-Russian relations. Fawkener received instructions to persuade Catherine to demilitarize any territory she insisted on annexing. Ewart failed to grasp the change in British policy and continued to advocate intimidation and intervention, much to Grenville's frustration.⁴⁰

In contrast to Ewart's lack of perspective, Fawkener's mission suffered from external challenges. Despite Pitt's retreat, Leeds's resignation, and Grenville's rapprochement, neither Fox nor Vorontsov relented in their efforts to ensure the impossibility of an Anglo-Russian war. In June, Fox sent his own agent, Robert Adair, to St. Petersburg to counter Fawkener's mission. Adair bore letters of recommendation from Vorontsov and received a warmer welcome at the Russian court than any of Britain's official representatives. Adair's mission seemed to vindicate Leeds's fears of the formation of a Russian party in the House of Commons.[41]

Despite the joint Russo-Whig victory, Fox's actions aroused concerns among some of his followers. The Adair mission in particular teetered dangerously close to treason and led to divisions within the ranks of the opposition.[42] In addition to the Adair mission, Fox maintained correspondence with the prominent French politician, Antoine Barnarve. Grenville expressed to Auckland his distaste for Fox's penchant for independent foreign policies on 29 July 1791:

> What do you think of Fox's letter to Barnarve? I cannot vouch for the words, but you may depend upon the fact that such a letter having been written. Is not the idea of Ministers from Opposition to the different Courts of Europe a new one in this country? I never heard of it before, and should think that if it could be proved, I mean legally proved, it would go very near to an impeachable misdemeanor. In the meantime, I trust it will not fail to get out into the public here, and to make the impression it ought to do.[43]

Pitt and Grenville recognized the destabilizing potential of Fox's parallel foreign policies and sought to neutralize the threat they posed from the end of the Ochakov Crisis until the outbreak of war with France on 1 February 1793.[44]

Ostensibly, Pitt's diplomatic retreat served to save the Triple Alliance system by preventing a political upheaval that would have replaced his administration with a Foxite ministry that did not share his vision for collective security. Instead, this maneuver destroyed British credibility throughout Europe. Officially, Frederick William II accepted the reversal of British policy gracefully, but the incident convinced him of the worthlessness of the Triple Alliance for his ambitions. He expressed his irritation by concluding a convention with Austria in July 1791 and entertaining Russian overtures for cooperation in Poland.[45] The British had hoped for a rapprochement between Austria and Prussia that would lead to Austria's inclusion in the Triple Alliance. Instead, the Austro-Prussian alignment marked Prussia's departure from Britain's intended collective security system. With the prospect of Triple Alliance mediation thereby reduced from unlikely to impossible, Catherine ignored British and Prussian suggestions regarding peace.[46] After further victories on both land and sea, she concluded a peace treaty with Sultan Selim III on 9 January 1792 in which Russia gained the Ochakov district and the right to integrate Crimea into the Russian Empire.[47]

In Poland, news of the ultimatum had raised hopes that Triple Alliance intervention against Russia might definitively secure Polish independence and expedite the stalled negotiations to bring Poland into the Triple Alliance. However, all Polish hopes for the protection of the Triple Alliance collapsed in May with news of the British retreat. Hailes wrote from Warsaw on 3 May 1791 that "as much as the spirits of people here were raised by . . . the appearance of coercive measures to oblige Her Imperial Majesty to accept peace upon the conditions of the strict status quo, so much are they now damped by the news lately arrived from Berlin . . . of the milder counsels adopted by England." Hailes observed that the incident destroyed all faith in Triple Alliance support for Polish independence from Russia. A desperate Sejm determined that Poland could rely on only its own resources to defend itself from Russian intervention. Therefore, it aggregated several previously mooted centralizing reforms into a new constitution that passed with overwhelming support on 3 May as Hailes wrote his letter. Not yet grasping the extent of the collapse of Anglo-Prussian cooperation, Hailes pleaded with Stanisław II to delay the new constitution until further negotiations could bring Poland into the Triple Alliance and ensure foreign support. The envoy predicted gloomily that Prussia would not accept the new constitution and that Catherine would support conservative dissenters in favor of the prior constitution to legitimize an invasion and restore Russian influence in Poland.[48]

Hailes's zeal to save Pitt's collective security system prompted him to travel to Berlin in mid-May to gain information on the best way of salvaging the deteriorating negotiations between Prussia and Poland. While there, he conferred with Ewart and received updated instructions from the new foreign secretary, Grenville. These instructions finalized the abandonment of Poland, ordering Hailes to cease his futile efforts to bring Prusso-Polish negotiations to a successful conclusion.[49]

Despite Pitt's recognition of Britain's strategic and economic interest in cultivating allies in eastern Europe, he lacked the ability to act on this belief. Pitt possessed insufficient domestic support to mobilize British resources for intervention in eastern Europe, and he lacked an ally committed to similar principals. Thus constrained, Pitt temporarily reverted to the more cautious policies of 1783–87, attempting to promote British interests on the Continent as much as possible without making any commitments that might require war.

The manner in which Hailes presented British views to the Polish government reflected this shift. Instead of attempting to reconcile Polish and Prussian views, he simply assured the Polish government that the ongoing negotiations with Russia would not neglect Polish interests.[50] After news of the Russo-Turkish peace reached Warsaw on 11 January, Hailes became completely passive. Further underscoring the collapse of British hopes for Poland, Grenville transferred Hailes to Copenhagen, replacing him with Colonel William Gardiner, who received instructions only to observe Polish affairs. Hailes had replaced Charles Whitworth at Warsaw in 1788 specifically as part of an effort to pursue closer Anglo-Polish relations and enlist Poland into the Triple Alliance, and his departure signified the end of that project.[51]

Having failed to establish Britain as a leader and mediator in European politics, British diplomacy stalled for a time. Contrary to British interests, the eastern powers formed a bloc dedicated to aggrandizement through partitions. In practice, if not in form, this left the United Provinces as Britain's only ally.[52] In the words of Auckland: "Under the palsied compositions of the Prussian Ministry we have, in effect, no continental alliance."[53] Pitt found little to salvage from the wreckage of his collective security system, and the rival alignment of the eastern partitioning powers seemed poised to dominate Continental affairs.

CHAPTER 4

Principled Neutrality and Political Recovery, 1792

From the Ochakov Crisis until the outbreak of war with France in 1793, the British distanced themselves from Continental affairs through strict neutrality toward the emerging conflict between the French Revolution and the Austro-Prussian alliance. Grenville wrote to Auckland on 4 August 1791, insisting on the importance of "avowing our determination of the most scrupulous neutrality in the French business."[1] With conflict between revolutionary France and the Austro-Prussian alliance looming, George III and his Cabinet felt no obligation or desire to assist either side. This distance and neutrality arose from two motivations. First, both the French and the German powers challenged Pitt's views on the European state system in different ways, making him reluctant to support either against the other. The German powers pursued goals of aggrandizement hostile to British interests, and revolutionary France remained unstable and unpredictable. Second, Pitt's reorganized Cabinet strove to restore the faith of Parliament and the public in his foreign policy before again taking an adventurous line. Success in this endeavor allowed them to take a firm stand against increasing French aggression toward the end of 1792 and face a French declaration of war in 1793 with confidence.[2]

The Austro-Prussian rapprochement after the Ochakov Crisis in 1791 arose partially from the impact of the French Revolution on European diplomacy. The dynastic ties of Leopold II with France through his sister Marie Antoinette's marriage to King Louis XVI made the safety of the French royal family amid an increasingly volatile revolution a matter of concern for Austrian prestige and honor. Catholics across the Continent looked to the Holy Roman emperor to stop the Revolution's rapacious policies toward the French church. More significantly, Leopold's position as emperor of the Holy Roman Empire included the responsibility of protecting the rights of the imperial princes.

Several of these princes found themselves in conflict with the French revolutionaries over their decision to shelter émigrés. Louis XVI's flight from Paris and subsequent capture at Varennes in June of 1791 exacerbated the danger the royal family faced and prompted Leopold to respond favorably in July to the Prussian proposals for cooperation in French and Polish affairs that followed the Ochakov affair.[3]

Through this alignment, Frederick William II replaced the apparently unreliable British with the Austrians as Prussia's primary ally. In return, Austria gained Prussian support for Austrian intervention in France. The treaty of alliance bound the two powers to support each other in their handling of French and Polish political crises. Projected compensation for mutual support included a Russo-Prussian partition of Poland for the Prussians and the Belgium-Bavaria exchange for Austria. Both powers thereby rejected the Triple Alliance's emphasis on the territorial status quo and protection of neutral states in favor of mutually supportive aggrandizement.[4]

Meanwhile, the Ochakov Crisis had cost Pitt's government the Triple Alliance and damaged its domestic base of support. With Parliament and popular opinion swinging against interventionism, caution and neutrality became necessities for Pitt's foreign policy as he worked to regain control over his own government.[5] Thus, Britain remained aloof from Austro-Prussian calls to rescue the beleaguered French king in both the Padua Circular of 25 July 1791 and the Declaration of Pillnitz of 27 August.[6] The Cabinet rejected these approaches just as it had ignored prior appeals from French émigrés. While George III expressed some sympathy for the situation of Louis XVI, Britain remained steadfastly neutral on the subject of French politics.[7]

No longer in close communication with Prussia, the British government viewed Berlin and Vienna with suspicion. After Austrian and Ottoman diplomats concluded peace at Sistovo under the supervision of Triple Alliance delegates on 4 August 1791, Grenville wrote to Auckland: "The conclusion of the Sistovo business has removed every difficulty which there was in the way of our speaking out and avowing our determination of the most scrupulous neutrality in the French business; and I now hold this language to all the Foreign Ministers in order that it may be clearly understood that we are no parties to any step the King of Prussia may take on the subject."[8] Expecting a Polish partition alongside a counterrevolutionary crusade, Pitt refused to join an international system so diametrically opposed to his own vision for collective security.[9] Grenville outlined the scope of British policy on 19 September 1791 in a letter to the British ambassador at Vienna. He declared that George III had observed "scrupulous neutrality" on all questions pertaining to the internal government of France and would continue to do so "unless any new circumstances should arise by which His Majesty should be of opinion that the interests of his subjects would be affected." Grenville declared that the British would neither support nor oppose an Austro-Prussian attempt to restore the authority of the Bourbon monarchy.[10]

In theory, the appeals from the Austro-Prussian alliance for cooperation against the French Revolution, which received endorsement from both Russia and Sweden, offered an excellent chance for Britain to regain a multilateral alliance directed against its old rival. However, two factors prevented any attempt to use this opportunity to rebuild the collective security system. First, the specter of Ochakov overshadowed British foreign policy after the middle of April. Having been forced to abandon his proactive policies by such a comprehensive political failure, Pitt prioritized caution over interventionism until he could recover from the defeat politically. On this point, Dundas noted privately and optimistically, "We are not without good hopes of being able to put things in such shape ... as will restore to us full confidence, and make our adversaries feel that all their expectations derived from the occurrence of last spring, will totally fail them."[11] Second, Pitt still clung to his foreign policy principles of expanded commerce, collective security, peaceful mediation, and the territorial status quo, even if the edifice he had constructed stood in ruins. Thus, he refused to participate in the system of the eastern powers, which rested on a predatory perspective of the balance of power that intended to maximize the aggrandizement of the participants at the expense of weaker states.[12]

Following their rebuff of Austrian and Prussian calls for concerted action against the revolutionaries, the British received a French envoy on 24 January 1792. Charles Maurice de Talleyrand-Périgord led this mission as an unofficial representative with credentials only as an individual well-informed on French policy. Talleyrand and Grenville discussed the possibility of an Anglo-French alliance, a mutual guarantee of territory, or simply a British declaration of neutrality. The French envoy's unofficial status prevented any formal action, but Grenville assured him of Britain's benevolent intentions. Talleyrand returned to France in March without securing any official British commitments, yet he was convinced that Britain would remain neutral in the event of a Continental war. That a French overture received benevolent assurances while the Austro-Prussian position generated a brusque assertion of neutrality reveals British attitudes toward both sides in early 1792. In fact, it suggests that the Cabinet viewed the Austro-Prussian alliance as a greater threat to British interests than the French Revolution.[13]

Additionally, the British insistence on official channels of communication reflected distrust, caution, and a commitment to neutrality. The perceived volatility of French politics rendered the accuracy of diplomatic exchanges questionable and contingent on circumstances. Written communications delivered through the British ambassador at Paris, George Granville Leveson-Gower, or a French ambassador in London, provided greater insurance against misinterpretation than informal discussions. Grenville recognized the great care necessary to ensure that good intentions toward France did not lead to Austrian or Prussian hostility.[14] Written missives also provided evidence of the administration's diplomatic efforts in case it needed to defend itself in Parliament. The French appointed Bernard-François, marquis de Chauvelin, as ambassador in April to provide this avenue for official communication.[15]

As tension between Austria and France escalated, French interest in Britain focused on London's policy toward the Low Countries—the likely theater of any Franco-Austrian conflict. Despite the prominent position of Belgium in British national security, Grenville confined British commitments to those contained in the Anglo-Dutch alliance and offered no formal statement regarding the Austrian Netherlands.[16] The Dutch protested, fearful of the consequences of a French invasion of the Austrian Netherlands.[17] Grenville acknowledged this danger but also emphasized the hazards of rash actions and expressed his doubts concerning

> the prudence of our mixing ourselves in such a scene of folly and bad conduct as the Austrian Government in the Netherlands. Surely, if mere military force is sufficient to maintain the Emperor's sovereignty, his 50,000 or 60,000 men will answer that purpose, without trouble or expense on our part, and without committing the Republic and us with the *Enragés* of France. If there is such a rooted hatred to the Emperor's Government there, that not even that army can keep them quiet, will 20,000 or 30,000 men from England and Holland do it? Or, if not, why should we have the disgrace of being involved in his failure? That we should not give them support or countenance I readily agree; and even that we should avow that determination whenever he will make it possible for us to do so; but I feel very strongly that this is not a time for embarking in gratuitous and unnecessary guarantees, particularly of forms of government, and still more particularly in the case of a Government wholly destitute of both wisdom and honesty.[18]

In addition to this polemical assessment, the Cabinet rightly suspected that Vienna might use its Prussian alliance and a war with France to jettison its unruly Belgian provinces in favor of a less troublesome territorial indemnity elsewhere.[19]

In early 1792, relations between Austria and France deteriorated rapidly. Leopold's connection with the beleaguered French royal family ensured tension and suspicion between the two states. Increasingly forceful French demands for the expulsion of the émigrés harbored in imperial territory moved

Austria and France closer to war.[20] Until his death in March, Leopold sought victory over the revolutionaries through posturing and intimidation. Both sides perceived their opponent as weak and incapable of effective resistance, and that misconception increased the mutual willingness to risk war.[21]

Following Leopold's death on 1 March 1792, the French declared war on his successor, Francis II, which opened hostilities between France and the Austro-Prussian alliance.[22] The rest of Europe remained neutral. Catherine offered only moral support for the war with France and focused her efforts on an impending invasion and partition of Poland in conjunction with Prussia. Madrid likewise supported the Austrian position yet remained averse to any direct Spanish intervention. Britain and the United Provinces remained thoroughly neutral and offered neither moral nor material support. The failure of the Triple Alliance in the Ochakov Crisis left the British government leery of incurring Continental commitments and suspicious of Russia and the German powers.[23]

The Triple Alliance, effectively an Anglo-Dutch defensive alliance after 1791, and the Austro-Prussian alliance constituted competing rather than cooperative power blocs. Although not in direct opposition, the two alliances represented opposing perspectives on the European balance of power. Given this gulf in perspective, the British had no motivation to involve themselves in the contest between the French Revolution and the German powers. Consequently, friendly overtures from both camps before and after the outbreak of war received only assertions of peaceful intentions and committed neutrality.[24]

The security of Britain's remaining ally, the United Provinces, was the primary foreign policy concern of the Pitt ministry after the start of Franco-Austrian hostilities in Flanders. Accordingly, Grenville's diplomacy maintained meticulous neutrality following the outbreak of war to achieve this end. The Cabinet recognized that such a policy required the pledge of a stable British government to defend its Dutch ally from both invasion and French subversion. Grenville expressed to Auckland concern about the latter point as early as 26 August 1791: "What I mentioned to you about the Netherlands in my last letter is continually striking me with fresh anxiety. It would, I fear, be very difficult to prevent the flame from spreading to Holland. If it did, France would play the same game there as in the [Austrian] Netherlands."[25]

Following the French declaration of war on Austria, Grenville expressed to Chauvelin his fears regarding a French invasion of the Austrian Netherlands. To preserve a good understanding between London and Paris, Talleyrand returned to London as a special envoy in late April 1792 to assist Chauvelin and request the aid of the Triple Alliance against Austria. After the British rejected alliance offers, the French envoys requested a loan to stabilize French finances and offered the island of Tobago as collateral. Grenville rejected this suggestion as well but offered a formal statement of policy promising British neutrality in accordance with existing treaty obligations, which required the French to respect the territorial integrity of the United Provinces and Prussia.[26] This statement demonstrates that the Pitt ministry still hoped to revive the Triple Alliance system either during or after the confrontation between France and the German powers.

As in the negotiations with Russia the previous year, Anglo-French diplomacy in 1792 became intertwined with domestic politics. In Britain, the centennial of the Glorious Revolution in 1788 had revived interest in reform societies celebrating Britain's revolutionary past. In addition to traditional groups, less reputable clubs emerged that more aggressively sought reform.[27] Both the older and newer organizations initially applauded the French Revolution as a model for political and social reform. Many societies celebrated Bastille Day on 14 July 1791 with language that ranged from reformist to revolutionary.[28] Celebrations of both the older and newer societies featured revolutionary songs, rhetoric borrowed from the French Jacobins, and addresses from French clubs. This established a connection between the British reform movement and the French Revolution that foreshadowed a radical swing of the former and began to trouble the government.[29]

In the eyes of the Pitt ministry, a dangerous tripolar threat emerged between the end of the Ochakov Crisis and the outbreak of war between France and Austria on 20 April 1792. Many of the reform societies identified themselves with the French Revolution and also received encouragement from the Whig opposition. The government knew that the Whigs, particularly Fox, maintained ties with the French embassy and the reformists. Finally, Gower reported from Paris that French envoys to Britain were given explicit instructions to undermine government authority. Throughout the spring of 1792, the Home Office received increasing reports of subversive French activities throughout the country. The Cabinet viewed these three mutually supportive groups—the reform societies, the Foxite Whigs, and French agents—as a serious threat to Britain's domestic stability and international influence. As demonstrated in the Ochakov Crisis, a united opposition party supported by foreign agents and public agitation held the potential to render Britain totally impotent in foreign policy.[30]

The immobilizing potential of British radical activity concerned The Hague nearly as much as it did London. On 15 May 1792, Auckland reported: "The anxiety of our Dutch friends on these subjects is not quite disinterested, for they feel that, in the present circumstances of Europe, the Republic is safe from any external attack, and from any interior commotion, so long as England maintains her tranquility."[31] Like the British, both the Dutch and the French recognized that the government of Dutch Stadtholder William V depended on the British government's freedom to act to maintain both internal and external security.[32]

The battle for British public opinion began simultaneously with the outbreak of war on the Continent. Reports of the French declaration of war coincided with Parliamentary debates over a political reform motion put forth by a member of the opposition in Parliament, Charles Grey, and sponsored by several reform societies. Although a reformer himself, Pitt spoke strongly against this proposal in the Commons on 30 April on the grounds that it venerated the increasingly radical and volatile French Revolution as a model to emulate. He contended that any reform based on a revolutionary model would only end in chaos.[33]

Following their defeat in Parliament, Grey and the reform societies threatened to appeal to the public, which gave the government some cause for concern in the context of the ministry's post-Ochakov weakness. In addition, on 14 May Pitt articulated growing concern about covert French efforts to encourage sedition.[34] Just as Leeds expressed concern about the possible emergence of a Russian party during the Ochakov Crisis, the Cabinet began to fear the development of a radical French party that identified with the revolutionaries in Paris.

Rather than passively rely on traditional political loyalties as it had during the Ochakov Crisis, the government took swift action to protect itself from the emerging threat. Dundas spearheaded this effort from his post as home secretary, a position he had assumed just as the French Revolution began to turn radical and violent and the fears of corresponding violence from British radicals became serious. He wielded his considerable influence in Scotland to promote proactive measures there to maintain order and contain riots. To gain security in Parliament, Pitt and Dundas communicated with conservative Whigs and gained their pledge of support for any public order measures deemed necessary.[35] To combat reformist appeals to the public, the government issued the Royal Proclamation against Seditious Writings on 21 May to alert the population to the dangers of seditious and inflammatory texts.[36] The ministry's overtures to the conservative Whigs enabled them to present the proclamation to Parliament with the support of a substantial number of Whigs.[37] In addition, in June, the government passed a bill to increase the strength of the London police to ensure public order.[38]

On 24 May, as the Cabinet fortified its domestic position, Grenville attempted to reinforce British neutrality. He offered Chauvelin a clarification of his earlier statement regarding Britain's resolution to honor the requirements of existing treaties. He explained that the alliances binding Britain to Prussia and the United Provinces required British action only in the event of a direct external attack. Prussia's decision to assist Austria against France failed to meet this requirement.[39] In reporting this to the National Assembly, Chauvelin criticized the ideologically charged attacks on the British government in the French press and opposed the policy of supporting the Whigs and radical reform societies. He asserted that these policies undermined his efforts to normalize relations.[40] Chauvelin warned that many French agents grossly overstated the extent of dissatisfaction with the Pitt administration throughout the country.[41] The government's efforts to maintain order through the Royal Proclamation against Seditious Writings bore fruit in the form of 1,341 petitions pledging loyalty received by late August 1792. This outpouring prompted many radical societies to cancel celebrations scheduled for Bastille Day, vindicating Chauvelin's observations and alleviating ministerial fears for the moment.[42]

The alliance with the United Provinces threatened to undermine British neutrality despite Grenville's clarifications. The Dutch Grand Pensionary, Laurens Pieter van de Spiegel, demonstrated less caution than Grenville in his approach to diplomacy. Spiegel supported Austro-Prussian counterrevolutionary intervention in France and pushed his British allies to participate.[43] Concurrently, residual Patriot unrest destabilized Dutch internal politics and provided an avenue for potential French interference. The Dutch took steps to ready their forces in case of emergency and sought continuous assurances of British support.[44] However, the Cabinet clung to neutrality as the course best calculated to keep Britain at peace, moderate the Revolution, and reintegrate France into the European community.[45]

The initial failure of French forces at Lille on 29 April 1792 reduced Dutch and British concerns about French intentions.[46] The subsequent collapse of French arms in the summer of 1792 seemed to foreshadow a quick and decisive Austro-Prussian victory. This concerned the British nearly as much as the initial French invasion of the Austrian Netherlands. The Pitt ministry anticipated that a triple alliance of Austria, Prussia, and France would follow a successful Austro-Prussian restoration of the French monarchy. As with Britain's Triple Alliance after the Dutch Crisis, such a league would preserve the new political order and compensate the intervening powers. Thus, the British faced the prospect of a revival of the string of alliances they had struggled to disrupt for the preceding decade. The prospect of French adherence to the predatory system of the eastern powers posed a serious threat to British security.[47]

Chauvelin and the French director general of the Department of Foreign Affairs, Guillaume de Bonnecarrère, also fearfully anticipated an Austro-Prussian victory in June and July 1792. At the behest of a new French foreign minister, Scipion-Louis-Joseph, marquis de Chambonas, Chauvelin attempted to convince the British of the dangers posed by the Austro-Prussian alliance. Simultaneously, Bonnecarrère provided Gower with an unofficial suggestion for an Anglo-French entente.[48] After some deliberation within the Cabinet,

Grenville responded favorably to the overtures, thereby bringing Britain close to a breach of neutrality in favor of the French.[49] However, owing to the French political upheavals in late July, such proposals came to naught. Chambonas lost his position on 23 July, and Bonnecarrère followed him during the collapse of the monarchy in August. Amid such instability and uncertainty, the British remained cautiously neutral. Traditional geopolitical rivalry, political distrust, and the war between France and the German powers prevented Pitt from pursuing an alliance with France as the basis for renewing his diplomatic system.[50]

In late July, the British government found itself under pressure from the counterrevolutionary camp to guarantee the safety of the French royal family. The infamous Brunswick Manifesto of 25 July articulated the determination of Francis and Frederick William to punish the revolutionaries severely should they harm the Bourbons. Pitt and Grenville received exhortations to follow suit from émigrés as well as from Gower. However, the British ministers refused to compromise British neutrality for an empty gesture.[51]

The Parisian reaction to the Brunswick Manifesto vindicated British caution but also rendered British neutrality more precarious. The storming of the Tuileries Palace on 10 August and the subsequent suspension of the monarchy demonstrated the ineffectiveness of threatening the revolutionaries.[52] Despite a genuine fear of Prussian retribution, rhetoric overpowered reason.[53] The suspension of the monarchy also interrupted formal diplomatic relations. Both the danger to Gower's safety and the nullification of his credentials prompted the Cabinet to recall him.[54] Such a step preserved British neutrality. Gower's continued residence in Paris would have implied recognition of the new republican government, placing Britain openly at odds with Austria and Prussia. The French reluctantly accepted the measure to maintain positive relations. To preserve lines of communication with France and avoid serious misunderstandings, the Cabinet allowed Chauvelin to remain in London in an unofficial capacity.[55]

Later in August, a new French foreign minister, Pierre-Henri-Hélène-Marie Lebrun-Tondu, resumed efforts to bring the British into the war as a French ally. He sent an additional envoy to aid Chauvelin with instructions to press the British to convert the commercial treaty of 1786 into a defensive alliance between the two powers. Lebrun took a conciliatory approach, reviving the offer to cede the island of Tobago in return for a British loan. In addition, he disavowed all notions of a French-sponsored revolution in the Dutch Republic and drew a sharp distinction between it and the Austrian Netherlands.[56]

Despite the favorable response to French overtures in July, the political upheaval and violence of August made the British reluctant to entertain the new French proposals. The September Massacres that followed turned British public opinion against the French Revolution.⁵⁷ Nevertheless, the British government refused to make a firm statement on the future government of France. Instructions to the British observer with the Prussian army on 12 September expressed the hope that the Austro-Prussian campaign would restore a moderate and stable government that "would protect other powers from a renewal of that spirit of restlessness and intrigue, which had so often been fatal to the tranquility of Europe."⁵⁸ Thus, these instructions suggest that Pitt's ministry hoped not for a restoration of royal authority in France but for a stabilization of some moderate government compatible with his vision for a collective security system.

While the British government and conservatives reacted with horror to the upheaval in France, British radicals took action to assist their ideological brethren. Many of the reform societies offered declarations and addresses to the French National Convention that pledged friendship and their determination to hold the British government accountable to its official policy of neutrality. Some addresses even went so far as to promise active resistance if the government took a hostile stance against the French revolutionaries, and Dundas, as home secretary, was inundated with reports and rumors of plots and conspiracies.⁵⁹ Although Chauvelin believed it wise to avoid direct contact with these radical societies, their decision to convey their addresses through the French embassy promoted the perception among both the public and the government of French activism in the reform movement. In addition, Lebrun sent the enthusiastic British reformers copies of *La Marseillaise*, which they proceeded to sing in their meetings.⁶⁰ The apparent threat of French agents inciting the British public to immobilize the government in the event of war bore an uncomfortable resemblance to Vorontsov's actions during the Ochakov Crisis the year prior.

Simultaneously, a stream of French refugees fleeing the September Massacres poured into Britain.⁶¹ This wave of émigrés posed a serious challenge to public order. The government feared that the steady stream of refugees would provide the desperate French government with an avenue to insert agents of purposeful subversion into Britain. In addition, the arrival of large numbers of former revolutionaries created significant opportunity for incidental subversion through contact with the local population. Through Dundas, the ministry acted to counter both possibilities. They sponsored émigré relief funds to monitor the activities of the émigrés and searched the émigrés' baggage for writings considered seditious, such as the works of Thomas Paine. Apprehensive vigilance replaced the confidence inspired by the demonstrations of loyalism earlier in the summer.⁶²

The reality of covert French activities in Britain fell far short of ministerial fears or the appearances given by the imprudent reform societies. Most agents dispatched from Paris carried instructions either to observe and undermine the counterrevolutionary activities of the émigrés or to secretly obtain food or military supplies for the French war effort. Some even crossed the channel just to keep Chauvelin under surveillance. While their instructions never excluded subversion, they generally posed little threat to the British state. Regardless, the sheer number of agents present combined with the fearful reports of émigrés and British conservatives provided the government with sufficient cause for concern.[63]

A reversal of military fortunes on the Continent further strained Anglo-French relations and heightened their public dimension. The French victory at Valmy on 20 September 1792 concerned London almost as much as it elated Paris.[64] On the heels of the ensuing Prussian retreat in October, French armies advanced on all fronts, invading Savoy, reaching the Rhine, and advancing into the Austrian Netherlands. This prompted Sardinian and Swiss appeals for British assistance on the grounds that French expansion represented unacceptable changes to the balance of power. The Cabinet rejected these approaches, unwilling to become unilateral protectors of the states on France's Alpine frontier. However, the ministers began to consider which French acquisition would constitute, in the language of the Sardinian ambassador, "*un nouvel ordre de choses*" and warrant British intervention.[65]

After spending much of the year on the defensive, French general Charles-François du Périer Dumouriez launched an offensive into the Austrian Netherlands on 3 November 1792. Following a resounding French victory at Jemappes on 6 November, Austrian forces evacuated Belgium, leaving nothing between the French army and the Dutch border.[66] The government of the Austrian Netherlands fled from Brussels to the city of Roermond, which was an exclave of the Austrian provinces within Dutch territory. Under-Secretary of State for Foreign Affairs James Bland Burges speculated that this step had the ulterior motivation of baiting the French into attacking the Dutch or otherwise sparking hostilities between France and the Anglo-Dutch alliance.[67] British ministers remained confident in the merit and ultimate success of Anglo-Dutch neutrality, but the proximity of French troops aroused considerable fear of invasion or subversion in the United Provinces.

News of Jemappes and the French advance lent new urgency to the question of Dutch security and French intentions. However, the British government remained dedicated to peace and neutrality. Grenville observed to Auckland on 6 November, "I continue fixed in my opinion . . . that both in order to preserve our own domestic quiet and to secure some other parts at least of Europe free from the miseries of anarchy, this country and Holland ought to remain quiet as long as it is possible to do so." He argued that war and foreign intervention exacerbated the radicalism of the French Revolution and speculated that peace would do more to restore order in France than foreign armies.[68]

Auckland replied by suggesting diplomatic steps to avert a crisis in the Low Countries. He proposed an Anglo-Dutch mediation between France and the Austro-Prussian alliance, not unlike the previous Triple Alliance efforts to mediate the wars in eastern Europe. As founding principles for such mediation, Auckland suggested the formal recognition of the French Republic in return for the safety of the royal family and French acceptance of the territorial status quo. To initiate the mediation, he recommended secret communications with Austria and Prussia to ascertain "their views and wishes relative to the manner of closing the war."[69]

In response to Jemappes and Auckland's suggestions, the government, via Grenville, initiated several measures that amounted to a policy calculated to deter French aggression and prevent Austro-Prussian aggrandizement. First, Grenville issued a statement of support for the Dutch government against any French interference in Dutch affairs, including both military invasion and political intrigue.[70] He instituted an Anglo-Dutch ban on grain exports to France in an effort to add material weight to his diplomatic assertion. In addition, he heeded Auckland's advice to initiate talks with the Austrians and Prussians concerning their war aims.[71]

Unlike the other proposed measures, the question of offering recognition to republican France required considerable deliberation within the government. Such recognition reversed British policy since the recall of Gower and threatened to alienate Austria and Prussia. Grenville requested the king's opinion on this point on 25 November.[72] Responding the same day, George III expressed reluctance to sanction the behavior of the revolutionaries. He doubted that the German powers would accept Anglo-Dutch mediation but conceded the necessity of exploring all options for maintaining peace.[73]

In addition to increasing tension, French victories also complicated Pitt's pursuit of domestic tranquility. Reform organizations openly applauded the success of French arms. This bold expression of support for the French added to the disorder caused by the steady stream of émigrés that crowded into Britain after the September Massacres. In addition, Catholic unrest in Ireland threatened to erupt into open revolt. Finally, to complicate the already tense domestic situation, a rainy harvest season foreshadowed a poor harvest and high food prices.[74] From the middle of October to late November 1792, Pitt's ministry received increasing reports of riots, strikes, French conspiracies, and planned urban revolts.[75]

The Pitt ministry acted quickly to restore public order. Traditional measures formed the backbone of the government's approach. Redeployment of garrisons to destabilized areas provided insurance against escalation, and modifications to the duties on grain alleviated concerns about food prices. However, the novel ideological and potentially foreign dimension to the disturbances demanded an equally unconventional response. The ministry built on the earlier Royal Proclamation against Seditious Writings and instituted several legal repercussions for producing or spreading subversive texts.[76] Additionally, Dundas traveled to Scotland to apply his influence and authority directly to contain unrest there. He and Pitt exchanged a flurry of letters throughout November to ensure their information and actions remained consistent.[77]

The French National Convention's November decrees finally ended hopes for an enduring peace between Britain and the French Republic and appeared to confirm conclusively British fears of French aggressive intent before mediation could even be attempted.[78] The decree of 16 November 1792 declared the Scheldt River open to navigation and asserted the right of French armies to pursue the Austrians into neutral territory. These claims violated the sovereignty of the United Provinces and unilaterally annulled the terms of prior treaties.[79] While the British found this unacceptable, the decree of 19 November caused even greater concern in London. In what became known as the decree of fraternity, the National Convention declared its intention to support revolutionaries abroad.[80] This effectively constituted a general statement of support for rebels and revolutionaries throughout Europe. Such a measure threatened both Britain and the United Provinces because of the presence of French-inspired radicals in both countries. Grenville described the decrees as "a concerted plan to drive us to extremities."[81] Both decrees represented the French rejection of neutral sovereignty and refusal to acknowledge existing treaties as the basis for international law and diplomacy. This aggressive unilateralism was incompatible with Pitt's defensive multilateralist vision.[82]

News of the French decrees reached Whitehall on 26 November 1792. Concurrently, Dumouriez received orders to pursue the Austrians into Dutch territory, and a French warship sailed for the Scheldt to support the assault on Antwerp. Grenville demanded that Chauvelin provide a satisfactory explanation for these actions. The Frenchman merely asserted the natural rights of French soldiers to pursue their enemies and of the Belgian people to enjoy the right of navigation on the Scheldt. An unofficial meeting between Pitt and Hugues-Bernard Maret, a member of the French foreign ministry, yielded similar explanations.[83] The British rejected these claims as unacceptable, insisting on the recognition of existing treaties and a renunciation of support for foreign dissidents.[84]

After receiving news of the French decrees, Grenville wrote on 26 November 1792 to Auckland to explain that the Cabinet believed the French wanted war. The foreign secretary also underscored the importance of securing public support by entering the war defensively: "A very few days must now probably decide this question, and we feel very unwilling to afford anything like a pretext which could diminish the strong impression to be expected here from so unprovoked an attack."[85] On the same day, Auckland dispatched his own views to Grenville and, like the foreign secretary, he emphasized the importance of maintaining public order to ensure the government's ability to fulfill its foreign policy obligations.[86]

Evidence for French-sponsored subversive activity is sparse. Dundas received an avalanche of reports and rumors of plots and insurrections in November and December 1792. However, these reports often came from questionable sources, such as bitter émigrés or xenophobic townsmen reacting to the presence of those same émigrés.[87] Auckland provided more reliable but still incomplete intelligence:

> Immense sums have been distributed in England by order of the *Conseil Executif*, to make an insurrection in different parts of the kingdom, in the last week of November or in the first week of this month. And the villains were so confident of success that they anticipated it in Paris, and I have accordingly seen Paris bulletins and letters, with all the details of a revolt in Westminster, similar to many of the horrid scenes of Paris.[88]

Despite inconclusive information, the Cabinet believed that sufficient evidence of a threat existed to take decisive measures to protect the government. On 29 November, Grenville announced to his brother that they intended to summon the militia.[89]

On 1 December, the government issued a royal proclamation to mobilize "two-thirds of all the Militias of the counties on the east coast from Scotland to London, which, together with Cumberland, Westmoreland and Kent, give us a strength of about 5,100 men." Grenville noted, "We have, I trust, secured the Tower and the City, and have now reason to believe that [the revolutionaries] are alarmed, and have put off their intended visit; but we are prepared for the worst."[90] The administration could legally take this measure only in response to insurrection or invasion. In addition, summoning the militia without Parliament in session required it to reconvene in fourteen days.[91] As Parliament stood prorogued until 3 January 1793, this measure precipitated an emergency meeting.[92]

Having summoned the militia, Grenville expressed confidence in a letter to Auckland on 4 December 1792. He professed that the French relied on their revolutionary foreign policy to render Britain impotent through internal dissent and emphasized the importance of firmness to dispel any delusions of the effectiveness of such a policy. The foreign secretary presumed victory in the battle for public opinion, asserting that "every hour's exertion gives vigor to people's minds, which were dispirited while nothing was apparently done; and I trust that the meeting of Parliament, on which all depends, will be very satisfactory."[93] Indicating genuine fears of insurrection, Grenville described the public opinion shift as "little less than miraculous."[94]

The emergence of loyalist societies in response to Francophile radicals seemed to justify Grenville's optimism. Conservative activist John Reeves founded one such society on 20 November 1792 at the Crown and Anchor Tavern. This society, the Association for the Preservation of Liberty and Property against Levellers and Republicans, constitutes one of the most prominent examples of these loyalist associations. The ministry profited from loyalist petitions from these organizations and garnered public support with moderate official statements. By encouraging these expressions of loyalism, the ministry successfully fought revolutionary diplomacy with British patriotism.[95]

The Cabinet took a more overt measure to prepare for war with France on 5 December by mobilizing "the Militias of the maritime counties from Kent to Cornwall, inclusive, and those of Berks, Bucks, Herts, and Surrey." Writing to his brother about this decision, Grenville explained the government's motivation: "The reason of the addition is partly the increasing prospect of hostilities with France, and partly the motives stated in your letter. Our object at first was to limit the number, in order not to give too great an alarm. The spirit of the people is evidently rising, and I trust that we shall have energy enough in the country to enable the Government to assert its true situation in Europe and to maintain its dignity."[96] In this letter, Grenville conveyed an overriding concern to engage in war with France only with definitive public support. The Ochakov affair of 1791 demonstrated the dangers and ultimate impossibility of embarking on a militant foreign policy without sufficient popular support. By assembling the militia in stages, the administration avoided public panic while the forceful demonstration of government authority also diminished the influence of radical reform groups.

In his address to Parliament on 13 December, George III justified the calling of the militia on the grounds of insurrection. The king's speech elicited substantial debate on the legality of the ministry's actions. In both the Lords and the Commons, members of the opposition indignantly denied the reality of any insurrection. Fox and his followers identified extensive loyalist activity as proof against the government's fears.[97] They accused the government of raising the militia illegally to prepare for war with France. Grenville defended the ministry's actions in the Lords, and Dundas spoke in the Commons. Both men emphasized the danger of French-backed radicals in Britain. They referenced the November decrees as evidence of French determination to pursue a revolutionary foreign policy. Although the government enjoyed general support in both houses, neither Grenville nor Dundas provided evidence of the supposed insurrection for which they had called the militia.[98]

The opposition's accusation that the fear of insurrection served as a cloak for warlike preparations gains credibility from Grenville's letters. The foreign secretary's aforementioned correspondence with both his brother and Auckland reveals an expectation of war with France. In addition, he acknowledged the inadequacy of the British army for meeting the twin challenges of internal and external security.[99] Any expansion of the army to meet these challenges required parliamentary consent. However, with Parliament prorogued, the administration lacked the means to obtain its approval. The act of summoning the militia provided a mechanism for the Cabinet to force Parliament to reconvene.[100] After the legislature gathered, the ministry quickly proposed new army estimates. The debate on these estimates as well as on a royal request for an augmentation of the army continued until 1 February 1793.[101]

While the Pitt ministry marshaled Britain's political and military resources, Chauvelin renewed French demands for formal diplomatic recognition as a precondition for further negotiations. This kept Anglo-French relations at a point of crisis for the remainder of December 1792 and into January 1793.[102] Grenville countered with his own demand that the French abandon expansionist policies in the Low Countries and the claim to annul treaties unilaterally on the basis of natural right.[103] The fruitless exchange of explanations and demands continued into January as Chauvelin and Grenville traded a series of nearly indistinguishable letters.[104] Despite the breakdown of diplomatic relations, neither side pushed the disputes far enough to draw a declaration of war.

Beyond direct military mobilization, Parliament's emergency meeting on 13 December 1792 allowed the government to proceed with transparency in its efforts to avoid war. As part of this effort, the administration published Chauvelin's inflammatory correspondence with Grenville.[105] In sharp contrast to the secrecy of negotiations surrounding the Ochakov Crisis, the ministry freely shared with Parliament the records of its diplomatic activities vis-à-vis the French Revolution. Over objections from the increasingly isolated Fox, the ministry enjoyed overwhelming support in both houses, including "the most respectable part of Opposition."[106]

Throughout December 1792, the ministry's victory became increasingly evident. After the government summoned the militia, surges of loyalism replaced reports of plots and riots. French agents proved less adept than Vorontsov at gauging the ebb and flow of British public opinion. On 5 December, a British agent in Flanders commented on the revolutionaries' misplaced confidence in subversive activity reducing Britain to impotence. He stated that "the French are induced to be insolent, from the addresses they receive from some of our insignificant clubs in England, who give themselves as the voice of the nation."[107] Grenville explained to Auckland:

> It is clear to me that the French rely, in the present moment, on their intrigues in the interior of both countries, and that they imagine they have brought us to a condition of inability to resist any demands which they may make. This is above all others a reason for firmness in the present moment, and for resisting, while the power of resistance is yet in our hands. . . . Our confidence on that head is very great indeed. The spirit of the country seems rising.[108]

Despite the observable loyalism in Britain, the French continued to place their faith in revolutionary diplomacy as late as 19 December. Lebrun delivered a heated speech to the National Convention in which he threatened to appeal directly to the British people if the government refused to accept French demands—a threat that rang hollow.[109] By the belligerence of their government and their missteps in Britain, Chauvelin and other French agents found themselves increasingly marginalized. This diminution of French influence culminated with Chauvelin's expulsion after the execution of Louis XVI on 21 January. In Parliament, Fox ranted impotently about Pitt's abuses of power while most of his friends and supporters deserted him. The government dominated parliamentary debates throughout the winter.[110]

The specter of Ochakov had hung heavy over Pitt and Grenville as they directed British foreign policy from the summer of 1791 until mid-December 1792. Cautious neutrality had disguised diplomatic impotence imposed on them by Vorontsov's skillful cooperation with the Whigs and manipulation of the British press and mercantile lobby. Over the course of 1792, Pitt and Grenville took several steps to deny Chauvelin the opportunity to achieve a similar feat. Significantly, while Vorontsov relied on economic arguments to rally opposition to the government, Chauvelin and other French agents utilized revolutionary political arguments. Successful government measures to restrict and marginalize radical reformers in 1792 limited the ability of French agents to use connections with them to influence policy. These measures also led to a division within the ranks of the opposition over the question of political reform. Reconciliation between the government and conservative Whigs secured the ministry from facing the embarrassment of a united, foreign-backed opposition party when raising questions of armament for intervention in Europe. Ultimately, skillful management of Parliament, popular opinion, and public diplomacy allowed Pitt and Grenville "to talk to France in the tone which British Ministers ought to use under such circumstances as the present."[111] Confident of political and popular support, Pitt and Grenville took an uncompromising stand against French demands regarding the Netherlands. While this stand led to a French declaration of war on 1 February 1793, the cumulative effect of the preceding precautionary measures allowed Pitt's ministry to enter the war without serious fears of domestic collapse.

Between news of the French November decrees reaching London on 26 November 1792 and the arrival of the French declaration of war on 9 February 1793, Anglo-French relations revolved primarily around this dispute over the legitimacy of prerevolutionary treaties and boundaries. Grenville demanded that the French renounce these decrees and accept the authority of existing treaties. Chauvelin countered by demanding that the British recognize the French Republic as a precondition of further discussion. Nevertheless, the final breakdown of Anglo-French relations involved a fundamental dispute over interpretations of the international order rather than the political structure of either nation.[112]

CHAPTER 5

BETWEEN REVOLUTION AND PARTITION, 1793

While the British Cabinet entered the conflict with France confident of its domestic political strength, Britain's strategic position had only marginally improved since 1783. The link to Prussia via the Triple Alliance had all but dissolved, leaving London with effectively only a Dutch alliance. Although the Cabinet remained convinced of the economic and strategic importance of this connection, it relied on Prussia to defend the United Provinces from any Continental threat. British and Dutch resources would likely be insufficient to repel a concerted French assault on the Dutch, much less carry the war to France and compel it to seek peace. As such, the British ministers first sought to avert conflict through armed mediation. After this failed, they strove to merge the numerous separate wars between France and its enemies into a general war between the French revolutionaries and a united coalition. Following the pattern of earlier efforts to build a collective security system, the Netherlands became the focal point of British strategy. The deployment of British troops to the Netherlands underscored this focus. Nevertheless, as with those earlier endeavors, Pitt refused to commit Britain to the predatory Austro-Prussian alliance, instead pressing them and other courts to adopt British collective security and status quo principles.

In December 1792, during Grenville's epistolary stalemate with Chauvelin over the French November decrees, the foreign secretary renewed British efforts to build a European consensus to mediate an end to hostilities. He unexpectedly received support for this policy from Catherine II. A Russian proposal of 19 November 1792 urged the British to end neutrality and join a coalition to overthrow the Revolution and restore peace.[1] Pitt and Leeds had hoped in vain for a similar Russian solicitation to make Britain the arbiter of Continental affairs before 1791, and Grenville sought to turn this proposal to good account with a careful reply that he also sent to the other courts of Europe except for France.[2]

Grenville's response to St. Petersburg addressed two main points: the steps needed to avert a general war through mediation and the military resources available to the coalition in the event of a general war occurring. To the first point, Grenville requested that the countries already at war with France clarify their aims and conditions for peace to enable a British-led bloc of neutrals to propose terms to France. After making this request, he suggested terms that the British found acceptable: the withdrawal of French armies, restitution of French conquests, revocation of "any acts injurious to the sovereignty and rights of other nations," and a public renunciation of French support for revolutionaries in other countries. These terms bore a strong resemblance to the 1791 attempt to force Russia to abandon its conquests and to secure Poland against both the military and political threat posed by St. Petersburg.[3]

In return for French acceptance, Grenville proposed that the states at war with France should end hostilities, renounce interference in French internal politics, and recognize the republican government of France. In the event that France rejected these terms, Grenville suggested that the mediating powers join the war against France to gain the terms of the mediation, to which he added the allowance that these powers might "look to some indemnity for the expenses and hazards to which they would necessarily be exposed."[4] With regard to the second point pertaining to the forces available to such a coalition, Grenville urged the neutral states to mobilize for war to strengthen the mediation and to communicate clearly the military force they could contribute.[5] While war preempted this initiative, it demonstrated British willingness to negotiate and accept any form of government in France that endorsed British principles regarding the European state system.[6]

Grenville sent copies of this message to Prussia, Austria, Spain, Portugal, and the United Provinces on 28 and 29 December. Each dispatch naturally included queries and exhortations unique to the target country. The original response to Russia and the copy sent to Spain emphasized the importance of aggregating overwhelming naval superiority, and those to the Dutch and Portuguese more generally emphasized the importance of military mobilization to both strengthen mediation and forestall French subversion. Perhaps most significantly, the dispatches to Austria and Prussia renewed British requests for some explanation of their war aims. Grenville had been pressing this point with increasing urgency throughout 1792, but both Vienna and Berlin remained silent on the matter. He now requested that all the target governments send a diplomat to The Hague equipped with full authority to participate in the mediation process to save time and achieve decisive results.[7]

In total, the dispatches represented a general acceptance of the original Russian proposal and a bid to translate that proposal into a multilateral alliance system. Unlike earlier British collective security efforts through the Triple Alliance, this mediation attempt sought *temporary* partnership to address an immediate crisis. Nevertheless, it represented the continuity of Pitt's foreign policy principles, and the dispatches suggested that cooperation based on this mediation could serve as the basis for a more permanent system to be formed in the peace settlement. Pitt's ministry hoped to supplant the aggressive, predatory system of the eastern powers with this security system and use it to restrain and overturn the revolutionary system of the French Republic.[8]

Contemporaries and historians criticize Pitt for not doing more to avert war by communicating this mediation proposal to the French as well. This criticism misunderstands the purpose of the proposed mediation, which was to overturn revolutionary foreign policy and conquests through a multilateral concert. Whether this was achieved by the mediation's success or through a united war based on the terms of the mediation was a secondary concern. Formally including France in the proposal would have provided the French Republic with de facto recognition, removing an incentive for it to accept the terms, and without prior agreement on the terms, the mediating powers could not present France with a united front. Additionally, if the French accepted the terms but the eastern powers did not, Britain could face the awkward choice of either joining the war on the French side to uphold the terms mediation (an untenable course) or undertaking a second humiliating diplomatic climbdown in as many years.[9]

The initiative depended largely on Austria and Prussia as well as still-neutral Russia. Successful mediation would require Austrian and Prussian diplomatic compliance and British knowledge of the terms they intended to demand. In the event of failed mediation, war with France to enforce the terms in question would require military cooperation with Austria and Prussia as well. Toward this end, the Cabinet sent an envoy, Sir James Murray, to the Prussian army's headquarters at Frankfurt to negotiate directly with Frederick William II in addition to the ongoing negotiations at Berlin and Vienna. Grenville charged Murray with pressing the plan for mediation and thoroughly discussing possible future military cooperation.

In Grenville's 4 January instructions to Murray, he apprehensively anticipated Austro-Prussian intentions to secure compensation through a new partition of Poland based on reports from Berlin, Vienna, St. Petersburg, and Warsaw. He declared that George III would never approve of seeking indemnification for the cost of the war with France through the partition of a neutral country. The foreign secretary then warned that if the eastern powers proceeded to incorporate a partition of Poland into their concert against France, Britain would be unable to be party to that concert. He acknowledged that Britain might still be forced into a war with France, "but it must be on principles and in a manner wholly distinct from the other Powers in whose views in such a case it will be impossible for the king to concur."[10] Even as the British ministers sought cooperation with the eastern powers for mediation, they recognized that those courts did not share the British principles for establishing a balance of power or protecting neutral states through the territorial status quo. As such Grenville's letter clearly indicates that in the event of war, Britain would fight a separate conflict rather than become a direct accessory to the predation of neutral states.

This letter and the implications of its assertions bears further emphasis as it illustrates how the diplomatic objectives and realignments of the 1780s defined the parameters within which the European states attempted to fight France in the War of the First Coalition. Speaking on behalf of Pitt and the rest of the Cabinet, Grenville identified a partition-based balance of power as antithetical to British views. Thus, he recognized that the Second Partition of Poland, which he predicted, would prevent any meaningful unity between Britain and the eastern powers. This prediction ultimately came true, and Britain fought a largely separate war with France than the one waged by the German powers. The partition and diplomatic gulf between Britain and the eastern powers arose in large part because of the British failure in the Ochakov Crisis in 1791, and both were apparent to most by the end of 1792. Thus, the forces and policies that fatally divided the coalition in the first war against revolutionary France were well established and even well understood even before the war began. In effect, as Sir James Harris had identified in 1785, the balance of power as enshrined in the Peace of Westphalia had become broken and obsolete beyond repair due to the rise of Russia and Prussia. In this context, the Russo-Turkish war of 1787 set off a series of diplomatic upheavals that developed into a contest over the future of the European states system that would not find its full resolution until the Congress of Vienna in 1815.[11]

On 12 January 1793, Grenville received a joint declaration from the Austrian and Prussian ministers in London regarding war aims. While they issued this statement in response to earlier inquiries, it effectively answered—and destroyed—the British initiative. The Austrians asserted their intention to secure compensation for the war by annexing Bavaria and installing its dispossessed elector in the Austrian Netherlands, which possibly would be augmented by some of French Flanders. The Prussians claimed their compensation in the form of Polish territory to be obtained through another partition already underway with Russian assistance.[12] Compounding this, Whitworth relayed that the Russians rejected the notion of recognizing or negotiating with a republican France.[13]

These replies proved unacceptable to the British and reduced the hope of avoiding war through mediation or forging an effective coalition before the outbreak of hostilities. Grenville replied to the Austrian and Prussian envoys that George III "would never be a party in any concert or plan" that sought "compensation for the expenses of the war from a neutral or unoffending nation."[14] The British appreciated the need for compensation if the failure of mediation necessitated the continuation of the war but insisted that indemnification should come from only the offending power: France. In addition, London categorically rejected Russian insistence on making the counterrevolution an integral part of any coalition. Despite enjoying an unprecedented opportunity to unite Europe against France, the British ministers rejected it on principle. In the attempt to halt the aggression of revolutionary France during the winter of 1792–93, Pitt's ministry viewed the predatory policies of the eastern powers as equally offensive if less immediately dangerous to the Anglo-Dutch alliance.[15] Consequently, Pitt's goal of maintaining British security through multilateral collective security agreements replaced the traditional policy of seeking to reduce French power in Europe and overseas.

Other courts responded positively to proposals for "a general system . . . between the leading powers of Europe for their common interest and security."[16] The Portuguese and Dutch professed a readiness to join the British diplomatically and militarily based on the recommended terms. The Spanish also embraced the overture, even suggesting a permanent alliance regardless of the outcome of the intended mediation. The Sardinian court accepted the British proposals as well, only reserving the right to observe prior obligations to Austria and requesting either a subsidy or loan to support its war effort. Many of the other Italian states expressed similar desires to work with Britain in return for the protection of the Royal Navy in the Mediterranean. Although positive, most of these replies trickled into London after the less palatable responses of the eastern powers.[17]

While the British would build on the positive contacts to cultivate wartime cooperation, the initial effort to preempt war through united mediation failed. Despite the Cabinet's best efforts either to avoid the war altogether or to fight only as part of an international concert, Britain was forced to go to war to defend the status quo and its Dutch alliance with no other ally committed to the same goals or principles. Paradoxically, as Britain went to war to defend its Continental interests, the two states most capable of military cooperation toward achieving British objectives—Austria and Prussia—pursued goals nearly as detrimental to British interests as those of revolutionary France.[18]

British ministers received an opportunity to revise their stance toward the German powers in an unexpected last attempt by the French to avoid war. On 23 January, Dumouriez requested a meeting with Auckland at the Dutch border to resolve Anglo-French differences over the navigation of the Scheldt and Dutch sovereignty. The Cabinet approved the conference, but Grenville explained both to Auckland and to the Austrian and Prussian courts that the British placed little faith in negotiations with Dumouriez beyond gaining more time to prepare for war. The negotiations never took place: by the time Auckland received approval from Grenville, the National Convention had already declared war.[19]

In communicating news of the Dumouriez initiative to Vienna and Berlin, the British revised the peace program they had proposed on 29 December. In addition to the broad terms of status quo ante bellum, Grenville made two additions: he included a demand for the safety of Queen Marie Antoinette and her two children, and he recommended divorcing the Austro-Prussian proposal for indemnification from the conflict with France. While Britain would not endorse either the partition or the exchange on principle, Grenville reasoned that neither project had any direct relation to the French war, therefore obviating any need to include them in a general peace. By separating Austro-Prussian territorial schemes from the French war, thereby granting tacit British acceptance, the Cabinet hoped to gain their acceptance of British views regarding the goals of the war. Grenville's proposals demonstrated British willingness to tolerate limited predations from the German powers in order to reach agreement on halting the more pressing danger of the continuing annexations and subversion of the French Republic.[20]

Pitt later explained this strategy during a Parliamentary debate over the treatment of French prisoners that expanded into a comprehensive discussion over the purpose of the war:

> [Pitt] was perfectly ready to admit that unjust measures were as hostile to his mind when adopted by crowned heads as when they were adopted on the part of a republic.... Let the present partition of Poland be as odious as it might, ... this was no reason why we should not cooperate [with the eastern powers] to a just end, to resist the operation of French power, to carry on the war with that vigor and effect which might lead to the conclusion of a sure and honorable peace, and to obtain indemnification for ourselves for the past and for the future to have a reasonable security for ourselves and for the rest of Europe.[21]

Pitt's search for security in Europe required a balance of realism and principle. In a move that his twentieth-century successors would repeat, Pitt pressed his countrymen to embrace the lesser evil in eastern Europe temporarily to stop a greater threat in the west. However, acceptance did not signify approval or support. Pitt above all sought to forge a broad coalition not limited to the German powers and Russia, and he recognized that questions of territorial indemnities posed the greatest threat to multilateral cooperation. As such, Pitt worked closely with Grenville and Dundas to ensure that British diplomatic proposals held the broadest possible appeal. Beyond a general acceptance of the principle of compensation, they carefully separated the issues of compensation and military cooperation. They also urged other states to send diplomats to London or The Hague to negotiate a multilateral convention that would include details of military cooperation and a pledge not to make separate peace until the French surrendered their conquests. To Murray at Frederick William's headquarters, Grenville described this proposal "as the only one which affords a reasonable prospect of forwarding the objects of common interest which all the different courts have in view."[22]

As the British government struggled unsuccessfully to assemble a coalition for mediation, the execution of Louis XVI on 21 January 1793 precipitated the breach in Anglo-French diplomacy that had been virtually inevitable after the November decrees. Louis XVI's death aroused tremendous anger throughout Britain, and, as noted, the British government ordered Chauvelin to leave the country by 1 February.[23] The French envoy returned to Paris on 29 January; three days later the outraged National Convention voted unanimously to declare war on Great Britain and the United Provinces. The Convention immediately ordered Dumouriez to invade the United Provinces and instructed Dutch Patriots to revolt against the House of Orange. In this way, war formally began between the Anglo-Dutch alliance and the French over the sovereignty and security of Britain's only ally on the Continent—the Dutch Republic. However, the French attempt to redefine international law in revolutionary terms by way of the November 1792 decrees remained the underlying issue that led to the more immediate rupture.[24]

Receipt of the French declaration of war on 9 February 1793 truncated the Dumouriez peace initiative.[25] The decision for war forced the British to transform preparations aimed at deterrence and mediation to a plan for war. Although the Cabinet had anticipated war with France, it had no clear solution to the strategic problems of fighting France and defending the Netherlands without a major Continental ally. As noted, Pitt had hoped Prussia would defend the Dutch Republic through the Triple Alliance of 1788, but five years later British ministers placed little confidence in Prussian adherence to that treaty. As early as 18 December 1792, Grenville voiced this sentiment in a letter to Auckland exhorting the Dutch to marshal their own resources to repel the impending French invasion: "Everything now depends on vigorous preparations in Holland, and even what cannot be done in fact should be done in appearance. If things come to extremities, the land forces of the Republic will, as it seems to me, be most miserably deficient, and it is the part in which we can least help her. I should be sorry that the whole reliance should be on Prussia."[26]

During the winter of 1792–93, Anglo-Prussian exchanges over defending the Dutch yielded little result. The British pledged to at least fulfill their chiefly naval treaty obligations while expressing hope that Prussia would direct its operations likewise to fulfill its treaty obligations to defend the Dutch by land. The Prussian response evaded the matter, suggesting vaguely that the continued operations of the Prussian armies on the French frontier would probably satisfy Anglo-Dutch needs.[27] Dutch approaches to the Prussians received similarly dismissive responses.[28]

Based on the relative weakness of the British and Dutch armies, the lack of Continental support, and his observations of French capabilities, Pitt harbored few illusions regarding the nature and difficulty of the impending war.[29] By February 1793, revolutionary armies had proven their ability to compete with old regime opponents all while France's dismal economic situation seemed to preclude the vigorous prosecution of a war. In a "Report on the Finances of France" among Pitt's papers dated January 1793, an unnamed author expounds on the strategic problems posed by war with the new revolutionary state:

> While France was a regular government and had ideas of national dignity or of established power, a successful attack upon either, was the best means of wounding her, and an insult upon her coasts ... the capture of her distant possessions or of her men of war was a national defeat. Both the feelings and the interest of the nation be different in the present struggle, and it must be considered where her sensibility is greatest in the present state of things, and what blow will most effectually hurt her. Thus, for instance, Bordeaux will now make a greater sensation if burnt than Brest.

The report follows this with more specific considerations on France's ability to wage war.

> The most important considerations which engage a statesman at the eve of a war are the objects of attack, the objects of defense, the means of both, and generally the finances and resources of the country with which war is meditated, and this last consideration is of the utmost importance, because on it principally depends the nature, the duration, and the probable success of the war. . . . It is most peculiarly so in the present instance; when France has not certain means of making even a first armament and yet may possibly bring into action resources of an extent and efficacy unknown in the history of any age or country.

> This is the peculiarity of the present state of France, deriving from anarchy and the confusion of all property immense powers of mischief and yet not able to answer with certainty for the expenses of a campaign or the equipment of a simple squadron.

The author speculated that revolutionary France might be an exception to the traditional rules governing the economics of war, a troubling prospect for the British whose military assets favored a strategy of attrition and economic warfare.[30]

In the conflict that became known as the War of the First Coalition, Britain engaged in a struggle with an unconventional foe to defend the sanctity of treaties, protect the sovereignty of neutral countries, and repudiate France's stated policy of intervening in the politics of other nations. In Parliament, Pitt explained that the goal of Britain's war with France was "seeing whether it was possible either by our own exertions or in concert with any other powers to repress this French system of aggrandizement and aggression" and "provide for the security of our own country and the general security of Europe."[31] Dundas added that the ministry would "endeavor to bring down every power on earth to assist them against France."[32] In 1792–93, as in 1788–91, Pitt sought to preserve the existing European state system and the balance of power from the predations of aggressive powers by forging a multilateral collective security system. This objective and its accompanying principles underpinned Pitt's strategy throughout the War of the First Coalition.

Lacking the means to secure its Continental objectives without the aid of another major power, British war policy prioritized efforts to persuade cobelligerents to accept Pitt's views as the basis for both the war as well as the ultimate peace with France. All other aspects of British strategy remained subordinate to this overarching goal. The government deployed Britain's military assets primarily as tools of diplomatic leverage either in return for allies accepting British views of the war or to secure French possessions to serve as leverage in the future peace negotiations. In addition, Britain's handling of the counterrevolution was chiefly governed by the Cabinet's assessment of how best to achieve a stable peace and integrate France into a postwar international system.[33]

Uncertain of any other powers' plans or depth of commitment to the war with France, London's initial military plans focused on using Britain's own resources to greatest effect while diplomacy continued to search for Continental solutions. In this context, Dundas pushed for a blue-water strategy reliant only on British resources and designed to secure British maritime and commercial dominance. In contrast, Grenville consistently advocated for waging war primarily with a view to maintaining the balance of power in Europe. Pitt

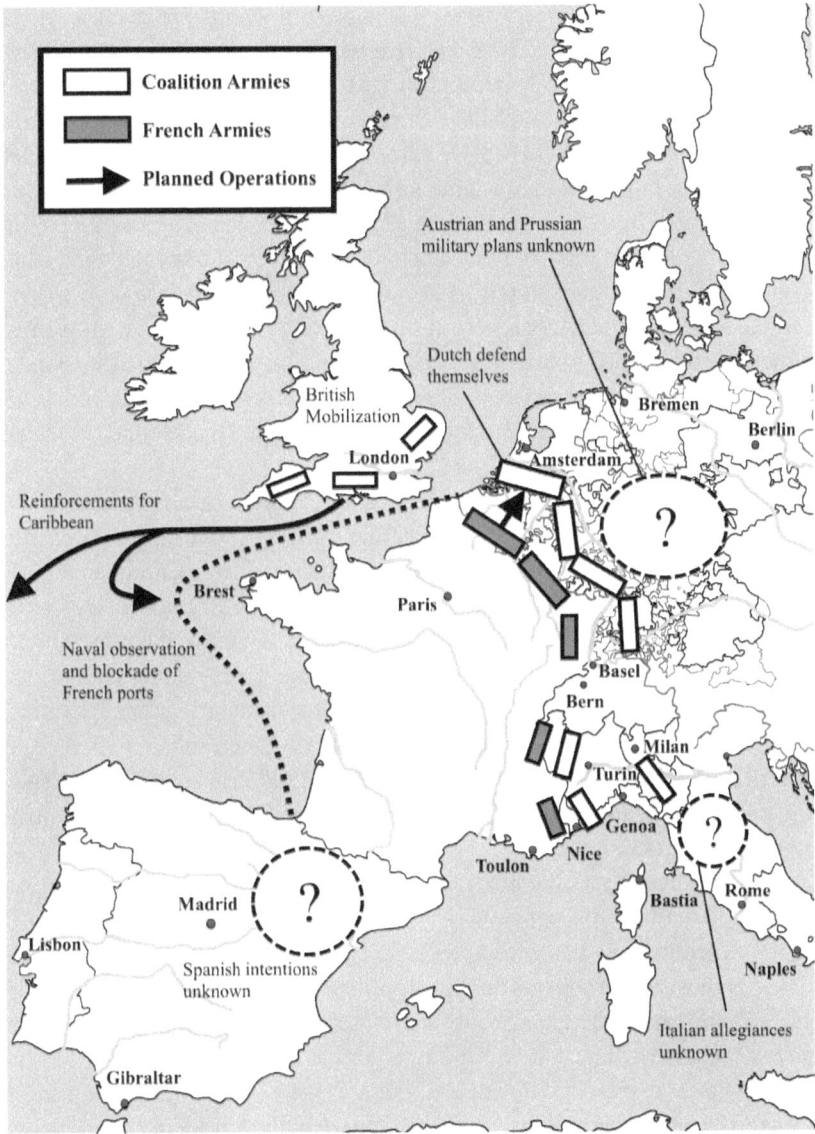

British plans for 1793

endeavored to balance the two perspectives, recognizing the pragmatic value of both views while adhering to his collective security goals.[34]

Although not expecting Britain's maritime resources to force the French to sue for peace, the Cabinet quickly deployed its seaborne assets to protect British colonies and commerce and then to strike at France's equivalents.

Preparations for economic warfare had formed a significant component of Grenville's prewar dispatches to the various courts of Europe. After French diplomacy radicalized in November of 1792, Grenville began urging neutral states to close their ports and halt all shipments of food to France. While aware of the revolutionaries' ability to bend traditional rules of finance, the Cabinet expected that food shortages would both hamper French military operations and accentuate hostility to the Revolution within France. Dundas especially urged operations to capture French colonies in the Caribbean to damage the French economy further and provide points of leverage in future negotiations for peace. Dundas acted partially in response to advice from French planter émigrés who had fled to Britain from slave revolts on the French sugar islands. On 10 February, he sent orders to Barbados for an attack on Tobago, and on 28 February he added instructions to assault Martinique, Guadeloupe, St. Lucia, and Marie-Galante.[35]

On the Continent, Auckland helped the Dutch organize the defense of the Netherlands against Dumouriez's impending offensive.[36] He begged Grenville for reinforcements on 15 February: "Men, commanders, ships, and money! We could not ask for more if this country were a part of Yorkshire; but I incline to think that it should be considered as such for the present; and if it is brought to a question whether we are to conquer it and to keep it, or whether Dumouriez is to do it, I have no doubt as to the decision."[37] Understanding the diplomatic, economic, and strategic importance of Britain's Dutch alliance, Auckland placed as much importance on defending the United Provinces as on defending Britain itself, and he believed that the Dutch could not repel a French invasion without assistance.[38]

On 17 February 1793, Dumouriez invaded the United Provinces, declaring friendship to the Dutch people and hostility to the House of Orange on behalf of the exiled Patriots that accompanied his army.[39] George III had already ordered Hanoverian troops to the Low Countries in the hope that they would arrive before the outbreak of hostilities. As they had not yet arrived, the British government heeded Auckland's advice and ordered three Guard battalions to prepare for embarkation. Prince Frederick, Duke of York and Albany, hastily sailed for the Low Countries on 25 February with 1,971 men.[40] The Cabinet hoped to inspire the Dutch to greater exertions until the mobilization of Dutch resources, the success of Austrian armies farther south, or French acceptance of British terms ended the French invasion.[41]

Although British reinforcements bolstered Dutch defenses and morale, facilitating a stubborn defense during the first half of March, Austrian success rather than any British or Dutch efforts turned the tide in the Low Countries in 1793. With a fresh army of 70,000 men, Field Marshal Prince Frederick Josias of

Saxe-Coburg-Saalfeld attacked and defeated the French army on 1 March 1793 at Aldenhoven and invaded Belgium.[42] Dumouriez withdrew from the United Provinces to confront Coburg but suffered defeats at Neerwinden on 18 March and Louvain on 22 March. With his army broken, the French general negotiated an armistice with Coburg that allowed all French forces to withdraw from the Austrian Netherlands.[43] In addition, the convention between the two commanders included an agreement whereby Dumouriez would lead his army to Paris to restore the monarchy. In return, the Austrian army would halt at the French frontier and receive the fortress of Condé as compensation.[44]

Throughout this campaign, Coburg continuously corresponded with the Duke of York and Prince William of Orange in an attempt to direct their operations. Although George III respected Coburg, he disapproved of this treatment of Anglo-Dutch forces. "Though it is impossible he should not be apprised that no concert as yet exists between this country and the two great German Courts on the best mode of repelling the French," he observed to Pitt, "yet he keeps calling both on the Duke of York and the Dutch as if he was empowered to call for unlimited assistance."[45] Despite his dispute of form, George fundamentally agreed with Coburg's plans. He issued orders for the Anglo-Dutch forces to advance to Antwerp by way of Bergen op Zoom and, if possible, from there to Dunkirk to harass the French retreat.[46]

Meanwhile, the Cabinet continued to view the British expedition as a temporary expedient to ensure the safety of the United Provinces until the danger had passed. Pitt suggested that the British and German troops under York's command would be best used to secure Dunkirk as a base to allow the British to supply the Austrian army in Flanders. Following that success, he hoped that the British force could be withdrawn, leaving Flanders to the Austrians. The British troops and German mercenaries in British pay would then be used to support Austrian operations indirectly through an amphibious assault somewhere in northern France to divert French reinforcements from Flanders.[47] Britain's ambiguous relationship with the Austrians and Prussians created an awkward military situation. While the British certainly hoped that Austro-Prussian military success would defeat France, no agreement forbade the German powers from making a separate peace with France without consulting the British. Additionally, neither Berlin nor Vienna was obligated to respect British interests in any such peace settlement. In this circumstance, the Cabinet sought to facilitate and support Austrian operations in the Low Countries without making British operations dependent on uncertain Austrian support. Instead, Pitt insisted on confining British deployments to operations dependent only on British or Dutch decisions, such as incursions along the French coast or an independent campaign in Flanders.[48]

In response to his negotiations with Dumouriez and the uncertainty surrounding the plans of each party with forces operating in the Low Countries, Coburg invited representatives from each army to a conference at Antwerp on 7 April 1793.[49] Grenville relayed the king's approval and specific instructions to Auckland on 3 April. The foreign secretary noted that "the two leading points are the general plan of future operations, and the advantages to which the powers at war may respectively look." These same two points had animated his dispatches of 29 December 1792. With regard to the former, Grenville favored the coastal plan of operations for British forces, which he viewed as providing flexibility amid uncertainty regarding Austrian intentions. On the latter, he urged Auckland to oppose the Belgium-Bavaria exchange and recommend the annexation of French Flanders instead.[50]

The Antwerp conference provided the British with an opportunity to achieve what Grenville had been unable to achieve in November and December 1792: an understanding with the German powers over the purpose of the war. A shift in the Austrian chancellery from pro-Prussian to pro-British officials improved the chances of agreement. On 25 October 1792, Frederick William II had issued the Verbal Note of Merle at his headquarters near Luxembourg, stating his intention to reduce Prussia's commitment to the war with France to that of an Austrian auxiliary. In addition, he asserted that Prussia would execute the planned partition of Poland immediately as compensation for its continued participation. The Austrians perceived the Verbal Note of Merle as little short of outright betrayal. Consequently, it weakened the foreign ministry of Johann Philipp, Count of Cobenzl, and Anton Spielmann, who had risen to prominence as supporters of a Prussian alignment. British resistance to the exchange mortally wounded the already reeling Cobenzl ministry. The moribund Austrian foreign ministry coasted until 23 March 1793 when Russian and Prussian envoys announced the Second Partition of Poland, dealing the final blow to Cobenzl's policy.[51]

As Austro-Prussian relations deteriorated in the spring of 1793, Francis II replaced his pro-Prussian minister with Baron Johann Amadeus Franz von Thugut. This change paired with a coolness from Berlin persuaded British ministers that an Austrian alliance might be both feasible and a better guarantee of the security of the United Provinces than the Prussian partnership. Paradoxically for the Austrians, such a connection would require Vienna to drop the exchange project, and Grenville renewed the British objections to it that he had abandoned in January. Thugut opposed Austria's alliance with Prussia and expressed willingness to abandon the Belgium-Bavaria exchange to secure a British alliance. However, this made Austria's search for territorial compensation to counter Prussian and Russian gains in the Second Partition of Poland a top priority of Thugut's foreign policy and one that would strain Anglo-Austrian cooperation.[52]

On the evening of 7 April, the Duke of York and Auckland joined their counterparts from the other armies. Stadtholder William V's eldest son and overall commander of the Dutch army, Prince William Frederick, and Grand Pensionary Spiegel represented the Dutch. The Austrian minister in Belgium, Franz Georg Karl von Metternich, and the Austrian ambassador to The Hague, Ludwig Joseph Maximilian von Starhemberg, represented Vienna, while Coburg and his chief of staff, Karl Mack von Leiberich, represented the Austrian army.[53] Field Marshal Alexander Friedrich von Knoblesdorff and Prussian ambassador to The Hague, Dorotheus Ludwig Christoph von Keller, attended the conference as Prussian observers without negotiating authority.[54]

Initial discussions at the conference addressed Dumouriez's defection and the appropriate response. The French general had met with Coburg on 4 April 1793 to arrange terms by which he would turn his army on Paris and declare for constitutional monarchy. Their meeting prompted Coburg to issue a declaration the following day detailing his support for Dumouriez and the Constitution of 1791. Coburg's declaration also renounced all possibility of conquering French territory as indemnities. However, Dumouriez's army refused to follow him except for approximately 2,000 infantry and cavalry.[55] During the conference, all of the delegates except for Coburg and Mack opposed the declaration and insisted on a new document to retract the first and more accurately state the intentions of the attending states. Metternich drafted the new statement and presented it to the conference on the evening of 8 April to general approbation. The new declaration, issued the following day, allowed Coburg to retract his previous statement with dignity.[56]

The delegates also developed a preliminary plan of operations subject to more extensive negotiations in the future. They determined that Coburg should besiege the French border fortresses with the main Austro-Prussian army while the Anglo-Dutch army took a position on Coburg's right flank toward the coast. Whether Austria would retain any conquests permanently or add them to the Belgium-Bavaria exchange remained undetermined.[57] Moreover, the conference failed to resolve the question of indemnities. Auckland's emphasis on the importance of retaining the fortresses of French Flanders to improve the security of the Austrian Netherlands gained support from Starhemberg and Metternich. Although noncommittal on account of the ministerial changes in Vienna, they both expressed personal distaste for the Belgium-Bavaria exchange and preferred the expansion of the Austrian Netherlands. They also noted that the Bavarian elector would likely accept the exchange only if it included the border fortresses in question. Leaving the fate of the fortresses undecided, the Austrian and British delegates at least agreed to conquer them.[58]

In addition to questions of Austrian indemnification, Auckland and the Prince of Orange both indicated that their respective governments would seek compensation for their contributions to the war. Auckland remained vague on the projected British indemnity but openly discussed with Metternich the options for Dutch compensation. He suggested cessions of territory from the Austrian Netherlands near Antwerp or Maastricht. Understandably, this suggestion paired poorly with simultaneous British pressure to augment the Austrian Netherlands either to strengthen the barrier or sweeten the exchange for Bavaria. The question of a Dutch indemnity never received a satisfactory resolution and continued to sour relations between the two alliances throughout 1793.[59]

To maximize British leverage over the peace settlement, Auckland secured Austrian approval for British command of the future siege of Dunkirk. Although a minor concession from the Austrians, the right to occupy Dunkirk in the name of George III provided a rare opening for Britain's meager army to secure substantial diplomatic leverage. British possession of Dunkirk offered the prospect of supplying the combined armies through that port rather than through Austria's lengthy overland lines of communication through Germany. British control over lines of supply theoretically promised greater British influence over the direction of operations. As one of the border fortresses that Vienna hoped to conquer, Dunkirk in British hands also offered leverage for persuading Austria to consider British views on postwar territorial adjustments. Additionally, the occupation of a French city in the name of George III rather than in trust for a restored French monarchy avoided commitment to any particular form of government for France, preserving Britain's careful neutrality on this point. Just as possession of Dunkirk would provide leverage over the Austrians, it would also secure for the British a voice in determining the coalition's stance on the future of the French government.[60]

Following the conference, the generals and diplomats returned to their posts. From this point, efforts to merge the Anglo-Dutch and Austro-Prussian wars with France chiefly relied on negotiations between the senior partners of each alliance: Britain and Austria. While the sheer power differential and the nature of the origin of the Anglo-Dutch alliance left no question as to the seniority in their relationship, Austrian leadership in the Austro-Prussian partnership resulted from a deliberate choice on the part of Berlin. Prussian ministers had consistently responded to British overtures since the outbreak of the war with vague replies deferring decisions to Vienna, insisting that Austria was the principal ally and Prussia merely the auxiliary. This assertion received its clearest expression in the aforementioned Verbal Note of Merle.[61]

At The Hague, Auckland continued to discuss Anglo-Austrian operations and the critical question of indemnities with Starhemberg and the governor-general of the Austrian Netherlands, Florimond Claude Mercy-Argenteau.[62] Although instructed to go to London and negotiate an official convention between Austria and Britain, Mercy's duties in Belgium continually delayed his departure. Meanwhile, Grenville continued his discussions with Austrian ambassador Johann Philipp, Graf von Stadion, in London while Auckland's younger brother, Sir Morton Eden, represented British interests in Vienna. The dispersal of negotiations reintroduced extensive delay to Anglo-Austrian communications, hampering efforts to capitalize on the agreement from the Antwerp conference. "It is much to be regretted," complained Auckland, "that there is not some person at the Austrian headquarters, on the part of that government, sufficiently informed of the system and views of the Combined Powers to give advice on the several new incidents, which are rather political than military."[63] Only Mercy possessed the authority to negotiate a definitive arrangement with Britain, thus rendering Grenville's talks with Stadion virtually meaningless and Eden's talks with Thugut redundant in expectation of Mercy's mission to London.[64]

As negotiations slowed to a crawl, Murray, now York's adjutant-general, brought the royal commander fresh instructions from London on 19 April 1793. The author of these instructions, Dundas, directed him to cooperate with Coburg but not to take orders from him or place any British troops under foreign command. The instructions established Dunkirk as York's primary objective pursuant to the agreement made at the Antwerp conference. Dundas emphasized the importance of continued British participation to ensure that Austria retained Belgium; the persistent uncertainty surrounding Austrian intentions reinforced this decision. A campaign for Dunkirk would bring the expedition closer to the coast and an escape route should Austrian policy change. While Thugut proved more amenable to British views than his predecessors in the Austrian Chancellery, the shifting administration and policy in Vienna reduced British willingness to take risks on the assumption of Austrian consistency in the absence of a binding treaty.[65] After Murray and York determined that the British expedition lacked the strength to assault Dunkirk, they moved the army south to assist Coburg with the siege of Condé.[66] Not losing sight of his instructions, York hoped "to take the attention of the enemy from Dunkirk" and influence them to divert reinforcements farther south to make a future British attempt on Dunkirk easier.[67]

The tentative union of the Austrian and British armies in late April mirrored a concurrent but no less tentative diplomatic convergence on the question of Austrian indemnification. On 14 April 1793, Thugut indicated willingness to abandon the Belgium-Bavaria exchange in favor of expanding the Austrian Netherlands, but he argued that if the British wanted Austria to take French Flanders instead of Bavaria, they must help conquer it.[68] Through Mercy and Stadion, he offered to renounce the exchange in return for either substantial British military assistance to conquer French Flanders or British diplomatic support for compensation in Poland.[69] While the Cabinet had washed their collective hands of Polish matters after the Ochakov Crisis, they could not so easily ignore the power struggle in eastern Europe that Pitt had so recently declared to be of paramount importance to British interests and security. Recognition of the interconnectedness of eastern and western European power politics had driven the British into the failed standoff with Russia in 1791, and that same connection colored nearly all negotiations surrounding the war with France two years later.

Thugut's proposal illustrated the fundamental difference between the two wars that he and Grenville sought to merge into one. For Thugut, the Austrian war remained essentially a struggle to maintain the balance of power in eastern Europe in which Austria was falling behind. From the Russo-Austrian war against the Ottoman Empire (1787–91), Russia gained substantial territorial and political concessions from the Turks while Austria made negligible gains in part due to British interference. The Second Partition of Poland similarly left Austria without compensation to balance Prussian and Russian gains. As such, Thugut insisted that an Anglo-Austrian accord pertaining to the war with France should include compensation for Austria to match Prussian acquisitions in Poland. In contrast, the British refused to sanction the odious Polish partition by including it in any agreement to which Britain was a party, just as Grenville had warned in January.[70]

Both London and Vienna viewed the defeat and containment of revolutionary France as imperative to their foreign policy goals. Regardless, they struggled to reach more than a temporary agreement on military cooperation because their objectives rested on fundamentally incompatible visions of national security and the balance of power. Thugut sought Austrian security through preserving the existing balance of territory, population, and revenue between the great powers. Imbalances would be compensated by extracting concessions from weaker neutral states. In contrast, Pitt sought security for Britain by rendering the prospect of war in Europe equally unappealing to all through a multilateral guarantee of the principle of the status quo.[71]

Austrian indemnification at French expense either along the border of the Austrian Netherlands or in Alsace and Lorraine emerged as the most probable compromise to satisfy Austria's competitive needs and Britain's opposition to predatory compensation from neutrals.[72] However, as the means of obtaining this compensation and each power's role in the campaign remained unclear, negotiations on all points continued well into the campaign. Grenville lamented to Auckland that the absence of full agreement on the purpose of the war hindered effective military cooperation. The two powers repeatedly reached temporary agreements on the immediate plan of campaign only to have military contingency force alterations that required renewed negotiations. The British sought a convention of cooperation to commit both powers diplomatically to the same ends thereby liberating their armies to cooperate without constant reference to their political superiors.[73]

Despite strides toward agreement, the negotiations with Austria remained fraught with difficulty. Both the Austrian and British governments sought firm commitments from the other while keeping their own options open, exacerbating the suspicion that had developed between them before the war. Grenville sought a permanent, written Austrian renunciation of the Belgium-Bavaria exchange as part of the war with France without committing Britain to securing an alternative for Vienna.[74] Conversely, Thugut pursued British support for an Austrian indemnity based on the principle of equivalent compensation for Russian and Prussian gains in the Second Partition of Poland. He shrank from committing to any specific source for this compensation to ensure that the acquisition of the Austrian indemnity did not depend on the fortunes of war. The ensuing diplomatic contest became one of principle: the Austrians sought British acceptance of a competitive balance of power secured by predatory compensation while the British sought Austrian acceptance of collective security through more limited compensation that respected the status quo in principle.[75]

The British faced challenges to this principle from their Dutch ally as well, which undermined efforts to reach an understanding with Austria. In return for continuing to support the offensive into France, the Dutch demanded territorial concessions from the Austrian Netherlands. The British attempted but failed to persuade the Dutch to take French colonies as their indemnity to alleviate Austro-Dutch tension in the Low Countries. The Dutch refused to make the expenditure necessary to mount a colonial expedition, and the British refused to do it for them. Although this proved to be a matter of significant embarrassment for Grenville, he could not avoid addressing the issue in his negotiations with the Austrians for fear of losing the aid of the Dutch army. Repeated British insistence on a campaign to secure Dunkirk and references to a Dutch indemnity aroused Austrian fears that London meant to retain Dunkirk at the close of the war and looked only for selfish gains for itself and its ally. The Austrians correctly anticipated that British possession of Dunkirk would allow Grenville to place conditions on the cession of the city, thereby forcing

Austria to accept British views on contentious issues like the Dutch indemnity. Discussion of the Dutch indemnity also made Grenville's earlier efforts to defer discussion of specific indemnities to the postwar peace negotiations appear hypocritical and disingenuous.[76]

Meanwhile, Austrian refusal to state their views on the matter of compensation caused British ministers to worry that the exchange or a slice of Poland remained under consideration.[77] Diplomats from both powers chastised their governments for needless intransigence. Eden wrote to Auckland: "I confess that the acquisition of Dunkirk appears also impolitic."[78] Concurrently, Mercy complained to Thugut of vague instructions for negotiating the matter of indemnities.[79] Unable to reach an agreement, both London and Vienna continued to "build too much on the supposed necessity of our proceeding in the operations against France," explained Auckland, "without further explanation, and in whatever may best suit their present and future views."[80] Auckland's criticism of the Austrians applied equally to British conduct.

The difficulties of the Anglo-Austrian negotiations of 1793 typified British efforts to secure multilateral cooperation based on principle without providing specific solutions to the territorial ambitions of the various states involved. This difficulty combined with the urgent need of military cooperation drove the Pitt ministry to abandon calls for a conference of diplomats at London or The Hague. Instead, Pitt fell back on the formula of the Triple Alliance of 1788 and sought to build a network of bilateral conventions more specifically tailored to meet the needs and concerns of each state. The Foreign Office thus obtained conventions of cooperation with Russia on 25 March, Sardinia on 25 April, Spain on 25 May, Naples on 12 July, Prussia on 14 July, and Portugal on 10 September.[81] Each treaty included some variation on pledges not to make a separate peace with France, not to export war materiel to France, to continue the war until the French had surrendered their conquests, and to cooperate militarily toward that end. Paradoxically, British insistence on separating the French war from measures distasteful to British principles ensured that negotiations on this basis could not provide the foundation for a comprehensive system acceptable to all powers as Pitt hoped.[82]

The negotiations for an Anglo-Russian convention emerged as a continuation of Russia's prewar proposals to form a coalition against France. After the French declared war on Britain, Catherine authorized Vorontsov to forge formal connections with Britain relative to cooperation in the war with France.[83] The Russian ambassador concluded two treaties with Grenville on 25 March 1793. The first concerned economics, encompassing a renewal of the Anglo-Russian commercial treaty of 1766 that Pitt had failed to renew in 1786 as well as agreements on policing neutral trade in the Baltic to keep war materiel out of French hands. The second included the determination to cooperate militarily to force France to restore its conquests, and the Russians offered a small squadron of ships as their contribution to the war effort. Grenville pressed Vorontsov for 12,000 Russian troops for service in Flanders as aid that Britain more urgently needed. Lacking the authority to make such an offer, Vorontsov persuaded Grenville to sign the preliminary treaties and refer them to St. Petersburg for modification.[84]

At St. Petersburg, British ambassador Sir Charles Whitworth discovered that Catherine demanded the impossible sum of £600,000 for 10,000 Russian soldiers to fight in Flanders. For reference, in April, the British obtained the use of 8,000 men from Hesse-Cassel for three years at the cost of about £56,000 per year plus nominal levy money. In September, a treaty with Baden secured 754 men for about £5,500 per year, and, in October, Hesse-Darmstadt contributed 3,000 men for about £41,000 per year. Thus, Grenville gained almost 12,000 men from Germany for roughly one-sixth of what Catherine demanded for the use of 10,000. This unreasonable demand effectively put an end to negotiations for Anglo-Russian military cooperation in 1793.[85] The commercial treaty survived and contributed to Pitt's strategy of choking France by sea, but Catherine refused to go any further. According to Whitworth, the collapse of these negotiations persuaded the British that "all which we have seen happen seems to justify the opinion I entertained from the beginning that it would be the policy of this court to engage as many as it could in the broil and to keep as clear as possible of it itself."[86] Whitworth had warned since February that Catherine encouraged Britain to war only to ensure that it could not oppose the Second Partition of Poland, and the result of the negotiations supports this view.[87]

In stark contrast to Anglo-Russian negotiations, discussions with Sardinia yielded rapid consensus. After responding positively to Grenville's proposal for British-led armed mediation, the Sardinians granted their ambassador in London full powers to negotiate a treaty for military cooperation and financial assistance. The latter concern proved crucial as the relatively small state was beginning to crack under the economic strain of a second year of campaigning. From Turin, British ambassador John Trevor supported the Sardinian case, arguing that they could not continue to deny the French access to the resources of Italy without financial support. The Cabinet concurred, and Grenville concluded a convention of cooperation with the Sardinian ambassador, Philip de St. Martin de Front, on 25 April 1793. The treaty pledged Sardinia to maintain an army of 50,000 men, which the British promised to support with a "respectable fleet" and an annual subsidy of £200,000 paid quarterly. Both states agreed not to make separate peace with France and to fight on until the French restored all of their conquests, especially the lost Sardinian territories of Nice and Savoy. A secret article further established that the first object of the Sardinian troops and British fleet would be the recovery of Nice. After accomplishing this goal, the Sardinians promised to place 20,000 of their required 50,000 men at the disposal of the British fleet to attack the French elsewhere in the Mediterranean. They kept this article secret and the treaty separate from other negotiations to avoid bringing the recovery of Nice and Savoy into discussions of indemnification with the Austrians and Spanish.[88]

Simultaneous negotiations with Spain emphasized the theme of a broader multilateral coalition. As in the convention with Russia, Anglo-Spanish negotiations emerged from Grenville's original proposal of 29 December 1792 for armed mediation. Anglo-Spanish negotiations proceeded relatively smoothly, unlike the concurrent talks with the Russians, but the project suffered from Spanish suspicion of other courts and the extreme delays of communication. Receiving Grenville's overture on 25 January 1793, nearly one month after it was dispatched, the Spanish embraced it and pressed for a military alliance and commercial agreement.[89] After this information reached Grenville on 6 February, he tasked Alleyne Fitzherbert, First Baron St. Helens, with negotiating the treaty.[90] In addition to drafting terms of an alliance, Grenville suggested that Spain should send an envoy to a coalition congress at London or The Hague with full authority to coordinate the Spanish war effort with the operations of other members of the coalition. Grenville then reiterated that he would "listen to no term which shall not provide that France shall in fact abandon her plans of conquest and aggrandizement and renounce all views of disturbing the tranquility or of infringing upon the rights of other governments." He also acknowledged the principle that any state obliged to defend itself from French aggression could reasonably seek indemnification from France. However, the foreign secretary recommended deferring discussion of this to a future peace conference.[91]

St. Helens proceeded to Spain at a leisurely pace, reaching Madrid on 12 March. While disputes over the commercial dimension of the treaty prevented the conclusion of a full alliance, St. Helens reached agreement with the Spanish on 25 March for a convention regarding military cooperation. Thereupon, he discovered that Grenville had neglected to provide him with documentation of his full authority to conclude the treaty, which resulted in the treaty being forwarded to London for royal approval.[92] This process took two months; St. Helens received the royal approval on 9 May and finally concluded the treaty on 25 May. The Anglo-Spanish convention included several of the same elements of commercial warfare against France as the Anglo-Russian treaty. Beyond this, the agreement bound the two states to support each other in case the terms of the convention led to conflict with a third party, and it included an agreement not to make a separate peace at least until France had surrendered its conquests.[93]

Aside from the extreme delays involved in concluding this treaty, it disappointed Pitt's designs in one other significant way. Regarding the proposal for a congress to unify the policies of the states arrayed against France, the Spanish declined, only offering to consider acceding to any agreement that Britain might make with Austria and Prussia. St. Helens explained that the Spanish did not trust Austrian or Prussian determination to continue the war and generally had poor relations with the German powers. The Spanish instead insisted that the Anglo-Spanish concert could be productive independent of Berlin or Vienna. Consequently, they suggested making the Anglo-Spanish convention the basis for a Mediterranean system by expanding it into an alliance that included the Portuguese and Sardinians.[94]

Negotiations to bring Naples into the war promised to strengthen this Mediterranean system. The addition of the modest but significant Neapolitan navy could protect the shipping of the coalition powers, and a Neapolitan expeditionary army could provide flexible support as needed. However, poor relations between the Neapolitan court and both the courts of Spain and Austria precluded the formal inclusion of Naples in a larger system.[95] Instead, the Anglo-Neapolitan convention followed the pattern of the Sardinian treaty, establishing terms for the British to employ Neapolitan forces as auxiliaries. The treaty also held limited value as it included a clause that left the court of Naples free to abandon the war and return to neutrality at its own discretion.[96]

Despite delays arising from both distance and contingencies, negotiations with the Mediterranean states yielded formal commitments sooner than the ongoing and uncomfortable negotiations with the more important German powers.[97] Efforts to ascertain Prussian intentions in the context of the treaties of 1788 had been largely disregarded by both the Prussian government in Berlin and Frederick William II at his Frankfurt headquarters. To bring matters to a point, the Cabinet dispatched Francis Seymour-Conway, Earl of Yarmouth, to Prussian headquarters with a mandate to conclude a new convention on the current war. Grenville charged Yarmouth with the task of reviving Prussian communication with both Britain and Austria, which had lapsed after the negative reaction of each to the execution of the Polish partition at the start of the year. This lapse in communication accompanied a decline in Prussian military activity, which Grenville also noted as a problem for Yarmouth to rectify. Revealing a lack of leverage, Grenville urged Yarmouth to convince or threaten Frederick William that alienating both Austria and Britain would leave him with no possible ally but a beleaguered France.[98] Returning to the positive objective of Yarmouth's mission, Grenville sent copies of the Russian and Spanish conventions, requesting that the Prussians agree to something similar regarding the purpose of the war and the means of waging it. He suggested giving Frederick William the option of joining the ongoing Anglo-Austrian negotiations to convert his separate engagements with each of them into a coalition of all three. Grenville added the proposition of also inviting the Dutch to accede to any such agreement to complete the merger of the two alliances into a single comprehensive coalition.[99]

Yarmouth's negotiations proceeded more quickly than previous Prussian silence had given reason to hope. The key to the speed and success of these talks was Yarmouth's willingness to abandon the idea of creating a multilateral treaty including Austria and the United Provinces as well. The Prussians categorically refused to consider anything but a bilateral convention. After Yarmouth conceded this point, he obtained agreement to a convention nearly identical to the Anglo-Russian treaty with no complaints from the Prussians. While theoretically a success, the agreement produced only a vague commitment to cooperate militarily, insistence on the restitution of territory that the French conquered from either signatory, and cooperation in economic warfare. This left Austria as the only remaining major power not formally connected to Britain.[100]

Lengthy sieges in French Flanders during the summer of 1793 reduced the prospect of forcing the revolutionaries to the negotiating table within the year. After York's army besieged Valenciennes from 23 May to 28 July, Pitt recognized the necessity of planning another campaign despite the lack of agreement with the Austrians. Amid Cabinet divisions, initial plans for the campaign of 1794 represented a compromise between blue-water and Continentalist strategies. Dundas preferred to leave Flanders to the Dutch and Austrians and use British soldiers to reinforce the Caribbean or make a more concerted descent on the west coast of France. The master-general of the ordinance, Duke Charles Lennox of Richmond, preferred to abandon such peripheral pursuits and concentrate all British resources on the army in Flanders.[101]

The initial plan, formed by Murray in July and adopted in late August, represented a compromise, calling for 30,000 men to defend the front in Flanders while two columns of 50,000 men each executed a pincer maneuver. One would advance west from the southern end of Flanders while the other landed in Normandy to raise a royalist rebellion and march east along the Seine to Paris. Pitt also designated another army of 50,000 men to invade Brittany and still another to attack Toulon to support existing rebellions in western and southern France. This unrealistic plan required 230,000 of the total 270,000 men in all coalition armies operating on the French frontier from Basle to the North Sea. In addition, the majority of these soldiers served under Austrian or Prussian rather than British or Dutch command, thus requiring extensive negotiations to acquire for British use.[102]

Amphibious operations to capitalize on French rebellions appealed to the Cabinet for several reasons. Strategically, landings in northern and western France would open an additional front to draw French armies away from Flanders and the Rhine. Additionally, major amphibious operations offered the chance of adding the strength of known and suspected royalists throughout northern France to the British war effort. Most importantly, this plan promised London more control over the direction of the war despite the relatively small contribution of the British army. Its dependence on British shipping gave London a significant claim to command. If adopted and successful, this plan offered the prospect of granting the British decisive influence over both the political settlement within France and the diplomatic settlement for all of Europe regardless of the lack of agreement with Vienna. Increased British influence would ensure that the postwar arrangement reflected the British principles of neutral rights and collective security rather than the Austro-Prussian preference for balance through partition.[103]

At the end of August, Anglo-Austrian military cooperation in Flanders finally yielded a firm diplomatic agreement despite a flurry of reversals and disappointments. After a slow but successful offensive in which coalition forces gained control of some of French Flanders, the British army's attempt to besiege Dunkirk in August and September 1793 ended in failure. French forces defeated York south of Dunkirk in the battle of Hondschoote on 6 September.[104] British aspirations of taking Dunkirk quickly faded in the face of this reversal. In addition to defeat at Hondschoote, several other diplomatic and military factors precipitated a change of priorities. Most importantly, Grenville and Starhemberg, who had replaced Stadion as the Austrian ambassador in London, signed an Anglo-Austrian convention of cooperation on 30 August 1793. This treaty followed the pattern of Britain's earlier conventions with other states by establishing an agreement to cooperate militarily, engage in economic warfare against France, and secure the restitution of French conquests. Like the Spanish treaty, this acknowledged the principle of obtaining indemnities from France by mutual consent and provided for mutual defense if attacked by a third party.[105]

The convention of 30 August 1793 represented the success of the British Flanders expedition as a diplomatic tool in the summer campaign despite

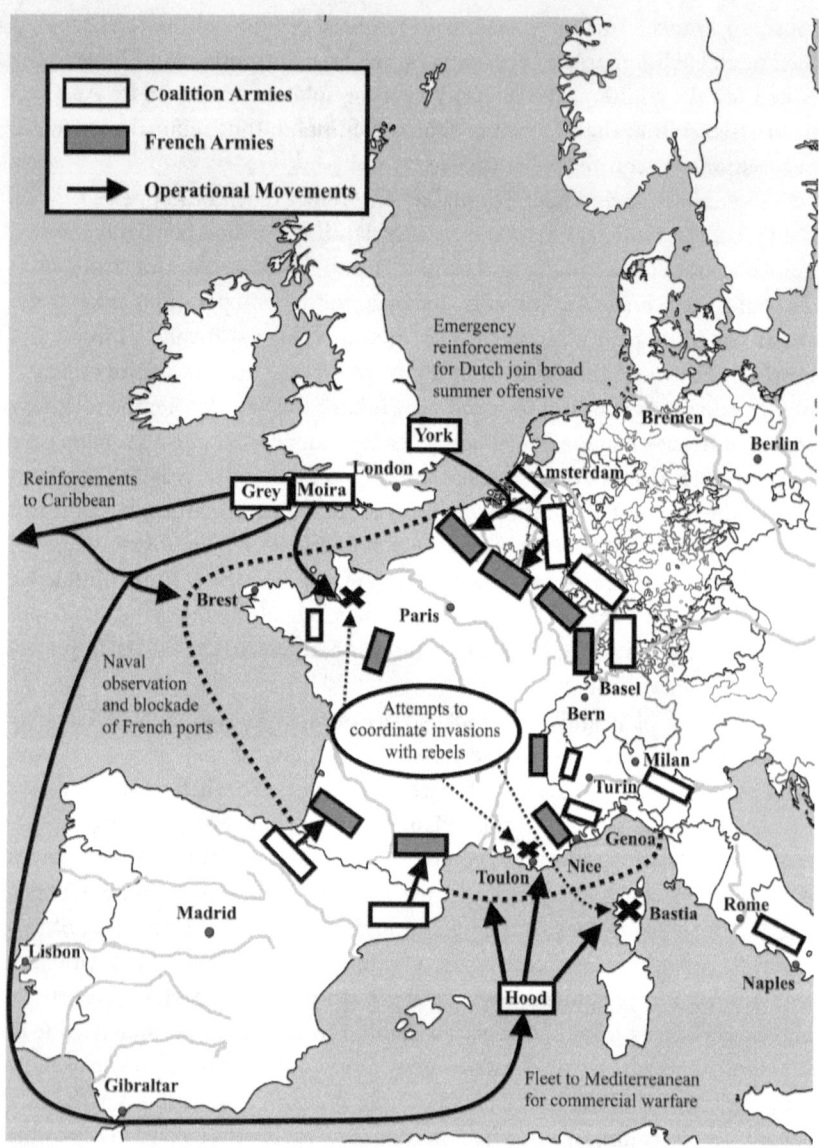

Operations of 1793

failing to achieve its military objectives. By committing the expedition to assist the Austrian armies in a campaign intended to conquer French Flanders, the Cabinet bolstered its negotiating strength to persuade Vienna to abandon the exchange project. Although the siege of Dunkirk failed, formal Austrian commitment to a British-approved peace program, however vaguely defined, rendered British acquisition of the city less important. After Hondschoote and the conclusion of the Anglo-Austrian convention, York retreated and reestablished a more secure defensive cordon in contact with Coburg's main army.[106] With the Anglo-Austrian convention of 30 August largely obviating the need for an independent British campaign, the Cabinet increasingly deferred operational decisions to York. Thereafter, he directed his army as a supporting element of the combined armies rather than as an independent British force. After a few minor defeats in October, York and Coburg stabilized their position and established winter quarters in November, retaining possession of most of the Austrian Netherlands.[107]

On 26 September, Pitt and Grenville completed their network of conventions to organize the war against France by concluding an Anglo-Portuguese convention. Throughout the negotiations with Spain, both the British and Spanish governments had expressed interest in enlisting the Portuguese as a third party to their convention and future alliance. Anglo-Spanish miscommunication combined with Portuguese hesitance to break with France prevented the inclusion of Portugal in the initial convention. Instead, Portuguese ministers in London and Madrid signed separate conventions with each court: the Spanish by the middle of July and the British by the end of September. Portuguese commitments resembled those of Naples, including modest military obligations, agreements regarding economic warfare against France, and a general pledge to act as an auxiliary to Britain during its war with France.[108]

Thus, by the autumn of 1793, British diplomacy had secured a network of bilateral conventions linking Britain to the other states at war with France. However, the form of these agreements represented wartime exigencies rather than an optimal diplomatic system. Most of these treaties had emerged from the negotiations initiated on 29 December 1792 by Grenville's proposals for armed mediation. Each convention acknowledged the restitution of French conquests as the goal of the war, and all agreed to an embargo of French trade as part of the effort to achieve this goal. Predating the war, the original proposal demanded that the French respect the sovereignty of neutrals and renounce support for foreign revolutionaries. In return, it required that France's enemies acknowledge France's republican government and disclaim any intention of interfering with France's domestic politics. The conventions forged after the outbreak of war between France and Britain abandoned these principles in favor of vague assertions of refuting hostile French principles. Regarding France's government, these treaties neither recognized the republic nor supported the counterrevolution. Conversely, they seized on a provision of the December proposals that acknowledged the right of states attacked by France to seek security from aggressive French principles through indemnification from France. The conventions acknowledged the legitimacy of this principle while remaining vague on the indemnities desired and postponing further discussion of them until the eventual peace conference.[109]

It is worth making a distinction between conventions and alliances. Alliances such as those constituting the Triple Alliance in 1788 specified permanent terms of mutual interest that both contracting parties engaged to defend on each other's behalf. In the case of the Triple Alliance, the core uniting principle had been the existing constitution of the United Provinces under the authority of the House of Orange, and the three powers added a mutual guarantee of territory to make it a full defensive alliance. Conventions like those concluded throughout 1793 included conditional and temporary commitments that could provide the basis for military cooperation while still leaving much room for interpretation and flexibility to escape the engagement later if desired. Alliances generally specified the obligations of each party numerically in men, ships, or money, granting each party the right to demand specific assistance from their ally in the event of a war relevant to the casus foederis. The looser pledges of cooperation in the 1793 conventions provided no basis for any such similar demands for assistance.[110]

While the network of conventions yielded agreement on these points and broad terms of military cooperation, their fragmented nature prevented efficacy. Understanding the strength of France and the difficulties of forging an effective coalition from so many diverse states, the British had proposed a general congress at London or The Hague. Grenville's dispatches requested that each state send a delegate with full powers to reach an agreement on the ends and means of defeating France to eliminate the extreme delay inherent in strictly bilateral communications over such great distances. Mutual jealousies and distrust among the states in question, particularly over indemnities and exacerbated by the ongoing Second Partition of Poland, precluded the success of this proposal. Even efforts on a smaller scale to unite Britain and the United Provinces to Prussia and Austria or to Spain and Portugal in a single treaty devolved into a series of bilateral commitments. The network of vague conventions represented a coalition of sorts but certainly not an alliance in any meaningful sense. Nonetheless, Pitt remained dedicated to the pursuit of multilateral collective security, writing to Yarmouth after the latter's successful negotiations with Frederick William:

> I augur most favorably as to the further consequences which may be expected from the apparent disposition of the King of Prussia and of his minister, and from your zeal and ability in improving it to the best advantage. The great object now to be aimed at, seems to be that of including Austria, Holland, and Sardinia,

in the engagements, stipulated by the convention.... It will, I trust, be the object of all the parties in the war, as it is ours, to strain every nerve for carrying on the operations as vigorously and as decisively as possible at a period when the internal distractions of France afford so favorable an opportunity.[111]

Although Pitt met with disappointment in his hope that the Prussian convention could provide the basis for a broader system, the noted "internal distractions of France" soon provided fresh opportunities to promote his views on the future of the European state system.

CHAPTER 6

Counterrevolution and Collective Security, 1793

After the defeat at Hondschoote on 8 September and the subsequent retreat to winter quarters in Flanders, British focus shifted to other theaters, which raised different diplomatic challenges. London increasingly turned its attention to Caribbean expeditions designed to cripple that avenue of French economic succor as the winter campaign season in the tropics approached.[1] However, Caribbean expeditions soon became secondary after unexpected opportunities arose in the form of counterrevolutionary rebellions within France itself. Cooperation with French rebels required the British to abandon their neutral stance on French politics and take an ideological position on the war. As in British dealings with coalition partners, principle triumphed over convenience, and the desire to create a stable and cooperative postwar international system guided Pitt's conditional support of counterrevolutionary measures.

After the French declaration of war preempted British mediation attempts, the Cabinet directed British military and diplomatic assets in a strategy of containment. They sought to repel French aggression and proselytization until either defeat, moderation, or counterrevolution led France to adopt a more restrained foreign policy. They also wanted to build multilateral consensus on this point without committing Britain to a war for extensive conquests. These efforts to achieve containment and consensus gained nominal success by the autumn of 1793. Despite broad, vaguely defined agreement across Europe, the diplomatic arrangements binding the coalition remained fragile and fragmented. Operations to constrict French trade by sea and repulse French armies on land had thus far achieved precarious and incomplete success.[2]

As the British waged war on these relatively limited terms, Pitt resisted pressure both from the opposition to make peace with the revolutionaries as well as calls from émigrés, foreign powers, and domestic conservatives to declare support for a Bourbon restoration.³ A British agent in Brussels recounted London's objectives in the war after lamenting the difficulty of bringing the émigré princes to understand them:

> It is a war to repel aggressions, to defend our constitution, to preserve our commercial interests, to restore order and tranquility, and to establish the balance of Europe on a clear and solid basis. Though, in proceeding on those grounds, the monarchy of France may be, and I imagine your Lordship will think must be, restored, still the restoration of the monarchy can never be held out as a motive for the war, and I shall see with pain whatever may tend to encourage the idea of its being a war undertaken for the interests of princes.⁴

British officials did make contact with royalist insurgents in the Vendée in northwestern France during this period but offered only logistical support. The rebellions against the Revolution held appeal primarily as a means of reducing the French capacity for war and hastening a negotiated peace with the republican regime.⁵

While the British and Austrian armies fought loosely connected campaigns in Flanders as part of their distinct and separate wars with France, the British discovered an opportunity to establish their own conditions for peace with France. Grenville had received a request from French foreign minister, Pierre-Henri-Hélène-Marie Lebrun-Tondu, for passports for a French emissary to travel to London to discuss peace terms in April. The foreign secretary declined this overture on 18 May. In his response, he asserted the British government's refusal to allow a French envoy in London until "those who are now exercising the functions of government in France" disavowed the revolutionary foreign policy that contributed to the breach between the two countries. Although averse to the mode of negotiation that Lebrun proposed, the British remained open to the prospect of making peace if the revolutionaries renounced the policy of exporting the Revolution by either force or subversion. Grenville's response also insisted that the revolutionaries provide security for the coalition through modest territorial cessions.⁶

A second draft of the reply—the one actually sent—took greater precautions to avoid affording implicit recognition of the revolutionary regime:

> His Majesty does not consider it expedient . . . to recognize under the present circumstances a new form of government in France, but if [the Revolutionaries are] prepared to terminate the war unjustly declared on His Majesty and his Allies and to give them a just satisfaction, security, and compensation, [they] may transmit in writing, to the generals of the armies on the frontier, the proposals which shall be made to that effect. This means of communication would avoid

the difficulties of form, and we might then judge of the nature of these propositions, and of the spirit which directs them."[7]

This response carefully maintained neutrality on the question of France's government by denying recognition to the new republic but also refusing to endorse the royalist cause. The form of the French government mattered far less to the Pitt ministry than the willingness of any French government to live at peace with its neighbors and respect the sanctity of treaties and neutral rights. The second draft asserts a willingness to consider peace if the revolutionaries adopted such policy changes, and it provided a method of opening negotiations that avoided the necessity of British recognition of the new government.[8]

In defending the necessity of the war to Parliament on 25 April 1793, Pitt articulated similar reasoning to Grenville's responses to Lebrun. He argued that Britain "was justly entitled to proceed on the war against France to repel her unjust attacks and to obtain indemnification for the past and security for the future. These were the principles on which they engaged in the war. These were the principles they must look to in carrying it on, and which they must keep in view at its conclusion."[9] He declared that he would consider peace if the French government repudiated revolutionary foreign policy or if success in the war rendered France impotent to act on those principles. The latter possibility justified British willingness to support compensation for the other powers of the coalition as long as it came from France. Although the National Convention repealed the decree of fraternity on 14 April 1793, the French made no move to overturn the annexations made in the name of the decree. Pitt preferred accommodation with the revolutionaries to a restoration imposed by force, but negotiations depended on French willingness to submit to the British interpretation of the traditional international order.[10]

Pitt considered the probability of bringing the existing revolutionary government to accept British terms unlikely but not impossible. In a debate over a motion from Fox to offer peace to France, Pitt articulated the government's position on working with counterrevolutionaries to overcome this obstacle to peace: "I declare that on the part of this government there was no intention, if the country had not been attacked, to interfere in the internal affairs of France. . . . But having been attacked, there is nothing . . . which pledges us not to take advantage of any interference in the internal affairs of France that may be necessary."[11] Leaving open the possibility of a counterrevolutionary strategy, Pitt offered a more detailed outline of the purpose of the war and the terms on which he would consider peace. In reference to the "indemnification for the past and security for the future," he placed particular emphasis on the security for the future.

And this security, it appears to me, can only be obtained in one of three modes: 1st, that these principles [aggressive revolutionary foreign policy] shall no longer predominate; or 2^{ndly} that those who are now engaged in them shall be taught that they are impracticable and convinced of their own want of power to carry them into execution; or 3^{rdly} that the issue of the present war shall be such as by weakening their power of attack shall strengthen [British] power of resistance.[12]

Foretelling the problems that would plague the Peace of Amiens a decade later, he added, "Without these you may indeed have an armed truce, a temporary suspension of hostilities, but no permanent peace, no solid security to guard you against the repetition of injury and the renewal of attack."[13] Pitt's highest priority remained a stable international system based on collective security principles; the form of France's government and the question of indemnities were secondary to this objective.

A series of defeats in September and October 1793 had frustrated the initial, tenuously united coalition campaign in Flanders to force the French Republic to abandon its aggressive views. Far from collapsing, as many had expected, the Revolution gained new strength through mass mobilization and extreme centralization. However, the conscription and institutionalized terror that enabled the French to repel the Anglo-Austrian advances in Flanders also multiplied the enemies of the Revolution within France. Royalist rebels in the Vendée region of northwestern France grew in number, and moderate republicans in southern France, known as Federalists, revolted against the increasingly radical government in Paris. While York was fighting at Dunkirk, Federalist rebels at the French Mediterranean port of Toulon surrendered the city and the French fleet to British admiral Samuel Hood on 26 August in return for food and protection. Already facing starvation from the Anglo-Spanish blockade, the threat of bloody vengeance from republican armies prompted the rebels of Toulon to seek British protection. Hood agreed on the condition that the rebels declare in favor of the Bourbon monarchy. They complied, allowing Hood to take possession of Toulon in the name of Louis XVII, the uncrowned son of the late French king, on 28 August.[14]

Requests from Breton royalists for financial aid, military supplies, and an émigré army reached Pitt on 7 September, and a courier delivered news of Toulon's surrender to him on 12 September 1793. The Cabinet took interest in both opportunities, but Toulon took precedence in their minds for two reasons. First, as a major hub of French commerce and the base of the French Mediterranean fleet, Toulon offered immediate and extensive advantages for the economic and naval war in the Mediterranean. Second, Hood's decision to occupy the city committed the government to forward action in southern

France while the absence of any commitment to the Vendéans left ministers the option of delaying intervention there. Pitt declared the surrender of Toulon "a most fortunate event" and asserted that "many things ought to be done immediately to make the best use of the advantage; and particularly I should think we ought again to press the Emperor, and perhaps Spain, to send troops to act in that quarter."[15]

In a letter to his brother on 15 September, Grenville dismissed the reversals in Flanders and outlined the administration's priorities. He argued that operations in Flanders "must be left to military decision" and expressed a strong reluctance to do anything to undermine other opportunities: "A few towns more or less in Flanders are certainly not unimportant; but I am much mistaken in my speculation if the business at Toulon is not decisive of the war."[16] With operations in Flanders halted, the ministry's diplomatic efforts to use military cooperation as a basis for broader diplomatic consensus shifted to the Mediterranean and exploiting the surrender of Toulon.

The Cabinet had contemplated attacking France's Mediterranean ports as early as 10 April. In July, they approved Murray's aforementioned plan of operations for 1794 that included a major assault on Toulon. Although drawn to the idea of attacking French ports as an operation largely achievable by Britain's own means, Pitt recognized that such an attempt would benefit greatly from the assistance of other Mediterranean powers.[17] Toulon's surrender at a time when much of Britain's flexible military assets were already allocated to either Flanders or the Caribbean or in consideration for the Vendée accentuated the necessity of gathering support from local allies. In this regard, Toulon represented as much difficulty as opportunity. To coordinate Mediterranean goals and operations, the British looked chiefly to Spain, Sardinia, Naples, and Austria. Negotiations with each of these states produced their own challenges.

Prior to the surrender of Toulon, British strategy in the Mediterranean had remained conservative, with an emphasis on interdicting French commerce, particularly in grain, and blockading French ports to reduce the revolutionaries' economic capacity to continue the war. The Spanish fleet quickly corralled the French Toulon fleet in port. Meanwhile, the small British squadron of six ships of the line based at Gibraltar patrolled the neighboring straits and organized British and Dutch merchant vessels into convoys while waiting for reinforcements.[18] After Hood arrived with sixteen British ships of the line in June, the British and Spanish fleets established naval supremacy and crippled French commerce. The economic hardship that this produced in southern France combined with purge of the Girondins from the National Convention during the first days of June prompted the Federalist revolt in Lyons, Marseilles, and Toulon. These revolts largely nullified French naval power in the

Mediterranean, primarily based in Toulon. Consequently, Hood could claim to have achieved his goals of halting France's commerce and protecting Britain's. He thus turned his attention to the primary gap in the blockade: neutral Genoa. With Genoa refusing to accept the draconian British interpretation of commercial neutrality, Hood informally extended his blockade to cover that port as well.[19]

Having attained their initial containment objectives, the Cabinet sought to exploit the advantage and put at least the Mediterranean portion of Murray's plan for the 1794 campaign into action early by gathering a multinational force for an amphibious assault on Toulon. In this effort, British diplomats throughout the Mediterranean theater generally found their host courts reluctant to entertain new, ambitious proposals. The Neapolitans proved most willing, mobilizing the six ships and 6,000 troops for British use according to the terms of the Anglo-Neapolitan treaty. Sardinia also owed a specific number of troops to the British based on their convention. However, the treaty made British use of 20,000 Sardinians conditional on the recovery of Nice. Placing a high priority on gaining this flexible manpower for British use, Dundas declared that retaking Nice "is to be our first operation of the campaign."[20] Despite Sardinian assurances and the withdrawal of significant French forces to deal with the Federalist revolt, British and Austrian liaisons with the Sardinian army reported that the army could not yet undertake a campaign, particularly with Alpine snow expected to obstruct transportation. The British attempted to persuade Vienna to assist in reconquering Nice, but Thugut insisted that new Austrian exertions on behalf of Sardinia would require territorial compensations from Turin. Already struggling to address Austrian concerns about indemnification elsewhere, the demand for more territory in Italy put an end to British efforts to retake Nice through Austrian aid.[21]

Unable to gain immediate assistance from Turin or Vienna to supplement the Neapolitans, the British looked to Madrid. Initial Spanish success on the Pyrenees front had faltered in the face of stiffening French resistance, making the Spanish court reluctant to divert troops or even ships to other British operations. As the Anglo-Spanish convention of 25 May included no obligation for Spain to provide men for any such expedition, the matter required fresh negotiations.[22]

Without sufficient resources to take offensive action in the Mediterranean before the end of the 1793 campaign season, the Cabinet resolved to remain on the defensive and aggregate military power in the Mediterranean for the 1794 campaign. On 27 August, Dundas noted, commenting in his capacity as head of the Home Office, which included the responsibility of being the ad hoc war secretary, that "nothing of vigorous exertion can be accomplished in the Mediterranean this campaign, and any attempt on our part to supply the deficiency of the Sardinian force would only cripple our other important exertions in Flanders and the West Indies."[23] Looking to the next campaign, Dundas developed an ambitious plan to pool 50,000 men in the Mediterranean in 1794, drawing from British troops across Europe as well as mercenaries from Switzerland and Germany. Ignoring the inevitable strategic consumption that would occur in British units abroad, he expected to be able to recall troops from a Caribbean expedition planned for that winter in time and in shape to contribute to the spring campaign in the Mediterranean.[24]

Dundas declared the government's intention to postpone serious operations in the Mediterranean until 1794 one day after Admiral Hood committed Britain to more active measures by accepting the defection of Toulon and the French fleet there in the name of Louis XVII. The enthusiastic reception of the news at Whitehall concealed the awkwardness of its timing. While Dundas had little prospect of delivering the expected troops to the Mediterranean in 1794, he stood no chance of mobilizing and deploying significant numbers sooner. In the king's assessment, with which Dundas concurred, "The misfortune of our situation is that we have too many objects to attend to and our force consequently must be too small at each place."[25] With British resources being insufficient to take advantage of their unexpected prize, both Hood and London necessarily relied on their local coalition partners.

Hood struggled to find reinforcements to hold his position against the approaching republican army under General Jean-François Carteaux. He faced complications in this effort as the Sardinians launched an offensive into Nice on 1 September, creating a competing need for reinforcements there. After entering the Mediterranean under orders to support coalition operations in the Alps and the Pyrenees, Hood had opened a new front and tried to convert it into the primary focus of the Mediterranean theater. To exploit this opening Hood had approximately 1,000 British soldiers and 3,000 Spaniards. While waiting on replies to his requests for aid from Turin, Naples, and London, Hood attempted to augment his forces by consolidating counterrevolutionary control of the city and drawing from the French population. He enlisted Toulonnais volunteers into units in British pay to help man the city's defenses and deported French sailors with republican sympathies to Brest to remove a potential internal threat.[26]

Although the Anglo-Sardinian treaty required the Sardinians to provide troops to the British for flexible usage only after the conquest of Nice, Turin agreed to send support, which amounted to 800 men. To fulfill British promises of naval support, Hood similarly allocated two ships of his fleet to aid the offensive into Nice. The small scale of this exchange highlights the overextension that characterized the 1793 campaign in the Mediterranean. Neither contribution was large enough to improve the tactical situation at their destinations significantly.[27] Not facing an immediate threat by land or sustaining an existing campaign, the Neapolitans responded more generously, dispatching six ships and the 2,000 troops they had ready out of the 6,000 that their treaty with Britain required. Vienna offered no support at all and remained largely uninterested in supporting the Mediterranean allies. Both the Neapolitans and the Sardinians arrived on 27 September, bringing the coalition forces at Toulon to a total of approximately 7,000. While respectable for such short notice, this remained barely sufficient to man the city's sprawling defenses, much less repel a determined attack or launch an offensive. In contrast, the same 7,000 men might have contributed significantly either to the Spanish army in the eastern Pyrenees or to the Sardinian offensive in Nice.[28]

Despite having concluded the impracticability of launching a campaign on the southern coast of France in August and remaining uncertain about the question of the French government, the Cabinet quickly determined in September to seize the military opportunity that Toulon represented and find reinforcements. The ministers agreed to withdraw 5,000 of York's German mercenaries from Flanders to go to Toulon, and they determined to send all they could spare from Gibraltar and from the planned expedition to the West Indies. Pitt rather optimistically estimated that these reinforcements coupled with an expected 3,000 from Spain, 6,000 from Naples, 9,000 from Sardinia, and 5,000 from Austria, would bring the coalition forces at Toulon up to 33,000. Ultimately, few of these expected reinforcements would reach Toulon.[29]

The question of the future government of France loomed large in the negotiations to gather reinforcements for Toulon from the Mediterranean coalition members because of the involvement of the Spanish Bourbons and their dynastic concerns. Madrid had responded to the emergence of the Federalist revolt by urging the British to help them steer that movement in a royalist direction by publicly committing to a Bourbon restoration and sending the Count of Provence to rally them to the standard of counterrevolution. On 19 July 1793, St. Helens conveyed a request from the Spanish foreign secretary for British views on

> the expediency of furnishing succors to the parties which have taken up arms in France for the purpose of effecting a counter revolution in that government, an object which . . . might now be easily accomplished by the intervention of a very slight portion of foreign assistance. And in this last view he particularly

wished to be informed of the sentiments of our court respecting Monsieur's [the Count of Provence] proposed journey to this country, saying that though no particular objection was entertained against it here, yet . . . the king his master had not thought proper to consent to it without being assured of His Majesty's concurrence and approbation.[30]

Having established neutrality on the subject and not wishing to rule out the possibility of negotiating with the revolutionaries, the Cabinet rejected this proposal.

On 9 August in a letter to St. Helens, Grenville expressed the British government's general support for restoring order in France on the grounds that "it may be doubted whether till this be accomplished permanent security can ever be acquired by other powers."[31] However, he cautioned that the French remained too divided in their political views for a coalition declaration in favor of any particular form of government to make a significant impact. In these circumstances, he contended that such a declaration would more likely unify the French against the invaders, as had been the case with the Brunswick Manifesto in 1792, than inspire widespread revolt and defection in the coalition's favor. Grenville's letter also rejected the more specific proposal of supporting Provence's pretensions as regent of France on behalf of Louis XVII, arguing that he and his advisers would likely cause more trouble than good. Grenville found the idea so absurd that he speculated that the Spanish mentioned it only so that they could blame London when they rejected Provence's request to come to Spain. He finished by advising St. Helens, "On the whole therefore the line to be adopted by your excellency in the present moment is to . . . prevent the court of Madrid from committing itself with any description of emigres or any party in the interior."[32] British caution regarding the future of France's government aroused Spanish suspicions that London sought to destroy its traditional rival rather than restore the beleaguered monarchy.

By accepting the surrender of Toulon in the name of Louis XVII and the undefined "constitution of 1789," Hood inadvertently forced his government to issue a formal policy statement on the question of the future government of France. By calling on and receiving reinforcements from the Spanish to hold the city, Hood also forced Pitt's ministry to consider Spanish views toward the counterrevolution. In response to Hood's request, the Spanish sent their main fleet and two infantry regiments as much to keep watch on the British as to contribute to the war against France.[33] Hood's precipitate unilateral decisions stemmed from the impossibility of waiting two months to put the question to the Cabinet and receive a definitive British answer. To defer the question to Anglo-Spanish diplomacy would take even longer.[34] Grenville's failed efforts to establish a coalition congress earlier in the year had been designed to address this problem of communication and allow for more flexible collective responses to changes in the military situation. In the absence of such a congress, the British ministry found itself reactively struggling to reconcile Pitt's foreign policy with Hood's actions.[35]

Unsure of what the "constitution of 1789" meant or how best to respond to Hood's achievement, the Cabinet chastised Hood for overstepping his bounds and prematurely committing Britain to a Bourbon restoration. In a letter to the British ambassador at Vienna, Grenville described the confusion of the British ministers: "It does not, however, clearly appear whether they intended to express their desire of adhering to the whole constitution as settled by the constituent assembly up to the period of their dissolution, or whether they refer themselves only to the few general articles respecting a monarchical government which were actually settled in 1789 and accepted by the king previous to his departure from Paris."[36] To soften Hood's unequivocal royalism amid this uncertainty, Grenville recommended that foreign powers defer decisions on the particulars of the French government to the French people. He suggested only that "the government of France should be founded on the general principles of justice and on the rights of society as established among civilized nations, and that it should be of such a nature as to be compatible with the safety and tranquility of the rest of Europe."[37] Notably, Grenville also mentioned that the British would insist that the French at Toulon accept the principle of postwar indemnification. This represented an effort to convince the coalition powers to look to Britain for leadership in both the conduct of the war and the fashioning of the peace.[38]

The Cabinet debated into October on the appropriate British response to the Toulon windfall as they prepared a commission for a provisional British governor of the city. Grenville resisted the need to specify any form of government for France in the government's declaration to the people of Toulon, but Pitt and Dundas persuaded him to include the recommendation of a monarchical restoration.[39] The declaration issued on 29 October stated:

> His majesty by no means disputes the right of France to reform its laws. It never would have been his wish to employ the influence of external force with respect to the particular forms of government to be established in an independent country. Neither has he now that wish, except in so far as such interference is become essential to the security and repose of other powers. . . . The king demands that some legitimate and stable government should be established, founded on the acknowledged principles of universal justice and capable of maintaining with other powers the accustomed relations of union and peace. His majesty wishes ardently to be enabled to treat for the reestablishment of general tranquility with

such a government, exercising a legal and permanent authority, animated with the wish for general tranquility, and possessing the power to enforce the observance of its engagements.[40]

It also specified a hereditary Bourbon monarchy beginning with Louis XVII as the ideal foundation of any French government; yet this declaration also allowed for future modifications to the monarchy and recommended constitutional limitations.[41]

Instructions to the provisional governor, Sir Gilbert Elliot, illuminated Pitt's rationale. Discarding Grenville's earlier concern that specificity would unite French factions against the invader, the instructions suggested that some form of constitutional monarchy offered the best basis for agreement both among Frenchmen and among the monarchies of Europe. Pitt and Dundas hoped that a moderate recommendation of limited monarchy would induce French rebels of all persuasions to join Toulon in seeking British protection. The British statement reflected a consensus that the existing revolutionary government could not be incorporated into the European community on acceptable terms.[42] Ultimately, Pitt indicated that "this idea by no means precludes us from treating with any other form of government, if, in the end, any other should be solidly established; but it holds out monarchy as the only one from which we expect any good, and in favor of which we are disposed to enter into concert."[43]

As the Cabinet finished organizing the British civil and military leadership for Toulon, the Count of Provence demanded that the British give him command of the city to galvanize royalist support in southern France. Knowing that Provence rejected limitations on the monarchy and that the Federalists only consented to a royalist settlement under duress, the British refused this demand and pressed the Spanish to do likewise.[44] A revived monarchy under Louis XVII would require a regency until the young king reached his majority, but the Cabinet disapproved of imposing Provence's regency on France by force. They preferred to defer the choice of regent and other nuances of governmental structure to the French people. Although Pitt rejected an aggressive revolutionary France as a member of the European state system, he also had no wish to restore an absolutist and threatening Bourbon monarchy.[45]

As Elliot took command of Toulon in November, the British Cabinet embraced a second counterrevolutionary opportunity in the Vendée. As noted, on 7 September the British received requests for aid from Breton royalists. The Cabinet remained undecided on the appropriate response to this request when news of Hood's occupation of Toulon arrived. Although the Mediterranean theater appeared more promising and absorbed much of the ministers' attention, on 17 October they pledged to send the logistical aid and émigré army that the royalists requested. Initial plans involved a joint émigré–royalist attack on the port of St. Malo to open communication between the rebels and the British fleet.[46] Émigré leaders shared British interest in this project. Just as Provence sought to gain control of the counterrevolution at Toulon, Charles, Count of Artois, expressed the desire to lead the émigré army designated for the Vendée. The Cabinet opposed this, instead advocating the statements in the declaration to Toulon as the basis for British intervention in northern France.[47]

A string of royalist victories in the Vendée and the stabilization of the Flanders front after the retreat from Hondschoote inspired Pitt and Dundas to organize a more extensive expedition composed of more troops drawn from York's army. The prime minister wrote of this opportunity on 16 November, "I am sanguine enough to think that it affords the best chance which has yet appeared of assisting, by a powerful diversion, operations in every other quarter and of giving the turn we wish to the whole of the war."[48] Thus, he urged the commander of the expedition, Francis Rawdon-Hastings, Earl of Moira, to gather his men and materials and embark as soon as possible.[49]

The Vendée ultimately resulted in disappointment for the British. This stemmed largely from the overextension of British resources and inadequate support from the coalition partners. Moira's expedition faced logistical difficulties, especially a lack of artillery and trained gunners. As in every other case in which the British army fell short of needs, Pitt called on the Austrians to supply the expedition's artillery from Coburg's army in Flanders. Although Coburg proved agreeable, the necessity of obtaining approval from Vienna before sending the requested troops delayed their departure until the expedition had already sailed and failed.[50]

Moira sailed for the Breton coast finally on 1 December 1793 but found no signals from royalists as the expedition sailed off the coast of Cherbourg and St. Malo. Republican armies had defeated the rebels, leaving no royalist army to support. While this spared the British the problem of trying to keep Artois and pure royalism out of the Vendée, it also ended an opportunity to open a new front almost entirely under British control. As with the planned conquest of Dunkirk and the occupation of Toulon, the Vendée expedition had theoretically offered the British a chance to hasten the end of the war and gain greater influence over the postwar settlement.[51]

The Mediterranean theater fared little better than the Vendée. When Elliot took command at Toulon on 16 November 1793, he discovered that Hood had exaggerated the strength of the defenses and underrated the extent of the reinforcements needed to profit from the position. Succors from the Mediterranean members of the coalition continued to trickle in but in insufficient numbers to meet the Cabinet's earlier expectations. The Neapolitans added 4,000 more men to the occupation as mobilization made them available. Already engaged in an Alpine offensive, the Sardinians had little to give but gradually committed several battalions totaling approximately 3,000 men.[52] Attempts to gain Austrian troops continued to stumble on strained Austro-Sardinian relations, particularly the Austrian demand for compensation for greater efforts. With difficulty, Eden persuaded Thugut to pledge 5,000 men for Toulon by avoiding all reference to assistance for Sardinia. Regardless, Thugut acted slowly, seeing Toulon as a largely useless diversion and significantly less beneficial to Austria than pressing the advantage on the Rhine or in Flanders.[53] The British themselves also failed to send reinforcements in significant numbers, partly because of overcommitment in Flanders, the Vendée, and the Caribbean and partly because of poor and conflicting communication between the government and its commanders. Ultimately, coalition forces in Toulon never exceeded 17,000 men—too few to do more than defend the port and, in the event, too few for that as well.[54]

Far from rallying counterrevolutionaries and Mediterranean states to British leadership, the occupation of Toulon exposed and exacerbated differences. Contributions from coalition partners to the defense of Toulon fell far short of expectations, and no mass uprising in southern France greeted the measured British declaration in favor of the Bourbon monarchy. Troops that Spain rushed to the scene constituted the majority of the coalition forces, supported by the Neapolitan, Sardinian, and British troops under British command. Correspondingly, Spanish commanders pressed for control over the occupation. Anglo-Spanish relations rapidly soured on this point. Grenville insisted that Toulon had surrendered to the British specifically, giving London the right to command the occupation.[55] Not interested in joining this contentious operation or wading into these Anglo-Spanish suspicions, Thugut indefinitely delayed sending the 5,000 Austrian troops he had promised.[56]

In the absence of a multilateral agreement defining war objectives, both London and Madrid relied on local command over coalition operations to increase their influence over the shape of the war and the peace. Neither power trusted the other. London feared that the Spanish sought only a Bourbon restoration for the purpose of reviving the family compact against British interests. Concurrently, Madrid worried that the British sought to cripple the French navy, giving the Royal Navy unassailable naval supremacy and leaving Spain without an ally capable of challenging British maritime hegemony. Additionally, British insistence on maintaining unilateral command at Toulon had aroused fears in Madrid that the Royal Navy would seek to retain the city as another outpost like Gibraltar. The October declaration of British intent to hold the city in trust for Louis XVII failed to allay this concern as it included conditional language that allowed for British retention should no other indemnity be provided. Hood had exacerbated this fear by identifying Toulon as "virtually English" in his correspondence with the Spanish admiral, Don Juan de Lángara—a phrase that offended the latter. Thus, enthusiasm for the common cause diminished as the Spanish resented growing British influence in the western Mediterranean; the window for consolidating the Anglo-Spanish rapprochement closed.[57]

Siege conditions left many of the coalition troops sick or wounded, and the disputed nature of command reduced the fighting effectiveness of the armies in the city.[58] By early December, the coalition army nominally of 17,000 men faced a French army of 40,000 men. On 16 December, the more numerous French stretched the coalition forces to their breaking point with simultaneous attacks on multiple positions in the incomplete defenses of Toulon.[59] In these attacks, the French gained control over the redoubts overlooking the harbor, thus rendering the position of the coalition garrison and fleet untenable in the opinion of their own engineers and artillery officers. A French artillery captain named Napoleon Bonaparte organized the French artillery on these positions to force the coalition armies to evacuate or surrender.[60]

Recognizing the impossibility of his situation, Hood held a council of war on the HMS *Victory* on 17 December to determine whether the army could retake the lost redoubts and, if not, to establish a plan of evacuation to minimize the danger to the coalition forces. The council agreed to withdraw on the 19th after destroying the French arsenal and taking as many French ships as possible. Plans for an orderly withdrawal collapsed almost immediately in the face of continued French attacks and coalition disunity. The Neapolitans discarded the plan and unilaterally evacuated the city on 18 December. With the 6,000 Neapolitans comprising approximately one-third of the coalition forces at Toulon, their departure made the coalition's position even more tenuous. Coordination continued to break down under the pressure of circumstances. Confusion between British and Spanish officers over the timing and responsibility for setting fire to the French arsenal and fleet resulted in some damage to coalition ships in the ensuing conflagration. The confusion also prevented complete destruction, allowing the French to salvage fifteen ships of the line and therefore reestablish the Toulon fleet. Amid this chaos and under fire, the coalition forces completed their evacuation on 19 December, having achieved little beyond sapping resources from other fronts of the Mediterranean theater and evacuating several thousand Toulonnais refugees.[61]

Poor communication contributed heavily to the failure of the Toulon campaign. The lack of a united coalition headquarters on the model that Grenville had sought on the eve of the war made military and diplomatic cooperation at Toulon dependent on bilateral communications between London and the local courts and commanders in the Mediterranean. The Cabinet spent the autumn of 1793 reacting to events in southern France and never mastered the situation. Hood's decisions forced British ministers to engage in a complicated political and diplomatic dialogue to try to reconcile the divergent views of French Federalists, Spanish Bourbons, and Pitt's foreign policy principles. In addition, Hood's reports overestimated coalition strength and underestimated difficulties, creating misplaced optimism about the opportunity that Toulon presented and erroneously minimizing the military urgency of the situation. After embracing the Toulon opportunity in September, the Cabinet had resolved the political questions attending the operation in October with the formation of Elliot's mission. They had dispatched Elliot in the hope of creating a local nucleus of British decision making to eliminate the dangers of slow communications with London. However, Elliot only reached Toulon to begin redressing Hood's optimism and unilateralism in mid-November. By then, time had run out to correct the situation. Weather prevented Elliot from sending his reports to London until after 27 November, and these reached the Cabinet only after French military success had forced the evacuation of the city.[62]

Amid the defeats of December, the British regrouped and looked ahead to 1794. The Mediterranean receded in importance after the fall of Toulon and the collapse of Federalist resistance. Following the failure of the expedition to the Vendée, London continued to probe for opportunities to exploit the waning royalist resistance there but lacked concrete plans for operations in that area. Failure at Toulon and in the Vendée rendered British amphibious plans for the 1794 campaign obsolete.

Nevertheless, Pitt remained resolute in his determination either to force the revolutionaries to recant their aggressive foreign policy or to secure a Bourbon restoration on terms favorable to British interests. In Parliament, Pitt defended the continuation of the war from another Foxite motion to send the revolutionaries peace terms:

> As to what were the objects of the war, . . . these objects were—first, that the system adopted by the French had developed principles destructive to the general order of society and subversive to all regular government. Secondly, that the French themselves, with a view, no doubt, of extending their system, had been guilty of usurpations of the territory of other states. Thirdly, that they had discovered hostile intentions against Holland. Fourthly, that they had disclosed views of aggrandizement and ambition entirely new in extent and importance and menacing in their progress not only the independence of this country, but the security of Europe. Unless it can be shown that we were originally mistaken; that these were not proper objects of contest; or that these objects are already gained; the obligations and necessity which originally induced us to undertake the war operate with equal force at the present moment.[63]

Pitt's argument involves a mixture of ideological rhetoric and pragmatic concerns. The theme of seeking the "independence of this country" through the "security of Europe" illustrates a Continental view of the war consistent with the founding principles of the collective security vision. Although Pitt employed conservative rhetoric to appeal to members of Parliament who did view the war in ideological terms, he noted "that if a peace could be made out upon terms of security to this country, no consideration of the crimes and horrors with which they were sullied ought to influence this country to reject such terms."[64]

Having explained the justification for the war and articulated a theoretical willingness to negotiate with a republican France, Pitt presented his reasons for believing that a peace required a Bourbon restoration. He argued that the revolutionary government remained too unstable to offer any certainty of a lasting peace. Pitt rejected Fox's assertion that the Bourbons posed a greater threat than the Revolution on the grounds that the Bourbon monarchy, however aggressive it had been in the past, "was regulated by certain principles and limited within certain bounds." Fundamentally, in the winter of 1793–94, Pitt believed he could trust a Bourbon monarchy to respect international agreements and the sovereignty of other states while he could not trust the revolutionaries to do the same.[65]

CHAPTER 7

THE PRUSSIAN BOND, 1794

Regardless of British preferences on the future of the French government, the loss of Toulon and the failure of Moira's expedition to the Vendée required an adjustment of the plans for 1794. Those unexpected opportunities had pushed into premature execution the partially prepared elements of Murray's plan of operations for 1794, and their failure rendered this plan untenable and obsolete. In 1794, ministerial attention shifted from the elusive counterrevolutionary opportunities of the previous fall to the more orthodox operations in Flanders and the West Indies. British operations in both of these traditional theaters of Anglo-French conflict would pursue objectives essential to British strategy. Caribbean operations supported the aim of strangling French commerce and held out the prospect of furnishing an indemnity for Britain at the conclusion of the war. Even this remained secondary to the overriding objective of securing the United Provinces by way of victory in Flanders through cooperation with Austrian, Prussian, and Dutch armies. Correspondingly, British ministers concerned themselves most with the campaign in Flanders.[1]

To strengthen coalition operations in Flanders, Pitt and Grenville built on their partial diplomatic success in 1793 and renewed their efforts to merge the Austro-Prussian alliance with the Anglo-Dutch partnership. Maintaining Prussia as an active participant in the war became the central object of British diplomacy in 1794. British ministers attempted to secure Prussian support through multilateral engagements encompassing the United Provinces, Austria, and even the Holy Roman Empire. However, British refusal to accommodate partition politics in this diplomacy precluded any comprehensive unity. As the diplomatic framework of the coalition remained fragmented, its military performance suffered, and coalition operations in Flanders in 1794 went from an abortive offense in the spring to a desperate summer defense and finally a disastrous autumn retreat.

The events of 1793 demonstrated that the Flanders campaign depended considerably on Anglo-Austrian cooperation. As such, the conclusion of the broad Anglo-Austrian convention on 30 August 1793 provided the basis for negotiating more specific plans for military and diplomatic cooperation. After concluding the treaty, Grenville penned new instructions for his minister plenipotentiary in Vienna, Sir Morton Eden, to solicit plans for 1794 from the Austrians. These extensive instructions merit analysis and consideration as they detail British priorities and intentions with a view to 1794. Grenville offered this thorough explanation of British policy in response to an Austrian proposal to convert their convention to a full defensive alliance. The foreign secretary expressed British eagerness to forge such an alliance but insisted on combining "this object with the others which must now fall under discussion and to postpone the actual signature of a treaty of alliance till some explanations . . . have taken place relative to the many points of common interest now subsisting between the two Courts." Pitt's persistent search for multilateralism loomed large in this statement of policy, and Grenville described the goal of reconciling Austrian views with those of other members of the coalition as "the principal point to be attended to."[2]

In this letter, Grenville took the opportunity to establish the necessity of continuing the war into 1794. He argued that whether one viewed the coalition's objectives as strictly defensive or counterrevolutionary or acquisitive, the campaigns of 1793 had stood little chance of bringing those goals to completion. Foreshadowing the government's response to Toulon, Grenville explained that the Cabinet did not believe a negotiated peace with the existing French government would be possible or desirable. "No certainty of present tranquility could be derived from negotiating while there is no one possessed even de facto of sufficient authority to answer for the conduct of France during the shortest period," he argued. Expressing confidence that Vienna would agree, Grenville added that "it is equally evident that the best security for success in our farther efforts will be the most complete understanding and concert between Great Britain and Austria as the two principal parties in the war and the regulating between them all the points which have immediate reference to it."[3]

Based on these assumptions, Grenville outlined five main points for Anglo-Austrian negotiations. First, he noted the necessity of reaching an agreement on war aims. Second, to establish mutual confidence and trust, he urged some formal commitment from both parties to continue the war until the attainment of those objectives. Third, he recommended cooperative action to secure the allegiance and support of other states. Fourth, the foreign secretary acknowledged the importance of forming a plan of operations to maximize the effectiveness of the coalition's military resources. Finally, Grenville argued that the negotiations should devote attention "to the permanent system to which we may look in case of a successful termination of the war in order reciprocally to secure our future tranquility and to consolidate whatever advantages we may have derived from our success."[4]

On the first subject of war aims, Grenville reiterated Pitt's mantra of indemnification for the past and security for the future.[5] The foreign secretary rejected the notion of achieving security by extending the coalition's indemnification to the point of rendering France impotent. Instead, he argued that security could arise only from the establishment of a stable French government able to guarantee respect for treaties. "It never has been the principle, nor is it now, the object of this country to make . . . war for the purpose of establishing any precise form of government in France. But it is on the other hand very doubtful whether that security . . . can be acquired until some form of regular government is established in that country." Grenville cautioned that "a premature step . . . might preclude us from deriving all the advantage which might otherwise result from such events as may . . . occur when any considerable progress of foreign troops shall be joined to the internal distresses resulting from the present anarchy." Correspondingly, he recommended that both countries avoid commitments on the future of France's government without conferring with each other.[6]

On the subject of indemnification, Grenville acknowledged the Austrian preference, after abandoning the Belgium-Bavaria exchange, for acquiring French territory "to as large an extent as . . . practicable in the Low Countries, in Alsace and Lorraine, and in the intermediate parts of the frontier of France." He then explained that any indemnity for Britain would come from French colonial territory. He made the case that Austrian growth on the French frontier enhanced the security of both powers and British commercial and maritime growth enabled London to better provide financial and military assistance for defending these territories.[7]

Although theoretically settled, the question of indemnification complicated the pursuit of firm mutual commitments to see the war to conclusion. Grenville recognized the importance of such commitment to endow military planning with confidence, but he expressed reluctance to commit Britain to continuing the war until Austria had secured its indemnification from France. While supportive of Vienna seeking compensation from France, Grenville recognized the political difficulties the Cabinet would face in transforming a defensive war to a war explicitly for conquest. As a compromise, the foreign secretary offered to avoid making a separate peace except on terms by which France would agree to cede its conquests and accept any conquests made by the coalition powers at the time of the treaty's conclusion or provide equivalent concessions.[8]

Regarding the cooperation of other states, Grenville described it as "the most important and the most difficult point of discussion with the court of Vienna." He indicated that other negotiations had secured the neutrality and commercial compliance of Denmark and Sweden, rendering it unnecessary to develop a joint policy toward them. Grenville also noted that "it does not appear that much can be done by Austria, at least in the present moment, towards securing the cooperation of Spain."[9] Spanish unwillingness to trust Austria or Prussia had become apparent in the negotiations for the Anglo-Spanish convention in 1793. In response to Grenville's proposal for a multilateral congress in 1793, St. Helens reported on 25 March 1793: "The fact is that the Cabinets of Vienna and Berlin . . . have for some time past treated this court not only with reserve but with the most marked slight and contempt, and it is therefore probable that the present minister declines explaining himself on the overture in question until he shall have seen whether his efforts to revive a friendly intercourse between Spain and those powers have been attended with success."[10] Correspondingly, Spain's adherence to the common cause largely depended on the bilateral relationship between London and Madrid. The foreign secretary also dismissed Russia, noting that efforts to bring St. Petersburg into active participation had failed and held little prospect of future success. He recommended that Anglo-Austrian diplomacy focus on uniting Switzerland and the Italian states against France and forging an effective union with Sardinia, the United Provinces, and Prussia.[11]

The instructions simply directed Eden to soothe Austro-Sardinian differences and press the Austrians to abandon their claim to compensation in northern Italy for any assistance to the court of Turin. This recommendation struck a hypocritical note when Grenville turned his attention to cementing Dutch allegiance. He indicated that the Dutch sought territorial compensation from the Austrian Netherlands in return for assisting Austria in acquiring territory from France. Grenville explained that the British government supported this claim to gain active Dutch support and viewed it as entirely reasonable despite opposing a similar Austrian claim on Sardinia. This discrepancy arose from the fact that Sardinian recovery of Nice and Savoy represented only a return to the status quo ante bellum whereas Austrian annexation of French Flanders would form a new conquest. In the British view, demands for compensation were justified as a price for supporting offensive objectives as in the case of Flanders but not as a price for supporting defensive objectives as in the case of Nice and Savoy. The Austrian view made no such distinction, viewing territorial gains as important compensation for military effort whether offensive or defensive.[12]

Grenville described the effort to procure active Prussian cooperation as "an object of far more importance and difficulty." He acknowledged the tension between Austria and Prussia but argued that the value of Prussian assistance outweighed the danger that Prussian activities in eastern Europe posed to Austria. Grenville tried to portray the Polish question as a separate matter from the French war, attempting to deny the interconnection of the two problems in Austrian and Prussian security concerns. He thus made the distinctly insensitive suggestion of making sacrifices to bring Prussia into full cooperation, recommending permanent Austrian renunciation of the Belgium-Bavaria exchange as a possible inducement for Prussia to continue fighting. That such a measure might lay a foundation for drawing greater assistance from Bavaria furnished an additional motivation.[13]

The instructions to Eden offered only vague ideas on the fourth point of future military operations beyond enumerating the three primary theaters of war: Flanders, the Rhine, and the Mediterranean. Grenville identified Flanders as the critical theater, and he included amphibious operations on the northern coast of France. He dismissed the Rhine frontier as a subject for Austro-Prussian cooperation, disclaiming any British intention of directing or assisting that campaign. The British expected the Austrians to leave Mediterranean operations to their discretion, just as they left the Rhine to Vienna. However, Grenville did request 15,000 Austrian troops to provide the British Mediterranean fleet with the capacity for decisive amphibious action. Despite the Cabinet's reticence to offer specific ideas, Grenville urged the Austrians to communicate their plans as soon as possible. "In referring the details of these points to subsequent explanation, it is by no means His Majesty's wish that they should be deferred. His Majesty feels on the contrary the pressing importance of their being brought forward early."[14]

With regard to the final point of discussion—the permanent alliance system—Grenville described it as a return to the old system that united the British, the Dutch, and the Austrians during the wars of Louis XIV: "The basis of such an alliance would naturally be . . . the same with that of the ancient system by which the two countries were formerly united: the securing a barrier against France; the retaining [of] the Netherlands under the lawful sovereignty of Austria; the security and augmentation of the commerce of the Maritime Powers; and the mutual guarantee of all possessions antecedent to the war." The dispatch then recommended inviting the other members of the coalition to accede to the alliance.[15] Despite the limited success of British overtures throughout Europe in 1793, British diplomacy continued striving toward Pitt's enduring goal of a collective security system.

The Austrian response to these British proposals merits consideration as well. Eden reported that Thugut agreed on most of Grenville's points. The Austrian minister concurred in the necessity of another campaign in 1794 and in the notion that Britain and Austria constituted the leaders of the coalition. Thugut agreed on the likely necessity of restoring the monarchy in France to obtain sufficient security for the future conduct of that country but also expressed willingness to defer to the British on the future of the French government. Grenville's explanation of British intentions to secure a colonial indemnity alleviated Thugut's fears about British plans for Flanders. Although the operation had failed, British insistence on taking Dunkirk in the name of George III had aroused concern in Vienna that London meant to keep that city. Thugut also expressed sympathy with Grenville's desire to secure mutual pledges not to make separate peace in the defensive war to repel French aggression without binding Britain to a protracted offensive war of conquest. Regarding a more permanent alliance system, Thugut offered preliminary agreement to Grenville's views and dispatched instructions to the Austrian envoy in London to negotiate a formal alliance.[16]

As Grenville had predicted, the question of building coalition unity proved the most difficult. The Austrians refused to budge in their dispute with the Sardinians over indemnification. Although generally willing to support British diplomacy in Italy and Switzerland, Thugut doubted the success of either. He was particularly pessimistic about the value of securing the Bavarian army, noting that the elector could barely furnish his contingent for the Holy Roman Empire, much less an independent army of any value for service in Flanders. Thugut also strongly protested the idea of a Dutch indemnity coming from the Austrian Netherlands but, under pressure from Eden, he conceded a vague promise that Austria would continue the war until the Dutch obtained a suitable indemnity.[17]

If compromises with the Dutch irritated Thugut, the prospect of making sacrifices for the Prussians elicited outright anger. He expressed the conviction that no Austrian sacrifice would bring the court of Berlin to feel a sense of obligation to continue the war vigorously. As proof of Prussian duplicity, he explained that Prussian acquisitions from Poland grossly exceeded what the Austrians had been led to expect, while the Prussian army had remained almost entirely passive after Brunswick's retreat from Valmy. Thugut recognized the connection between these problems and sought to redress the deficit of Austrian gains relative to Prussian equivalents, preferring to distance himself from Prussia and seek gains on his own terms. According to Eden's report to Grenville, Thugut argued that "if His Prussian Majesty's duty and interest as a sovereign to put a stop to the French Principles, his engagements with this court, and those very recently contracted with his Majesty will not secure his cooperation, nothing can; particularly where that cooperation has in view also an indemnification for this court, and no new aggrandizement for His

Prussian Majesty." Thugut ultimately agreed to continue discussions and to provisionally support British efforts to secure active Prussian cooperation, but he shunned the notion of further sacrifices for such uncertain gains.[18]

Regarding plans for military operations in 1794, Thugut believed that they could decide nothing until the outcome of the 1793 campaign was clear. However, he did promise to discuss plans in the future. He explicitly promised that the Austrians would maintain at least the same number of troops in Flanders as they already had there or potentially add to that number. The ambiguity on the part of both powers regarding military plans for the next year reflected the uncertainty characterizing their relationships with the other states involved in the war.[19]

After the fighting in Flanders slowed in November 1793, the Duke of York took the initiative to clarify some of these ambiguities. He sent one of his aides-de-camp, Major Charles Craufurd, to Vienna to discuss the reasons for the failure of the coalition offensive in 1793 and to develop plans for 1794. Craufurd began his trip by consulting Mercy in Brussels before traveling to Vienna on 12 November to meet with Thugut. The major departed the Austrian capital on 16 November to return to London and make his report to the Cabinet.[20]

Craufurd provided a memorandum of these conversations to George III, synthesizing the ideas of the Austrian ministers. According to him, the Austrian officials blamed insufficient artillery in both the British and Austrian armies, failure to pursue a decisive battle, slowness in conducting sieges, and failure to exploit the coalition's advantage in cavalry for the disappointments of 1793. Thugut and Mercy consolidated these observations into four broad reasons for the failure of the 1793 campaign:

- 1st   That the preparations for the opening of it were not sufficiently rapid and extensive.
- 2nd   That there never was any well digested, settled plan of campaign, which occasioned much delay and indecision.
- 3rdly   That the Allied Army was never numerous enough to make so rapid a progress as was necessary on so strong a frontier.
- 4thly   That there was not an officer at the head of the Austrian army capable of conducting the operations.[21]

The memorandum further explained that the Austrians would lack the resources to continue fighting in 1795 should the 1794 campaign fail. In the interest of avoiding such failure, the Austrian ministers expressed a willingness to cooperate closely with the British to conduct an effective joint campaign. To produce such a campaign, the Austrians suggested that the ministers consider three leading points to be the basis upon which our successes must rest.

> 1st   An extensive and timely preparation.
> 2ndly   A well digested and detailed plan of campaign, as far as a plan of campaign can be detailed.
> 3rdly   Either a Commander-in-Chief, or an executive person in the entire confidence of the Commander-in-Chief, who is capable of conducting the operations in chief.[22]

To settle these points, Thugut and Mercy urged Emperor Francis II to travel to Brussels in the immediate future. They expected the emperor's presence to shorten lines of communication between the Austrian and British governments, enable quicker decisions on changes in command, and bolster the Austrian army's morale.[23]

The emperor's prospective trip to Brussels became the first of several miscues of the 1794 campaign. Through Eden, Grenville urged Thugut to accompany Francis and visit London. The two ministers agreed to take the opportunity to meet and settle diplomatic and military plans for 1794.[24] Francis had initially planned to arrive at Brussels in mid-October, but news of continued French offensives repeatedly convinced him to delay the trip. After the front stabilized, the journey suffered further delays as he awaited messengers from Italy, Poland, Flanders, and the Rhine to minimize the administrative disruption occasioned by his absence from Vienna.[25]

Repeated delays of the emperor's departure prevented the development of a joint Anglo-Austrian plan of campaign for 1794. In a typical dispatch to Eden on 8 October, Grenville offered vague observations on the strategic situation before stating, "I omit entering for the present into any other particulars as this dispatch will not arrive at Vienna till a considerable time after the departure of the Emperor and Monsieur Thugut for the Low Countries."[26] Perpetually expecting to meet each other in the near future, Grenville and Thugut omitted military plans from their dispatches to their respective ambassadors. On 14 November, Grenville wrote to Eden:

> The expectation of the Emperor's journey to the Low Countries has for some time past prevented my writing to you at Vienna and communicating such particulars as are material in the present state of affairs. But there seems to be a great probability that this journey which according to the last accounts received from you on that subject was fixed for the fifteenth instant will again be deferred, especially on account of the risk of insults from the enemy to which the Emperor's residence in the Low Countries might be exposed during the winter. And as

there are some points of a very pressing nature to be arranged with the Austrian government I have determined to send off this messenger without waiting for any further intelligence respecting the motions of the Emperor.[27]

He went on to plead for Thugut to send an Austrian general in the emperor's stead to develop a plan for the coming campaign. He lamented that "the delay... in entering into these discussions is much to be regretted, particularly as it obliges this government to form its plans on separate ideas and exposes both countries to the inconvenience of a want of full concert and cooperation."[28] Consequently, as the armies recovered in winter quarters and 1793 gave way to 1794, the coalition possessed no plan of operations.

In January 1794, Grenville continued to press Vienna for plans and preparations for the approaching campaign. On 3 January he wrote to Eden, complaining bitterly of delays both to the emperor's journey and to the selection of some officer to negotiate a plan. He noted that Coburg had proposed a plan through York without prior approval from Vienna. British concerns about the Austrian government's confidence in Coburg created "a great degree of uncertainty as to the weight and attention to be given to that plan."[29] Grenville then articulated the need for an officer that commanded more respect from both the armies and governments of the coalition powers. He speculated "that the return of general [Karl Mack von Leiberich]... would at least have the effect of inspiring confidence which does not prevail in the present moment."[30] York conveyed similar sentiments to George III on 4 January:

> As long as Prince [Frederick William of] Hohenlohe[-Kirchberg] remains in his present situation of Quarter Master General... nothing of consequence can be expected.... It would therefore be very much to be wished that... the Emperor could be persuaded to let... Mack return to the army. His presence alone would restore confidence to the troops, and instill a degree of spirit into the plans and execution which has been miserably wanting since he has been removed.[31]

Increasingly, the British clamored for Mack to deliver them a plan and revive the morale of the Austrian army. On 7 January, Grenville expressed the Cabinet's dissatisfaction with the inactivity of the armies in the winter months and suggested "that from all that can be collected respecting the opinion of the Austrian army, the return of General Mack is an object of very great importance to the common cause."[32]

Recognizing the increasingly pressing need to develop a plan of operations for 1794, Thugut agreed in early January to send Mack to tour the front and develop a plan. After meeting with the British, Mack would return to the Austrian army to assume the role of quartermaster general.[33] Although not a replacement for the emperor, Mack enjoyed the esteem of both the British and Austrian armies as well as Pitt's administration. On learning that Mack would rejoin the Austrian army for the 1794 campaign, York commented: "The return of General Mack to his former situation about the Prince of Cobourg will, I am sure, restore that spirit and confidence to the Austrian troops which I am sorry to say the misfortunes and faults committed at the end of the last campaign have greatly destroyed."[34] The Austrian general departed soon after his appointment and traveled to the Rhine to assess the condition of the recently defeated Austro-Prussian army while on his way to Flanders.[35]

Mack reached Brussels on 31 January 1794 and met with York on 2 February. At that meeting, the Austrian general agreed to travel to London after the planned council of war with the coalition commanders in Brussels to answer any questions. On 4 February, the commanders convened to receive Mack's plan.[36] Thereafter, Mack and York departed for London, arriving on 12 February. On 13 and 14 February 1794, Mack met with the British Cabinet. These meetings marked the culmination of British diplomatic efforts to unite the coalition's war aims and efforts, but they were poor substitutes for the coalition congress that Pitt and Grenville had been seeking since 1792.[37]

The plan Mack presented called for a cordon of 340,000 men between Switzerland and the North Sea. Of these, he planned for 95,000 Austrians to concentrate on the border fortresses of Landrecies, Avesnes, Maubeuge, and Cambrai to breach the string of fortifications on the frontier. The remaining 125,000 Austrian, British, Dutch, and Prussian troops in Flanders would cover the flanks of this advance while 120,000 more Austrian, Prussian, and imperial troops held defensive positions on the upper Rhine. Mack expected the successful execution of his plan would lay the groundwork for a triumphant march on Paris in the spring of 1795.[38]

The Cabinet received Mack's plan readily and abandoned Murray's obsolete ideas. The Anglo-Austrian convention of 30 August 1793 reduced the diplomatic imperative of exerting British control over combined operations. In addition, the loss of Toulon and failure of the Vendée expedition reduced the prospects of coordination with counterrevolutionary forces. The Cabinet insisted only that both the main attack force and the coastal covering force include contingents from both the British and Austrian armies. Thus, the plan received British approval "subject to such political measures as it seemed right to insist upon on the part of this country."[39]

As of February, coalition forces on the eastern frontier of France numbered no more than 270,000—70,000 short of Mack's ideal 340,000. His plan divided the responsibility for furnishing the difference between the members of the Coalition, calling for 20,000 from the British, 10,000 from the Dutch, 15,000

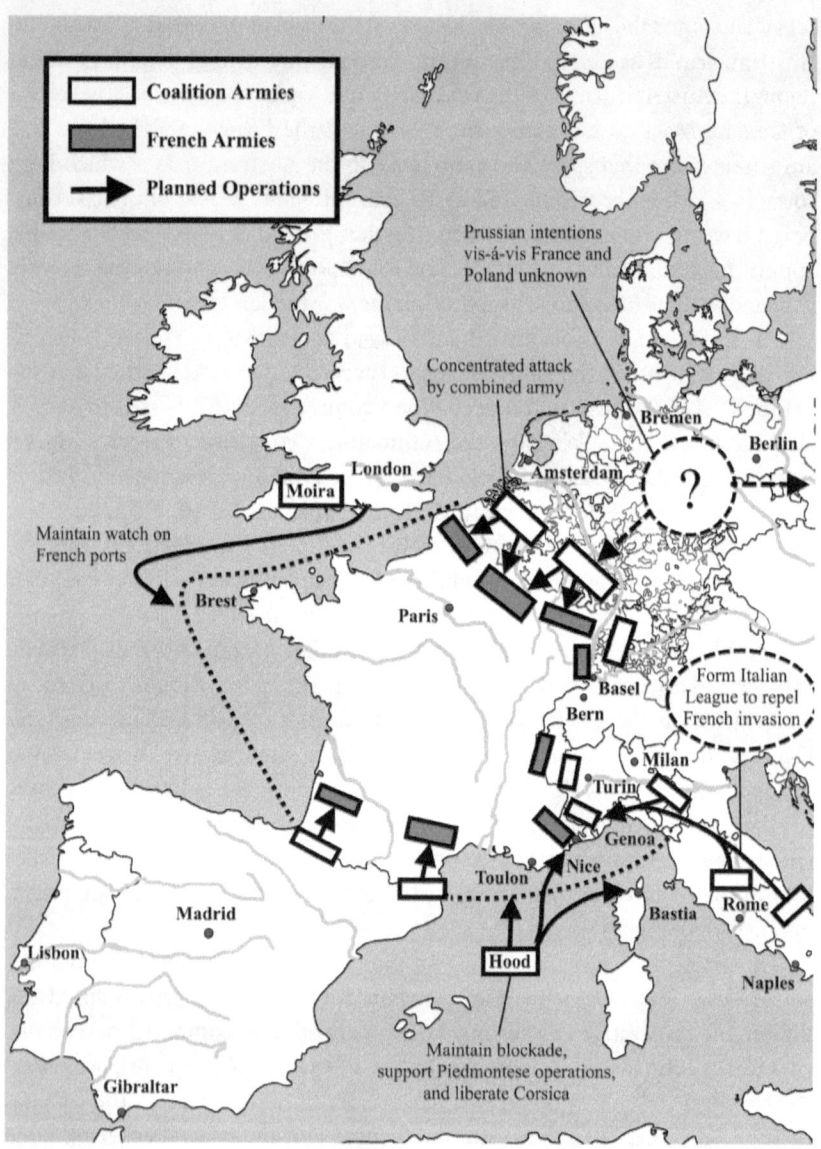

British plans for 1794

from the Prussians, and at least 25,000 from Austria.⁴⁰ While this settled matters between Austria and Britain, Berlin and The Hague resisted Mack's ideas as Grenville and Thugut had anticipated in their exchanges in September 1793.

The Dutch had been pressuring the British since April 1793 to secure some territorial compensation for their military exertions. Grenville and Thugut disagreed over the issue of a Dutch indemnity throughout 1793, and the problem remained unresolved in 1794.[41] Grenville hoped to convince Thugut to cede territory from the Austrian Netherlands to the Dutch after acquiring and retaining French Flanders. Conversely, Thugut saw no need for an Austrian cession and urged Grenville to placate the Dutch with colonial territory in the East Indies. Grenville attempted this but found the Dutch unwilling to accept the colonial lands they had unsuccessfully demanded as part of the 1788 alliance negotiations.[42] Lacking assurances of concrete gains in Europe, the Dutch remained irresolute on the issue of their military contributions to the offensive campaign. Having received repeated firm refusals from Thugut, Grenville attempted to incorporate a solution to the problem of Dutch compensation into the negotiations to motivate the Prussians.[43]

Mack's reliance on substantial Prussian participation in the campaign of 1794 lent urgency to ongoing Anglo-Prussian negotiations. Despite Yarmouth's successful conclusion of an Anglo-Prussian convention on 14 July 1793, that agreement did little to increase Prussia's role as an active participant in the war.[44] In fact, Girolamo Lucchesini, the leading Prussian diplomat accompanying the army, had delivered notes to Yarmouth and the Austrian observer on 23 September 1793 expressing Frederick William's reluctance to continue the war with France for another year. These notes explained that the war with France coupled with the necessity of militarily securing the Prussian portion of the Second Partition of Poland against Polish resistance placed an unmanageable strain on Prussian finances.[45] The Prussian king also, not entirely unreasonably, asserted that the recovery of the Austrian Netherlands satisfied the terms of his alliances and absolved Prussia of its obligation to continue the war. Consequently, Frederick William demanded a guarantee of Prussia's newly acquired Polish lands as well as a subsidy as his price for participation in the 1794 campaign.[46]

Grenville advised Pitt to reject the Prussian demands unequivocally, but Pitt hesitated to alienate such a major Continental ally. Instead, the prime minister suggested that the British and Dutch request from Prussia the 32,000 troops stipulated under the 1788 Triple Alliance. Similarly, Vienna would request the 20,000 men that Prussia owed them under the terms of the Austro-Prussian alliance. In compliance with the terms of these same treaties, Prussia's allies would provide for the expenses of these forces. Pitt also suggested making an additional offer to subsidize further Prussian troops under the same terms as the mercenaries from the smaller German states. In a Cabinet meeting on 9 October, they reached a compromise that rejected the guarantee of Prussia's Polish territory, reflecting continued British refusal to incorporate what they viewed as a detestable partition into broader diplomatic solutions. However, they did offer to cover the expenses of the troops required of Prussia under the Triple Alliance.[47]

The Prussian minister in London offered a negative view of this proposal, arguing that Prussia was not bound to provide the assistance stipulated by the 1788 alliance for two reasons. First, he insisted that the terms of that treaty required Britain to field an army of at least 45,000 men before demanding Prussian assistance. Second, he contended that the Anglo-Prussian convention of 14 July 1793 superseded the previous alliance as the governing agreement for cooperation in the war with France. Frederick William received the British counteroffer in early November and reiterated his demands, insisting that he simply lacked the resources to remain active in the war with France. He embraced the rationale of his envoy for refusing support to Britain under the terms of the Triple Alliance and added a third reason. He argued that because Prussia had not called on Britain or the United Provinces after being attacked by France in 1792, London should not invoke the terms of that alliance to fight the same enemy.[48]

This Prussian rejection left negotiations at an impasse and prompted Grenville to dispatch a special mission to Berlin to resolve the differences between the two courts. The Cabinet selected Malmesbury, the architect of the 1788 Triple Alliance.[49] Grenville's instructions to Malmesbury refuted the Prussian objections to furnish support under the terms of the Triple Alliance. Grenville observed that Frederick William could not claim to be the primary target of a French attack (and thus in a position to request aid rather than give it) and simultaneously claim to be an auxiliary of Austria as repeatedly asserted in the summer negotiations. He also argued that the British understood the July convention to be an additional commitment specifically regarding the war with France without replacing or superseding the 1788 alliance. This assertion lay at the heart of Malmesbury's mission, as Grenville explained:

> If the King of Prussia's determination cannot be altered, it will then become necessary to . . . refute these pretexts in a formal memorial . . . which shall expressly declare the Treaty of Alliance to be annulled by the refusal of the King of Prussia to fulfill his obligations. The object of your lordship's mission is, however, rather to endeavor if possible still to bring the King of Prussia to a just sense of what he owes to his engagements . . . than to terminate the connection hitherto subsisting by a declaration, which . . . would . . . be productive of inconvenience to the cause in which [George III] is engaged.

The British government insisted on the same respect for treaties from its allies that it demanded of the French revolutionaries.[50]

The Cabinet instructed Malmesbury to ascertain the validity of Frederick William's protestations of poverty. They hoped to determine whether the king's evasion of his treaty obligations arose from actual weakness or simply out of a desire to deny any gains to Austria. In the former case, they authorized Malmesbury to offer financial assistance for troops provided in accordance with existing treaties. However, the instructions insisted that any such negotiations would need to be "concerted with Austria and Holland and adopted with respect to those countries as well as with respect to Great Britain."[51] In a letter to his brother, Grenville expressed doubts about the outcome of Malmesbury's mission: "Lord Malmesbury is going to Berlin to bring our good ally to a point—ay or no. I think it will end in no."[52]

Malmesbury left on 22 November 1793 and charted a course from London that allowed him to visit the coalition's armies and the Dutch government before proceeding to Berlin, following the directive of involving the Dutch in measures to secure Prussian cooperation. At The Hague, Malmesbury found eager support for the British position. The Prince and Princess of Orange welcomed him and provided as much encouragement and information to aid him as they could. Primarily, they corroborated accounts of Prussian financial difficulties and advised Malmesbury on the current flow of influence at the Prussian court.[53]

Reuniting with his old friend, Grand Pensionary Laurens Pieter van de Spiegel, Malmesbury indulged in an extensive conversation in which the two men outlined ideal diplomatic plans. Like Malmesbury, Spiegel could claim to be a leading architect of the Triple Alliance. Malmesbury found Spiegel still dedicated to that alliance's collective security goals, and the pensionary outlined a vision for uniting the coalition. He argued that the four leading powers in the war against France—Britain, Prussia, Austria, and the United Provinces—should form a unitary alliance based on four points of agreement and deferring points of disagreement for future discussion. His four points of necessary agreement included the future of the French government, a plan of operations, honest mutual accounts of each power's military assets, and plans for seeking indemnification from France. According to Malmesbury:

> On these four cardinal points . . . he considered the fate of the war and with it the fate of Europe to rest. It was on similar principles that the Grand Alliance in 1701 was formed, and history furnishes us with many examples that all leagues without such a previous accord have constantly failed. Separate conventions between each power will not answer the end . . . they must all be united by one strong and common political chain. . . . For this purpose, the four courts should . . . appoint a place for a meeting of their respective plenipotentiaries; in this meeting all those points should be settled and methodized and it should be afterwards considered as the center on which all the operations should turn and to which all doubts and differences should be referred.[54]

Malmesbury thought these ideas so obviously agreeable with British aims that he declined to offer additional commentary. While Pitt and Malmesbury had looked to the future rather than the past in conceiving the collective security system in 1787, Spiegel's reference to the Grand Alliance of 1701 reflected the new realities of that goal in the context of war with France.[55]

While Malmesbury found the Stadtholder's family and Spiegel helpful and agreeable, they also cautioned him about the limits of Dutch support. Regarding Dutch political stability, Spiegel indicated "that for the present all parties were as much united as persons thinking so differently ever could be."[56] He lamented the propensity of Dutch bankers to prefer lending to other countries before their own and the political restrictions that allowed him to commit only a fraction of the Dutch army to field operations in Flanders. To Spiegel's mind, a guarantee of territorial concessions from the Austrian Netherlands would further unite the people and remedy many political difficulties.[57]

Malmesbury spent some time in Brussels to assess the situation of the armies in Flanders and meet with Count Mercy before traveling to Berlin and meeting with Frederick William II on 24 December 1793. Despite the king's high opinion of the British diplomat from their extensive interactions in 1788, he offered no better assessment of Prussia's ability to continue the war. Frederick William reiterated his lack of money, and Malmesbury quickly confirmed this claim. According to Malmesbury's report on Prussian finances, Frederick William II had inherited 87 million crowns from Frederick II. Of these, he spent 9 million immediately to pay his outstanding debts, 6 million for the invasion of Holland in 1787, 20 million to mobilize the army to enforce the Convention of Reichenbach on Austria, 7 million to perpetuate that armament through the Ochakov Crisis in preparation for war with Russia, 1 million to support émigrés in 1791, 18 million for the campaign of 1792, and 10 million for the campaign of 1793. In total, Frederick William had spent 71 million crowns while his more lavish lifestyle and patronage increased the government's annual expenses to the point of reducing Frederick II's 3 million crown annual surplus to zero and even incurring a deficit.[58]

After two weeks of studying conditions in Prussia, Malmesbury dispatched a report to Pitt on 9 January 1794 with his assessment:

> It seems to me that there is every reasonable ground to suppose that the King of Prussia is at this moment as eager to go on with the war as we are that he should not withdraw himself from it. The irresolution and weakness of his character is indeed such that I cannot venture to pronounce that, if he is allowed to cool, this disposition will last.... I only venture to vouch for his present feelings, but... I am still more certain that they will be of no avail if they are not secured by a compliance, in some shape or other, with his demand of pecuniary assistance.[59]

Malmesbury proceeded to elaborate on the dismal state of Prussian finances before offering a simplified perspective on the problem:

> The question reduces itself to a very narrow compass. Can we do without the King of Prussia or can we not? If we can, he is not worth the giving of a guinea for; if we cannot, I am afraid we cannot give too many. We must only look to making the best and quickest bargain possible, to purchasing him as reasonably, and to binding him as fast and as securely as we can.... The greatest difficulty is to secure the hearty cooperation of His Prussian Majesty till the end of the war, and on this point, I confess I am quite at a loss what is to be done.[60]

Malmesbury's reductionist question aptly summarized the British strategic dilemma at the start of 1794.

Even before receiving Mack's plan in February, Grenville's dispatches suggest that the Cabinet believed that they could not do without the King of Prussia. He observed to Eden on 7 January that he saw the Prussian army as "almost indispensable with a view to the prosperous issue of the next campaign."[61] On 16 January, Grenville explained to the now-retired Auckland, "The question of Berlin['s] cooperation all turns on money. If that (to a very large amount) could be found, it seems likely that we might have the effective support of 100,000 men under Möllendorff.... The subject is full of difficulty, and yet something seems of absolute necessity to be done."[62]

Following Malmesbury's report, the Cabinet debated the merits of obtaining a Prussian army by subsidy while waiting for the emperor's journey to Brussels. On 28 January, they proposed that Prussia furnish 40,000 troops under its treaty obligations, with 60,000 more procured through a joint subsidy of £2,000,000 from the coalition.[63] On 14 February, Mack's plan of operations appeared to affirm the Cabinet's decision to pursue continued Prussian participation by subsidy if necessary. They assumed that Mack's reliance on Prussian troops for his plan indicated Austrian willingness to support Anglo-Prussian subsidy negotiations. Correspondingly, Grenville requested Austrian consent to the subsidy scheme on 18 February.[64]

Pitt conceived a joint subsidy for Prussia as a means of finally merging the Triple Alliance with the Austro-Prussian alliance. The plan divided the burden of the subsidy into fifths with Britain paying two-fifths and Austria, the United Provinces, and Prussia each paying another fifth. Pitt insisted on all four states sharing the financial burden as a means of overcoming the suspicions and divisions between them. The subsidy, arranged in this manner, would serve as a shared investment in the war effort that would give all parties a clear interest in the success of the Prussian army. More generally, by combining the obligations of each alliance in the unitary subsidy agreement, the Cabinet hoped to impart unity to the coalition's military resources, planning, and objectives. Grenville explained to Eden, "You will see by the enclosed copies of the two letters which I have written by His Majesty's command to Lord Malmesbury the measures which have been suggested for the purpose of enabling this country and Austria to make a united and vigorous effort in the course of the present year."[65] Much to the chagrin of the British ministers, Thugut refused to contribute to a subsidy for Prussia. He asserted that the plan Mack developed ignored his instructions to place no dependence on Frederick William II and the Prussian army.[66]

Personally disillusioned with Prussia, Grenville sympathized with Thugut's position. Nonetheless, the Cabinet collectively remained convinced of the necessity of obtaining active Prussian participation in the coming campaign.[67] Consequently, the foreign secretary modified his offers to include only the maritime powers as contributors to the subsidy, rendering the prospects of comprehensive coalition unity in 1794 remote. On this basis, Grenville continued haggling with his Prussian counterparts via Malmesbury throughout March 1794. To mitigate the time lost in relaying messages, Malmesbury persuaded the Prussians to continue the negotiations at The Hague. Writing to inform Grenville of this, he prophetically observed, "As the only benefit which can arise from the Prussian cooperation depends on its being insured in time, I hope you will not think I have done amiss in consenting to remove the negotiation to The Hague."[68] By 28 March, the differences between the British and Prussian positions diminished to surmountable proportions, and Grenville instructed Malmesbury to reach an accommodation with the Prussians for a subsidy treaty.[69]

Despite his unwillingness to subsidize the Prussians, Thugut undertook his own projects for rectifying the deficiency of troops. He appealed to Russia and the Reich as the most likely candidates to compensate for Prussian inaction. Although Catherine II continued to remain aloof from the war while providing verbal support for the counterrevolution, the Reich proved more receptive. The Reichstag at Regensburg rejected the Austrian suggestion of arming the citizens of the Rhineland but accepted the proposal to form a Reichsarmee of 110,000 men to serve alongside the coalition armies on the upper Rhine. Regardless, the Reichsarmee failed to provide an effective replacement for the Prussian army. By March, the Reichsarmee numbered only 80,000, including 55,000 Austrians. Although an Austrian field marshal commanded the army, he possessed limited authority within the imperial constitution and faced constant resistance from the German princes.[70]

As British and Austrian ministers struggled to find more soldiers, the combined armies in Flanders waited expectantly for reinforcements before initiating the planned offensive. In fact, few of the reinforcements required to execute

Mack's plan arrived. Despite readily agreeing to Mack's plan, the Cabinet failed to mobilize the 20,000 men that constituted Britain's share of the reinforcements. The Dutch and Austrian armies also remained below their prescribed strength. Throughout March, the Prussian army on the Rhine remained uncommitted amidst ongoing subsidy negotiations.[71]

On 21 March, York and Mack met at Valenciennes to discuss the execution of the plan. They agreed to move into forward positions within a week and initiate offensive operations as soon as the weather turned favorable. Already, Mack determined that the deficiency of troops from the coalition powers required modifications to his plan. According to York, Mack had decided that the absence of Austrian reinforcements precluded the broad offensive and simultaneous sieges. Instead, he recommended keeping the central army concentrated and conducting sequential sieges.[72] Beginning on 26 March, the coalition armies maneuvered into position to launch a belated offensive while they waited for reinforcements and the arrival of the emperor.[73]

By the beginning of April, the British, Dutch, and Austrian commanders had organized their armies into three main divisions in rough compliance with Mack's vision. Austrian general François de Croix von Clerfayt commanded the right wing of the combined army that received the task of defending a sixty-mile front across western Flanders from Nieuwpoort on the coast to Orchies and Marchiennes. He possessed an effective strength of about 24,000 men for this assignment. Believing this number to be inadequate, he only reluctantly accepted the command. Field Marshal Franz Wenzel von Kaunitz-Reitberg commanded the left wing of 27,000 men. These he stretched across a forty-two-mile front from Bettignies to Dinant. Command of the center remained divided between York, Coburg, and Prince William Frederick of Orange-Nassau, although Emperor Francis's impending visit offered the prospect of at least nominal unity of command. Within this center group, York led 22,000 British, Hessian, Hanoverian, and Austrian soldiers on the right. The Prince of Orange commanded 19,000 Dutch on the left. Between them, Coburg led the main Austrian army of 43,000 men. Each commander retained separate headquarters: York at St. Amand, the Prince of Orange at Bavai, and Coburg at Valenciennes.[74]

On 1 April 1794, Malmesbury and Prussian foreign minister Christian August Heinrich Kurt von Haugwitz reached agreement on the terms of the subsidy, signing the resulting treaty on 19 April. By its terms, Prussia offered 62,400 men for service in the war with France in return for an initial payment of £400,000 as preparation money and an additional monthly stipend of £150,000. To provide for a Dutch indemnity, the treaty declared that any conquests made by the subsidized army would be held in the name of the maritime powers. The British expected to cede such conquests to Austria in return for a cession to the Dutch Republic in the final peace settlement.⁷⁵ Significantly, the question of command of the subsidized army remained ambiguous. Haugwitz refused to give the Dutch or British total control over the army to avoid the appearance of Frederick William renting out his troops like common mercenaries. Instead, the treaty stipulated the formation of a coalition military commission to consult with the Prussian generals on the army's movements. To assuage Prussian financial concerns, Malmesbury assured Haugwitz that his government would deliver the preparation money and April installment of the subsidy quickly.⁷⁶

Austria also needed financial assistance to continue the war effectively, but the initial British reluctance to subsidize the Prussian war effort led Thugut to instruct Starhemberg to seek a private loan from a British bank instead. He succeeded in negotiating a loan of £3,000,000 from Boyd, Benfield, and Company through the sale of bonds. Fatally, the projected tax revenue from Belgium provided the security for the loan. Pitt approved this measure on 6 May, but the arrangement quickly collapsed with subsequent military reversals.⁷⁷

Amid this haggling over finances, popular Polish resentment of the Second Partition grew into an open revolt. The resistance began with the refusal of Polish commanders to obey Russian orders to disband their units in and around the Russian-occupied capital of Warsaw. As one of the foremost Polish nationalists and reformers, Kościuszko took the mantle of dictator at the behest of the Polish army at Kraków on 23 March 1794. From there he issued an act of insurrection on 24 March, effectively declaring war on Russia and Prussia. Russia drew the most ire from the patriots due to its occupation and forceful manipulation of the country. On 4 April, Kościuszko led his rebels to victory over Russian forces near Kraków at the Battle of Racławice. Following this victory, patriots in Warsaw and Vilnius expelled the Russian occupation forces on 17 and 23 April, respectively. These initial Russian defeats brought Kościuszko's uprising to the attention of the German powers. Frederick William became concerned for his eastern frontier just as his foreign minister signed a subsidy treaty binding him to a war in the west. Although the Treaty of The Hague ostensibly committed him to the war with France, the activity of the Prussian army remained contingent on the receipt of subsidy payments and the formation of a multilateral military commission to determine operations.⁷⁸

While the coalition reorganized its projected offensive and a distraction brewed in the east, the initiative began to slip away. On 29 March, French general Jean-Charles Pichegru made an abortive attack on Coburg's Austrians at Le Cateau-Cambrésis. Another French attack near Tournai on 7 April met with similar results. Although the Austrians repulsed both attacks and inflicted significant casualties, they nonetheless began the campaign on the defensive rather than the offensive as planned.⁷⁹

As the French probed the coalition line, Emperor Francis embarked on his long-awaited journey to the Belgian front on 2 April together with his brothers, Archduke Charles and Archduke Joseph, and several key ministers. Although supportive of it earlier, Thugut now opposed the trip, thinking that it would render Austria unable to respond effectively to the rapidly changing situation in Poland. He failed to persuade the emperor of this and satisfied himself by remaining in Vienna to handle incoming reports from the uprising in Poland before following on 9 April.[80] That same day, 9 April, Francis reached Brussels and continued to Austrian headquarters at Valenciennes on 14 April. Coburg recommended Mack's amended plan to the emperor, whereby the coalition center would concentrate on sequential rather than simultaneous sieges. Mack and Coburg convinced Francis that this approach better suited the understrength coalition forces, and the emperor took ostensible command of the combined force with this plan in mind.[81]

On 16 April, Francis assembled the army at Le Cateau-Cambrésis, where he established his headquarters. The coalition armies began a tentative advance on 17 April, driving back light resistance to secure a position to cover the siege of Landrecies.[82] The advance and accompanying skirmishing continued to 20 April. On that day, the Prince of Orange drove the French from their positions around Landrecies and opened siege trenches against the city. Having successfully surrounded Landrecies, Coburg left the Prince of Orange in command of the siege and organized the rest of the coalition center into a covering force. York's British contingent formed the northwestern flank, taking a position southwest of Le Cateau-Cambrésis.[83]

This initial advance inspired tremendous optimism in Britain. George III lauded "the brilliant opening of the campaign, which I trust is a fortunate augur of the conduct that will be shown in the prosecution of it."[84] Auckland offered a diplomat's perspective: "Mack seems to have opened the campaign in a manner which justified the opinion formed of his talents. . . . Our prospects are nearly restored to what they were at the capitulation of Valenciennes and with the additional advantage of having secured our indemnity in the islands."[85] He also expressed optimism about the Cabinet's efforts to renew Britain's ties to Berlin: "I conceive that the Prussian treaty . . . will be received with good humor at present, and the wisdom and efficiency of such an exertion will be more and more felt every day."[86] Initial signs suggested that despite the delays, the coalition offensive might succeed.

A combination of British and Austrian cavalry repulsed a French attempt to advance and drive a wedge between Coburg and Clerfayt at the Battle of Villers-en-Cauchies on 23 and 24 April. Undaunted, on 26 April, Pichegru launched another broad advance at the central coalition army to relieve

Landrecies, but the superior Anglo-Austrian cavalry again foiled the attack at the Battle of Beaumont.[87] While Landrecies fell on 30 April, French attacks on the flanking divisions of the combined armies enjoyed greater success, forcing Coburg to reinforce them from the center and delay resuming the offensive. The southern division of the army managed to recover, but French pressure on the northern division under Clerfayt gradually drew the coalition army into a full engagement there.[88] Coburg sent York's command north in early May, and Emperor Francis soon followed with more troops to reinforce Clerfayt.[89]

On 15 May, Francis arrived at Tournai with Austrian reinforcements to bolster York's position.[90] The French forces assailing Clerfayt and York numbered approximately 82,000 men while the coalition possessed 62,000. Both armies remained scattered across a broad front of broken terrain. Mack devised a plan of attack on 16 May to destroy the French army, which resulted in the Battle of Tourcoing on 17 and 18 May. After York's column enjoyed initial success, a resolute French counterattack destroyed Mack's battle plans. The other coalition columns failed to make progress, and the French mauled York's column, nearly capturing the duke along with his entire contingent and driving the coalition back to Tournai.[91] In recalling the battle, one British soldier commented, "It is a happy thing for us mortals that we cannot see into futurity.... If we had known ... what our next day's work was to be, we should not at least have slept so sound that night."[92]

The main coalition army regrouped at Tournai on 19 May, and the commanders resolved to attempt another offensive. Again, the French preempted their operations. Pichegru attacked the combined armies around Tournai on 22 May, but after initial success a determined counterattack threw the French back. Although the combined armies held their positions at Tournai, the action marked the effective demise of Mack's grand offensive plan. Insufficient reinforcements and the absence of the Prussians had reduced coalition operations from a broad offensive to a limited advance and finally to a desperate defense. Mack refused to confront the collapse of his masterpiece and resigned on 23 May.[93]

The Duke of York also took time on 23 May to write a full report to his father on the recent battles and provide his opinions on the campaign.

> Ever since [the Battle of Tourcoing there] has existed in the Austrian headquarters a degree of pusillanimity and alarm which still continues in spite of the success yesterday, and which, I am afraid, will be productive of the very worst consequences. During the whole engagement yesterday, they were talking of nothing else than of passing the Scheldt and taking a position before Ath, in order to cover their magazines.... I could not help telling them that England had

as yet given them every assistance in her power, but that, as certainly one of the great objects of that assistance was to protect Flanders for the sake of Holland, should His Imperial Majesty choose to give up Flanders without attempting anything for its relief, he must not be astonished if your Majesty employed the forces which you have in this country for the purposes most advantageous to yourself and to your allies the Dutch without any regard whatsoever for him.[94]

York went on to suggest that the emperor took his words seriously, resolving to hold the position around Tournai in the subsequent council of war. Despite this tenuous maintenance of unity at the front, all discussions of future operations revolved around defending current positions rather than resuming the offensive. Concerned with Austrian resolve to defend Flanders, York suggested that the troops in British pay should be united into a single, unified army. In the brief period of full Anglo-Austrian military cooperation between the 1793 and 1794 campaigns, ministers from both courts had agreed to merge their armies. By the end of May 1794, military and diplomatic friction between the two powers had soured relations at the front.[95]

With diminishing prospects of success in Flanders, Francis deemed the administrative and personal inconvenience of his absence from Vienna no longer worth the questionable military benefit of his presence at the front. He expressed the desire to return to his wife's side for the last stages of her pregnancy with their third child. Thugut supported this impulse, eager to restore flexibility to Austria's ability to respond to events in Poland. On 29 May, the emperor announced his intent to return to his capital, restoring overall command to Coburg.[96] Francis remained in Belgium two weeks further before leaving for Vienna on 13 June. The emperor's departure on the heels of significant military reversals and the resignation of the army's chief of staff seemed to amplify a sense of defeatism in the Austrian army.[97] By 17 June, the wife of a British general observed: "I see a great deal of the Austrians; I think they have less hope than we have, and they seem to have no plan, no management, no money, no troops, to cope with the power against them; and their army is so dwindled that if the Prussians come they will do little more than replace their losses."[98]

Before his departure, however, Francis further damaged coalition unity during a council of war. There, he discussed with his military leaders the prospect of reducing Austrian commitment in the west to make more military assets available to protect Austrian interests in the east. Both the British and Austrian officers saw this as a prelude to the total abandonment of Belgium by Austria and a betrayal of the coalition cause. Conversely, Francis thought only of husbanding Austria's limited resources to protect the monarchy from Russian and Prussian ambitions in Poland. Francis, known for lacking resolution in the face of opposing opinions and detached from his more determined foreign minister, may have simply reflected the Austrian generals' distaste for the campaign in the Netherlands in particular and the war with France in general.[99] Thugut had no intention of abandoning the Austrian Netherlands and strove to counter this impression. After learning that Coburg as well as Mack's replacement as quartermaster, Christian August, Prince of Waldeck and Pyrmont, had been the source of this rumor, Thugut had both recalled, leaving Clerfayt in command of the Austrian army in Flanders.[100] This misunderstanding regarding official Habsburg policy had the unfortunate consequence of completely deflating the morale of the Austrian army and thoroughly embittering the British.[101]

Meanwhile, the British government did not initiate the process to remit the subsidy payments for the desperately needed Prussian reinforcements until 20 May: two days after the main coalition army in Flanders suffered the disastrous defeat at Tourcoing. Frederick William II waited one full month for the arrival of British money and the coalition military commission after the conclusion of the treaty in early April. In the absence of either, he withdrew 20,000 men from his army on the Rhine and led them to Poland to crush Kościuszko's uprising on 14 May.[102] On 24 May, Grenville sent Malmesbury back to the Continent with instructions to go to Möllendorff's headquarters at Mainz and persuade the Prussians to advance to support the combined armies in Flanders. The Cabinet also dispatched Cornwallis to serve as the British delegation to the military commission intended to direct the operations of the subsidized Prussians. Malmesbury and Cornwallis both reached Maastricht on 1 June to meet with Haugwitz and press him to order the Prussian army forward. While he accepted the proposed usage of the Prussian army, Haugwitz declined to order the movement until the British met their financial obligations under the subsidy treaty. British reluctance to pay the subsidy on time and Prussian reluctance to move their army hamstrung efforts to incorporate Möllendorff's army into the coalition's cordon throughout the summer.[103]

With coalition forces in Belgium convinced that the emperor intended to abandon the province, combined operations became a thin disguise for an unnecessary retreat.[104] On 17 June, Ypres fell to Pichegru, and General Jean-Baptiste Jourdan laid siege to Charleroi the next day. Coburg chose to concentrate his forces against Jourdan in the south to raise the siege of Charleroi, leaving York and Clerfayt to hold Pichegru in the north. Unable to maintain their positions, both commanders retreated to the Scheldt, ceding northern Belgium to the French. On 25 June, Charleroi surrendered to Jourdan before Coburg's attack came the following day.[105]

Although militarily indecisive, the resulting Battle of Fleurus on 26 June 1794 had tremendous consequences. Despite holding the upper hand at the end

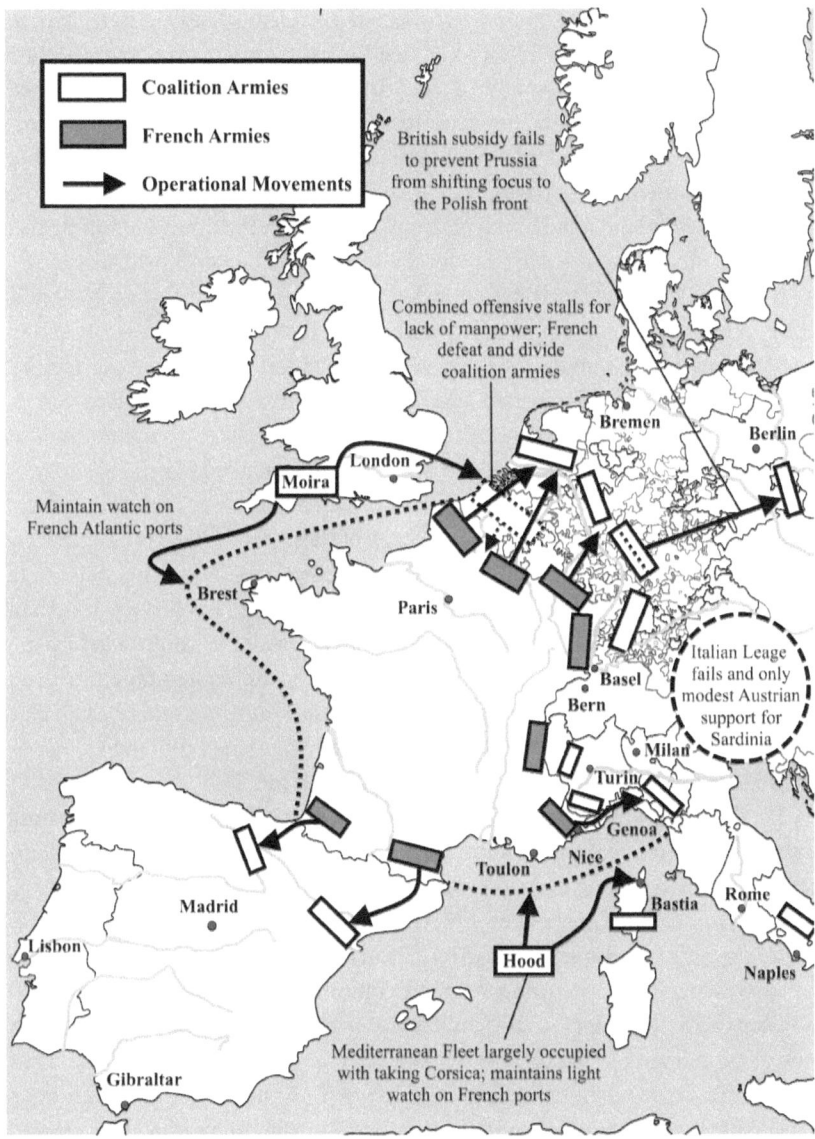

Operations of 1794

of the day's fighting, Coburg chose to break off the attack and retreat, having learned earlier of the fall of Charleroi. Believing that the emperor placed no value on the defense of Belgium, Coburg saw little point in a large, bloody engagement with Jourdan without the prospect of relieving Charleroi.[106] It appeared to the British that the Austrians retreated from a battle they had won, further confirming their perception of Austrian perfidy. After Fleurus, cooperation between Austrian and British forces collapsed. As noted, Clerfayt replaced Coburg as commander of the Austrian army, and he slowly retreated out of Belgium, repeatedly compromising the British position. York accordingly retreated to Rozendahl in Holland, unable to hold his position without support and unwilling to try for such a dubious ally. By the end of October, the Austrian Netherlands had completely fallen to the French, leaving the British army in Holland and the Austrian forces on the right bank of the Rhine.[107]

Repeated military and diplomatic delays and miscommunications between the end of the 1793 campaign in November and the start of the 1794 campaign in March weakened coalition operations in Flanders before they started. By their own standards, the British and Austrians had failed comprehensively in their plans for 1794 by the beginning of June. Major Craufurd's memorandum of November 1793 prescribed timely preparation, a detailed plan, and unity of command to rectify the mistakes of 1793. However, Emperor Francis's journey to the front inadvertently undermined each of these points. Perpetual expectation of the journey combined with repeated postponement of his departure delayed the formation of a joint plan of campaign until 14 February, less than one month before the opening of the campaign season. Without a firm plan, coalition preparations proceeded haphazardly and ultimately failed to meet expectations. Although Francis's arrival at the front in April granted ostensible unity of command to the combined armies, they remained divided along national lines and maintained independent headquarters.[108]

By the more specific standards of Mack's plan of operations, the spring campaign in Flanders fell far short of expectations. The intended grand offensive began by repelling French probes while awaiting reinforcements and the commander in chief. Instead of inflicting major defeats on French field armies while executing multiple simultaneous sieges, the coalition launched only one offensive operation. The understrength combined army advanced timidly to envelop one fortified location—Landrecies—while desperately parrying French efforts to relieve it. With their second planned advance preempted by a major French attack at the Battle of Tourcoing on 18 May, the campaign ground to a halt. After stabilizing the army's position at Tournai on 22 May, Francis and Mack abandoned the front, leaving Coburg to supervise a defensive campaign in the summer.[109]

At the beginning of 1794, British ministers retained hopes of building a more unified coalition based on the loose network of conventions created in 1793. With the will and ability of the Mediterranean states to unite under British leadership declining after the debacle at Toulon, British diplomacy focused instead on the German powers. British efforts to create an effective coalition as a foundation for a collective security system relied on the Triple Alliance to bridge the gap between the Anglo-Dutch and Austro-Prussian wars with France. Pitt tried to use Prussia's commitments to the Triple Alliance and to its alliance with Austria in the French war as a common thread between the two hitherto conflicting alliances. Insensitive British diplomacy and Austro-Prussian jealousies doomed this to failure. After failing to impose a British interpretation of the balance of power in eastern Europe in 1791, London refused to engage with the predatory partition politics of the eastern powers in that sphere at all, artificially treating the Polish and French questions as discrete issues. By insisting on this separation, British diplomacy failed to resolve the Austro-Prussian differences in the east that hampered cooperation in the west. Thus, British proposals for a collective security coalition could not encompass the full scope of Austrian and Prussian security dilemmas. Accordingly, cooperation in the west faltered as the eastern security problems of the German powers escalated without the prospect of finding a solution to them in the west.

CHAPTER 8

Division and Defeat, 1794

The failure of the offensive in Flanders in the spring of 1794 marked the beginning of the end for Pitt's original vision for the coalition. From a British perspective, diplomatic efforts had been steadily reconciling the differences of the coalition powers into a functional network of cooperation. However, efforts to produce a general treaty that committed all signatories to wage war for the establishment of a genuine multilateral security system had not yet succeeded, and its absence allowed a resurgence of bilateral jealousies that widened the gap between the coalition partners. In the remaining months of 1794, military setbacks rekindled enduring suspicions among the coalition partners and produced a series of diplomatic failures that unraveled the strained ties that bound them. Spanish insecurities over British naval power in the Caribbean and the western Mediterranean diminished Madrid's support for the coalition and drew the Spanish into negotiations with the French. Concurrently, London's inability to reconcile Austro-Prussian differences resulted in both powers seeking security solutions in the east at the expense of their commitments to the French war.

While cooperation in Flanders faltered in the spring and summer of 1794, the semblance of unity in the Mediterranean collapsed altogether. The chaotic evacuation of Toulon on 19 December 1793 marked the final joint Anglo-Spanish operation of the war as each power proceeded to pursue independent objectives. Auxiliaries from Naples and Sardinia returned home, and the Spanish fleet hastily dumped its share of Toulonnais refugees at Livorno and returned to the Spanish coast to support the campaign in the eastern Pyrenees. With the evacuated British troops and some 14,000 French refugees on board, Hood anchored his fleet in the Bay of Hyères, approximately fifteen miles east of Toulon.[1] The dismal results of the Toulon campaign did little to impress Britain's Mediterranean allies. Far from uniting them in a single campaign for a single purpose, Toulon had devolved into an acrimonious struggle for command over fundamentally insufficient resources, exacerbating Anglo-Spanish distrust and crippling cooperation. Despite British protestations and declarations to the contrary, Madrid remained extremely anxious about the increase of British power in the western Mediterranean and the potential for London to retain Toulon as another outpost on the model of Gibraltar.[2]

On 20 November 1793, the British leaders at Toulon issued a declaration denying any intention of taking an indemnity on the continent of Europe. In a letter to St. Helens on 30 November, Grenville elaborated that the British hoped to indemnify themselves with French islands in the Caribbean while they encouraged Spain to take border territories from France. Although a similar expression to Thugut regarding Dunkirk had alleviated Austrian concerns about British intentions, it had the opposite effect at Madrid. As a maritime rival of Great Britain both in Europe and overseas, the Spanish viewed with jealousy the increase of British naval and colonial power in any region.[3]

Spanish anxieties about British colonial expansion grew in response to a successful British campaign in the West Indies that accelerated in the spring of 1794. Before the outbreak of war, Home Secretary Dundas had been in contact with royalist French planters to discuss the transfer of French possessions into British protection. Local British resources at the disposal of the acting governor general of Jamaica, Sir Adam Williamson, secured the island of Tobago and a foothold in St. Domingue in 1793. British ministers planned to send further reinforcements to the Caribbean in September, but emergencies in Flanders and opportunities in southern and western France siphoned troops from that purpose and delayed the departure of the intended reinforcements. The British West Indian expedition under the command of General Sir Charles Grey and Admiral Sir John Jervis finally sailed for the Caribbean on 26 November and arrived at Barbados on 6 January 1794. For the first six months of 1794, the Grey–Jervis expedition conquered most of the French islands, leaving only the challenge of suppressing the slave revolt on St. Domingue to take possession of the eastern third of Hispaniola.[4]

Grenville claimed to see no reason for the Spanish to be concerned by these operations, insisting that the British had provided Madrid "little cause for jealousy. . . . The immense territorial possessions of Spain in America . . . furnish ample scope for the exertions of all the industry, capital, and skill which Spain can employ." He also suggested that while Spain and Britain had strategic interests in St. Domingue, "it is by no means conceived that these projects entertained by the two courts are incompatible with each other. The extent of that island and the distance of the Spanish quarters from the parts nearest to Jamaica leaving full scope for arrangements being taken . . . such as may be mutually beneficial to both countries."[5] St. Helens reported on 14 January 1794 that the Spanish wanted St. Domingue as their indemnity, setting them at odds with similar British intent. St. Helens optimistically echoed Grenville in proposing a partition of the French part of the island, which, according to his report, Spanish prime minister Manuel Godoy y Álvarez de Faria received favorably.[6]

This cordiality proved a thin facade to conceal enduring suspicion and jealousy that the Anglo-Spanish convention of the previous year had failed to efface. Immediately after signing that convention, St. Helens observed that "[my] chief antagonist is the minister of the marine, M. [Antonio] Valdés [y Fernández Bazán], who, in common with but too many other persons, has persuaded himself that the secret aim of Great Britain in the present war is to engage the French and Spaniards to batter each other's ships to pieces and so secure to herself in future an uncontested superiority over both."[7] St. Helens proceeded to opine that despite Godoy's apparent sincerity in wishing to establish an Anglo-Spanish connection, the minister's lack of knowledge and experience would cause him to follow the lead of men like Valdés.[8] Anglo-Spanish relations also suffered from the staunchly Anglophobe Spanish ambassador in London, Marqués Bernardo del Campo. On 1 December 1793, del Campo's hostility reached such a pitch that Grenville wrote to St. Helens to request a statement from Godoy on the matter:

> It is ... necessary that your excellency should ascertain whether the form and language of [del Campo] were provided to him by his court or whether they arise solely from his ill disposition toward this country of which he has given repeated proofs. And if the latter should be found to be the case, your excellency will ... adopt some proper expedient by which [Godoy] may be apprised how little Monsieur Del Campo's conduct appears calculated to promote union and good understanding between the two countries.[9]

In both London and Madrid, prominent Spaniards resisted the connection with their old rival.

This aversion remained strong as operations in theaters of overlapping interest amplified differences. In his letter of 14 January 1794, St. Helens attributed an unexpected Spanish refusal to acknowledge the principle of indemnification publicly despite private acceptance "to the influence of ... the ancient French or Bourbon interest at this court, the partisans of which ... are still but too numerous and powerful."[10] Despite his consistently optimistic appraisal of Godoy, St. Helens revealed tension in his relationship with the Spanish prime minister in recounting their discussions over the debacle at Toulon. "Since [the evacuation of Toulon], we have avoided, as by tacit agreement, the entering into any explanation respecting the circumstances of it, being aware that, as there are grounds of complaint on both sides, such an *éclaircissement* must necessarily have led to unpleasant disputes without answering any useful purpose."[11] By the spring of 1794, St. Helens's assessment of the Spaniards from 29 May 1793 "that they are infinitely more intractable and difficult to deal with as friends than as enemies" would find broad agreement at Whitehall. The Spanish appeared to feel the same way about their partnership with the British.[12]

In this context, an opportunity at Corsica that proved irresistible to the British appeared to confirm Spanish fears of Britain's expansionist intentions in the western Mediterranean. Corsica had been an object of considerable British interest for strategic and opportunistic reasons since the Corsican declaration of independence from Genoa in 1755. The lack of response from the British government when Genoa sold the island to France in 1768 led to harsh criticism and the subsequent fall of the administration of Augustus FitzRoy, Third Duke of Grafton. After French forces took control of Corsica in 1769, the Corsican leaders that resisted the French invasion were forced into exile. Chief among them, Filippo Antonio Pasquale di Paoli took refuge in London where he established a good relationship with British elites, including King George III. Paoli returned to Corsica after the National Assembly offered amnesty to exiles in 1790. He was elected president of the Department of Corsica but began seeking opportunity to escape French control after the execution of Louis XVI. In May 1793, a general assembly of the Corsican people voted to secede from France and invest Paoli with dictatorial powers for the duration of the struggle. British diplomats in Italy viewed the taking of Corsica as a feasible operation that would provide Britain with a forward base in the western Mediterranean without, they presumed, excessive difficulty or risk of offending the Italian states.[13] The idea gained currency at Whitehall, and Godoy even suggested that Corsica might serve as the British indemnity in the final peace settlement in response to St. Helens's March 1793 suggestion of a joint Anglo-Spanish expedition to take the island.[14]

However, as with every other aspect of the Anglo-Spanish connection, Godoy's seemingly agreeable disposition toward British interests in Corsica did not extend to other Spanish officials, nor did it persist in the face of reversals. Hood received appeals for assistance from Paoli on 25 August 1793, but events at Toulon prevented him from immediately responding. Nevertheless, he dispatched a small squadron under Commodore Robert Linzee on 21 September to assess the situation and provide aid. Owing to its small size and erroneous intelligence received from the Corsican rebels, the squadron achieved little beyond angering the Spanish.[15] Hood's decision siphoned desperately needed resources from Toulon even as Spanish troops arrived in answer to his earlier call for support after taking the city. In the context of concurrent British demands for unilateral command at Toulon, Hood's similarly unilateral move to support Corsican rebels seemed to confirm Spanish fears that the British only sought their own gain at Spanish and French expense. On 8 November, St. Helens reported extensive Spanish complaints about the Corsican expedition and described the court as being in a state of great "pique and ill-humor."[16]

Undaunted and with the tacit support of his government, Hood continued to provide support to the Corsicans and planned to undertake a more concerted effort to conquer the island in the spring of 1794.[17] He sent Captain Horatio Nelson with another squadron early in December even as Toulon began to collapse. Ultimately, Hood was forced to recall Nelson to assist in the evacuation of Toulon on 18 and 19 December. Following the evacuation, Hood regrouped in the Bay of Hyères where he received a renewed overture from Paoli in early January. This spurred Hood to act on his prior intentions of undertaking a spring campaign to gain control of Corsica. He dispatched envoys to obtain information and settle the details with Paoli, including the anticipated transfer of the displaced British governor of Toulon, Sir Gilbert Elliot, to oversee British-controlled Corsica.[18] Meanwhile, St. Helens reported that the Spanish remained deeply dissatisfied with Hood's unilateral Corsican operations despite professing no interest of their own in the island.[19]

Hood's Corsican operations reinforced British unilateralism in the western Mediterranean despite Pitt's multilateralist intentions. After the failure to link coalition operations in the Alps and the Pyrenees into a broader southern offensive through combined operations at Toulon, British focus in the south shifted to supporting operations in Italy. Anglo-Spanish disputes over military command and support for the counterrevolution rendered close cooperation unappealing. Hood's moves toward Corsica both reflected and reinforced the estrangement of British and Spanish forces. Elliot reported to Dundas that "a correspondence which has already taken place between Admiral Lángara and Lord Hood on the subject of Corsica seems to promise some trouble if anything should be undertaken in that quarter. But . . . it is to be hoped that these inconveniences may be avoided."[20] As Elliot discovered in May 1794, this decision and the ensuing British operations on Corsica destroyed any remaining willingness on the part of the Spanish to cooperate with the British in the Mediterranean. After encountering Lángara at Livorno, he reported to Grenville that the Spanish admiral "repeated several times with some emphasis that the British and Spanish fleets were no longer combined."[21] The British minister at Madrid belatedly reported this disposition on 22 October, noting among other Spanish complaints about British behavior that "there predominates at this moment a strong aversion to engage with His Majesty's forces in any combined operation whatsoever."[22]

At the beginning of 1794, Hood turned toward Italy partially because Spain appeared neither to want nor to need British help in the eastern Pyrenees. To make a difference in Italy, the British fleet needed a reliable local port. Port Mahon on Minorca was too distant, and the use of Spanish ports had become uncomfortable amid disputes over the responsibility of paying for supplies and repairs. The ports of Naples and the island of Sardinia were too distant to serve as a base for reliably supporting land operations on the Alpine front. Tuscany and Genoa possessed the only other ports capable of serving British needs, and neither state favored the coalition. Tuscany supported the British under duress due to the heavy-handed diplomacy of British minister John Augustus Hervey. Genoa favored the French to the extent that Hood found it necessary to blockade Genoese ports to prevent them from supplying the French troops fighting the Sardinians. Hood and the Cabinet wished to emancipate the British fleet from its reliance on reluctant foreign governments or distant Gibraltar, and Corsica furnished an ideal solution. Thus, securing that island became a prerequisite for adding substantial British military support to its fiscal and diplomatic aid in the Italian theater.[23]

Elliot provided several reasons for acquiring Corsica in a report to Dundas following his conference with Paoli and a tour of the island. He argued that keeping Corsica's supply of good timber in British rather than French hands would improve Britain's naval position in the Mediterranean. Elliot also speculated that Corsican recruits could bolster both the British army and navy, with its landsmen suited to be light troops and its sailors experienced in Mediterranean commerce. Corsica's strategic location also featured prominently in Elliot's report. He noted that while France did not need Corsican ports because of their close proximity to the French coast, they provided an enormous extension of the Royal Navy's reach, hitherto tethered to Gibraltar. In the case of the ongoing war, Elliot noted that if France could "prepare at her leisure in that island an expedition against the Italian states, I do not know that the utmost superiority we can ever obtain at sea would [be] a sufficient security to the Italian coasts." For Britain, he suggested that "the harbor of that Island must render us at once formidable to France and independent of the little Italian states whose ports are not good and whose friendship is but slippery."[24]

The means of politically establishing British control over Corsica to obtain these advantages occasioned some discussion as well. Elliot had suggested supporting Corsica as a fully independent country, but Paoli, recognizing Corsican weakness, pressed for incorporation as a possession of the British Crown. In an earlier letter to Dundas, Elliot had posited such a possibility as the most advantageous arrangement if the Corsicans would accept it. Thus, Elliot and Paoli agreed that Corsica could fit easily into the British administration in the form of a viceroyalty as it already possessed a functioning constitution and popular assemblies.[25]

Beyond strategic and logistical considerations, the establishment of the British monarchy in Corsica also held the prospect of playing an important diplomatic role in British efforts to forge collective security. "In a political view," suggested Elliot in the same report, "[Corsica] gives us a solid and permanent footing as a Mediterranean power, and by keeping us constantly in the view of the Italian states as a formidable enemy or as a powerful protector, it ought to give us a leading and steady influence in the politics of Italy and tend either to avert war or to strengthen us in the prosecution of it when unavoidable."[26] On 22 February, he explained his goals for increased British influence in Italy:

> I have often thought ... that some permanent league of the Italian states for their mutual defense would be a great security not only to that country itself, but to the peace of Europe. The want of it is particularly perceptible at this time. ... I think possible that if some systematic confederacy in Italy is thought a desirable thing ... it might be brought about, and if we are settled in Corsica, I should hope still more from the influence of Great Britain in treating that affair.[27]

By making George III effectively a king in Italy and giving Britain closer ties to the continent in that region, Elliot hoped to facilitate a local collective security system.[28]

In March, Elliot received confirmation of his ideas and the steps he had taken, and he received a modification to his commission that required him to report simultaneously and separately both to Home Secretary Dundas as the Cabinet's political representative in Corsica and to Foreign Secretary Grenville as a key agent for British diplomacy in the region. Dundas wrote on 31 March to approve the incorporation of Corsica into Great Britain as a dependent kingdom and charged Elliot with overseeing the process.[29] Before receiving Elliot's speculation about an Italian confederation, Grenville invested him in early March with the task of constructing a similarly conceived system. Grenville declared that "the establishment of such a system you are to consider the leading object of your present instructions."[30] After receiving Elliot's reports, Grenville wrote in a second letter, "You will not fail to observe how much [our] sentiments agree with the ideas stated by your excellency. In particular, you will perceive that the whole of the [object] to which the king's views are [directed] turns upon the establishment of a confederacy among the different states of Italy for their common defense."[31] Grenville went on to note that while the government had always sought this goal, it had not been considered within the reach of British influence until the Corsican connection provided a more direct and stable link.[32]

The prospective Italian league offered a means of compensating for the loss of Toulon and the decline of Spanish enthusiasm for the war. The French recapture of Toulon and corresponding collapse of the Federalist revolt freed French troops to reinforce the Alpine and Pyrenean fronts. While the Spanish front appeared stable in the spring of 1794, British ambassador John Trevor reported from Turin that the Sardinians struggled to maintain their defenses, facing shortages of money and manpower despite the British subsidy. British efforts to reconcile Austrian and Sardinian differences to bring the former to support the latter more vigorously had thus far yielded little result. Thus, under his new commission, Elliot sought to overcome those differences by including Sardinia and Austria in a more broadly defined collective security system that encompassed any and all Italian states, with Naples and the emerging Anglo-Corsican Kingdom playing leading roles. If successful, such a system could compensate for the additional pressure on Sardinia following the evacuation of Toulon and for the loss of effective Spanish cooperation.[33]

Elliot's Corsican and Italian commissions ultimately failed to meet expectations and proved less complementary in practice than the British had hoped. Elliot managed to make only a brief tour of Italy in May to pursue the ambition of an Italian league before the demands of managing Corsica forced him back to that island for the rest of the year. Moreover, during his tour, Elliot's efforts were complicated by a lack of clarity surrounding his authority to conduct negotiations as well as additional issues that distracted him from his primary objective. In addition to the Italian league, Elliot also bore responsibility for finding sanctuary for the Toulonnais refugees. Furthermore, Elliot inherited the unenviable task of resolving the Anglo-Genoese disputes over Genoa's continued trade with France and its refusal to oppose a French invasion through its territory on 6 April. Armed with a special commission but no credentials to certify him at any specific court, Elliot faced questions about his authority throughout Italy.[34]

Elliot's efforts to form an Italian league resulted in a meeting at Milan on 7 May with Austrian Archduke Ferdinand, brother to Emperor Francis II. The conference, also attended by Trevor and Francis Drake, the British envoy to Genoa, enjoyed an auspicious start as the archduke acknowledged that he had instructions to support the creation of an Italian league. The Austrians had, in fact, already made a proposal for a similar league and received a negligible response. According to Ferdinand, only the duchies of Parma and Modena had shown any interest, and he discounted their ability to contribute in any meaningful way. Elliot attempted to resurrect the project by starting with written agreements, but Ferdinand demurred on the grounds of Elliot's ambiguous authority. Ferdinand refused to take any further steps without the emperor's express approval. However, in the midst of Elliot's efforts, Francis embarked on his long-delayed trip to Flanders, which extended the lines of communication between the Austrian court and Italy. Elliot complained that the trip that the Cabinet had so hoped would achieve success in the north had brought all Austrian activities in Italy to a halt.[35]

Even Trevor's more confined efforts to enlist greater Austrian support for Sardinia yielded little result. Beyond the outstanding Austrian demand for Piedmontese territory as the price of cooperation, the Austrians preferred caution due to a manpower shortage of their own. The overwhelming focus of the Austrian army remained the Flanders theater as indicated by the emperor's journey there. This commitment deepened as it became clear that the armies in Flanders and on the Rhine would require additional reinforcements to compensate for the passivity and ultimate withdrawal of Prussian troops. Prussian actions also induced Vienna to retain a substantial body of troops in reserve to defend itself in the event that Austrian refusal to endorse Berlin's Polish gains precipitated a Prussian attack. In this circumstance, British envoys estimated the Austrian forces at the disposal of the government in Milan to be no more than 15,000 men. With this small force and lacking confidence in the Sardinian army's ability to defend the Alpine passes, Ferdinand and his military advisers preferred to preserve and concentrate their forces to meet any French breakthrough on the open plains of Piedmont. They feared that dispatching divisions to support the defense of the Alpine passes would only risk defeat in detail without the prospect of making a significant difference.[36]

After meeting with Ferdinand, Elliot returned to Corsica to coordinate Anglo-Corsican operations. Over the course of 1794, Anglo-Corsican forces eliminated the French presence on Corsica but more slowly than anticipated. The fortress of Fornali fell on 17 February, and the French evacuated San Fiorenzo the next day. After a laborious campaign, Bastia fell on 15 May, leaving only Calvi. Anticipating reinforcements from France that never came, Calvi resisted until 10 August. During the last siege, the Corsicans officially offered their crown to King George III, which Elliot accepted in his stead, inaugurating the Anglo-Corsican Kingdom.[37]

Elliot wrote to Grenville on 27 August to describe his situation and explain why the lofty expectations of a deft insertion of the British Crown into Italian politics had been disappointed. He noted that the Corsican business had prevented him from returning to Italy to pursue his diplomatic charge there. However, he also observed that he could do little without more extensive credentials, which he never received. Elliot was left to work through correspondence with existing British diplomats at Italian courts to circumvent that problem, adding a layer of delay to the process. He relayed that Ferdinand had proposed a new project of an Italian concert, but Elliot dismissed it as so vague as to be practically meaningless. He lamented that the success of any Italian league would depend on Neapolitan support, yet the growing threat of a revolution in Naples and Sicily prevented the Neapolitan Bourbons from even sending northward the aid they owed Britain by treaty and had furnished at Toulon. Elliot observed that "although the prospect is not encouraging, yet a concert of the Italian states is so important and so interesting an object that I am unwilling to abandon or lose sight of it without a trial, but when a favorable opportunity will occur of making the experiment, I am unable at present to foresee."[38]

Far from boosting the coalition's position in the western Mediterranean and facilitating the addition of an Italian league to a larger collective security arrangement, the British turn toward Corsica largely achieved the opposite. The unilateral action offended the Spanish and hardened them against the prospect of military cooperation with the British fleet. The move to annex Corsica also caused alarm in Italy. The Genoese took offense that the British did not acknowledge Genoa's historic claim to the island. The court of Tuscany expressed irritation at the prospect of the Anglo-Corsican Kingdom becoming a powerful commercial rival. The benefits Elliot had predicted from possession of Corsica that might have compensated for these diplomatic costs failed to materialize in 1794 because of the stubborn French defense of Bastia and Calvi, which prevented Elliot from consolidating British control over the island.[39] Even after Calvi surrendered on 10 August, the Anglo-Corsican Kingdom made no contribution to the Italian campaign beyond denying the French access to the island's ports and resources. Elliot discovered that the modest British expedition of approximately 2,000 men barely answered the needs of defending Corsica and could not be spared to assist with the defense of Piedmont. Recruitment of Corsican units failed to produce sufficiently reliable recruits to relieve the British garrison for service elsewhere. With Britain's primary diplomatic and military effort in the Mediterranean absorbed by Corsica, the idea of supporting Sardinia with an Italian league remained little more than a fantasy.[40]

Throughout the summer of 1794, as Elliot waited impatiently for the surrender of Calvi and the combined armies in Flanders suffered defeats, the situation on the Spanish front deteriorated. The Spanish offensive into Roussillon had stalled for lack of manpower, and several Spanish ministers argued that carrying the war any further was neither within Spain's interests nor its abilities. Confirming this apprehension, a French counteroffensive in the eastern Pyrenees in April and May ejected the Spanish army from Roussillon, pushing it back into Spanish territory. Another French assault in the western Pyrenees in June and July drove Spanish forces back beyond their own frontier there as well. French pressure continued into the autumn as the outnumbered Spanish armies struggled to respond. These setbacks finally persuaded Godoy to seek peace, although he still pursued an honorable peace that included some concession for the young Louis XVII. Proposals to this effect that he communicated to General Jacques François Dugommier, the commander of the French Army of the Eastern Pyrenees, received only scorn.[41]

The behavior of the coalition toward Spain offered little to counteract this growing pacifism. After rejecting the British calls for a congress, Godoy had issued proposals to Austria and Prussia for bilateral conventions much as the British had forged with the members of the coalition in 1793. In his letter of 14 January, St. Helens reported from Madrid that the Spanish had received responses to their "repeated overtures for the establishment of some kind of concert between Spain and those powers, but neither of these answers is by any means satisfactory." The Austrians declined any convention, instead only pledging to notify (rather than consult) Spain before making peace with France. From Prussia, the Spanish received notification of Frederick William's intent to continue to provide the Austrians with only the minimum support required by their treaty. The Prussian note offered to contribute more in return for financial assistance. Both of these replies showed a total disregard for Spain as a partner in the common cause.[42]

Of the major powers of the coalition, only Britain had attempted to treat Spain with any respect or courtesy, but that relationship had soured nearly as soon as it began in 1793. Constant Anglo-Spanish disputes over indemnities, command of combined operations, and the future of the counterrevolution gradually disillusioned both powers. Both London and Madrid pursued independent policies and operations, and they complained to each other about the lack of communication. On the part of the Spanish, this complaint appears somewhat justified. In early February, St. Helens departed Madrid to assume his new post as Auckland's replacement at The Hague. This left only the low-ranking secretary of the British embassy, Francis James Jackson, to manage Anglo-Spanish relations while Grenville dealt with the prickly del Campo in London. The Cabinet planned to have Morton Eden transfer to Madrid from Vienna to replace St. Helens, but the greater urgency of Anglo-Austrian negotiations relating to the Flanders campaign detained Eden until the summer, whereupon he decided he preferred to keep the Vienna post rather than move to Madrid. After Eden declined the position, the Cabinet made little effort to find a replacement for the Spanish embassy until the summer of 1795.[43]

Moreover, Grenville's correspondence with Jackson throughout 1794 primarily addressed minor legal disputes over recaptured ships or wrongfully detained merchants. Grenville made almost no mention of larger plans for waging war or obtaining peace beyond making suggestions for the deployment of the Spanish fleet. Such communications hardly alleviated Godoy's irritation at the "neglectful conduct of Great Britain towards Spain and the want of cordiality which has all along prevailed."⁴⁴

Despite this poor relationship, the British remained faithful to the principles of cooperation as specified in the Anglo-Spanish convention and to Pitt's collective security principles in advocating Spanish views at other courts. Most notably, Grenville instructed Eden in November 1794 that "you will . . . state to [the Austrian government] the wish of the court of Spain to engage in a like concert for the common defense in the south of Europe, especially if an opportunity should offer of creating a diversion by offensive operations against the French territories on that side." In mentioning "a like concert," Grenville referred to the other topic of that letter: renewed efforts to work with the Austrians to create an Italian league to strengthen the defense of Italy for the 1795 campaign. However, the negotiations initiated in this dispatch remained unsettled until May 1795, by which point the Spanish had given up on the coalition.⁴⁵

While Madrid contemplated secession from the anti-French coalition in the summer and autumn of 1794, Berlin also turned away from western war to attend to its eastern interests. British tardiness in honoring the subsidy agreement of 19 April 1794 contributed to Prussian disillusionment with the coalition much as Anglo-Spanish command disputes had alienated Spain. Early in the subsidy negotiations, Frederick William had pledged to personally lead the subsidized Prussian army, which would firmly fix Prussian attention on the war with France. However, the laborious negotiations to produce the final agreement had taken long enough to cool the Prussian king's enthusiasm for that cause. In addition, Kościuszko's revolt in Poland signaled the need for additional Prussian resources in that quarter. British delays in producing the agreed subsidy payment convinced Frederick William to prioritize his clear interests in the east over his more nebulous commitments in the west. On 4 May, the Prussian king had left for Poland, focusing Prussian attention there instead of on the Rhine as originally planned.⁴⁶

One month later, on 13 June, Francis II had left the defeated coalition army in Flanders to return to Vienna. Events in Poland contributed to this decision as much as they had the Prussian move. Thugut also urged him to return to his capital. While the Austrian minister believed strongly in the need to fight France vigorously, the concentration of Austrian power in Flanders caused him concern in view of the larger picture. In a letter of 15 February, Eden recounted Thugut's views: "He strenuously argued that [the advantage of concentrating all of Austria's armies in Flanders] would be more than overbalanced by the circumstance of the Austrian army being entirely cut off from [Austria] since it would leave the King of Prussia arbitrator of our operations and of the pacification."⁴⁷ Frederick William's eastward shift in May exacerbated these fears and caused Thugut to expect that Russian and Prussian campaigns against the Polish rebels would inevitably result in a third partition. While he recognized that such an event could only be disadvantageous to Austria, he also understood that the Habsburg monarchy could not prevent it while embroiled in a war with France. To maintain the balance of power in eastern Europe, Thugut determined that Austria must be party to the new partition, and the Austrian share must outweigh the Prussian share to compensate for Austrian exclusion from the Second Partition.[48]

Continued military disappointments in Flanders reinforced the resolution of the German powers to seek compensation in Poland for their efforts. Following Francis's departure from the front, Austrian morale plummeted because of the expectation that the emperor intended to abandon Belgium. Mack's replacement as quartermaster general, Prince Waldeck, cultivated this notion, incorrectly surmising the abandonment of their Belgian provinces to be the secret wish of the Austrian government. This impression increased as Francis withdrew 20,000 men to reinforce Galicia in preparation for any expansion of the Polish upheavals.[49]

Relations between the British and Austrian armies deteriorated as York and other British officers complained of Austrian passivity and mistreatment of British troops. Through George III, York pressed the Cabinet to end the misuse of British troops by disentangling the British and Austrian armies and forming all troops in British pay into a single army.[50] The Cabinet initially resisted this idea as antithetical to their goal of using military unity to foster diplomatic unity. However, Austrian retreats forced them to adopt exactly the measure York had recommended in order to prevent the French from overrunning the British lines of communication that ran to the coast.[51] From July to October, French armies pursued the now divided Austrian and Anglo-Dutch armies out of Belgium. Coburg retreated along his lines of communication east into Germany, and York retreated with the Dutch to prepare the defense of their frontier.[52]

With the situation in the Low Countries collapsing, Pitt, Grenville, and Dundas developed new measures to attempt to rally the German powers for a united effort against France. Pitt prepared a memorandum that outlined the resolutions emerging from the discussions of the three ministers. In it, he divided the proposals for Austria and Prussia into discrete lists. Pitt wrote seven for Austria and only three for Prussia. This separation of proposals reflected the failure of the preceding eighteen months of British diplomacy to produce the desired multilateral consensus. Pitt's proposals for Austria primarily included ideas to coordinate Anglo-Austrian operations, to reconcile differences over the future peace, and to convert their convention of cooperation into a defensive alliance. In contrast, the proposals for Prussia primarily demanded compliance with the terms of the subsidy treaty. This difference indicated recognition of the Prussian determination to continue only as an auxiliary, leaving Austria as Britain's primary partner in the war. Nevertheless, the summary struck a multilateralist tone as one of the proposals for Prussia sought Prussian consent for any Austrian acquisitions and accession to a collective guarantee of the postwar territorial status quo by all coalition members.[53]

While Frederick William oversaw Prussian operations in Poland to crush Kościuszko's uprising, Anglo-Prussian diplomacy ground to a halt. Prussian ministers and Field Marshal Möllendorff demanded prompt and complete payment of the subsidy as a prerequisite for the Prussian army complying with the directives of the maritime powers. They complained of delays and misunderstandings in the delivery of the payments and pleaded the absolute inability of the army to move without immediate financial assistance. Meanwhile, the British repeatedly complained of the total inactivity of the Prussian army and demanded some evidence of its compliance with their wishes to justify the remittance of the subsidy payments.[54] British envoys at Berlin and at Prussian army headquarters suggested that the Prussians appeared to have no desire or intention of providing the agreed assistance.[55] This made the Cabinet reluctant to continue making payments on an army it could not control. In September, Grenville threatened to cancel the subsidy payment for October if the Prussian army did not advance to force the French to lift the siege of Maastricht.[56]

Although British diplomatic efforts at Berlin received Austrian support, that support had little impact. The Austrian ambassador at Berlin urged the Prussians to comply with the demands of the maritime powers, to furnish the aid they owed to Austria by the alliance of 1791, and to provide the contingent they owed to the Reichsarmee to help defend the Rhine. Thugut had hoped to compensate for the effective loss of Prussian participation through this Reichsarmee in much the same way as the British hoped to compensate for the loss of Toulon and declining Spanish support by forging an Italian league. Pitt supported this Austrian initiative to activate the collective security mechanisms of the Holy Roman Empire, but it enjoyed little more success than the British Italian project. While some of the smaller states of the Holy Roman Empire mobilized resources for the Reichsarmee, Prussia flatly refused to contribute to it. Ultimately, the limited ability and will of the German states to contribute to the Reichsarmee reduced it to little more than an Austrian army shackled by the legal constraints of the Holy Roman Empire.[57]

While Austrian diplomacy supported British efforts to keep Prussia engaged in the west, the operations of the Austrian armies undermined this objective. The decision to withdraw 20,000 men from the army in Flanders to reinforce Galicia and the subsequent retreats both in Flanders and along the

Rhine appeared to confirm suspicions of Austria's reorientation eastward to match that of Prussia. Making matters worse, Austrian retreats in July left Möllendorff's Prussians exposed as the foremost coalition unit in the way of the French advance. The British envoy at Berlin reported that while the Prussian ministers formally rejected the notion, rumors abounded that the Austrians had intentionally retreated to expose the Prussian army to attack.[58]

By the end of September 1794, the Cabinet accepted the failure of the Prussian subsidy. Regardless of mistakes made in transmitting the money to the Prussians, the British government had paid more than £1,000,000 and received no return on the investment. On 30 September, Pitt informed Jacobi that the subsidy would be suspended until the Prussian army marched to the Netherlands as requested. On 24 October, Jacobi delivered Frederick William's reply, which expressed surprise and denied any breach of the treaty on the part of the Prussians. Notably, Jacobi took the opportunity to communicate to Grenville the new orders the Prussian king had issued to Möllendorff. The Prussian army on the Rhine was to abandon the front and retreat to Prussian territory to aid in the suppression of the Polish resistance. All possibility of Prussian adherence to the broader coalition appeared to vanish with this bitter separation.[59]

Meanwhile, London and Vienna recommenced their negotiations for a more extensive alliance. Divergent views regarding Dutch indemnification and the Prussian subsidy in combination with the upheavals in Poland had stalled Anglo-Austrian alliance talks after the conclusion of their convention of cooperation in August 1793. By the summer of 1794, military and financial necessity drove the two powers to renew negotiations to overcome these differences. Thugut sought a loan on the British financial market while Pitt needed Austrian troops to defend the United Provinces in Prussia's stead. Although Austria had successfully managed the enormous expenses of the war in 1792 and 1793, the struggle began to deplete Vienna's resources in 1794. Having observed the unproductive haggling and recriminations that attended the Prussian subsidy negotiations, Thugut elected to raise a loan with private British bankers to avoid the unwanted British demands that would undoubtedly arise in talks for a direct subsidy. He hatched the scheme in February 1794 for a loan of £1,000,000, expanding it to £3,000,000 in April, and the sale of the corresponding bonds opened in May with Pitt's knowledge and approval. Unfortunately, Thugut offered Austrian revenues from Belgium as the security for the loan, so the collapse of the Flanders campaign in the summer of 1794 caused investors to avoid the bonds despite Pitt's endorsement.[60]

This difficulty induced Thugut to send Mercy from his post at Brussels to London to obtain a British guarantee of the loan as well as further financial and military assistance as part of a full alliance. Thugut particularly emphasized the importance of pressing the British to strengthen York's army and unite it with the Austrians to mount a counteroffensive rather than maintaining an ineffective cordon defense of Dutch territory. He also urged Mercy to seek British acceptance of the Belgium-Bavaria exchange, providing the former included territory taken from French Flanders. The Austrian minister warned that if the British could not adequately support this project, Austria would seek indemnification from Poland instead.[61] The choice of Mercy for this delicate mission indicated its high priority. As a veteran statesman and Thugut's patron and friend, Mercy enjoyed the full confidence of the Austrian government. Mercy had also garnered considerable respect in London, and, as the governor of the Austrian Netherlands, the Cabinet viewed him as someone sympathetic to the needs of both countries as well as the realities of the war in Flanders.[62]

Before Mercy arrived, the British Cabinet had reached a similar conclusion on the need for a closer Anglo-Austrian alliance to bring order and purpose to the haphazard coalition and began organizing a special diplomatic mission to that end. In addition to British disappointment with the Prussians, the resolution to seek an independent Austrian alliance emerged from domestic political shuffling. In May 1794, the Pitt ministry dramatically increased its political strength by joining forces with the conservative wing of the Whig party. The resulting coalition government left a weak Foxite rump of the Whig party as the only opposition in Parliament.[63]

This political alliance represented the culmination of Pitt's post-Ochakov efforts to prevent domestic divisions from weakening British foreign policy. The more conservative Whigs had disliked Fox's near-treasonous opposition during the Ochakov affair, and the French Revolution brought that issue to a point. In December 1792 and January 1793, the Cabinet's careful self-justification and preparations for war won the support of the Whigs under the leadership of William Cavendish-Bentinck, Third Duke of Portland. However, Portland refused to separate from Fox openly over the issue of the war with France, despite their opposing views. An impatient group of his followers led by William Windham broke rank to support the government formally as a sort of third party. Over the course of 1793, Pitt's ministry used offers of political and diplomatic offices to entice this third party to unite with the government and bring the remaining Portland Whigs with them. As with the initial formation of Pitt's administration in 1783, Dundas played a key role in conducting the social and political maneuvering necessary to seal this alliance. By regularly consulting the Windham and Portland Whigs on domestic legislation and foreign policy and including their members in the execution of these measures, Pitt gained their confidence.[64]

Malmesbury and Elliot are two notable examples of Whigs pressed into service. Pitt enlisted Malmesbury to return to diplomatic service after having lost his position by opposing the government during the Regency Crisis. The inducement of a government stipend helped reconcile Malmesbury's conscience to the prospect of breaking with Portland and lending his experience and familiarity with Frederick William II to Pitt's Prussian diplomacy in late 1793. After some hesitation and consultation with other Portland Whigs, Elliot accepted Pitt's offer to serve as provisional governor of Dunkirk after York's army occupied that city. Unexpectedly, he found his commission transferred with minor modifications first to Toulon and then Corsica. Both of these rogue Whigs played important roles in shaping and executing British war policies.[65]

In May 1794, Pitt and Dundas worked through Windham to negotiate a reorganization of the government that reunited the Windham and Portland branches and gave members of both prominent positions within the government. Most notably, Portland became home secretary, Earl George Spencer became Lord Privy Seal, and Windham secretary at war. The former home secretary, Henry Dundas, assumed the newly created office of secretary of state for war, or war secretary.[66] In foreign policy, the Portland Whigs advocated a strong alliance with Austria and both firm commitment to and vigorous support for the counterrevolution. Thus, the inclusion of these new Cabinet members amplified the Cabinet's shift toward favoring Austria over Prussia as the central pillar of Britain's collective security system. The British mission to Vienna being organized in July 1794 reflected the influence of the new additions to the government. The Cabinet entrusted its leadership to the new Lord Privy Seal, George Spencer, and added Thomas Grenville, the older brother of the foreign secretary, as a supporting delegate. The choice of Grenville's older brother for the mission also signified the foreign secretary's personal interest in an Austrian alliance.[67]

In his instructions to Spencer on 19 July 1794, Grenville urged the importance of securing close military cooperation to halt the French advance in the Low Countries and thereafter to counterattack to relieve several besieged fortresses. The foreign secretary pressed for resuming offensive operations "for the purpose of bringing the war to a successful issue on such terms as can alone afford a hope of security to the continental powers and to the rest of Europe." To this end, Grenville furnished the envoys with a combination of demands and offers to present to the court of Vienna. He insisted on a change of command in the Austrian army to remove Coburg and Waldeck, who appeared to be unwilling to fight for the Austrian Netherlands, and he recommended Archduke Charles as the most desirable replacement. Regardless of the replacement chosen, Grenville established the change of command as "a sine qua non condition of all future cooperation on the part of the British troops." He asserted that London would not offer cooperation to an army in which it could place no confidence.[68]

The remainder of the instructions left more room for negotiation. Discussion of deployments and operations remained vague under the continuing uncertainty regarding the Prussian army. Nevertheless, Grenville generally recommended a defensive on the Rhine with a counteroffensive to recover the Netherlands, especially the fortresses of Condé and Valenciennes, both of which were then under siege by French troops. He requested that the Austrians increase their army in the Netherlands from 70,000 men to 100,000. In return, Grenville pledged to reinforce York's army from 38,000 to 50,000 men and to pressure the Dutch to expand their army from 12,000 to 20,000.[69]

Having outlined these military points, Grenville authorized the envoys to address Austria's financial needs. He noted that Britain could not afford to subsidize Austria while still upholding its existing financial commitments to Sardinia, Prussia, and the several German states with armies in British pay. Unaware of the details and difficulties of the Austrian loan, he offered to provide some support to Vienna through British credit. After a conversation between Pitt and the treasurer of the Austrian Netherlands on the matter on 25 July, Grenville informed the envoys of lackluster bond sales but did not explicitly extend the offer of British credit to cover the failing loan.[70] In an accompanying letter, Grenville proposed transferring the main émigré army commanded by Louis Joseph, Prince de Condé, from Austrian to British service. Condé had rallied the émigrés at Koblenz after fleeing France in 1791 and, following the outbreak of war, formed them into an army to fight alongside Austrian forces on the Rhine. Transferring that army into British pay would alleviate the Austrian financial burden of maintaining it and allow London to redeploy that army from its current position alongside the Austrians on the Rhine to reinforce the faltering Flanders campaign.[71]

With regard to indemnification and concerns that Austria might seek a separate peace with France, Grenville renewed offers to commit Britain to securing the border fortresses of French Flanders for Austria. To formalize this concession and alleviate Austrian fears about potential Prussian treachery, Grenville proposed a mutual guarantee of territory and a full defensive alliance. He also mentioned the need to secure an Austrian pledge for indemnification for the United Provinces in order to preserve the popularity of the Stadtholder's government and prevent the Dutch from seeking a separate peace. However, Grenville acknowledged that the Austrians would likely find this demand distasteful at best and urged the envoys to omit discussion of it until after securing agreement on all other points.[72]

Neither the British nor the Austrian mission succeeded. The Spencer-Grenville mission arrived in Vienna in early August and found Thugut extremely interested in a British alliance and eager to continue the war. However, they struggled to reach agreement on nearly every other point outlined in their instructions. By agreeing to replace Coburg, Thugut at least met the minimum requirement for continuing the negotiations but objected to the replacements that the British requested and only offered Clerfayt in return, which the British found disagreeable. He rejected the transfer of Condé's army, insisting on its importance for defending Germany, and the envoys largely let that secondary component of their instructions drop thereafter. More alarmingly, Thugut demanded that the British guarantee the entire £3,000,000 loan and transfer the 1794 Prussian subsidy to Austria in 1795 in return for the continuation or expansion of Austrian military efforts in the Low Countries. As this exceeded Grenville's instructions, they referred the matter back to the anticipated negotiations arising from Mercy's mission to London.[73]

The negotiations never took place. The aging Mercy fell ill in transit from Brussels to London and died in the British capital on 25 August 1794, having achieved nothing beyond passing his instructions to the resident Austrian ambassador, Starhemberg. Although capable, Starhemberg possessed less diplomatic talent than Mercy, and his relationship with the British had been strained by the preceding year's difficult negotiations. The promise of a fresh start to Anglo-Austrian relations that accompanied Mercy to London died with him, and the focus of negotiations shifted back to Vienna. Starhemberg did convey the essence of Mercy's instructions to the Cabinet, echoing Thugut's discussions with Spencer and Thomas Grenville. He expressed three primary Austrian needs to Grenville: immediate financial aid for the Austrian army for the 1794 campaign, a guarantee of the Austrian loan, and further financial assistance for 1795.[74]

With faith in the Prussians at a nadir and military fortunes rapidly worsening, this proposal found Pitt agreeable but determined to obtain clear and explicit military value for any British financial contribution. In conveying the Cabinet's initial response to Spencer and Thomas Grenville, the foreign secretary emphasized the desire to unite with Austria "both for the prosecution of the present war and for all future measures of mutual security." Yet he declared that the extensive Austrian demands for financial support "not only justify but require the fullest previous explanation on all points which relate to the means of realizing the plans now in question, of securing the advantages held out by them, or of obviating the difficulties to which they may lead."[75] To meet Austria's immediate needs, the prime minister instructed York to provide the Austrian army with up to £150,000 from the British army's coffers, insisting in return that the Austrians should retreat no further and counterattack to relieve the fortresses of Condé and Valenciennes.[76]

To answer Austria's long-term financial concerns, Grenville dispatched a more comprehensive project on 29 August. Reflecting the Cabinet's wariness of financial aid in the wake of the Prussian subsidy debacle, he emphasized the need to ensure that such enormous supplies of British money produced corresponding military results. He expressed doubts about the prudence of the project but acknowledged that the ministers thought "that the experiment ought to be hazarded, provided it is accompanied with such conditions as appear to them absolutely necessary to ensure its success." The British proposed to accept the requests to guarantee the Austrian loan and to furnish a subsidy for 1795 by transferring to Austria the subsidy agreement concluded with Prussia in April 1794.[77]

Nevertheless, the Cabinet demanded steep prices for these fiscal boons. Grenville's letter insisted that the Austrians accept Charles Cornwallis as commander in chief of the coalition armies in Flanders and reiterated the request for the transfer of Condé's army. For the subsidy, London demanded that Vienna expand its army in Flanders by the number of troops specified in the original Prussian treaty. In addition, the proposal requested that the emperor use his influence within the Holy Roman Empire to persuade the German states to pay a subsidy to induce the Prussians to continue the war in 1795. Anticipating resistance on this last point, Grenville explained that it served to obviate Austrian fears of Prussian treachery in Germany or Poland. He argued that binding Prussia to defend the Rhine through a subsidy that depended on Austria for its success offered the surest means of preventing Berlin from taking advantage of Vienna's extensive commitment to the war against France.[78] The proposal thus reprised the 1793 idea of creating a link of shared interest among the coalition powers through shared financial obligations. This attempt to include a Prussian subsidy also reflected Pitt's lingering desire to build toward an effective collective security system by linking new connections to his original Triple Alliance foundation.[79]

Thugut found this offer insulting and refused to discuss either the prospect of a British *generalissimo* or the notion of the empire furnishing a new Prussian subsidy. The former arrogantly implied that the Austrians had no general fit to command their own armies, and the latter suggestion galled Thugut since he had denounced the Prussian subsidy as foolish from the beginning. He complained that if the empire had the ability to pay such a subsidy, he would have sought financial aid there instead of London. Finally, Thugut refused to transfer Condé's army on the grounds that Vienna planned to advance it into Franche-Comté as part of their offensive in 1795 to raise the banner of royalism and inspire uprisings. Interestingly, even as Thugut refused to place Austrian troops serving in Austrian territory under British command, he demanded that the Sardinians accept an Austrian commander in chief in return for Austrian support in the 1795 Italian campaign.[80]

Before receiving Thugut's response, Grenville dispatched a new offer in response to the swift surrender of the Austrian garrisons at Condé and Valenciennes and Clerfayt's continued retreat. With a new offensive in 1794 both less likely and less important as a result of these surrenders, this new proposal reduced both the promises and demands of the previous offer. It simply offered to guarantee the Austrian loan in return for maintaining a minimum army of 80,000 Austrians in the Low Countries. Grenville pledged that Britain would maintain an army of its own of at least half of the Austrian strength and pressure the Dutch to maintain a force of at least a quarter of the Austrian numbers. He revoked all mention of Cornwallis as commander in chief and of the prospect of a subsidy either for Austria or Prussia. In addition, the British accepted the Austrian inclination to a defensive posture in the Low Countries, deferring to them the choice of concentrating either on the Rhine or in Italy for offensives there. Grenville reiterated British support for an Austrian indemnification in the form of unspecified French border fortresses, and he recommended that the proposed convention include an article stipulating the future conclusion of an alliance.[81]

Although reasonable, the tone of the new offer contributed to the collapse of negotiations. Grenville attached accusatory demands for explanations of the recent surrenders of Austrian garrisons and the retreat of Austrian armies. The equally dismal performance of York's army and Britain's Dutch ally made this additional commentary appear hypocritical as well as arrogant.[82] Understandably angered by this tone and unimpressed with the offer, Thugut rejected it as insufficient for Austria's needs. In the wake of this icy reception, negotiations broke down entirely. Lord Spencer and Thomas Grenville prepared to leave Vienna in defeat, but Thugut made them another offer before they departed. He suggested that the British double the Austrian loan to £6,000,000 in return for an expansion of Habsburg forces in the Low Countries to 100,000 men. Armed with this offer, the British envoys departed for London on 7 October. The collapse of Anglo-Austrian negotiations at Vienna coincided with the decision to cancel the Prussian subsidy, marking a period of severe disillusionment toward both German powers.[83]

Nevertheless, Pitt still held out the possibility of renewing the defunct Prussian subsidy if the Prussian army took an active role in measures to defend the Dutch provinces. Berlin also left open the possibility of renewed cooperation. Before Malmesbury departed his post at Berlin for a new commission, he received a proposal for a new subsidy arrangement from the Prussians. The new project described Prussian participation in the war as a favor to the British and Austrians for which they would furnish unspecified financial support proportional to Prussia's needs. It also stipulated that the subsidized army would remain under Prussian command. Grenville found the proposal incredible and unacceptable, complaining of its "unfriendly and unconciliating tone." He argued that Prussia could hardly demand "such immense sacrifices" from the coalition "in terms which give to the whole transaction a color of concession and favor on the part of the King of Prussia while it is in fact a relaxation of those demands which the allies have a right to make and from which they desist only on account of the alleged necessities of Prussia."[84] Malmesbury argued against taking any such proposal seriously, suggesting "that the alteration in the conduct of Prussia was simply one of language and not of intention, and that their goal was to get the whole subsidy and do nothing for it.[85]

The cancellation of the Prussian subsidy coincided with the opening of Austro-Russian negotiations for a third partition of Poland. Thugut had refused to ratify the Second Partition agreement between Prussia and Russia, leaving Frederick William anxious about Austrian intentions on his eastern frontier. In September 1794, with Galicia reinforced, Thugut approved negotiations with the Russians to redress the imbalance created by the Second Partition of Poland and Prussian refusal to assist in acquiring a proportional indemnity for Austria from France. Concurrently, Kościuszko's stubborn defense forced the Prussians to lift the siege of Warsaw by 6 September, and a Polish counterattack even pressed into Prussian territory. Meanwhile, the Austrian army in Galicia remained idle, refusing Prussian requests for assistance, thereby giving every appearance of seeking to take advantage of Prussian distress for Austrian gain. Yet Russian armies crushed the Polish insurrection by the end of November, and Catherine opened separate negotiations with Austrian and Prussian delegations for the Third Partition of Poland.[86]

While the affairs of eastern Europe kept Berlin preoccupied, the situation in the Netherlands continued to deteriorate. The prospect of a French invasion cowed supporters of the Stadtholder and emboldened the hitherto suppressed Patriots, raising the prospect of revolution as well as defeat. The Dutch population increasingly viewed the British as the source of their hardships and became obstructive and hostile to the British expedition.[87] Wracked by internal divisions and dissatisfied with the coalition, the Stadtholder's government begged the British to open general peace negotiations. The Cabinet refused, viewing revolutionary France as still too volatile and untrustworthy for any peace to provide sufficient security for the other states of Europe. Therefore, while reiterating London's commitment to defend their ally, British ministers recommended that the United Provinces seek separate peace with France. They reasoned that a separate peace that secured all or most of the independence of the United Provinces would be preferable to pressing the Dutch to remain in the war only to suffer more extensive loss through revolution. The Dutch embraced the opportunity, but the negotiations yielded no agreement. The French sought revolution to secure the Dutch as an ally of France; anything less held no interest for them.[88]

During a lull in the fighting in Flanders from October to December, the Cabinet began considering changes to their strategy for the 1795 campaign. This included recalling the Duke of York, in whom the ministers had lost faith, ostensibly for consultation but with no intent to return him to the army. Command of the British expedition devolved on Lieutenant General William Harcourt. This decision achieved little beyond annoying George III. With such meager resources and uncertain allies, Harcourt fared no better than York.[89] Less contentiously, Pitt made use of the new talent acquired from the Portland Whigs to alter the leadership of the navy. Although he delayed the measure until December, he appointed Spencer as first lord of the admiralty to replace his own brother, John Pitt, Second Earl of Chatham, who had become deeply unpopular.[90] In addition to the question of command, the Cabinet also reevaluated foreign sources of support. Although negotiations between Grenville and Starhemberg on the Austrian loan continued, the foreign secretary turned the attentions of his office to Russia while Pitt and the Portland Whigs considered counterrevolutionary options.[91]

Efforts to gather intelligence and establish reliable contacts with counterrevolutionaries both in and out of France had continued after the failure of the Vendée and Toulon adventures in 1793. Correspondence with French rebels in Brittany had gained some regularity over the course of 1794 under the direction of the British spymaster in the Channel Islands, Philippe d'Auvergne, prince de Bouillon. Through this correspondence, the British government had established contact with Joseph-Geneviève, comte de Puisaye, a talented leader of the Breton resistance who shared the British preference for a moderate, constitutional restoration of the Bourbon monarchy. Puisaye traveled to London in September 1794 to secure support for his movement just as the Cabinet was losing faith in the Prussian army and the Austrian negotiations. The Portland Whigs, Windham chief among them, expressed great enthusiasm for the royalist cause.[92] Dundas and Grenville remained skeptical, the former declaring to Pitt that "it is impossible for me to be sanguine on the ideas of the C[omte] de P[uisaye]."[93] In contrast, Pitt resolved to pursue the opportunity in western France in light of the disappointments on its eastern frontier. The prime minister wrote to his brother that the deterioration of negotiations with Austria meant that "we must look to more limited exertions on the side of Flanders and turn our principal efforts to the French coast."[94]

However, the very disappointments in Flanders that turned Pitt's attention to western France obstructed his ability to immediately supply the British army of 10,000 men that Puisaye sought. In his letter to Chatham on 24 September, Pitt urged the adoption of the project "if we can find the force, which though difficult, is, I trust, not impossible."[95] His hopes rested primarily on what remained of the original expedition gathered for the Vendée in 1793. After its failure, Moira's Vendée expedition had been maintained in hopes of making another attempt, but the Cabinet had deployed it to Flanders in June 1794 to stabilize York's position. By September, Moira had returned to Britain and partially reconstituted his expedition, again preparing for a descent on the French coast. Pitt and Windham struggled unsuccessfully to assemble the resources for the operation in October and November until finally abandoning the effort in December. Based on the intelligence available to him, Moira judged the British and Breton forces at hand insufficient for the task and questioned the wisdom of opening such a campaign in the winter without a clear line of retreat or reinforcements.[96] Pitt sent money and supplies but postponed plans for direct intervention.[97]

Another counterrevolutionary appeal for British financial backing arrived in September 1794 from Condé and the main émigré army. Condé shared British annoyance with Austria's relatively passive prosecution of the war, and he contacted Pitt in the hope of finding more active support and employment for his forces. Pitt embraced the chance to establish a link with another counterrevolutionary asset and advanced £15,000 to Condé immediately. An agent sent to the army found it in poor condition but eager for action if properly supported.[98] Although Thugut had resisted suggestions to transfer the army to British service, a direct communication from Condé renewed the possibility of gaining the support of his army in the Low Countries or at least in support of a British plan of operations for 1795. The strength of Condé's army fluctuated amid the uncertainties of the royalist cause, but it generally mustered approximately 5,000 men after the outbreak of war. British hopes for making Condé useful relied on the expectation that he would be able to increase the strength of his army from the pool of French exiles in Germany if supported by British funds.[99]

Additional contacts increased the importance of the links with Puisaye and Condé. In October, French constitutional monarchists in Switzerland sent the British government proposals allegedly from royalists and moderates in Paris. The overture amounted to a comprehensive settlement encompassing both a European peace and a moderate restoration of the French monarchy in return for British support for a royalist coup in Paris.[100] In response, the Cabinet dispatched William Wickham, a friend of Grenville, to Switzerland to establish regular contact with the counterrevolutionaries and especially in the former bases of the Federalist revolt. Wickham's instructions referenced and bore a strong resemblance to the directives given to the British commissioners at Toulon the previous year and the declaration to that city. The British government remained ambivalent toward the exact form of the future French government, only insisting that it be stable enough to offer the other powers some hope of security. As in the declaration to Toulon, Wickham's instructions tentatively recommended a restoration of the Bourbon monarchy as the most likely to provide this stability but left the question of constitutional limitations to the decision of the French people. Regarding the context of the war, Grenville specified that any agreement with these royalists pertaining to the suspension of hostilities and future peace required the consent of all coalition partners to succeed. Wickham fulfilled his role as spymaster in Berne under the cover of first supporting and then replacing the existing envoy to Switzerland, Sir Robert Fitzgerald.[101]

In November, Wickham determined that the overture lacked substance. He discerned no group capable of immediately delivering on those promises. However, he also determined that resistance in central and southern France continued to simmer despite the triumph of republican armies in 1793 and the restoration of the Girondins after Thermidor. Wickham projected that this resistance could be cultivated into a full revolt centered at Lyon at the discretion of the British government. The Cabinet thus made Wickham's position permanent, equipping him with funding to pursue that aim, and he consolidated his counterrevolutionary network during the winter of 1794–95.[102]

Through Puisaye, Condé, and Wickham the British began to produce a comprehensive counterrevolutionary arm of strategy for 1795. If sufficiently coordinated and supported with coalition resources, counterrevolutionary activity held the prospect of significantly weakening France and reinvigorating the war effort. An Anglo-émigré landing in western France would draw French forces from the eastern front while a new uprising in Lyon would similarly distract French armies and threaten the logistics of those at the front. The émigré army on the Rhine would then strengthen an Austrian attack on that weakened French line. Success of these counterrevolutionary vanguards with coalition support could draw more royalists to the cause with the ultimate prize of a coup in Paris to end the war. However, the relative weakness and uncertainty of these components meant that they could provide only a supporting role rather than replace major allies.

On 26 November 1794, the British government formally reappointed Sir Morton Eden as ambassador to Austria, complying with his change of heart regarding the embassy of Madrid. Eden's instructions directed him to resume the task of the failed Spencer–Grenville mission to secure a new convention between the two courts to supplement the existing one and plan for the 1795 campaign. The Cabinet tasked Eden with establishing unity in British and Austrian policies toward other states and toward the counterrevolution. In Eden's instructions, Grenville acknowledged that the British advised the Dutch to make peace and justified it as a measure that would relieve Britain and Austria of the burden of trying to defend the Netherlands. To forestall any Austrian concerns arising from that measure, he reiterated Britain's commitment to make no such separate peace. The British sought Austrian support for renewed efforts to create an Italian league for the mutual defense of those states and for a larger defensive system that included all of southern Europe, including Austria, Spain, and the Italian states. In another effort to bridge the gap between Vienna and Madrid, Eden had instructions to request Austrian thoughts on the Spanish suggestion to recognize Provence as regent of France. Grenville noted that the British viewed such recognition as a tool in the counterrevolutionary strategy to be used only at a time and in a manner that would have the greatest effect on the war.[103]

Regarding the means and ends of the 1795 campaign, the instructions authorized Eden to resume negotiations with Thugut on the question of providing Austria with financial assistance but remained vague on specific offers beyond again requesting the transfer of Condé's army to British control. Instead, the foreign secretary asked the Austrians to explain the operations that varying degrees of British funding would allow them to undertake. The uncertain future of the Dutch also proved a vexing obstacle to forming military plans, leading Grenville to observe that "all the ideas entertained here . . . are liable to be varied from day to day by the turn which affairs are taking in Holland." Correspondingly, he offered two broad suggestions based on the two possibilities. If the Dutch successfully made peace, he suggested that the British army withdraw entirely, leaving on the Continent only the mercenaries in British pay. The former would then join émigré forces to attack the west coast of France while the latter would unite with the Austrian army for an offensive across the Rhine and into France. In the event that Dutch negotiations failed, Eden was to request that the Austrians provide at least 40,000 men to join the British army to mount a counteroffensive in the Low Countries.[104]

Meanwhile, Anglo-Russian relations remained relatively unchanged since the conclusion of their convention in March 1793. Catherine's exorbitant demands for a subsidy for the use of Russian troops had persuaded the Cabinet that her commitment to fighting the French Revolution extended only to exhorting other courts to action. By December 1793, Catherine had offered direct Russian support in the war only in return for a British guarantee of Russian territory, including the new Polish acquisitions. To fight for British security in western Europe against France, Catherine demanded a reciprocal British commitment to Russian security in eastern Europe against any Prussian or Turkish attack. The Cabinet reluctantly expressed willingness to meet these demands in January 1794, but Kościuszko's uprising caused Catherine to withdraw this offer.[105] She refused to consider new obligations until the Polish rebels had been crushed. After Russian forces defeated Kościuszko and captured Warsaw in October, Grenville instructed Whitworth in November to renew the British requests for Russian support.[106]

Anglo-Russian negotiations proceeded little further in December as St. Petersburg negotiated the Third Partition of Poland with Austria. However, discussions on the French war in Vienna and London seemed to gather momentum as 1794 drew to a close. Before receiving any word from Eden, Grenville informed the ambassador on 18 December 1794 of the Cabinet's willingness, after further deliberation, to offer a British guarantee of the full £6,000,000 loan. In return, he required Austria to field 200,000 men in 1795 and send 80,000 of those to work with the Britain's mercenaries to drive the French from the Low Countries. Grenville urged an offensive across the Rhine with the remaining 120,000 men and emphasized the importance of coordinating the timing of that offensive to coincide with British landings in Brittany to maximize the impact of these maneuvers. He deferred to Thugut to determine when the Austrian army would be ready for such action. The foreign secretary posited that the British army could be ready for the new offensive by late March if the Austrians could quickly relieve it from its position in the Low Countries.[107]

In this new dispatch, Grenville took occasion to reiterate several of the points in his original instructions to Eden and revealed his own desire to make the Anglo-Austrian connection the new foundation for Britain's European policies. He requested Austrian assistance in gathering an Italian league against France and, to that end, pressuring recalcitrant Tuscany and Genoa into compliance with the coalition's diplomatic and economic policies. Reflecting the maturation of a comprehensive counterrevolutionary strategy, Grenville urged the Austrians to take all necessary steps to raise and support royalist rebellions in central and southern France concurrent with the offensives. By way of encouragement on this point and as a show of confidence, the foreign secretary informed Thugut of the secret British communication with French dissidents through Wickham. Notably, Grenville explicitly declared that he placed no reliance on the Prussians for the 1795 campaign despite some indications of Berlin's willingness to resume the fight for the right price. He acknowledged this possibility but emphasized the importance of a strong Anglo-Austrian alliance, which he pledged to sign after the conclusion of the loan convention.[108]

On the same day, Eden relayed a comparable proposal from Thugut to London. Thugut reached a similar conclusion on the necessity of resolving Anglo-Austrian differences to secure an effective alliance and financial aid and agreed to most of Grenville's proposals. The Austrian minister reiterated his request for a £6,000,000 loan to finance 200,000 men but acknowledged that a loan of £4,000,000 would meet the minimum requirements for Austria to wage an offensive campaign. While Grenville had excluded Italy from his calculation of 200,000 men for the Austrian army, Thugut's proposed 200,000 men included Austrian forces in Italy. Nevertheless, Thugut accepted Grenville's broad plan of campaign and pressed for the conclusion of a defensive alliance as quickly as possible. Through Eden, Thugut also expressed support for the idea of a concert of southern Europe and informed London of Vienna's intention to launch an offensive into the Genoese Riviera. Sardinia and Austria had finally reached an agreement establishing an Austrian commander in chief for their armies and a joint military council at Milan to direct operations. The Austrian minister requested British support in obtaining from Naples the 6,000 men owed to Britain by treaty to support the Italian offensive. Thugut also endorsed Grenville's view of acknowledging Provence as regent as a tool to be saved for a later date. He persisted in refusing to transfer Condé's army and reiterated his plan to use that army to spark and support a royalist rising in Franche-Comté. Lastly, Thugut asked the British to support Austrian requests for Russia to exert pressure on Berlin to continue fighting France or at least maintain a benevolent neutrality toward the coalition. He also recommended that the British seek a Russian army to bolster British operations in western France.[109]

With the gap between the British and Austrian positions substantially narrowed, the Cabinet authorized Eden on 13 January 1795 to conclude a treaty based on either proposal. Grenville's letter on this point carried approval for a loan of £6,000,000 if the Austrians agreed to field 200,000 men north of Switzerland in addition to 40,000 in Italy or a loan of £4,000,000 if the Austrians could supply only 200,000 men across all fronts. Grenville also reciprocated the good faith Thugut appeared to demonstrate in lowering the Austrian offer by recommending that Eden should increase the loan to £4,500,000 to cover the money that the British had already advanced to the Austrians if Vienna chose the second, reduced option.[110]

Grenville relayed the Cabinet's consent to Thugut's plans for Italy but warned of the dangers of leaving the direction of the campaign in the hands of a committee. Nevertheless, he promised to support Austrian diplomatic efforts to rally the Italian states and to press Naples to send 6,000 men to Piedmont. The foreign secretary cautioned that the Neapolitan troops would likely be of such poor quality that they would provide very little benefit. Grenville also conveyed the government's acceptance of Thugut's plans for Condé's army, only urging that his advance "to establish in Franche-Comté a center of counterrevolution" should coincide with the similar British efforts to the west.[111]

Despite this auspicious renewal of Anglo-Austrian negotiations, Thugut took issue with the details of the loan agreement, complaining of the method of raising the loan as well as the interest rates, which he viewed as excessive.

Grenville failed to provide Eden with clear details of the loan's terms, leading Thugut to misinterpret them as unduly harsh. Thugut had previously agreed to pay a higher interest rate than the British government's rate of approximately four percent, but he interpreted the agreement to mean that Austria's rate would be at seven and one-half percent, which he viewed as too high. In reality, the Cabinet had arranged for the Austrians to pay a more modest rate of six percent.[112] Thus, the Austrian minister rejected the offer in January, and weather delayed messages between Eden and Grenville that could have resolved the misunderstanding. Grenville's offer of 18 December 1794 only arrived in Vienna on 15 January 1795 after being delayed crossing the channel. Eden's letter of 21 January enclosing Thugut's rejection of the loan arrived in London on 20 February. Grenville's response of 24 February to clarify the loan terms then arrived on 13 March, finally ending almost two full months of stalled negotiations. Despite agreement on nearly all other points, this financial misunderstanding and the accompanying weather delays prevented Anglo-Austrian agreement on a strategic plan for 1795 and the conclusion of a full alliance until after the 1795 campaign had already begun. The delays and missteps in the efforts to unite the British and Austrian war efforts in 1795 bore a strong resemblance to the similar difficulties they had encountered in 1794.[113]

The absence of a centralized coalition headquarters like that proposed by Pitt's ministry in the winter of 1792–93 continued to haunt the coalition members as they relied solely on sluggish and disjointed bilateral diplomacy to coordinate multilateral operations. In the autumn of 1794, each member of the coalition conducted operations in pursuit of goals largely disconnected from those of the other members. Isolated British and Dutch troops in the Netherlands suffered repeated defeats as the links to Austrian and Prussian armies on which they depended for support dissolved. Vienna moved troops to Galicia and began negotiating the Third Partition of Poland with Russia while Berlin opened peace negotiations with the French and shifted its focus to defending Prussian Poland from anticipated Austrian intrigues. In this atmosphere of division, Pitt clung desperately but without success to his goal of creating a broad collective security system to unite all states at war with France in a single common cause. Conversely, Grenville and the Portland Whigs began pushing for a more selective pursuit of alliances with Austria and Russia and a strategy more wedded to the counterrevolution while Dundas urged greater focus on colonial campaigns to secure and expand British assets overseas. Events in 1795 would initially exacerbate this division before ultimately forcing Pitt to make some concessions to the pragmatism of the other members of the Cabinet.[114]

CHAPTER 9

THE PEACE OF BASEL AND THE NEW TRIPLE ALLIANCE, 1795

As Prussia and Spain moved toward peace and the Netherlands collapsed before a relentless French onslaught, efforts to forge bonds with new allies gained urgency as a means to salvage rather than strengthen the coalition. Austria and Russia formed the new pillars for the system Pitt sought to create. He also sought to exploit opportunities to rally a strong counterrevolutionary movement. Following the evacuation of British forces from Flanders, cooperation with French rebels offered the best prospect of aggregating sufficient strength to sustain a renewed British presence on the Continent. Negotiations to reshape the coalition in 1795 and develop a new plan of operations suffered from the pressures of trying to prevent Prussia and Spain from making peace with France while at the same time attempting to wrest Austrian and Russian attention from Poland. Pitt's reluctance to abandon a multilateral approach in favor of more targeted alliances began to fracture the unity of the Cabinet. In addition, his refusal to embrace partition politics in eastern Europe slowed diplomatic progress, preventing the new coalition from taking shape until the summer of 1795. Amid this uncertainty, effective military planning proved impossible, and the hasty attempt to coordinate Austrian offensives with a royalist uprising and an Anglo-émigré landing in western France failed. By the end of the year, British diplomacy secured the new Triple Alliance with Austria and Russia, but the Allies' best hopes of combining their resources to achieve victory had already foundered.

In the winter of 1794–95, the perfect storm of the termination of the British subsidy, French and Polish military success, and potentially hostile Austro-Russian negotiations persuaded Frederick William to heed the advice of his ministers and reduce his obligations through a separate peace with France. His decision gained urgency after a conference between Russian, Austrian, and

Prussian ministers in St. Petersburg on 19 December 1794 definitively revealed a Russian disposition to favor Vienna over Berlin in the Third Partition. Rumors of Franco-Prussian negotiations circulated almost immediately following the cancellation of the subsidy. By 20 December, the new British envoy to Berlin, Sir Arthur Paget, referenced these negotiations as something already known to the Cabinet and projected that they would be successful.[1]

In fact, Möllendorff had been in communication with his French counterparts on his own initiative during the 1794 campaign. After the Thermidorian Reaction caused peace with the French Republic to seem more attainable, he dispatched an envoy to negotiate with the local French ambassador in Basel, François de Barthélemy, under pretense of discussing the exchange of prisoners.[2] Official negotiations began in December. Frederick William sent the sickly former Prussian ambassador to France, Wilhelm Bernhard von der Goltz, to discuss terms of peace. The Prussian king initially hoped to obtain an extended truce and salvage some prestige by establishing a basis for future peace between France and the Holy Roman Empire.[3]

Paget reported these developments to London with concern. In addition to Goltz's mission, Paget took note of an additional emissary having been sent to Paris with a rumored commission of making peace and a subsequent Franco-Prussian alliance. In response to his complaints that these measures violated Prussia's agreements with Britain, Paget received unsatisfactory responses.

> It is ... asserted by this ministry that His Prussian Majesty, far from thinking of entering into any separate compact with France, is ... solely actuated by the desire of ... putting an end to the war and thereby consolidating a permanent and honorable peace for himself and his allies, and that the sole object of Count Goltz's mission is to concert with some of the princes and circles of the Empire for the furtherance of these views."[4]

Although the Prussian explanation partially addressed the issue of collective security within the bounds of Holy Roman Empire, Paget continued to press in vain for the necessity of a broader multilateral solution. He wrote, "I have endeavored to show that the only means of attaining this desirable end would be to establish a general and well-directed concert among the belligerent powers backed by the most vigorous preparations for the continuation of the war, but I meet no sort of proposal tending to the execution of such a measure."[5]

Despite Paget's frustration with the Prussian communication, the course of negotiations at Basel seemed to support the moderate Prussian assertions. Before his death on 5 February 1795, Goltz achieved a Franco-Prussian armistice, but the French demanded more for formal peace than Frederick William was willing to concede. Disgruntled by the French demands for a full alliance,

Frederick William conveyed to Malmesbury his desire to resume active participation in the war if he could receive a new British subsidy to support these efforts. Reinforcing the king's second thoughts, the Anglophile Karl August von Hardenberg replaced Goltz at Basel. Hardenberg also wished to resume the war and pledged to Malmesbury to procrastinate in his mission to give time for fresh Anglo-Prussian negotiations. Malmesbury doubtfully forwarded these approaches to London while similar reports arrived from Berlin.[6]

These reports sharply divided the British government, setting Pitt's desire to rescue the Anglo-Prussian connection he had established in 1788 and Dundas's preference for having Continental powers do the Continental fighting against the disillusionment that Grenville, George III, and Parliament felt toward Prussia as an alliance partner. The question of whether to renew approaches to Prussia as a partner in the larger coalition or abandon Berlin to focus solely on developing relationships with Austria and Russia split the Cabinet.[7] Pitt took an idealistic view, seeing no need to choose between the two approaches and clinging to his ambition that a universal collective security system would overcome all such petty jealousies. The Triple Alliance of 1788 represented the first incarnation of this endeavor, and as much as Anglo-Prussian differences had weakened that bond since its inception, it theoretically remained in place. Pitt was reluctant to abandon this diplomatic foundation entirely, preferring to aggregate new links with the hope of combining them all into a single system as mutual guarantors of the communal peace settlement after victory over France. Any state making a separate peace would undermine this aim, so the prime minister placed a high priority on keeping Prussia in the war, even at the expense of complicating relations with Austria and Russia.[8]

Pitt proposed renewing the 1794 subsidy agreement in modified and simplified terms. In return for an army of 60,000 men operating in the Low Countries, he proposed to pay £1,600,000 per year in monthly installments. To circumvent the difficulty that the ambiguity of command of the army had created in 1794, Pitt proposed large bonus payments for achieving British defined territorial objectives. He offered £400,000 for crossing the Yssel River, £400,000 more for pushing the front back to the Waal River, and £1,200,000 for completely restoring Orangist control over Dutch territory.[9]

Dundas supported this proposal on the pragmatic grounds that he did not believe victory possible without Prussian support. He argued:

> The exertions of the next campaign will be sadly crippled indeed if we are not in some shape or other able to bring forward a respectable Prussian force to act from Westphalia for the recovery of Holland. Without this exertion it may perhaps be a safe campaign, but it will neither be a brilliant nor a decisive one, and

if we should unfortunately be disappointed in our hopes founded on the joint effect of the interior distress of France and the offensive operations on the coast, we shall then at the end of the campaign be under the necessity of making peace in the same ignominious state we now are in at the beginning of it.[10]

Dundas preferred to cast the broadest net possible for the 1795 campaign to bring every available resource to bear against France. He feared that the alternative course might result in the other members of the coalition accepting separate peace with France and leaving the British to do the same from a weak and isolated position.

In contrast, Grenville led the opposition to this, espousing a different pragmatic perspective of abandoning a demonstrably failed connection in favor of new links with greater potential. Grenville found Pitt and Dundas's willingness to attempt another Prussian subsidy difficult to comprehend. He could not understand why they expected the Prussian government to respond to a subsidy agreement in 1795 any better than in 1794. The military situation was considerably worse, and, unlike the previous year, the Prussians were known to be in negotiations for peace with the French. In addition, he observed that the failure of the 1794 subsidy had damaged support for the war in Parliament, and he cautioned that another such disappointment would irrevocably undermine confidence in the government's handling of the war. He also believed that a renewal of the Prussian subsidy would alienate Austria and Russia. Grenville pinned his hopes for ultimate victory in the war with France on consolidating the Anglo-Austrian relationship and bringing in Russia as a full partner as well. Tensions in Poland suggested to Grenville that renewal of the Anglo-Prussian connection would upset Vienna and St. Petersburg as it had in 1785, 1788, and 1791. He contended that "the hope of uniting those three courts in one common system is one which neither our past experience nor any view of their present situation and disposition towards each other seem to justify." He believed that Vienna and St. Petersburg would resist the inclusion of Prussia in any new system, thereby making overtures to Prussia counterproductive rather than simply useless.[11]

Grenville acknowledged the enormous utility Britain would derive from the full cooperation of the Prussian army but doubted that any British offer could secure Prussia's vigorous activity. He contended that no amount of money could motivate the Prussians to shoulder the burden of a war from which they stood to gain nothing more than British money to cover their expenses. In Grenville's view, financial support could yield positive results only when allocated to a power fully committed to the war for independent reasons, such as Austria, or when conducted on a contractual basis that yielded total control of the forces purchased as in Britain's arrangements with the minor German states. George III echoed these sentiments and conveyed his disapproval of Pitt's new scheme.[12]

Although not blind to these considerations, Pitt remained convinced that renewed Prussian participation in the war offered the best means of achieving Britain's formal war aims. In 1793, the British had gone to war to defend the sovereignty and security of the United Provinces, and Prussian armies offered the best chance of recovering Dutch territories, if not Austrian Flanders as well. This geostrategic logic had underpinned the 1788 Triple Alliance, and it remained persuasive to Pitt. In a broader sense, he wished to preserve that system as a foundation for the broader collective security system that he sought to forge in the midst of the war. The prime minister acknowledged Grenville's argument that Austria's overall commitment to the war seemed more reliable and therefore more deserving of British financial support. However, the Austrian abandonment of Belgium in the autumn of 1794 demonstrated that the British could not necessarily rely on Austrian armies to secure British objectives in the Low Countries. Without a stark contrast between the reliability of the two German powers, Pitt preferred to attempt to reconcile them rather than choosing one or the other.[13]

The debate over the new Prussian subsidy continued from February to April. With Dundas's support, Pitt's view gained ascendancy in the Cabinet and over George III on 1 March, prompting an unimpressed Grenville to offer his resignation, effective at the end of that Parliamentary session. However, more reports arrived after the Cabinet meeting of 1 March that undermined confidence in Prussian intentions. The Cabinet cancelled its support for the subsidy, and Grenville withdrew his offer of resignation accordingly.[14]

The idea faded until early April when new information from Malmesbury and another new envoy at Berlin, Henry Spencer, suggested that Prussian attitudes had taken a British turn. The appearance of an improving chance of securing Prussian support by subsidy coincided with an extreme need for Prussian support to salvage the military situation. Pitt needed the Prussian army to undo the forced evacuation of the British and Dutch armies from the Netherlands. Extremely cold temperatures during the winter of 1794–95 had frozen Dutch waterways solid, largely nullifying their recourse to inundating the countryside as a defensive measure. This had allowed the French to continue the campaign in the Netherlands through the winter, forcing York and the British army back to Germany. By the time Pitt received the new Prussian overtures, Dutch revolutionaries and French armies had forced William V to flee the United Provinces and transformed the country into the Batavian Republic.[15]

In this situation, a Cabinet meeting on 8 April 1795 resolved to offer to Prussia the new subsidy as initially conceived by Pitt in February. Notably, this offer added to Pitt's original plan a pledge to maintain a corps of 25,000 British and Hanoverian troops and German mercenaries to support the Prussian army. Pitt remained dedicated to maintaining a direct British presence and influence on the Continent, resisting the temptation to abandon vexing Continental operations in favor of a solely maritime strategy. Grenville again protested against placing any faith in Prussia. Rather than resign this time, he simply refused to have anything to do with the measure.[16] Therefore, on 10 April, Dundas dispatched instructions in Grenville's stead to Spencer at Berlin, authorizing him to propose Pitt's subsidy plan. The proposal arrived too late. After receiving no indications from the British of a disposition to provide a subsidy, Hardenberg signed a peace treaty with Barthélemy on 5 April, removing Prussia from the war.[17]

Frederick William's willingness to delay the peace also diminished as the fate of Poland remained ominously unsettled from his perspective. His negotiator at St. Petersburg had failed to secure any promises from either the Austrians and Russians.[18] In fact, the Austrian envoy sent to St. Petersburg to negotiate the Polish business had signed agreements on 3 January with the Russian ministers regarding the Austrian and Russian shares of the Third Partition. They concealed this from the Prussians and agreed to defend their gains from Berlin if necessary. Frederick William and his ministers suspected this and sought peace to prepare for any eventuality.[19]

The Franco-Prussian Treaty of Basel removed Prussia from the War of the First Coalition and effectively ended British hopes of securing a Prussian army by subsidy. While the British viewed the treaty as a betrayal, its terms reflected the views Prussian ministers had expressed to Paget in December 1794. Beyond simply establishing peace and subsequent neutrality, Hardenberg secured for the states of northern Germany the same relatively equitable terms for restoration of prisoners and commerce. The French also agreed to accept Prussian mediation in peace negotiations with any other state of the Holy Roman Empire. Frederick William's attempt to stand as guardian of the empire even as he abandoned a *Reichskrieg* received further clarification on 17 May 1795 with the publication of the secret articles of the original treaty. These secret articles established all of northern Germany as a zone of neutrality closed to the operations of any belligerent in the War of the First Coalition. Hardenberg pledged that Prussia would maintain a corps of observation to enforce the neutral zone. In return for peace and respecting Prussia's efforts to protect northern Germany, the French insisted on continuing to occupy Prussian and imperial territories on the left bank of the Rhine. Although the French clearly intended to annex these territories, the treaty deferred formalizing any annexation and compensation of dispossessed princes, including Frederick William, to peace negotiations between France and representatives of the Holy Roman Empire. The Treaty of Basel ultimately allowed Frederick William to pose as the protector of the Holy Roman Empire while simultaneously freeing him from the war with France. Thus absolved of his obligations to the west, he could take a stronger stand in the terminal partition of Poland.[20]

Although the Franco-Prussian treaty specified other German states as targets for Prussian mediation, Spain actually proved the first to take advantage of this option to make peace with France. After a brief respite during the winter, in 1795 the campaigns in the Pyrenees had resumed to Spain's disadvantage as French armies pressed into Navarre and Catalonia. Facing defeat in a fight to defend the son of a dead king as part of a coalition that appeared to care little for Spain, Godoy became convinced of the need for peace.[21] In addition, changes in the French government appeared to improve the prospects of obtaining an acceptable peace through negotiation. The Thermidorian coup on 27 and 28 July 1794 had shattered the radical Committee of Public Safety's stranglehold on French policy, allowing more moderate voices in the National Convention to be heard.[22] In this context, Godoy sent the former Spanish ambassador to Poland, Don Domingo d'Yriarte, to Basel to open negotiations for peace with the French ambassador there, Barthélemy.[23]

Yriarte negotiated a Franco-Spanish treaty in conference with Hardenberg and Barthélemy between 16 May and 22 July 1795. The primary points of negotiation involved territorial exchanges and the future of the French Bourbons in the person of the young Louis XVII. For the Spanish, the war had always been one of dynastic concerns, and Yriarte doggedly pressed the French to release the prince into Spanish custody or agree to his establishment in some minor principality. Barthélemy just as persistently refused these demands, initially threatening to deadlock negotiations. However, on 8 June 1795, Louis XVII died in the custody of the revolutionaries from a combination of his own poor health and extensive mistreatment from his captors following his mother's death. While the prince's death evoked anger and sorrow in Madrid, it also cleared one of the primary obstacles to peace. The French made no difficulties about turning Louis XVI's daughter over to Spain, and without dynastic concerns at play, Yriarte and Barthélemy quickly reached an agreement on the exchange of territory. The Spanish conceded San Domingo to the French in return for the restitution of territory conquered by French armies in Navarre and Catalonia. Barthélemy only insisted that individuals and villages who had welcomed the French advance should not face retribution for their actions after the restoration of Spanish authority. Like the Prussian treaty, the Franco-Spanish Treaty of Basel contained an offer of Spanish mediation to secure peace between France and Portugal, Sardinia, and the other states of Italy.[24]

Through their peace negotiations at Basel with both Prussia and Spain, the French undermined British efforts to unify the coalition in northern and southern Europe. Ironically, the French enjoyed greater success in seeking multilateral agreement at Basel than Pitt's best efforts since 1791. In 1792 and 1793, Grenville's diplomacy failed to persuade Berlin and Madrid to attend a congress to establish agreement on the future of Europe during and after the war, yet the French achieved almost exactly that at Basel, albeit under duress. In the north, no major power respected Prussia's line of neutrality, but several of the smaller German states did use it as an excuse to abandon the war. On 28 August 1795, Hesse-Kassel became the first state to seize this opportunity by concluding a separate peace with France at Basel and withdrawing from the Reichskrieg. More states followed suit in 1796. George III even consented to Hanoverian accession on the prudential grounds of the impossibility of Hanover standing alone against both France and Prussia's Army of Observation.[25] The Spanish treaty had less immediate influence on the diplomatic landscape. On 9 February 1795, the Grand Duke of Tuscany made peace with France, but neither Portugal nor the other Italian states showed any inclination to take advantage of Spanish offers of mediation despite a dismal military situation.[26]

Beyond its diplomatic impact, the Peace of Basel also struck at the two primary avenues of British influence in Europe. Through the Dutch Crisis of 1787 and subsequent Triple Alliance, Pitt had anchored Britain to the Continent through a Dutch alliance and a supplementary Prussian alliance collectively supported by George III's control of the Electorate of Hanover. After the outbreak of war in 1793, the addition of a tenuous connection with Austria further supported this British connection to the Continent by virtue of Vienna's control of Belgium. French conquest of the Low Countries and the Prussian-led neutrality of northern Germany effectively severed those links. Similarly, Pitt had endeavored to forge new links to the Continent in southern Europe during the war through diplomatic connections with Sardinia, Spain, Naples, and Austria and through direct British occupation of first Toulon and then Corsica. The Franco-Spanish peace rendered Britain's access to its Mediterranean connections through the Strait of Gibraltar significantly less secure.

Ultimately, the cumulative Peace of Basel represented the failure of British diplomacy to capitalize on the limited diplomatic successes of 1793 to build a more cohesive coalition against France. Although the British had secured conventions of cooperation with every state at war with France in 1793, they failed to unite them in a single alliance to resolve outstanding suspicions and coordinate measures for prosecuting the war. Without a prior consensus on war aims and plans of operation, those matters fell to bilateral negotiations, which led to delays and complications in continued efforts to build a broader consensus. This absence of a larger multilateral agreement undermined Britain's relationship with all of its partners and catastrophically so with both Spain and Prussia.

As Prussia and Spain withdrew from the war, Austria increased in importance as the lynchpin that connected operations and diplomacy in Italy, Germany, and eastern Europe. The Cabinet had recognized the importance of an Austrian connection to wage an effective war against France since the beginning of the conflict. Before French mass mobilization, Austria had possessed the largest army in Europe, and Habsburg rule in Belgium gave Vienna a shared interest with London in defending the Low Countries from French aggression. However, from 1792 through 1794, the course the Cabinet charted to secure an Austrian alliance had first passed through The Hague and Berlin. Rather than form a new and separate alliance, Pitt had sought to bring Austria into a broader system by reviving the defunct Triple Alliance with the Dutch and Prussians and merging that with the Austro-Prussian alliance through the common link of Prussia. The animosity between Berlin and Vienna generated by the Second Partition of Poland and subsequent Russo-Prussian campaigns in Poland crippled this avenue of approach, and the Third Partition and Peace of Basel destroyed it.[27]

Allied planning remained largely vague and noncommittal during the early months of 1795 while Anglo-Austrian and Anglo-Russian negotiations plodded along and Prussia, Spain, and the United Provinces moved toward peace with France. The Cabinet concentrated on maximizing British assets by extricating the British army from the Continent via Bremen and probing for openings to exploit new counterrevolutionary connections. They planned for a British expedition to western France but remained skeptical of the Breton, Lyonnais, and Parisian royalists with whom they had established contact in 1794. In a plan of campaign for 1795 that Dundas provided to the Cabinet on 11 February 1795, he considered the possibility of being "disappointed in our hopes founded on the joint effect of the interior distress of France and the offensive operations on the coast." He recommended taking any necessary measures to secure a Prussian army for the 1795 campaign to avoid relying too heavily on counterrevolutionary activity.[28] As late as May 1795, Grenville cautioned Wickham that an extensive and vigorous rebellion "cannot be reckoned upon in the formation of any plans, though it would undoubtedly be highly useful that the Allies should if possible be in a situation to profit [from] such a circumstance if it should occur."[29] Nevertheless, Pitt advocated the counterrevolutionary opportunities, Dundas embraced the Breton expedition in his plans, and Grenville encouraged Wickham to support émigrés and rebels as part of the war effort.[30]

Counterrevolutionary opportunities appeared to decline early in 1795, vindicating Dundas's skepticism. In February, Breton guerillas signed a truce with republican commanders, diminishing prospects of success in that quarter. On the other side of France, Wickham expressed confidence in the existence of widespread discontent in central and southern France that would explode at the approach of Condé's forces, but such an operation required Austrian backing.[31] Thugut alleged that Austria planned to use Condé as part of their offensive across the Rhine to raise the counterrevolution in Franche-Comté and so refused British offers to place that army on London's payroll. The Cabinet remained skeptical of the Austrian will and capacity to follow through on their planned offensive, and Grenville urged Eden to renew the request in nearly every dispatch.[32]

Concern about Austrian intentions and abilities grew out of the repeated Austrian delays in settling the aforementioned loan convention early in 1795. In one letter to Eden, Grenville complained, "I observe indeed in your letter to Sir Charles Whitworth that you state the court of Vienna to have already agreed to the finance part of [the loan convention], but . . . no such intimation has yet been given here, and the whole of that subject [is] still in a state of uncertainty, which is in the highest degree inconvenient to the public service."[33] He enumerated these inconveniences, including the inability to take any further steps to secure the money for the loan and the similar inability to develop military plans with any certainty regarding Austrian action. To save as much time as possible, Grenville dispatched a proposal for a defensive alliance to Eden on 24 April 1795 with instructions to conclude it as quickly as possible after finally completing the loan negotiations.[34]

While poor weather and misunderstandings had obstructed Anglo-Austrian agreement and military planning during the winter of 1794–95, Anglo-Russian negotiations continued at St. Petersburg.[35] Talks proceeded slowly at first as Catherine maintained the same coy disposition she had throughout 1793, but two events persuaded the empress to come to terms with the British. First, the third Polish partition agreement signed between Austria and Russia largely relieved Catherine's concerns for her southwestern frontiers. In July 1794, Catherine had invited both Vienna and Berlin to send delegates to St. Petersburg to discuss a final partition. Both powers had complied, but the Prussian envoy quit the negotiations after hearing Catherine's proposal, which favored Austria. The Austrian and Russian delegates thereupon concluded a bilateral arrangement on 3 January 1795 along the lines that Catherine proposed, and they pledged to uphold it by force. They agreed to invite the Prussians to accede to the new partition only after the Austrian and Russian courts ratified the agreement. This

Austro-Russian treaty not only provided the two countries with new boundaries but also secured Austrian acceptance of the Second Partition and pledged Austria to support Russia against the Ottoman Empire if necessary.[36]

Second, the military collapse in Flanders began to truly alarm St. Petersburg. From December 1794 to February 1795, French armies overran Dutch defenses and ejected the British army from the Netherlands. In January, William V fled to Britain, and the French occupied Amsterdam. London began to view the United Provinces as effectively lost, looking to the safety of the British expedition rather than making any hopeless attempt to defend the Dutch. On 8 February, the Cabinet resolved to withdraw the British expedition, leaving only its cavalry to act with Britain's German auxiliaries in support of the Austrian armies farther south. Perhaps the most dramatic and most concerning episode of the collapse occurred on 23 January 1795 when French hussars captured the main Dutch fleet frozen in port at Den Helder. This loss made the British less averse to receiving Russian aid in the form of ships rather than troops, and it made the Russians more eager to provide that aid.[37]

Thus, finding the Russian court agreeable, Whitworth managed to conclude a provisional defensive alliance with Russia on 18 February 1795. By the terms of the treaty, both powers agreed to defend each other from any new attack on any of their European or colonial possessions. The British pledged to assist Russia with twelve ships of the line while the Russians promised the support of 12,000 men. The public terms of the treaty provided no help for Britain in the French war, but a secret article committed the Russians to send a fleet of twelve ships of the line and six frigates to cooperate with the Royal Navy in the Atlantic.[38]

Significantly, the twentieth article of the Anglo-Russian alliance established the willingness of both the British and Russians to invite other states to accede to the alliance. The rationale for this emerged in a letter from Grenville to Eden on 10 March 1795. In response to rumors of the finalization of a Franco-Prussian peace, Grenville wrote to alleviate potential Austrian fears on that count. He explained "that [the Anglo-Russian treaty] if favorably improved by Austria may lead to the establishment of a permanent and solid political system between this country and the two imperial courts by which the influence of Prussia and of France even in case of an intimate union between those powers would be decidedly counteracted." Grenville proposed that "after the signature of the [Anglo-Russian and Anglo-Austrian alliances, they] should by some general article or agreement be consolidated into one system of union and defensive alliance by which the Three Courts should guarantee to each other all their possessions such as they shall stand after the conclusion of a peace made by common consent." He also explained that the British had agreed to exclude the French war as a casus foederis for the Anglo-Russian alliance on the condition that the Russians send to Austria the corps of 12,000 men that they would have owed the British without that exclusion.[39] Beyond this, Whitworth had instructions to secure an additional larger Russian corps by subsidy to serve either on the Rhine or in British coastal operations. However, he found Catherine persistently averse to this measure as long as there appeared a possibility of a Prussian challenge to the Third Partition of Poland.[40]

Eden and Thugut finally signed a convention on 4 May that stipulated a loan of £4,600,000 and a total Austrian army strength of 200,000 men. After further negotiations, Eden also secured an Anglo-Austrian alliance on 20 May based on the proposal Grenville had sent him on 24 April.[41] The alliance provided for mutual support in case of attack and included a reciprocal guarantee of territory, including any gained in the future peace with France. A separate article of the Anglo-Austrian treaty also pledged the two powers to invite Russia to accede to the alliance to form a unitary triple alliance, much like the twentieth article of the Anglo-Russian treaty.[42]

Thus, fortunes seemed to change in April and May. Despite the Franco-Prussian peace of 5 April, planning for the year's campaign accelerated. The Anglo-Austrian alliance enabled London to count on the continued activity of the Austrian army. From Berne, Wickham reported growing unrest in France. Contacts in Brittany that had gone silent after the February truce began to re-emerge and express eagerness to rise again.[43] Even the negative events of April and May reduced the variables that clouded the decision-making process. The French had effected a revolution in the United Provinces, installing their clients, the exiled Patriots, as leaders of the new Batavian Republic. This new government made peace with France at the expense of some border territory, and promptly rejoined the war as a French ally, thereby eliminating the immediate need or opportunity to revive a campaign in the Low Countries.[44]

In these circumstances, the Cabinet tried to coordinate the remaining strategic threads into a plan of operations. Grenville exhorted the Austrians to take the offensive across the Rhine and into Franche-Comte in conjunction with Condé's army. To this end, he sent Colonel Charles Craufurd to Condé with cash and instructions to coordinate his operations with Wickham's royalist contacts in Lyons.[45] The foreign secretary also pressed for the Austro-Sardinian forces to support Condé with a major offensive on the Italian front.[46] Simultaneous with these offensives, the Royal Navy would carry another émigré army under Puisaye to the Quiberon Peninsula on the southern coast of Brittany to establish a base from which the British would incite and support a royalist

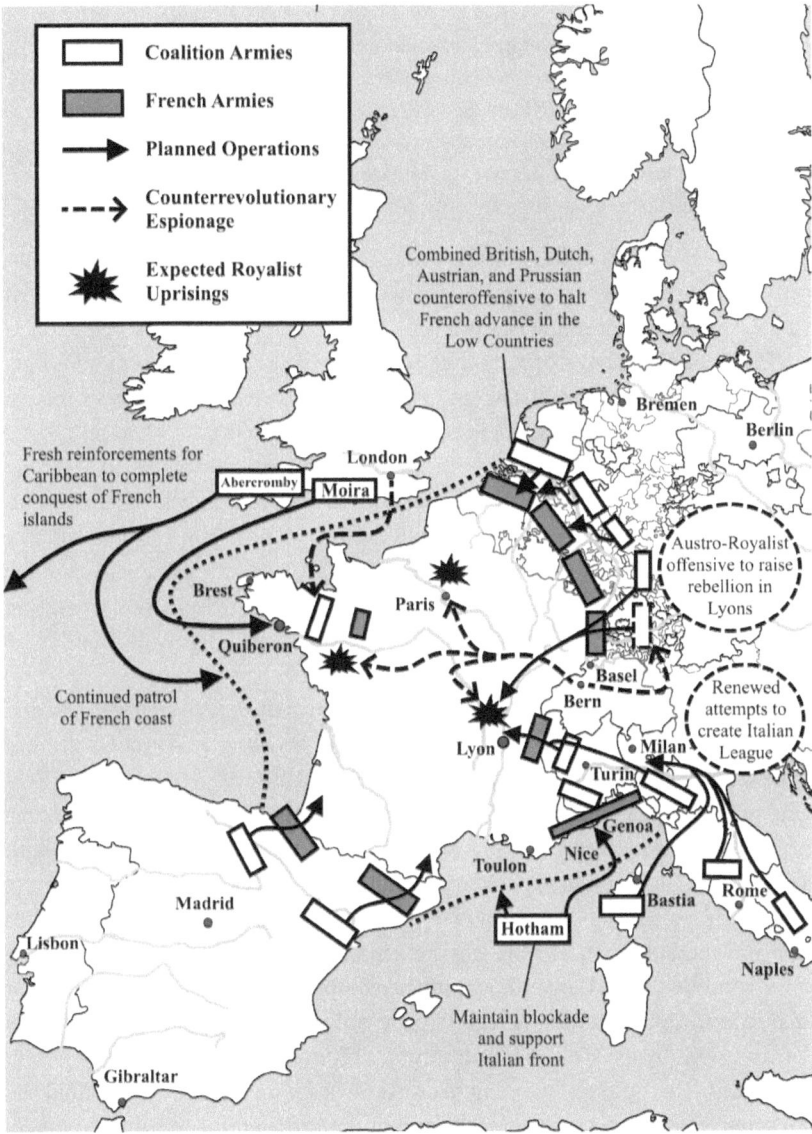

British plans for 1795

uprising. British ministers hoped that their landing would prevent the French from reinforcing their armies on the Rhine while the Austrian attack would bolster royalist confidence and strengthen the uprisings throughout France. Clear and prompt communication would be key to the effective execution of this plan as Grenville explained to Eden:

However general may be the engagements of the treaty now negotiating between the two courts and however impracticable it may be for this country to cooperate with Austria upon the continent under the present circumstances, the necessity of full communication and concert between the two governments is not on that account less apparent whether with a view to the general success of the common cause or to the direction of such separate efforts as both parties may be enabled to make against the common enemy.[47]

The Cabinet discussed the overall plan extensively throughout April and May until, encouraged by Eden's promise that Thugut had ordered Clerfayt to advance, they set it in motion in June.[48]

The Allied offensive of 1795 that commenced in June did not unfold according to the plan the British government had developed in the spring. In Britain itself, preparations for the émigré expedition to Brittany had proceeded quickly. An act to regularize the formation of émigré regiments in 1794 had produced dividends, providing the prospective expedition with a readily available core. To bring the expedition up to sufficient strength, Puisaye issued a call to arms to French exiles throughout Europe, and the British government sought volunteers among French prisoners of war. On 17 June, the expedition sailed with a strength of approximately 3,500 men, reaching its destination by the end of the month.[49]

On the Rhine, Thugut ordered the Austrian armies to take the offensive and raise the French siege of Luxembourg. Despite bristling at the suggestion of Cornwallis as commander in chief in 1794, Thugut agreed with the dismal British assessment of Coburg's leadership and replaced him with Clerfayt in August of 1794. However, Clerfayt's appointment failed to produce the change that both Vienna and London desired. From the autumn of 1794 through the spring of 1795, the new commander retreated despite orders from Thugut to hold his position and counterattack. In June 1795, he remained stationary, complaining of the poor condition of his men and insufficient supplies.[50] The British government shared in the blame for the lack of urgency, only informing Clerfayt of the plans for the amphibious royalist expedition on 12 June, less than one week before it embarked. The Cabinet had long planned for such an expedition and told the Austrians as much several times before, but the British ministers did not finally commit to the operation until early June. Thus, both Vienna and London based their own operations on only partial knowledge of those of their ally. On 22 June, to the dismay of both the British and Austrian governments, Luxembourg capitulated to the French, and still the Austrian forces remained inactive.[51]

Partially in anticipation of Clerfayt's unwillingness to take the initiative, London hoped to use Condé's army to jump start the Rhine campaign and spark a new revolt in Lyons.[52] Craufurd pressed for an attack with increasing urgency throughout June as the Breton expedition took shape. He forwarded thousands of pounds to strengthen and motivate the émigré army, but Condé fundamentally lacked the strength or the will to attack without Austrian support or approval. Despite urging from London and orders from Vienna, Clerfayt refused to advance. His concerns about Prussian intentions following the Peace of Basel dominated his conversations with Craufurd. Clerfayt complained that the Prussians maintained a menacing posture both in the redeployment of substantial forces to Silesia and in their pressure on the other imperial states to come to terms with France. He also reported (and Craufurd corroborated it) that Prussian agents were purchasing already scarce supplies to sell to the French. This rendered the strained logistical situation of the Austrian army even more precarious, leading Clerfayt to prefer to maintain a defensive posture.[53]

Even as initial hopes for a major revolt in central France supported by an Austrian offensive diminished, the British considered new possibilities for unifying the disparate components of the counterrevolution into a single, powerful movement. This required smoothing over differences between the various counterrevolutionary factions, ranging from pure absolutists to moderate constitutionalists, over the future government of France. It also required Britain to treat the leadership of the counterrevolution as a diplomatic partner rather than simply a military asset. The government began to consider establishing formal relations with the self-proclaimed regent, Provence, to coordinate with him terms for a moderate and flexible restoration and to obtain his sanction for British-sponsored émigré operations. The death of the imprisoned Louis XVII on 8 June increased the motivation for British ministers to reformulate their policy toward Provence, who proclaimed himself Louis XVIII immediately after learning of the child's death. In June, the British government prepared a diplomatic mission to treat with Provence and attempt to reconcile his views with the more moderate counterrevolutionaries. Concurrently, the Cabinet invited his brother, the Count of Artois, to join the expedition to Brittany to bolster its appeal and soothe the misgivings of some émigrés about serving alongside what many viewed as a peasant revolt.[54]

In July, the British plan of campaign culminated and failed. On 3 July, the royalist expedition secured a coastal fort on the Quiberon Peninsula in cooperation with royalist rebels.[55] By 10 July, local forces mustered from the countryside numbered approximately 4,000, doubling Britain's émigré units. Despite this successful start, disputes over command of the expedition and the best approach to the campaign caused the royalist forces to sit idle for five days. Puisaye officially held overall command in the British-ordained structure of the army, but émigré officers and rival rebel leaders challenged his authority.[56] Appeals for cooperation met with either reluctance or refusal. In theory, Artois could have imposed unity by his presence, but he joined the Breton operations too late to save the Quiberon expedition, only accepting the British invitation in early July and arriving in Britain on 7 August.[57]

On 16 July, Puisaye attempted to attack the republican army commanded by General Louis Lazare Hoche, but confusion in the command structure and poor coordination led to only one of several intended columns attacking. Hoche repelled this assault without difficulty, and only British naval fire prevented his counterattack from destroying the royalist force. Undaunted, Puisaye planned a second attack for 20 July after receiving 1,500 more émigrés from the British fleet, but a French attack on the night of 19 July preempted this and effectively destroyed the expedition. The cause of this debacle was the questionable decision to include volunteers from the French prisoners of war. Some betrayed the expedition, informing republican forces of weaknesses in the fort that the émigrés used as their base. Some of the royalists, including Puisaye, escaped to the British fleet, but many surrendered only to be executed a few days later.[58]

Meanwhile, the British government prepared to send a force of 9,400 British reinforcements under General Moira to support the landing and secure other coastal islands as supply points. The lateness of this reinforcement arose due to its source. Moira assembled this expedition from the British army that had returned from the Continent—what had been York's expedition to Flanders and were now the only troops available. These troops had embarked from Bremen in April and arrived in Britain considerably understrength and in dismal condition from their disastrous winter retreat. The government spent May and June replenishing the ranks of these units and restoring sufficient discipline to make them fit for active service.[59] News of the original expedition's catastrophic defeat on 20 July and the Franco-Spanish peace on 22 July called into question the wisdom of sending reinforcements. By the time Artois arrived in Britain to join Moira's reinforcements on 7 August, the Cabinet was questioning the value of sending any more resources to western France.[60]

As royalist fortunes rose and fell over the course of July in the west, Clerfayt remained passive, holding the Austrian army in a defensive position. By the end of July, Thugut lost faith in Clerfayt altogether and transferred the majority of his army to the more energetic septuagenarian, General Dagobert Sigmund von Wurmser, with clear instructions to take the offensive.[61] Farther south, Austro-Sardinian forces launched an offensive in the Ligurian Alps. At the same time, Grenville belatedly suggested that these forces attack Savoy instead to support French royalists in Franche-Comté in lieu of any decisive action from the Austrians on the Rhine.[62] Beyond the inconvenience of reorienting an offensive already in motion, the Austrians and Sardinians preferred the assault

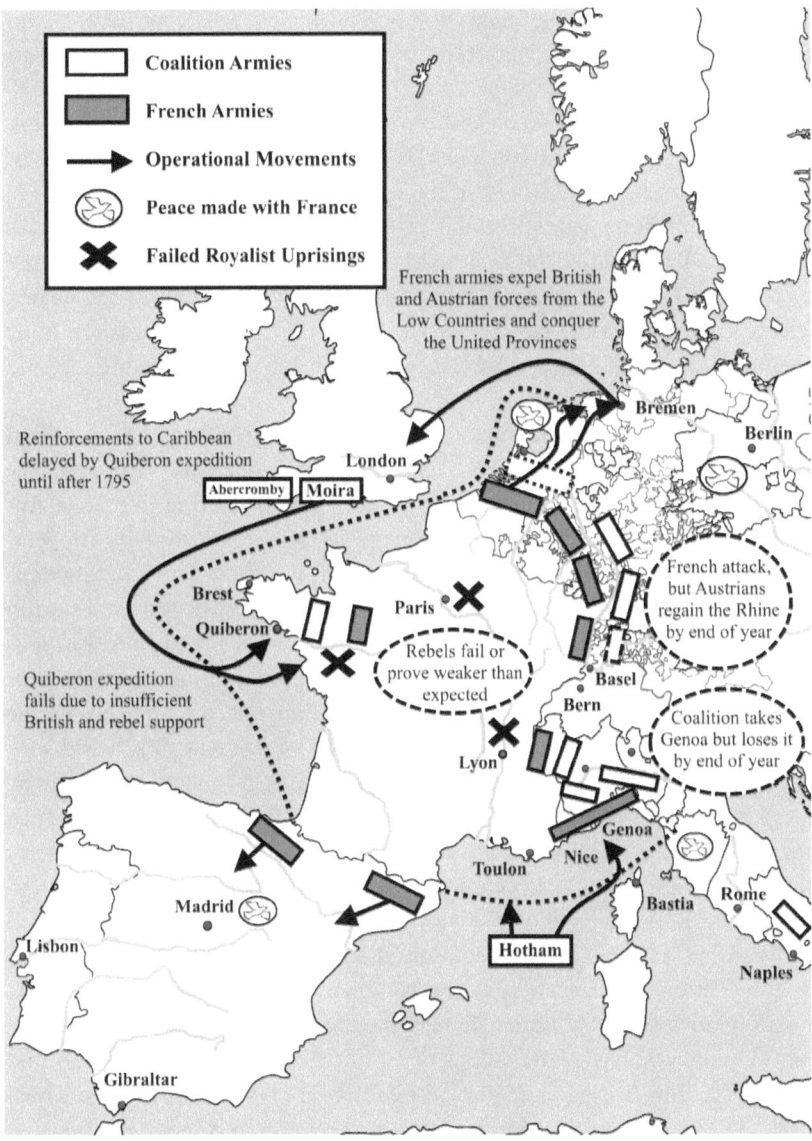

Operations of 1795

on the coast to shield their vulnerable southern flank and to gain the advantage of British naval support. Initial successes seemed to confirm this decision and destroyed any British hope of a redeployment for an assault on Savoy in 1795 in support of an uprising in Lyon; Grenville correspondingly ceased to advise such a maneuver.[63]

Following the disappointments of July, British plans for a coordinated campaign that incorporated counterrevolutionary assets unraveled beyond repair in August and September. Moira set sail at the end of August with Artois, half of his originally planned force, and conservative orders. His new instructions limited his operations to coastal islands and excluded a landing on the mainland. Moira resigned in protest of his loss of resources and control; without him, the expedition sought a viable target in vain for most of the month of September. By the end of the month, this small force had secured Île d'Yeu, and a summons from Artois yielded partisans ready to cooperate on the nearby French coast. However, Artois refused to undertake the personal risk of joining them. In November, the expedition received orders to abandon the attempt and return to Britain.[64]

Efforts to coordinate the counterrevolution from other directions also fared poorly. The Cabinet dispatched Earl George Macartney to treat with Provence in July, and he reached the prospective French king's court at Verona in August. The government charged Macartney with securing Provence's cooperation in British efforts to coordinate the counterrevolution. In his instructions to Macartney, Grenville warned that formal recognition of Provence's claim would require agreement among the Allies yet unofficially identified him as "the King" in the text of the instructions. Grenville recommended that Louis XVIII publish a moderate manifesto of his intentions but commit to no specific government form and endeavor to appeal to all individuals dissatisfied with the Revolution. The foreign secretary urged him to follow such a declaration by quickly joining Condé's army to raise the banner of the monarchy on French soil. By the time Macartney arrived, Provence had already issued a declaration in favor of a restoration that was unlikely to hold broad appeal. Although Provence accepted the notion of a constitution, in all other regards he proposed to undo the entirety of the Revolution, turning the clock back to the spring of 1789 before the formation of the National Assembly. Thus, Macartney's mission failed before it began. He remained with Provence through the winter, indulging tentative discussions of an alliance between Louis XVIII and George III. This hinged on British recognition of Louis XVIII as king, which itself depended on some progress of either the counterrevolution in France or the Allied armies making sufficient progress to support a restoration.[65]

Even with a more moderate declaration, events on the Rhine would have prevented Provence from returning to France with Condé's army. First, in August, the Austrians declared that they had no immediate plans to use Condé, contradicting Thugut's earlier assertions about Condé's army being essential to the Austrian position on the Rhine. Then, on 6 September, a massive French army crossed the Rhine with the Austrian armies retreating precipitously before it. One of Wurmser's divisional commanders, Peter Vitus von Quosdanovich, managed to halt the retrograde movement on 24 September by defeating Pichegru at Handschuhsheim.[66]

Four days after the battle of Handschuhsheim, Whitworth, together with the Russian government and the Austrian ambassador, signed a declaration merging the alliances that connected each of the three powers into a single Triple Alliance. Articles regarding this possibility in both the Anglo-Russian alliance of March and the Anglo-Austrian alliance of May indicated that all three powers agreed on the propriety of the measure. However, the slow pace of coordinating diplomacy over the enormous distances separating London, St. Petersburg, and Vienna rendered the actual creation of a Triple Alliance extraordinarily difficult. As a tripartite arrangement would necessarily rest on the foundation of the existing agreements between each of the three powers, negotiations could not begin until all three were certain of the ratification of each alliance. Owing to Catherine's insistence on hosting the negotiations at St. Petersburg, talks depended on the speed of information reaching the most distant of the three governments. Whitworth received the British ratification of the Anglo-Russian Alliance on 11 May; the older Austro-Russian alliance needed no further confirmation. Only the much-delayed Anglo-Austrian alliance prevented the progress of negotiations. Grenville did not receive the formal Austrian ratification of the treaty until 25 July. He then dispatched instructions to Whitworth on 5 August authorizing him to conclude the Triple Alliance, which Whitworth received on 25 August. Thus, by the time delegates at St. Petersburg had all the information and authority to consolidate the three alliances into a single system, the military campaigns of that year were already underway.[67]

The coalition suffered from this delay as Catherine asserted that she would take direct action against France only after the conclusion of the Triple Alliance. On this basis, Russian ministers refused Whitworth's repeated requests for a Russian army to fight in the west in return for a subsidy. The Russian court defended this refusal by expressing anxiety over the situation of Poland and the need to defend Russia from a potentially hostile Prussian response to the Austro-Russian Third Partition agreement. In June, after learning of the Franco-Prussian peace, Catherine requested British subsidies in the event of a war with Berlin.[68] The Cabinet refused this, arguing that the British government did not want to help create a war in eastern Europe by providing the Russians with the means to push any dispute to the point of breach. Thus, St. Petersburg sent nothing to aid the war with France in 1795 beyond a squadron to fight alongside the Royal Navy in the Atlantic.[69]

News of the ratification of the Anglo-Austrian alliance and corresponding instructions for concluding the Triple Alliance between the three powers arrived amid negotiations between the Russian, Prussian, and Austrian ministers on the final division of Poland in late August. On 9 August 1795, the Russian and Austrian representatives at St. Petersburg informed their Prussian colleague of the bilateral agreement for the final partition that they had concluded in January. The Austro-Russian convention together with the Anglo-Austrian and Anglo-Russian alliances presented Berlin with a fait accompli. Although furious, Frederick William II recognized the impossibility of challenging Vienna, St. Petersburg, and London combined and accepted the portion of Poland allotted to him.[70]

Negotiations for the new Triple Alliance finally proceeded in September with all parties reaching rapid agreement. On 28 September, delegates of all three powers issued declarations acknowledging that they viewed their bilateral links as constituting a unitary Triple Alliance and pledging to adhere to all measures common to the three bilateral treaties. Displaying a consistency of principle, the Cabinet had insisted that the Triple Alliance carefully avoid any statement that would explicitly make Britain party to or guarantor of the second or third Polish partitions. Thus, with difficulty, Pitt replaced the lapsed Triple Alliance of 1788 with a new Triple Alliance binding Britain to two of the chief antagonists of the former system: Austria and Russia.[71]

In the remaining months of 1795, the Allied campaign continued to deteriorate in every theater except, strangely enough, Germany. All remaining British forces on the western coast of France returned to British ports, leaving the rebels to the mercy of republican armies. Similarly, royalists in Paris rose in open revolt in early October partially in response to the presence of Artois at Île d'Yeu. They seemed poised to seize control of the capital as Wickham had insisted was possible. However, General Bonaparte famously defeated the royalists in a battle outside the hall of the National Convention with a "whiff of grapeshot" on 5 October (13 Vendémiaire by the republican calendar).[72] The withdrawal of Artois and the failure of the Vendémiaire uprising ended the coalition's best hope of securing peace through a royalist coup. Resistance in Brittany crumbled, Condé remained inactive, Provence proved unattractive both to the British and the rebels, the core of royalism in Paris had been defeated, and Wickham reported that the resistance movement at Lyon was beginning to disintegrate.[73]

Only after the conclusion of the Triple Alliance and Prussia's corresponding acquiescence to the Third Partition did Austrian forces show any degree of vigor. After halting the French offensive on 24 September, Wurmser and Clerfayt conducted an energetic campaign in October that drove the French back to the Rhine. However, the enthusiasm of the Austrian commanders ended at that boundary, and Clerfayt concluded a local armistice at the end of the year to rest his exhausted troops. The October victories were also tempered by an Austro-Sardinian defeat at Loano on 23 and 24 November. After this reversal, the Austrian and Sardinian armies retreated into winter quarters in Piedmontese territory, ceding the Ligurian coast to the French and nullifying the year's gains.[74]

As in 1794, the sluggish pace of communications and the division of the attention of all parties among several spheres of interest had hampered the formation and execution of an effective military plan in 1795. Unlike 1794, the Cabinet faced the approach of the 1795 campaign season with no reasonable certainty of which states would remain in the war, how many troops they would field against France, or where they might deploy their armies. Despite overtures to other courts, the British government consistently and correctly viewed Vienna as its most reliable partner in the war. Therefore, British military planning for Europe again hinged on Anglo-Austrian negotiations. Diplomatic delays in these exchanges in conjunction with Thugut's struggle to find a commander willing and able to take the offensive led to a disjointed Allied campaign in the summer and autumn of 1795. Poor coordination therefore squandered what was arguably the last great chance for the First Coalition to achieve victory through force of arms. Wurmser's success in Germany in October proved that Austrian commanders and armies on the Rhine were capable of defeating their French counterparts. Meanwhile the Vendémiaire uprising in Paris demonstrated that British hopes of opening a western front with the aid of French royalists and inspiring a counterrevolution to bring about peace were not unfounded. Nevertheless, the failure to achieve diplomatic unity earlier in the year prevented the coordination of these campaigns in an overarching strategic offensive. Thus, despite the successful conclusion of a Triple Alliance between Britain, Austria, and Russia, the Italian and Breton fronts ended the year in failure, contributing to Austria's inability to capitalize on the autumn success of its armies in Germany.

Although a success in the context of the war, the circumstances surrounding the new Triple Alliance made it, in some ways, a failure for the diplomacy of Pitt's administration. Arguably, it represented more of a Russian than British achievement. After Pitt failed to settle the Polish question with the eastern powers through the principle of collective security in 1791, they sought security on their frontiers through a laborious and volatile partition process under Russian leadership. After rebuffing British pressure for alliances in 1793 and 1794, both Vienna and St. Petersburg changed their tone and embraced a British connection as Prussian compliance with the Third Partition became doubtful. Thus, the preservation of the partitions of Poland more than collective security against the aggression of revolutionary France served as the foundation for the Triple Alliance of 1795 despite continued British efforts to remain wholly unconnected with the partition politics of eastern Europe.[75]

The new Triple Alliance also reflected Pitt's reluctant concession to the need to choose between Austria and Prussia because of their irreconcilable differences primarily in Polish affairs. Pitt accepted this need only after the Franco-Prussian and Franco-Spanish peace treaties destroyed his hopes of reconciling all the major powers in a more comprehensive system. Pitt had originally sought to gather most, if not all, of the states of Europe in a single system based on the principles of collective security, armed mediation of disputes, and commercial agreements. In contrast to this, the Triple Alliance of 1795 constituted a narrowly defined defensive pact, including only two other states with little prospect of adding more. Pitt's shrinking list of viable Continental allies and British defeats in Flanders contributed to the increased British interest in working with the counterrevolution. Although not an optimal situation from London's perspective, the new Triple Alliance and counterrevolution did at least theoretically serve Pitt's overarching objective of preserving British connections and influence in Europe.[76]

The lack of alliance prospects arose from successful French diplomacy in 1795. The Republic gained its first formal ally, the Batavian Republic, in May, and the remaining members of the coalition feared similar Franco-Prussian and Franco-Spanish alliances after those countries signed peace treaties with France. In addition, Sweden and the Ottoman Empire began to warm to the new French government, and a renewal of historical French links with those countries appeared plausible. In this context, the Triple Alliance of 1795 became one of two nascent power blocs in Europe competing for the allegiance and resources of neutral states. Subsequent British diplomacy in 1796 therefore focused primarily on trying to salvage influence where possible and maximize leverage for peace negotiations. The Cabinet did not totally abandon hope for military victory through Austria's German and Italian campaigns, but British diplomatic focus shifted to prepare for the worst. Before the war, the Foreign Office had pursued Pitt's collective security through mediation. After the start of war, diplomatic methodology necessarily shifted toward laying the groundwork for postwar collective security in wartime conventions and alliances. As the tides of war turned against London, British diplomacy began to consider seeking collective security through multilateral peace negotiations instead. This too failed in 1796 and 1797.

CHAPTER 10

WAR AND PEACE, 1796–1797

By the time Pitt's diplomacy finally obtained a multilateral alliance against France in the autumn of 1795, the opportunity for combined operations to defeat revolutionary France had largely passed. The evacuation of the British army from Bremen in April 1795 and the subsequent failure of the Quiberon expedition over the course of the summer effectively ended direct British involvement in the campaigns on the Continent. Prussia's neutralization of northern Germany also led to the loss of most of the German mercenaries that the British left behind to cooperate with Austrian forces.[1] In southern Europe, peace between France and Spain rendered British access to the Italian front tenuous. Finally, the abortive Vendémiaire uprising in October had destroyed any realistic hope of reviving direct British participation through a royalist uprising. In these circumstances, British forces could not effectively reach or coordinate with the primary remaining Continental ally, Austria. British ministers determined that unilateral amphibious operations were unlikely to succeed and thus were not worth risking limited British manpower. In this context, Pitt began transitioning from attempting to defend British interests in Europe through a coalition rooted in collective security to seeking multilateral commitments to a negotiated peace. His foreign policy principles remained constant, but he necessarily adapted his methods to military realities.

Two considerations convinced Pitt to adjust his objectives from victory to negotiation in the waning months of 1795. First, the French government seemed to become more moderate after Vendémiaire with the establishment of the Directory. After the overthrow of Robespierre, the Thermidorian Convention dismantled the institutions of the Terror and endeavored to safeguard a moderate interpretation of the French Republic from threats from both radical Jacobins and revived royalism. To this end, its members produced a new constitution on 22 August 1795 that created the government known as the Directory. A rigorous separation of powers distinguished the Directory from the preceding government of the National Convention. The Constitution of Year III divided the legislature into two houses and the executive among five Directors. Evidence began to suggest that the Directory might be more able and willing than its predecessors to negotiate and respect an equitable peace that afforded London some degree of security.[2]

Second, while the prospects of military victory had diminished, the coalition recovered some strength both diplomatically, with the formation of the Triple Alliance between Britain, Austria, and Russia, and also militarily, at sea and in Germany. Opening negotiations from a position of strength held greater appeal than waiting for French armies to force Austria and the Italian states to make a separate peace. The Triple Alliance that the British and Austrians viewed as so important in 1795 ultimately had more diplomatic than military significance. The great distance separating Russia from the frontiers of France limited the direct aid that the court of St. Petersburg could provide to the Allies. Although capable of sending a considerable force either overland through the Habsburg dominions or by sea to Britain for use in amphibious operations, such an army would necessarily depend on the already strained Austrian or British logistical systems for subsistence. The time necessary to make and complete such arrangements rendered any military plans dependent on timely Russian assistance, which was dubious at best. In addition, Catherine's persistent evasion of any commitment to send troops to western Europe persuaded the Cabinet to place minimal reliance on military support from the empress. Russia's allegiance served primarily as insurance against overt pro-French moves from Prussia, Denmark, Sweden, and the Ottoman Empire, which bolstered Austrian resolve to continue the war. Thus, the formation of the new Triple Alliance partially compensated for French diplomatic victories in separating the Dutch, Prussians, and Spanish from the coalition.[3]

Militarily, the Allies still held a strong position in the winter of 1795–96. Austrian and Sardinian forces continued to defend the Alpine passes, and the Austrian and imperial armies remained intact in Germany despite their retreat. In the maritime war, the British held the advantage. Expeditions to the West Indies had achieved significant though incomplete gains, and British forces in the East Indies had also fared well. Following the Dutch revolution and defection, British forces successfully seized most of the strategically significant Dutch colonies with the cooperation of exiled Stadtholder William V.[4] Moreover, the Toulon episode of 1793 had severely damaged the French Mediterranean fleet. On 1 June 1794, a large naval battle off Brest resulted in a major victory, known in British history as the Glorious First of June, that crippled the main French Atlantic fleet. The Royal Navy stood ready to defend Britain's possessions around the world. This situation handed Pitt the option of reviving the old Whig practice of trading colonial conquests for European concessions. After three years of mostly military disappointments, Pitt believed that the Allies could and should open negotiations from a position of some strength rather than waiting for further setbacks.

For these two reasons, British diplomacy and military operations in 1796 and 1797 largely abandoned the elusive goal of total victory and instead focused on maximizing leverage for negotiating a compromise peace. Over the course of these two years, Pitt made several unsuccessful attempts to achieve peace. Externally, these efforts suffered from poor or slow communication with allies, French military success, and French political shifts. Internally, Pitt refused to accept harsher French terms that would have reduced Britain to the same dangerous isolation from Europe that he had worked so hard to end.

The first British initiative to obtain peace began in September 1795. The Cabinet decided to consult Austria on possible terms for a tripartite peace while Austrian armies were retreating through southern Germany. The ministers feared that Vienna might make a separate peace with France as had Berlin and Madrid, and they hoped to forestall this by opening talks regarding a general peace. The Cabinet also perceived a need to demonstrate willingness to make peace in order to maintain support in Parliament. If Pitt failed to produce a convincing attempt to secure peace and prospects of victory remained poor, he would present the Foxites the opportunity to accuse the government of waging war without purpose, thereby eroding both confidence in his management of the war and his support in Parliament. On 20 September, Pitt explained to Portland his views on the necessity of approaching Vienna.

> With a view to prevent the Emperor being alarmed into a separate peace . . . as well as in order to satisfy the public mind here at the meeting of Parliament, it would be very useful to come immediately to such an explanation with Austria as may put it in our power . . . to make use of any opening for ascertaining on what terms the new [French] government may be disposed to treat and may . . . establish in time a full concert for the prosecution of the war, if necessary, next year.[5]

Anticipating the objection that any such approach should wait until new reinforcements destined for the West Indies could achieve some success and further strengthen the British position, Pitt added, "By waiting for the actual success in the West Indies, we may run some hazard of losing the benefit of the cooperation of Austria at least on the Rhine, and that our relative situation may thus upon the whole become less favorable instead of moreso."[6]

While Pitt urged the necessity of maintaining clear communication with Austria regarding terms for peace, he also planned for the continuation of the war and made a list of possible circumstances for the campaign of 1796, highlighting the uncertainties facing him. Pitt noted that if Sardinia, Naples, and Austria all remained in the war with the support of the Holy Roman Empire, excluding the states that had already made peace, "this affords the best possible prospect of success." If the Empire made peace, Austria would be limited to fighting in Italy, which Pitt suggested could still create a powerful diversion, indicating a hope to force France to negotiate. Last, Pitt supposed that the war must end if both the Empire and Sardinia made peace, leaving no means for Austrian and French armies to reach each other. Compounding the unknowns, Pitt noted that Spain, Denmark, and Sweden might all join France. The extent of Dutch willingness to take an active role on the French side of the war remained unclear, and with the new Triple Alliance and Third Partition of Poland not yet settled at that time, Prussian and Russian intentions remained in question.[7]

These considerations prompted a series of dispatches from Grenville to Eden advocating continued military pressure into 1796 to give strength to peace negotiations while also requesting an explanation of Austrian views regarding such negotiations. Grenville's letters urged the Austrians to act quickly in Germany both to prevent more German and Italian states from following the Prussian and Tuscan example in making peace and to provide British ministers with evidence to present to Parliament to justify continued financial aid to Vienna. He argued that "if these smaller princes or states saw even now that Austria was at hand, able and willing to protect them, it would not be difficult to convince them how much more advantageous it must be for their interests to connect their pacification with that of Great Britain and Austria than to attempt to procure from France such terms as a victorious and insolent enemy may be willing to grant." Grenville remained vague on the question of operations, only recommending a renewed attempt to execute the plans of 1795 and indicating that British operations would depend on Austria's plans.[8]

Above all, Grenville's dispatches urged the preservation of diplomatic unity and extensive communication, particularly pertaining to Austria's views regarding peace. To discourage any disposition for a separate peace, he explained that French war weariness "is such as affords the best grounds of hope that by union and firmness, the Allies may even in the worst events obtain honorable and advantageous terms for themselves and even such conditions as may in a great degree provide for the security of the rest of Europe." Regarding the terms of negotiation, Grenville conveyed British rejection of any insistence on monarchy in France and expressed hope that the Directory might prove a reasonable member of the international system. He instructed Eden to press the importance of keeping the Austrian Netherlands out of French hands but did not insist that it be returned to Austria. The foreign secretary merely asked for ideas on the best means of keeping those provinces and the conquered territories on the left bank of the Rhine from France. Notably, he observed, "The situation of this country, both at home and abroad, being such as would leave His Majesty little difficulty in concluding a beneficial peace for himself if he could overlook the interest he has in the maintenance of the balance of power in Europe." Despite the resources expended in the maritime war and corresponding British success overseas, Pitt's ministry prioritized Britain's European interests.[9] While waiting for an explanation of Austrian views, the Cabinet sent Francis Jackson to reinforce Eden and deliver their views more clearly than letters could convey.[10]

Jackson arrived in Vienna by 1 November after the dramatic Austrian counteroffensive in Germany, which preemptively fulfilled one of the objectives of his mission. News of the Triple Alliance and Third Partition of Poland arrived near the same time, further reinforcing the push for Allied unity. Nonetheless, Thugut responded vaguely to Eden and Jackson, and the eastern developments caused as much difficulty as they erased. Thugut recommended consulting Russia on peace terms and operational plans despite British protests over the extreme delays it would cause. Moreover, he pressed the British for assistance in securing significant support from Russia and the German states. He equivocated on the Austrian Netherlands, explaining that Francis II had no desire to regain the territory but would never allow it to remain in French hands. While he did not explicitly advocate the Belgium-Bavaria exchange, his language indicated that solution to be his preference.[11] For his part, Eden relentlessly pressed the importance of Austria retaining the territory despite the flexibility of Grenville's instructions on this point. Eden also exceeded his instructions on the question of British financial assistance. He interpreted Grenville's warning that the Cabinet would be unable to pledge another loan without significant Austrian military success as a flat refusal of another loan. Thugut requested £3,000,000, but Eden asserted the impossibility of such a measure. The Austrian minister remained vague on the desired terms of peace and generally displayed a disinclination to discuss the matter with either of the British envoys. He argued repeatedly that they could discuss the details of peace terms as soon as French peace overtures created the need.[12]

Just as military success in October 1795 halted discussions of possible peace negotiations amid fresh Austrian confidence, the disappointments of November and December renewed the British conviction of the need for such a conversation. As noted, French forces defeated the Austro-Sardinian armies on the Italian front, undoing the progress the Allies had made there since the beginning of 1795. In Germany, Austrian armies retained their gains, but Clerfayt's armistice signaled the exhaustion of his army and halted the campaign for the winter. These reversals reduced the prospect of a vigorous renewal of Austrian campaigns in Italy and Germany in 1796. In addition, Catherine made the dispatch of any Russian troops to aid the Austrians conditional on Prussian acquiescence, ostensibly for logistical reasons. In effect, this nullified any faint hopes of obtaining a significant Russian army to support a new offensive in 1796.[13]

Concurrently, the prospects of improving the Allied position through maritime success diminished as the Cabinet's major reinforcement for the Caribbean suffered delays. Originally scheduled to embark in September, logistical difficulties and weather prevented the convoy from sailing until February. Pitt and Dundas had hoped that success in the West Indies would strengthen the coalition's hand and persuade the French to seek terms rather than continue fighting in 1796.[14] The delays meant that the expedition could not have such an impact before the start of the 1796 campaign even if such hopes were reasonable. Spurred by this disappointment as well as a growing bullion shortage brought on by British subsidy payments and the upkeep of armies abroad, the Cabinet made a more extensive and explicit peace proposal on 22 December 1795 to both Vienna and St. Petersburg.[15]

This second effort to secure consensus expanded on Jackson's November mission to ascertain Austrian views on opening peace negotiations and similarly proposed measures for strengthening the war effort as well as a program for peace. To bolster military operations, Grenville directed Whitworth to secure an army of 55,000 Russians through a subsidy of £1,000,000 to support the Austrians on the Rhine. He expressed the hope that this could compensate for Britain's inability to raise an army for Austria from the German states due to the Prussian neutrality zone. To aid Austria directly, Grenville conveyed an offer to guarantee a £3,000,000 loan in the near future. He admitted that Britain's specie shortage prevented immediate measures on that subject but offered to reexamine the financial circumstances within two months. Aside from the bullion shortage, he cautioned that Thugut's refusal to disclose Austrian peace aims would prevent the Cabinet from approving a new loan. In a supplemental dispatch, Grenville suggested that Austria could attempt to raise a loan in one of the German or Italian cities to avoid the difficulties facing a loan from the Bank of England; he added that the British government would happily guarantee such a loan immediately.[16]

Regarding mutually agreeable peace terms, Grenville provided a clear explanation of British views. He first insisted on amnesty for French royalists and émigrés as essential to fulfill Britain's obligation to those French exiles under its protection. A second point asserted London's intention to take some indemnity from among the captured colonies in British possession but also a willingness to return most colonial conquests to secure British interests in Europe. This brought the discussion to the question of the future of Austria's territories. In the absence of any clear suggestions from Thugut, the British suggested that Austria should retain Belgium and improve its defensibility by annexing Liège and retaining the territory that the French had added to Belgium from the Dutch provinces. In southern Europe, Grenville's dispatch recommended only the return of Nice and Savoy to Sardinia. For states that had not lost territory, the proposal urged a simple return to the status quo. The instructions insisted that all states involved in the coalition war should become signatories to the final peace settlement, creating a mutual guarantee of the result and thereby laying the foundations for a new collective security system. To persuade the French to seek terms, Grenville's letter recommended a declaration to the war-weary French people regarding the Allied disposition to make peace on honorable terms.[17]

The December proposal met with mixed responses. Catherine had committed herself to support the exiled Bourbons and refused to consider a peace that required formal recognition of a republican regime.[18] In contrast, Thugut proved largely agreeable. He argued that the Russian rejection served as a cloak for continued evasion of any measure to provide military aid to Austria. He proposed instead that the British provide funding for Austria to raise an army of 17,000 men from Germany on cheaper terms than the intended Russian corps. The Austrian minister also agreed to attempt to raise a loan in Hamburg based on Grenville's suggestion. This time, Thugut seemed receptive to the notion of seeking peace quickly while the Allied military position remained strong. In his letter of 22 January 1796, Eden reported that Thugut himself had proposed a declaration of peaceful intent to the French people and so approved of the British suggestion of the same. Thugut only recommended delaying any such declaration until a proper time to prevent it from reducing confidence in Allied military preparations. The Austrian minister even agreed with the British proposal for Vienna to retain an enlarged Belgium. Regarding the smaller states, Thugut supported the Sardinian claim to Nice and Savoy and suggested that Portugal and Naples could receive some commercial concessions from France to indemnify them for their efforts. Grenville received Eden's letter containing Thugut's response on 5 February.[19]

In January, intelligence from France suggested that a declaration in favor of peace might produce a good effect on the French people. In addition, a proposal emerged from Berlin for Prussian armed mediation in favor of the Allies provided that Prussia receive funding from the British and an indemnity in Germany. By 1796, the Prussians, together with other states within the northern German neutrality zone, had formed a corps of observation to defend a line of demarcation for that zone. The Cabinet suggested that the Prussians take that army to the Netherlands to overthrow the unpopular Batavian Republic and reinstate William V as Stadtholder, followed by a proposal for a peace conference that would include all belligerent states. Should this peace negotiation fail, Prussian reentry into the war would potentially assist in bringing Russia to play a more active role as well. Grenville relayed the suggestion that either the Dutch should reimburse Prussia for the campaign or the British would do so from the revenue of captured Dutch colonies. The foreign secretary forwarded both the desire for an immediate pacific declaration and the Prussian mediation proposal to Vienna with a pledge not to act on either without Austrian consent.[20] Eden received the letters on these topics in early March and relayed Thugut's negative response to both. The Austrian minister placed no faith in Prussia and insisted that any immediate declaration in favor of peace would undermine military preparations. However, he did agree to send an envoy to join Wickham in Switzerland to test the French disposition.[21]

Amid uncertainty regarding the intentions of Vienna, St. Petersburg, and Berlin, the Cabinet resolved to ascertain French attitudes toward peace in February 1796. As with the Prussian and Spanish negotiations of 1795, Barthélemy in Switzerland became the point of contact, and Wickham conveyed to him the British inquiry for terms on 8 March. The French response on 26 March indicated that France remained fundamentally aggressive in intent. Barthélemy demanded the restitution of all British conquests overseas while France retained conquered territory extending to its natural frontiers in Europe: the Rhine, the Alps, and the Pyrenees.[22] This represented an insistence on total submission and rejected any notion of conceding to British demands in Europe to obtain the return of conquered colonial possessions. As in the prewar negotiations between Grenville and Chauvelin, the government published the exchange to demonstrate its desire for peace and the necessity of continuing the war against such an unreasonable foe.[23]

With the Directory intransigent, British hopes of obtaining a negotiated peace would rely on a counterrevolutionary shift in the French government. The limited prospect of a counterrevolutionary coup after Vendémiaire hinged on contact with General Pichegru, but this idea collapsed after his dismissal in March 1796.[24] Thereafter, the British concentrated on Wickham's support of moderates and conservatives to cultivate a peace party within the French government. This approach had little hope of success until the next election in 1797, when Wickham's accumulated influence might produce tangible political changes.[25]

London continued to prepare for continued military operations while seeking an avenue to peace. Reinforcements for the Caribbean finally sailed in February, and the Cabinet agreed in April to provide cash advances of £150,000 to Austria each month for the 1796 campaign in lieu of another loan.[26] However, the arrival of spring brought a resumption of military disappointment. General Bonaparte's Army of Italy broke through the Alpine passes in a skillful campaign. After defeating the Austrians in the Battle of Montenotte on 11 and 12 April, he drove a wedge between the Austrian and Sardinian armies. Facing the victorious French army alone, Sardinia sued for peace on 28 April 1796. After Napoleon's 10 May victory at Lodi, the Austrians withdrew from Milan to their fortress at Mantua, which the French besieged. Having chased the Austrians from Lombardy, Napoleon turned south, persuading the terrified Neapolitans to sign an armistice at the end of May and extracting resources from the other Italian states throughout the month of June. In response, the Austrians redeployed part of their forces from Germany to the Italian theater, which caused their weakened army on the Rhine to retreat after two French armies crossed the river in June.[27]

Austrian setbacks in Germany and Italy convinced Pitt that Vienna could not win the war or even maintain an effective defensive campaign into 1797. This consideration added to the gloom occasioned by the loss of the Italian states, Russian and Prussian passivity, the inauspicious prospects of an internal French political solution, and London's diminishing finances. Rumors of Franco-Austrian peace negotiations strained the confidence initially generated by the amicable exchanges at the start of the year. By June, these factors persuaded the Cabinet to make another effort to negotiate peace and prepare the country to fight alone against a growing French coalition. Pitt reluctantly agreed to a proposal from Grenville to renew the request for Prussian armed mediation. "But though I think it should be tried," he wrote to Grenville, "I do not flatter myself with much chance of success. On the whole, my notion is that most likely, either now or a few months hence, we shall be left to sustain alone the conflict with France and Holland, probably joined by Spain, and perhaps favored more or less openly by the northern powers. But with proper exertion we can make our party good against them all."[28]

A Cabinet meeting on 28 July refined Grenville's idea into a formal proposal. To secure Prussian armed mediation, the British planned to suggest that Prussia rather than Austria would gain Belgium in the peace while Austria annexed Bavaria to balance Prussian expansion. Grenville hoped that the prospect of British support for these territorial gains could replace the financial support that London could no longer afford to provide.[29] In July, the Cabinet dispatched George Hammond to visit first Berlin and then Vienna to obtain the consent of the respective governments. This plan represented a concession to partition politics, which Pitt accepted hesitantly based on the apparent necessity, and George III protested strongly from the perspective of a German prince.[30]

Hammond's mission proved to be stillborn. Although he had an agreeable meeting with Frederick William II, Hammond found the Prussians cold and completely uninterested in any British proposal. Their reserve arose from a secret convention signed with the French shortly before Hammond's arrival that confirmed Prussian neutrality in return for French consent to the annexation of the bishopric of Münster after the final peace. The British offer of land that required a resumption of war with France and a laborious campaign of conquest could never have competed with the French offer of land for nearly no effort at all. Thus, Hammond found no opening to make Grenville's proposal for Prussian armed mediation.[31] Austrian disapproval finally nullified his mission. Eden informed him of Vienna's attitude in August, making any progress with Prussia irrelevant as well as unlikely. Although he did not know the details of Hammond's mission, Thugut felt betrayed by further British courting of Prussia after he learned of it on 13 August. He insisted that no good could come of the approach and reminded Eden of the numerous examples of Prussia's bad faith toward the Allies during the preceding years.[32] Persuaded that his mission had no hope of success, Hammond returned to London in September.[33]

The ongoing and unsuccessful Italian campaign further discouraged the Austrians as well as the British. After Napoleon ransacked southern Italy in June 1796, an Austrian offensive to relieve Mantua forced him to focus on the north in July. Although the Austrian maneuver forced Napoleon to lift the siege, he successfully parried their advance at the Battle of Castiglione and resumed the siege.[34] Thugut pleaded with the British to send more financial aid and to support Austrian efforts to rouse the Russians to action. In September, he requested a new loan of £5,000,000 and an increase of monthly advances to £200,000.[35]

Although sympathetic to Austrian needs, the deterioration of Britain's own strategic situation in the summer of 1796 rendered London unable to offer aid to Vienna on the scale requested. On 19 August 1796, the Spanish signed an offensive alliance with the French Republic. This did not immediately result in a declaration of war on Britain but rendered it likely and confirmed the Cabinet's worst fears of Spanish hostility. The looming prospect of Spanish entry into the war dramatically expanded the demands on the Royal Navy. Spanish hostility and Napoleon's domination of Italy left Corsica as the only base for the British fleet within the western Mediterranean. From his post in Corsica, Elliot never abandoned the goal of using the Anglo-Corsican Kingdom to lead an Italian league to resist the French invasion. In June 1796, he even considered an invasion of Tuscany in conjunction with papal forces. However, Elliot never possessed forces large enough to attempt such a bold operation, and the commander of the Mediterranean fleet, Admiral John Jervis, deemed the attempt impracticable. Napoleon's campaign through central and southern Italy in June and July ended the possibility of such an operation. Nevertheless, Elliot continued to plead with the Cabinet to send substantial British reinforcements to pursue his increasingly quixotic ambition of rallying an Italian league against the French.[36] Like Jervis, the Cabinet deemed this project no longer practical or safe. The Franco-Spanish alliance posed a threat to Gibraltar, the only tenuous link between Britain and the Mediterranean. Unwilling to risk substantial British military resources under these conditions, the Cabinet dispatched orders for British forces in the Mediterranean, including the garrison on Corsica, to evacuate to Gibraltar and then Lisbon.[37]

In the Atlantic, the union of France, Spain, and the Batavian Republic recreated the maritime threat that had proved so dangerous to the British in the American War of Independence. That a small Russian fleet now supported the British cause provided little comfort. As in the American War, the aggregation of Continental naval power raised British fears of invasion, which required the expansion of the militia for domestic defense and an increase of naval exertions in home waters.[38] British forces remained dominant in the East and West Indies, but this did little to aid the defense of the home islands and only supported diplomacy if the enemy would barter colonial holdings for European concessions, which the French had thus far refused to do.[39]

These rising demands on British military resources led to increasing expenses as well. The growing specie shortage eroded British credit and caused an economic slump. This made Pitt's efforts to meet extraordinary military expenses through a loan both politically and economically difficult. Although personally inclined to aid Austria, he conceded the impossibility of a formal loan in the circumstances of economic and political strain in the summer of 1796. He did increase the monthly advances to £200,000 as Thugut had requested but could do little more.[40]

Before learning of Thugut's new appeal to Russia and the failure of Hammond's mission, the overall dismal strategic situation prompted the Cabinet to initiate a new attempt to secure a balanced, multilateral peace. In discussing this new approach, British ministers outlined a peace plan revised from earlier proposals that Grenville recorded in his notes of the Cabinet's proceedings on 2 September. Regarding the form of the negotiation, they resolved that the French must allow the British to invite the Austrians to join the peace conference. Anticipating resistance on this point, Grenville recorded several arguments to make in favor of the measure. According to Grenville:

> The interests of Great Britain cannot be so separated from those of the Continent.... No peace can be concluded between Great Britain and France, nor even any progress made in the negotiation, without constant reference to the manner in which it may be proposed to arrange the affairs of the continent and particularly the interests of Austria to whom His Majesty is bound by a community

of interest as well as by the ties of good faith.... Such a mode of treating has always been found the only effectual mode of restoring peace to Europe when engaged in general or extensive wars.... If, therefore, the Directory sincerely wish peace, they cannot refuse acceding to the only proposal which can produce that object.[41]

Once again, the British government sought multilateral negotiations as the basis for building collective security into a peace settlement.

If the French agreed to multilateral negotiations, the British envoy would request peace terms or, if the French insisted, provide a British peace program. Grenville's notes suggested that negotiations commence from either the status quo ante bellum or *uti possidetis* and offer concessions from either point to reconcile the views of all parties involved.[42] In either case, the British offered to accept the Spanish cession of San Domingo to France and to return most of Britain's colonial conquests to France and its allies, only insisting on retaining Ceylon, the principality of Cochin in southern India, and the Cape of Good Hope. In return, they demanded the restitution of all Austrian territory that France had conquered. However, Grenville's notes also acknowledged the probability that France would insist on keeping Belgium while Austria would not be eager to recover it. In this case, the British proposed to accept the French conquest of Belgium if Austria received indemnification elsewhere. The notes recognized the French conquest of Nice and Savoy as acknowledged in the Franco-Sardinian peace and similarly accepted the French conquest of all German territories on the left bank of the Rhine except those owned by Austria.[43]

In this new peace initiative, the Cabinet outlined as the minimum requirement for British security a strong and independent Austria coupled with unfettered British access to and dominance of India. Although this reflected a sober recognition of the military situation in Europe, it did not represent an abandonment of Europe. On the contrary, the British ministers were willing to return most overseas gains to secure the restoration of their primary ally's territory or suitable compensation for any of its losses.[44]

Having twice failed to obtain Prussian mediation, London turned to neutral Denmark to open these negotiations. Denmark was one of the few remaining countries capable of fulfilling this role. Prussia, the North German states, and the Italian states were both unwilling and theoretically bound by treaties with France. The Ottoman Empire was neutral, but lingering tensions in the Balkans made Vienna and St. Petersburg unlikely to accept Turkish mediation. Sweden remained aloof from the Continental war but tended to favor the French. Denmark enjoyed cordial relations with all parties as well as a strong friendship with Russia. Through the Danes, the British requested a passport from the French for a British negotiator to travel to France to discuss the possibility of beginning formal negotiations that other states might join. The Danes agreed but the Directory would provide a passport only if the British asked them directly. The Cabinet consented to this direct approach and received the passport in early October. They then entrusted the mission to their veteran, Malmesbury, who proceeded to France, arriving on 18 October.[45]

During September and early October 1796, while Malmesbury's mission took shape, the ever-fluctuating state of the war influenced Pitt's ministry to increase the minimum demands from Grenville's initial sketch. Although Spain declared war on Britain on 5 October, Grenville received good news from St. Petersburg and Vienna. Against all expectations, the fresh Austrian appeal to Russia had prompted Catherine II to offer an army of 60,000 men in return for a payment of £300,000 at the beginning and end of the campaign and £120,000 each month.[46] Grenville countered with an offer of £300,000 at the start of the campaign, £100,000 per month, and a pledge for £600,000 redeemable after the conclusion of peace in return for the same 60,000 men. To further motivate Catherine, Grenville authorized Whitworth to increase the postwar pledge to £1,000,000 and accept as few as 40,000 men. In addition, he offered to transfer Corsica to Russia if Britain retained commercial privileges and basing rights on the island.[47]

This proposal reversed the Cabinet's decision to evacuate Corsica and the Mediterranean as London hoped that Catherine might accept it and commit forces to the Mediterranean as well.[48] Concurrently, Archduke Charles rallied the Austrian army in Germany to halt the French advance in Bavaria in August. As in 1795, the Austrians then launched a counteroffensive that pushed the French back across the Rhine in October. The Austrian position in Italy had not improved, but Mantua continued to withstand the French siege and preparations to relieve it were underway.[49]

Improving military prospects influenced the Cabinet to update Malmesbury's orders and instruct him to adopt a slightly tougher stance toward the French. This decision received reinforcement when the Austrians denounced the new peace approach as inappropriate and damaging to the image of the Allies across Europe. The negative Austrian reaction disappointed the British ministers, but they pressed ahead with the negotiation.[50] Grenville amended his instructions to Malmesbury to emphasize further the necessity of restoring all Austrian territory or equivalent compensation and to insist on the talks being preliminary to a general peace that included Austria. Thugut's demand that Britain honor its obligation to prosecute the war with vigor and not make a separate peace dampened the Cabinet's enthusiasm and hopes for the new negotiations with France.[51]

Malmesbury arrived in Paris on 22 October to open the peace negotiations and encountered difficulties immediately. French foreign minister Charles-François Delacroix shrewdly sought to exploit the diverging opinions prevailing in London and Vienna to persuade Malmesbury to accept a separate peace. Grenville had clearly instructed Malmesbury to reject any such proposal and insist on unity with Britain's Continental allies, but Thugut's complete rejection of the British peace initiative left little hope of an Austrian diplomat joining the discussion. Caught in this inflexible position, Malmesbury appealed to Grenville who wrote to Eden more insistently regarding Austrian participation in the negotiations.[52] He demanded that Austria send an envoy to Paris to join Malmesbury or provide him with authority to negotiate on their behalf. In the event of Thugut's continued refusal, Grenville threatened to cease all financial support and to negotiate a peace without Austrian participation on the basis of France restoring to Austria all conquered territory. This satisfied the conditions of both the Anglo-Austrian convention of 1793 and the more recent alliance of 1795. Grenville expressed British willingness to accept the Austrians annexing Bavaria as a replacement for Belgium but proposed that if Vienna did not retain Belgium, then it should pass to Berlin to continue serving as a barrier against the aggressive French Republic.[53]

Further fluctuations in the diplomatic and military position in November softened Thugut's attitude. Archduke Charles pushed the French back across the Rhine but proved unable to cross it himself to continue the offensive. In Italy, Napoleon preempted another Austrian attempt to relieve Mantua with a resounding victory in the Battle of Arcole.[54] Simultaneously, the British fleet and army abandoned the Mediterranean, not receiving the Cabinet's new resolution to hold Corsica until after conducting the evacuation as initially ordered. This proved less significant for Anglo-Russian diplomacy than it might have because Catherine II died suddenly on 16 November. Her successor, Paul I, reversed his mother's apparent trajectory toward direct involvement in the war, withdrawing the offer of troops and rejecting the proposal of Corsica. Paul harbored greater respect for Prussia than Austria, and his withdrawal from the precipice of war as part of the new Triple Alliance reflected this sentiment.[55] The British retreat from the Mediterranean also led Naples to expand its armistice with France to a formal peace treaty, removing the last hope for any aid to Austria in Italy.[56]

Losing faith in his allies, Thugut took the British demands seriously if still with great annoyance. He complained bitterly of the suggestion of ceding Belgium to Prussia while Austria annexed Bavaria. The Austrian minister categorically refused to support any further Prussian gains. Beyond that consideration, he argued that the British proposal made no provision for the Bavarian elector.

According to Eden, Thugut "asked me what we would do with the [Bavarian elector]—would we strangle him or send him to Botany Bay?" While seemingly a pious condemnation of British insensitivity to imperial politics and the need for adequate compensation, the accusation rings hollow, considering an earlier proposal from Thugut. In November 1795, he had suggested that Austria annex Bavaria and give Belgium to an independent prince outside the House of Wittelsbach that Britain might approve.[57] Forgetting his earlier willingness to dispossess the Bavarian elector entirely, Thugut countered this proposal by insisting on the Belgium-Bavaria exchange in its original form with the addition of a guarantee of the new Wittelsbach principality in the Low Countries to mollify British concerns. He also pressed for a restoration of the Holy Roman Empire's lost territory and the formation of a solid barrier against the French in Italy as well. Although Thugut still refused to participate in the British negotiations, his proposals gave tacit assent to the British claim to negotiate on behalf of Austrian interests.[58]

Based on Thugut's response, the Cabinet framed new instructions for Malmesbury to allow him to proceed without the presence of an Austrian colleague. His new instructions provided five key points as the basis for the negotiations. First, France should return Belgium to Austria or allow Austria to execute the exchange project and leave Belgium independent thereafter. Second, the Holy Roman Empire should regain its lost territory or at least enough to reconnect it to Belgium. Third, the instructions directed Malmesbury to press for the restoration of Austrian territories in northern Italy, or, if their military fortunes in that quarter improved, to demand an expansion of the Archduchy of Milan. Fourth, Grenville provided Malmesbury with several ideas for rearranging the Caribbean to prevent France from gaining San Domingo from Spain. Finally, the new proposal maintained the demand for the Cape of Good Hope, Ceylon, and Cochin while agreeing to return other Dutch possessions to the Batavian Republic.[59]

After having stalled for two months, Malmesbury gained fresh purpose from the instructions. He had been skeptical of the negotiations from the start, but the fact that the French allowed him to stall and linger while waiting for the new instructions suggested to him that they were also eager for peace. Malmesbury delivered his new peace program to the French on 17 December. In an extensive discussion with Delacroix, the gulf between British and French views became clear. The French minister protested that the Directory could not cede territory integrated into France as part of the current constitution while Malmesbury insisted that the status of the territories before the war made them liable for negotiation. In addition, Delacroix complained that French Continental concessions grossly outweighed the British colonial compensations.

However, he placed greater value on the colonies when discussing those that Britain intended to keep. Malmesbury viewed the prospect of successful negotiations as grim but believed that the negotiations would at least continue. Two days later, the Directory rejected the proposal without further discussion and ordered Malmesbury to leave the country within two days, which he did on 21 December.[60]

The failure of Malmesbury's mission confronted the British government with the necessity of continuing the war with limited chances of ultimate victory. Austrian operations in Germany and Italy had ground to a halt, and the death of Catherine II removed the flicker of hope for Russian support. Nevertheless, the strained Anglo-Austrian alliance remained the only chance of persevering long enough to bring the French to greater moderation in negotiation. Thus, the Cabinet reluctantly offered the Austrians a new loan of £2,400,000 to support their war effort into 1797 despite the financial troubles in London.[61]

Like the Allies, the French constantly adjusted their attitudes and expectations based on the latest reports of the fluctuating military situation. Much as the escalation of British demands arose from reports of military success, the sudden termination of Malmesbury's mission arose from French anticipation of significant operations. Specifically, a French expedition of 20,000 men sailed for Ireland from Brest on 16 December to raise a rebellion and initiate an invasion of the British home islands.[62] The Directory attempted to delay this expedition after receiving Malmesbury's offer but, finding that it had already sailed, the Directory decided to await its outcome. In addition to the question of the Irish expedition, news of the death of Catherine II arrived in Paris on 14 December; Malmesbury concluded that this news played a significant role in the outright rejection of the Allied peace proposal.[63]

The French expedition slipped past the Royal Navy's relatively lax watch at Brest but weather ultimately spoiled this opportunity. The ship carrying the expedition's senior officers became separated from the main body, and winter gales prevented the French from attempting a landing despite having reached Bantry Bay. While that attempt failed, the Cabinet anticipated another, receiving reports throughout December of French plans to concentrate the French, Spanish, and Dutch fleets at Brest to gain control of the English Channel. Corroborating this concern, the Dutch appeared to be preparing an invasion force on the island of Texel. Accordingly, the British government took measures to prepare coastal counties for defense, including augmenting the militia and removing livestock from coastal pastures.[64]

British concerns were well-founded as the expedition that retreated from Bantry Bay was the first component of a three-pronged invasion. The second expedition sailed for Newcastle in January but also failed to reach its target owing to the weather. However, the third expedition succeeded in landing 1,400 French troops commanded by a bitter, aging Irish American, William Tate, on 22 February 1797 at Fishguard Bay in southern Wales. The British government's preparations yielded a bold defense from the local militia and volunteers. Although the French outnumbered the Welsh militia, their morale was low, having no avenue of retreat and suffering from desertion. The British commander bluffed that he had overwhelmingly superior numbers and persuaded Tate to surrender unconditionally on 24 February.[65]

While the attempted French invasions had negligible military significance, they had a disproportionate impact on the British economy. Already suffering from an economic slump brought on by the shortage of specie, the fear of invasion escalated the pressure on banks across Britain as people demanded their money in panic.[66] Runs on two banks in Northumberland caused them to fail on 20 February. Banks across the country struggled to stave off panic and sent desperate messages to the Bank of England requesting more coinage to stay open, but the Bank of England's bullion shortage left it unable to assist. The French landing transformed widespread anxiety into a full sense of panic that augured economic disaster. Rumors of French invasions had already led to the withdrawal of £200,000 from the Bank of England on 23 and 24 February; confirmed reports of invasion seemed certain to cause a run on the Bank of England, likely collapsing the whole edifice of British finance.[67]

Timing proved significant in the outcome of the invasion scare. The date of the French landing, 22 February, was a Wednesday. Reports of this landing percolated through London on Saturday, 25 February, arriving too late for residents to express their panic through a full run on the Bank of England. The bank would not open again until the morning of Monday, 27 February, leaving the Cabinet the reprieve of Saturday afternoon and Sunday to devise a solution. In two lengthy meetings on Saturday, the ministers discussed possible solutions and agreed on the necessity of taking decisive action through a royal order in council. Accordingly, they requested that George III come to town for an emergency meeting of the Privy Council. Although effectively summoning the king in such a manner was highly unusual, George III recognized the severity of the situation and complied. The king and the Cabinet met for most of the day on Sunday, 26 February, to forestall a financial crisis. During this time, news of the surrender of the French expedition reached London, providing some measure of reassurance.[68]

The Sunday meetings resulted in an Order in Council to the Bank of England suspending cash payments until Parliament could be consulted. The Cabinet sent the Order in Council to the bank on Sunday evening, and the bank published it before opening its doors on Monday, 27 February. The crowd that gathered for making withdrawals found their purpose thus thwarted. The Bank of England therefore retained its limited supply of bullion and continued to issue bank notes. This alone may not have dissuaded the anxious London crowd, but a meeting of several important London business leaders agreed to continue accepting the bank's notes, thereby preserving confidence in them. By the end of the day on Monday, Pitt reported, "Confidence . . . revives, and things in the City wear a better aspect than for some time."[69] Although the atmosphere of London remained tense and anxious, Pitt's assessment ultimately proved accurate. The suspension of cash payments coupled by the willingness of London businesses to continue accepting the bank's notes as legal tender allowed the Bank of England to recover its coin reserves gradually. This stability at the core of the British financial system radiated outward to the provinces, restoring confidence everywhere over time.[70]

Pitt built on this success on 28 February by pushing through Parliament a bill to allow the Bank of England to issue paper notes for as low as £1 instead of the previous low of £5, which partially compensated for the shortage of coin in daily transactions. Although it took until May to pass through Parliament, Pitt secured the passage of another bill mandating that the Bank of England's notes would be guaranteed to be accepted for payment of taxes and debts, thereby boosting confidence in the bank and its paper currency still further.[71]

Confidence received a further boost after news arrived on 3 March that the former Mediterranean fleet under Sir John Jervis had defeated a larger Spanish fleet near Cape St. Vincent on 14 February. Jervis's victory prevented the French and Spanish fleets from uniting in the Channel, thus diminishing immediate fears of larger invasion attempts. For these reasons, Britain experienced a recession followed by a slow recovery rather than a debilitating economic crash.[72]

Although the naval and economic dimensions seemed to have stabilized, the winter months offered no respite from military disappointments on the Continent. In January, Napoleon crushed another Austrian attempt to relieve Mantua, leading to its surrender on 2 February. In March, Vienna pulled Archduke Charles from his successful command in Germany to attempt to halt the seemingly inexorable progress of General Bonaparte's army. Even the most talented commander in Austria failed to arrest French progress. Napoleon continued to advance, repeatedly defeating Charles over the course of March in Venetian territory. On 31 March, after French forces reached the Austrian hereditary lands, Napoleon proposed an armistice.[73]

No longer in a position to influence the Continental war militarily, the British focused on finding support for Austria both diplomatically and financially. Despite being formally allied, Russia proved largely unhelpful. After initially recalling the Russian fleet from the North Sea, Tsar Paul did at least consent to its continuation there in support of the Royal Navy. Also, he eagerly sought a new commercial treaty. While welcome in London, these friendly measures fell far short of a major Russian army supporting Austrian forces in Germany and Italy.[74] Attempts to win Spain back to the coalition through diplomacy at Lisbon and similar efforts to rally German and Italian states yielded no result. A Prussian overture in February for armed mediation on behalf of the Allies occasioned wary interest from the Cabinet. However, British ministers learned the following month of the secret Franco-Prussian neutrality convention of August 1796 that included French support for Prussian annexation of the bishopric of Münster as compensation for territories lost on the left bank of the Rhine. This revelation reinforced the inclination of British ministers to place no faith in the court of Berlin.[75]

The British offer of a new loan of £2,400,000 arrived in Vienna in early February, delayed by the same weather that obstructed French invasion plans. Thugut was unimpressed with the smaller size of the loan in comparison to those of previous years and rejected the offer.[76] By the time Thugut's rejection reached London, the suspension of cash payments from the Bank of England effectively precluded any immediate British financial assistance, including the usual advances. Before British aid could have made any difference, Austria withdrew from the war. On 8 April, as Napoleon continued to advance, the Austrians accepted his offer of an armistice. On 18 April, they signed a preliminary peace with the French general at his headquarters at Leoben, approximately eighty-five miles from Vienna.[77]

Before learning of this, the British took measures to preserve some semblance of unity with their ally. Finding no realistic source of support for Austria on the Continent, the Cabinet decided in early April to comply belatedly with Austrian requests for a British fleet to be sent to the Adriatic.[78] Pitt also obtained Parliamentary support for a loan of £3,500,000 for Vienna on 29 April. However, his overriding objective at this point was not to bait the Austrians into continuing the ruinous war but to keep them strong enough to resist making a separate peace. On the same day that Vienna agreed to Napoleon's armistice, Pitt outlined a peace program to George III. He proposed seeking Russian mediation, potentially including Prussia as well, for a general peace conference. He urged the importance of essentially conceding any point the Austrians might demand in the name of obtaining a multilateral peace that would preserve the Anglo-Austrian connection and entail multilateral commitment to upholding the resulting settlement and thereby preventing renewed aggression.[79]

The Cabinet embraced Pitt's idea on 9 April and dispatched George Hammond to Vienna to seek Austrian acquiescence to this fifth attempt to secure peace, this time through Russian mediation. The suggested terms in Hammond's instructions included numerous concessions to both Austrian and French demands in previous overtures. The British would accept French annexation of Belgium provided Austria received indemnification most likely from Italy or Germany. Britain would also return all colonies except for Ceylon and the Cape of Good Hope. As in the proposals of December 1796, the new program adhered to the principle of maintaining the alliance of a secure British maritime empire and a strong Austrian monarchy to preserve the balance of power in Europe but with greater concessions to French military success.[80]

Hammond's mission might well have enjoyed a positive reception in Vienna had it arrived earlier. Pitt dropped all proposals regarding Prussia or the Austrian Netherlands that Thugut had generally found objectionable. In addition, Thugut sought Russian mediation on his own accord during the armistice, but the relentless pace at which Napoleon dictated both his campaign and his diplomacy prevented Thugut from stalling long enough to receive a response. Ultimately, Thugut obtained terms from Napoleon that he could hardly hope to improve through mediation. Napoleon compensated Austria for the loss of the Netherlands and Milan by granting French approval for Austrian annexation of the Venetian mainland and colonies. After enduring constant disputes with the British on the question of Austrian indemnification, Thugut determined that the proposed compensation in the current military circumstances outweighed the questionable value of the British alliance. Hammond reached the Austrian capital on 30 April, twelve days after the signing of the preliminary peace at Leoben.[81]

For the second time, Hammond left a European capital without making the proposal he had been tasked with transmitting. He and Eden found themselves totally excluded from policy discussions in Vienna. British ministers learned of the Peace of Leoben on 3 May and quickly concluded that multilateral peace had escaped them. They declared an end to the cash advances to Austria, which had already been halted during the Bank of England crisis, and pressed Starhemberg to raise a new loan to repay the sum already advanced as per the original conditions of those advances. Acknowledging the matter as a fulfillment of an engagement already made, Starhemberg signed Austrian consent to a loan of £1,620,000 on 16 May. Unexpectedly, Thugut refused to ratify the new loan, arguing that Starhemberg had lacked authorization for such a measure and that the terms were ruinous to Austria. He went further and refused to make payments on the loans already concluded in 1795. Austrian refusal to ratify the loan and to communicate the terms of the Peace of Leoben effectively nullified the Anglo-Austrian alliance. On 3 May, St. Petersburg offered to call for a general peace conference without posing as mediator. With Britain as the only major power still at war with France, the Cabinet rejected the proposal as pointless after receiving it on 28 May.[82]

With the loss of Austria in April 1797, British ministers faced the choice of continuing the war alone or seeking peace without the support of a major Continental ally to improve their bargaining position. Prospects for continuing the war seemed poor. Although the ministry had successfully weathered the peak of the financial crisis in February, it continued to face many foreign and domestic dangers. The French, Spanish, and Dutch fleets remained at large if not united, and intelligence suggested that the French and Dutch were organizing another invasion attempt in the Netherlands. Concurrently, mutinies wracked the Channel fleet and the North Sea squadron from April to June, paralyzing Britain's primary means of defense.[83]

The government resolved the mutiny in the Channel fleet by 15 May through judicious concessions to the relatively modest demands of the mutineers. However, the leaders of the revolt in the North Sea squadron, which began on 12 May, proved less agreeable. The Cabinet refused their more extensive demands, opting to strengthen the coastal defenses and outlast the mutineers.[84] With the North Sea fleet immobilized, only the Russian squadron that Paul consented to remain in London's service allowed the British to maintain a watch on the Dutch ports.[85] At the height of the crisis, rumblings of discontent in the army seemed to forecast a mutiny on land as well, and a flood of petitions for peace testified to the weariness of the people.[86]

On 1 June, Pitt delivered an address from George III to Parliament that called on the British people to support the government against the mutineers. In the following days, Parliament passed the two acts making any encouragement of or intercourse with the mutineers a felony punishable by death.[87] As in the crisis of December 1792, the country rallied around Pitt's administration, leading to a surge of volunteers, financial donations, and pledges of support from privately owned vessels. In addition, no revolt in the army materialized, and preemptive measures to address unrest among the soldiers ended that threat. Just as the business leaders of London supported the government through the Bank of England crisis, popular army and naval officers assisted the government in resolving the unrest in the fleets and the guards in London. Facing a united country against them, the mutiny in the North Sea squadron began to collapse and finally ended by 16 June.[88]

While the crisis in the British armed forces ended without leading to invasion or political collapse, news of the Peace of Leoben arrived during its darkest moment. Apprehensive about continuing the war with the loyalty of the military in question and without a major Continental ally, Pitt led the

Cabinet to undertake another peace initiative. George III complained of the humiliation of applying to the French again, gloomily observing, "I do not see the hopes that either war can be continued with effect or peace obtained but of the most disgraceful and unsolid tenure."[89] Convinced of the need to negotiate if possible, Pitt overcame the reservations of the king and the Portland Whigs and produced a new peace proposal. In it, he insisted that Portugal must be included in the negotiation on Britain's side while France should invite the Spanish and Dutch to join as well. Pitt still sought to keep the peace settlement anchored in a broad European consensus.[90]

Despite the king's dismal forecast, hopes for successful negotiations received encouragement from within France itself. The elections of March and April 1797 had resulted in major victories for royalists and those in favor of peace throughout the government. Wickham maintained contact with these royalists from his post in Switzerland and began to close the gap separating them from the exiled Louis XVIII. In March, Louis issued a more moderate proclamation of his intentions at British urging. After failing to restore the French monarchy by force, the British grew increasingly optimistic about the possibility of a restoration through France's own political process. In this context, Pitt took a direct approach, writing to the French foreign minister, Delacroix, to request a passport to send another mission to Paris to discuss peace.[91]

On 14 June 1797, the Cabinet received a reply from Delacroix that included a passport and directed the British to send a negotiator to Lille with authority to sign a strictly bilateral peace between Britain and France. The demand for a separate, bilateral peace violated the core of Pitt's foreign policy principles. Even in June 1797, Pitt clung to the hope of securing some sort of multilateral settlement that prevented total British isolation. Although most of the coalition had made peace, Portugal remained active as a British ally. Russia also continued a nominal participation, and Pitt hoped to include both allies in any peace settlement. In addition, the Peace of Leoben had been only preliminary, leaving open the possibility of Austrian participation in a general peace conference. Even the inclusion of the Dutch and Spanish as France's allies, neutrals like Prussia, Denmark, Sweden, or the remaining Italian states would provide a broader network of consensus to preserve any general settlement.[92]

The French message caused considerable division within the government. Grenville and George III viewed the French demands as unacceptable, and they received support from the Portland Whigs who despised the notion of a negotiated peace with a republican France at all. In contrast, Pitt and, with less conviction, Dundas pressed for at least attempting negotiations on the terms proposed so as to avoid recreating the dangerous isolation of 1781–87. With difficulty, Pitt carried his point over Grenville's second formal dissent.

After arriving at the decision to negotiate on French terms, the Cabinet selected Malmesbury to go to Lille and make a second attempt to obtain peace.[93]

Malmesbury reached Lille to begin the negotiations on 4 July 1797. His instructions demanded the Cape of Good Hope and Ceylon for Britain as a sine qua non for any peace settlement, which reflected Dundas's imperialist outlook.[94] Beyond that, Malmesbury should press for the cession of Cochin and one or more of the Caribbean islands, only conceding those in return for French concessions in Europe pertaining to the fate of the Austrian Netherlands and Sardinia's lost territories of Nice and Savoy. Malmesbury's instructions emphasized Spanish or Dutch possessions as primary targets as a mechanism for broadening the negotiations to include other states. Reinforcing this move, Malmesbury was directed to negotiate on behalf of Portugal as well. In reference to the original Anglo-French breach over the sanctity of treaties, Grenville instructed Malmesbury to press the French to acknowledge the binding nature of previous treaties, including the Peace of Utrecht, the Peace of Aix-la-Chapelle, the 1763 Peace of Paris, and the 1783 Peace of Paris.[95]

The French responded to Malmesbury's proposal within the first week of July with several preliminary demands. First, they insisted that George III renounce the ancient claim of English kings to the throne of France. Regarding the more contemporary matters of the war, they also demanded restitution of or reparations for the French ships taken from Toulon in 1793. Finally, they required that the British annul their claim to Belgian revenues as collateral for the Austrian loans.[96] While Pitt was willing to discuss these proposals, the French sent a further demand on 15 July for the return of all overseas territory under British occupation as a precondition of negotiations. The Directory argued that its treaties with the Dutch and Spanish prevented it from making their territories a subject of negotiation until the British agreed to abandon them. As Malmesbury predicted to the French envoys, London rejected this assertion, and negotiations devolved into a fruitless debate over the applicability of France's pre-existing commitments to its allies.[97]

Malmesbury's position weakened in August after the Portuguese ambassador in Paris signed a peace treaty on his own authority. A small British army was in Lisbon at Portugal's request, and the former Mediterranean fleet used that city as a base for patrolling the Spanish coast. Thus, the Portuguese peace threatened to remove Britain's last active ally and the last sphere in which the British wielded even minor military leverage in Europe. No longer able to plead for the inclusion of Britain's allies, Malmesbury could argue with the French only about the inclusion of theirs.[98]

The fate of the Lille negotiations ultimately depended on increasingly tense French politics. The royalists pushed for moderate reforms and maneuvered to increase their control of government functions, initially without resistance from the moderate Directors led by Lazare Carnot. However, the more resolute republican director, Paul Barras, organized a coup against the royalists with the support of Napoleon, who sent one division under General Pierre Augereau from Italy to assist the coup. On 4 September 1797, Barras and his supporters executed what became known as the Coup of 18 Fructidor according to the republican calendar. The conspirators arrested and deported numerous royalists, annulled the spring elections, and began censoring royalist publications. The coup effectively restored to power the Jacobins after their ouster during the Thermidorian Reaction of 1794.[99]

From a British perspective, the Coup of 18 Fructidor meant the likely death of negotiations. The royalists and moderates had represented the popular desire for peace while the Jacobins represented a firm commitment to retain all the gains of the Revolution and a distinct lack of interest in a peace based on balance or compromise.[100] The new regime replaced the French delegation at Lille on 11 September. Five days later, the new delegation demanded that Malmesbury accept the principle of restoring all British conquests. On 17 September, Malmesbury insisted that any such question must form a part of the peace negotiations rather than be a precondition for them.[101] The French declined to discuss the matter further, ordering the British envoy to leave within one day, which he did.[102]

The collapse of the Lille negotiations effectively ended the last British attempt to end the War of the First Coalition through multilateral consensus. In September and October, Pitt and Dundas, to the disgust of George III and Grenville, contemplated clandestine French offers for peace in return for bribes, but all failed. The proposals involved exorbitant demands but offered no assurances. In addition, the secrecy necessary for such transactions would prove impossible to reconcile with the need for Parliamentary approval of the sums involved.[103] Pitt continued to consider such secret approaches throughout the remainder of the year, but he placed little hope in them after the initial overtures failed.[104]

The final Franco-Austrian peace signed at Campo Formio on 17 October 1797 left Britain almost alone in the war with France. By the end of the year, even the pretense of the alliance with Russia had crumbled. Paul rejected British appeals based on the 1795 Triple Alliance, simply asserting his inability to fulfill his obligations under that treaty. Only Portugal remained allied to Britain and at war with France, as the government in Lisbon had rejected the treaty its minister had signed in Paris.[105]

Unable to obtain a peace that addressed Britain's European interests, Pitt determined in 1797 that continuing the fight posed less danger to Britain than concluding peace on the terms that the French Republic demanded. Successful recovery from the crises of the spring bolstered his confidence in making this decision. Confidence in the economy was growing, and the Bank of England began to rebound from the specie shortage as payments to British troops abroad and allies lessened. The country had adapted to an increased reliance on paper money without a catastrophe. An election in 1796 had reinforced government majorities in both houses of Parliament, and Pitt's repeated efforts to negotiate an acceptable treaty prevented the opposition's calls for peace from undermining his political ascendancy.[106]

Militarily, British success at sea and in the colonies combined with the significant enlargement of the militia and volunteer forces in the home islands increased confidence in Britain's defensive capabilities. The rapid seizure of Dutch colonies secured communications with Asia, and the dedication of significant resources to the Caribbean ensured the safety of the British West Indies. Jervis's victory at Cape St. Vincent had temporarily crippled the Spanish navy, and the Channel and North Sea fleets resumed their vigilant patrols off Brest and the Texel after the ministry ended the mutinies. Further good news arrived on 13 October 1797. Admiral Adam Duncan had crushed a Dutch fleet in the Battle of Camperdown, capturing eleven Dutch ships of the line. Camperdown, Cape St. Vincent, and the renewed naval vigor that followed the mutinies reduced the prospect of a combined French, Spanish, and Dutch fleet gaining ascendancy in the Channel and conducting a major invasion of the British Isles. Thus, Pitt could look to the continuation of the war with confidence while seeking new openings to recover his lost European connections.[107]

Conclusion

Successors and Success, 1798–1815

In a speech in the House of Lords on 8 January 1799, Auckland offered a summary of the British strategic situation that applied equally to the end of 1797: "So far as the mere safety of these islands is in question, we are safe in our own courage and resources, but in looking towards the wished-for period of pacification, we must never forget that the security of Europe is essential to the security of the British empire. We cannot separate them."[1] This single statement contains the guiding principles of Pitt's foreign policy throughout the 1780s and the War of the First Coalition. Pitt took office in 1783 on the heels of the loss of the thirteen American colonies in a confrontation with a coalition of the strongest maritime powers in Europe—a catastrophic demonstration of the dangers of embracing a policy of "splendid isolation" from the European continent.[2] Pitt consistently endeavored to remove these dangers by taking an active role in European politics and seeking British security within the European state system rather than in Britain's wooden wall. According to Pitt's view, British security in Europe required a multilateral alliance system to protect the territorial status quo and mediate disputes on the basis of existing treaties without wars or conquests.[3] This foreign policy vision that emerged prior to the Revolutionary and Napoleonic Wars provided the future foreign secretary and Pitt protégé, Robert Stewart, Viscount Castlereagh, with a firm belief in the need to establish a concert of Europe. Although Pitt failed to achieve his lofty ambitions, Castlereagh's adherence to Pitt's principles contributed heavily to the creation of the Quadruple Alliance in 1814 and the Vienna Congress System in 1815.

The line of continuity between Pitt and Castlereagh is supported by the historiography surrounding the latter minister. Most often, historians attribute Castlereagh's advocacy for the Quadruple Alliance and the Vienna Congress System to his experiences as Pitt's war secretary during the War of the Third Coalition.[4] In the 1804–5 winter, Pitt produced a peace plan calling for "a general agreement and guarantee for the mutual protection and security of different powers and for reestablishing a general system of public law in Europe."[5] Castlereagh acknowledged that these principles formed the basis of his policies as foreign secretary from 1812 until his death in 1822.[6]

Several historians, including Peter Jupp, Piers Mackesy, and John Sherwig, argue that Pitt derived his 1805 program from Grenville's earlier ideas for creating the Second Coalition in the winter of 1797–98. At that time, Grenville pressed for the creation of a quadruple alliance encompassing Austria, Prussia, Russia, and Britain and recommended designating a central location for an allied conference to coordinate operations and reconcile diplomatic differences. On 14 January 1798, he wrote to the British ambassador in Berlin that London sought "the formation of a system of Quadruple Alliance," security for the Holy Roman Empire, a "maritime peace" acceptable to Britain, and a mutual guarantee of territory among all the states of Europe.[7] Thus, Grenville articulated a project that strongly foreshadowed both Pitt's plan of 1805 and Castlereagh's subsequent policies of 1812–22.[8]

Attributing the origin of these later policies to Grenville and his efforts to forge a second coalition against France in 1797 and 1798 raises two problems. First, distinguishing between Pitt's foreign policy views and Grenville's is difficult. Although Pitt left the execution of foreign office duties to Grenville, they collaborated closely, together with Dundas, on the formation of nearly every aspect of British domestic and foreign policy.[9] That Pitt and Grenville did not always agree is abundantly clear. Grenville's record of opposing his cousin's policies included opposition to the ultimatum to Russia in 1791, protest against the Prussian subsidy proposal of 1795, and resistance to the idea of approaching France for peace in 1797. The first of these occasions nearly caused the collapse of Pitt's ministry, and the latter two prompted threats of resignation followed by the rare occurrence of a cabinet minister registering formal dissent to George III in response to Pitt overruling Grenville's views.[10] Beyond simply furnishing examples of disagreement between the two men, these incidents demonstrate that Pitt did not always bow to Grenville's will as is often portrayed. Instead, Pitt felt confident enough in his own ideas to confront and overrule the foreign secretary. Therefore, any foreign policy initiatives actually undertaken, such as Grenville's concert proposal in January 1798, reflected at least Pitt's full concurrence if not his own original thinking.[11]

Attributing Castlereagh's push for a cooperative balance of power during and after the War of the Sixth Coalition to either Pitt in 1805 or Grenville in 1798 leads to a second problem. Pitt's 1805 plan is often presented as a new solution developed in response to the aggression of revolutionary and Napoleonic France in which Pitt adapted old ideas of "barriers" from the wars of Louis XIV to new circumstances. Similarly, Grenville's 1798 quadruple alliance proposals are explained as simply a reaction to the failures of the First Coalition. However, such explanations ignore Pitt's foreign policy from 1783 to 1793. He rejected traditional island insularity and permanent Francophobia in favor of multilateral guarantees and a new cooperative diplomatic system to prevent war and aggression before the French Revolution transformed the political landscape of Europe. These goals predated Grenville's presence in the Cabinet and changed little after the outbreak of war with revolutionary France.[12]

Pitt's foreign policy took shape slowly between 1783 and 1787. Caution characterized his early years in office as he balanced the goal of ending hostile French hegemony in Europe and the resulting British isolation with the more pressing demands of national recovery from the late war. During this period, Pitt rejected any alliance that seemed to place Britain in a dependent position or commit it to aggressive projects. This stance led to poor relations with the ambitious and expansionist Austro-Russian alliance, but it also yielded a nascent rapprochement with the Bourbon monarchies. However, the endurance of the Franco-Austrian alliance of 1756 along with lingering mutual suspicions within the British and French governments prevented this trend from developing into a complete diplomatic realignment. The Dutch political crisis in 1787 partially revived the Anglo-French antagonism and brought Pitt to a crossroads. During the crisis, Carmarthen and Malmesbury influenced Pitt to depart from his earlier caution and embrace more active interventionism to pull the strategically critical Dutch Republic out of the French bloc. Pitt's active involvement in the conduct of foreign policy during the Dutch Crisis contributed to successful Prussian intervention without a war with France.[13]

Pitt used his success in the Dutch Crisis to forge the Triple Alliance of Britain, Prussia, and the United Provinces, which he hoped to use as the foundation for a broader collective security system that encompassed as many states as possible. From 1788 to 1790, Pitt repeatedly attempted to expand the Triple Alliance and establish it as a system for arbitrating European conflicts. As France collapsed into financial crisis and revolution, Pitt endeavored to supplant Versailles as the protector of Sweden, Poland, and the Ottoman Empire from Russian aggression. This effort failed largely because of a difference of vision between Pitt and the Prussian court. While Pitt sought security through multilateralism, commerce, and commitment to the status quo, the Prussians sought security in opportunistic aggrandizement and subjugation. The maritime nature of British military resources meant that Pitt could not achieve his European objectives without a major Continental ally that shared his vision, and, in this regard, the Prussian alliance proved to be a disappointment.[14]

This conflict proved most pronounced in the case of Poland in 1791. Pitt hoped to solve the problem that the growth of the eastern powers posed to the balance of power by incorporating a revitalized Poland into his collective security system. If successful, Pitt hoped to gain for Britain a valuable economic partner with considerable military potential while also eliminating Poland as a sphere of competition and partition between Austria, Prussia, and Russia. While a strong, independent Poland in a British-led alliance system may not have resolved all the regional security concerns of the eastern powers, it could have preserved a buffer between them, thus minimizing the tension that so severely undermined the First Coalition. Regardless of Poland's potential as a member of the Triple Alliance, the attempt to wield British influence in eastern Europe failed during the Ochakov Crisis of 1791. Pitt sought to mediate the 1787 Russo-Turkish War as a mechanism to bring other countries, especially Poland, into the Triple Alliance and even gain the allegiance of Vienna and St. Petersburg in the aftermath. The attempt foundered as the Prussians used their influence in the collective mediation effort to attempt to enact a complex partition scheme primarily at the expense of Poland and Austria. Pitt issued an ultimatum to Russia to preempt Prussia's plans but found himself forced into a humiliating retreat by his failure to persuade Parliament to accept his interventionism in eastern Europe.[15]

The failure at Ochakov led to significant diplomatic realignments detrimental to Pitt's goals and created the rifts that irreconcilably divided the future members of the First Coalition. Prussia effectively abandoned the Triple Alliance to forge a new connection with Austria based on the principle of using aggressive partition politics, specifically against Poland and France, to counter the growth of Russian power. This new alliance not only conflicted with Pitt's status quo and collective security vision but contributed to the beginning of the French Revolutionary Wars and two partitions of Poland. Consequently, when the French revolutionaries declared war on Austria in 1792, unknowingly starting the first of seven coalition wars, Pitt favored neither the predatory German powers nor the unstable and unknown revolutionary government in Paris. He thus guided Britain through a studious neutrality in 1792, seeking to strengthen his domestic position to allow Britain to defend itself and even stand as a mediator in the conflict.[16]

British attitudes shifted with military fortunes on the Continent in the summer of 1792. As the French ejected Vienna's armies from the Austrian Netherlands and adopted an increasingly aggressive posture toward the United Provinces, the threat posed to Britain's primary ally eclipsed concerns about the German powers. Pitt attempted to revive his collective security ideals and end the war through Anglo-Dutch mediation in November 1792. However, the French National Convention preempted this effort by rejecting neutral Dutch sovereignty and proclaiming its intent to support foreign revolutionaries. The November decrees ended hopes for peace between Britain and the French Republic and confirmed British fears of French aggressive intent. Anglo-French diplomacy failed to resolve the matter, leading to a French declaration of war on 1 February 1793. Thus, Britain entered the War of the First Coalition not to humiliate an old rival or seize its colonies but to defend the sovereignty of neutrals and preserve a European balance of power that included Britain. This consideration also governed British attitudes toward the possibility of negotiating with the revolutionaries or supporting the counterrevolution. Pitt consistently made the question of peace with France contingent on the restoration of France's European conquests and the renunciation of its aggressive policies rather than on extensive colonial concessions or a change of government.[17]

Throughout the War of the First Coalition, Pitt continued to adhere to his foreign policy principles of collective security. In late December 1792, prior to the outbreak of war, Pitt attempted to unite the neutral states of Europe to end the war through armed mediation. This initiative failed to bear fruit before the French declaration of war and thereafter became an attempt to unify the efforts of the states at war with France into a single system. Notably, Pitt repeatedly refused to accede to the predatory Austro-Prussian alliance system, which would have made Britain party to the Second Partition of Poland in 1793. Instead, building on earlier mediation proposals, he called for a coalition congress at The Hague to settle all differences and create a united front based on the principles of collective security. This initiative failed in 1793 and 1794 as the eastern powers insisted on some resolution to their disputes over the allocation of Polish territory from the Second Partition, an issue in which Pitt was unwilling, on principle, to involve Britain in any way.[18]

During the war, Pitt accepted the necessity of indemnification but insisted that it must come from the aggressor, France, rather than a neutral state like Poland. Despite this principle, Pitt harbored no desire to destroy or cripple France. He explicitly rejected the idea and suggested only modest colonial acquisitions for Britain's indemnity. Pitt's administration placed much greater emphasis on the future shape of Europe and the restoration of France's conquests there than on the fate of France's colonial holdings. This position failed to address the unique concerns of each coalition member, which in turn prevented them from being united in a single system. The Spanish viewed with suspicion British maritime success and equivocation regarding the French Bourbons.[19] British failure to provide a European indemnity for the Dutch contributed to a revival of their simmering domestic factionalism and undermined their war effort.[20] Pitt's principled refusal to engage with the Polish partitions prevented him from addressing the full scope of the eastern powers' security concerns and uniting them against France.[21]

In 1795, the Third Partition eliminated the Polish question entirely, thus paving the way for a new Triple Alliance of Britain, Austria, and Russia, but only after Prussia, Spain, and the United Provinces had made peace with France and the latter two pivoted to become French allies. By this time, the hope of building the collective security system out of the wartime coalition had largely failed. The new Triple Alliance could not provide for the needs of the war, much less for a grander design transcending the war. Russia provided nominal assistance, leaving Britain dependent on an exhausted Austria to wage war on the Continent. Pitt's diplomatic focus in 1796 shifted from obtaining security through a united coalition designed to subdue France by force to obtaining security and unity through multilateral peace negotiations. Amid a rapidly fluctuating military situation in Italy and Germany and an unstable political scene in France, these negotiations failed. Unable to find a military answer to General Bonaparte, Vienna made peace, leaving Britain to face France alone, primarily at sea and in the colonies.[22] Thus, by 1797, Britain's diplomatic position looked much as it had when Pitt took office in 1783: isolated, facing a largely hostile European continent, and reduced to waging war almost exclusively at sea and in the colonies. Nevertheless, this represented an uncomfortable necessity rather than a resurgence of the insular, Tory, blue-water thinking of the 1760s and 1770s.[23]

In the unpleasant circumstances of 1797, Pitt resolved to continue the war with France based on his agreement with Auckland's assertion that "the security of Europe is essential to the security of the British empire."[24] Britain's colonial conquests minimized the French, Dutch, and Spanish threats to Britain's overseas empire and yielded significant economic benefits. Thus, colonial success allowed the Royal Navy to focus on defending home waters, unlike in the American War of Independence. The preservation and expansion of colonial commerce furnished financial resources to sustain Britain's war effort in the face of hostile French domination of western Europe. Nevertheless, Pitt preferred to trade this militant and watchful security for security based on balance and cooperation within Europe. Finding the French unwilling to accept such an exchange, Pitt resolved to continue the war until either the internal situation of France's politics and economy forced the revolutionaries to terms or British diplomacy forged a new coalition to impose British views of security by force.[25]

Castlereagh's later efforts to bind the members of the Sixth Coalition and consolidate British security in Europe through the Congress of Vienna followed the principles Pitt had established but achieved greater success.[26] After the outbreak of war between Russia and the French Empire in June 1812, the ministry of prime minister Robert Jenkinson, Second Earl of Liverpool, readily offered Russia logistical and naval assistance without optimism regarding the outcome. Even after Napoleon began his retreat from Moscow, the Cabinet hesitated to attempt to base a new coalition on Russian success. Its members doubted that Tsar Alexander I would carry the war into central Europe. Should he decide to do so, London questioned whether his intentions would coincide with British interests. Disappointment in five previous coalition wars had instilled in the British a caution that overrode optimism.[27] This attitude changed following the Russo-Prussian Treaty of Kalisch on 28 February 1813. In it, Prussia joined the war on Russia's side on the condition that St. Petersburg should continue the war until Prussia regained territory sufficient to return it to its strength prior to the war of 1806.[28]

Following the Treaty of Kalisch, Castlereagh instructed his envoys to the Prussian and Russian courts to offer British subsidies in return for military persistence and to secure both the rejection of a separate peace and the acceptance of a multilateral alliance, including a unified council to coordinate war aims and operations. To his ambassador to Russia, Earl William Cathcart, Castlereagh explained his views on the future general peace settlement:

> The political arrangement of Europe, in a larger sense, is more difficult at this early moment to decide on. . . . The main features we are agreed upon—that to keep France in order we require great masses—that Prussia, Austria, and Russia ought to be as great and powerful as they have ever been—and that the inferior states must be summoned to assist or pay the forfeit of resistance. I see many inconveniences in premature conclusions, but we ought not to be unprepared. As an outline to reason from, I send you as a private communication a dispatch on which the confederacy in 1805 was founded; the Emperor of Russia probably has not this interesting document at head-quarters (interesting it is to my recollection as I well remember having more than one conversation with Mr. Pitt on its details before he wrote it). Some of the suggestions may now be inapplicable, but it is so masterly an outline for the restoration of Europe that I should be glad your lordship would reduce it into distinct propositions and learn the bearings of his Imperial Majesty's mind upon its contents.[29]

Thus, Castlereagh offered as the basis for the War of the Sixth Coalition and subsequent peace the plan for a permanent collective security alliance system that Pitt had proposed in 1805 after refining through two wars the ideas that animated his policies since he took office in 1783.[30]

As Castlereagh's proposals led to separate Treaties of Reichenbach with Russia and Prussia on 14 June 1813, he faced as much difficulty as Pitt in his efforts to create a larger alliance system. Austrian foreign minister, Prince Klemens Wenzel von Metternich, largely ignored the British in his arrangement of an armistice between Napoleon and the Russians and Prussians earlier that same month. During the summer armistice, Metternich proposed Austrian armed mediation, demanding from Napoleon the dissolution of the Grand Duchy of Warsaw, the restoration of much of Prussia's lost territory, Austrian recovery of the Illyrian provinces, and the liberation of the Hanseatic cities. Castlereagh indicated British acceptance of these terms in an effort to close the diplomatic gap between Britain and the eastern powers. However, like Pitt in 1796 and 1797, Castlereagh offered to return the colonies Britain had conquered from France and its allies only if the Continental peace better reflected British concerns than did the Austrian proposals. He insisted as his price for British concessions the independence of Holland and appropriate provisions for Portugal and Spain.[31]

After French refusal of Metternich's terms brought Austria into the war in August, Castlereagh redoubled his efforts to promote British views on the Continent and secure them through a multilateral alliance. On 18 September 1813, he dispatched new instructions to his envoys in central Europe urging the necessity of combining the Peninsular War and the War of the Sixth Coalition into a single struggle through a common alliance. He proposed inviting all states at war with France to accede to a single treaty rejecting a separate peace and establishing a perpetual defensive alliance to repel any aggression in Europe whether from Napoleon or another sovereign. Castlereagh's September proposals mirrored Pitt's efforts from 1788 to build a collective security system to repel any aggression. In addition, Castlereagh's struggle to merge two different wars against a common foe into a single combined effort bears a strong resemblance to Pitt's similar efforts to unite the Anglo-Dutch and Austro-Prussian alliances in 1793 and 1794.[32]

Castlereagh suffered from the same slow communication that plagued the diplomacy of Pitt and Grenville in the 1780s and 1790s. His September proposals reached the British envoys on 20 October, only after the Battle of Leipzig had completely transformed the strategic situation. Further delays in the envoys' efforts to coordinate their negotiations between themselves prevented any communication of Castlereagh's ideas until after Metternich had submitted his Frankfurt Proposals to offer peace to Napoleon if France would return to its "natural frontiers." This proposal, which left Belgium and the great arsenal of Antwerp in French hands, was as unacceptable to the British in 1813 as it had been in 1793. Napoleon's rejection of the proposals annulled the prospects of a peace concluded on such a basis that left British concerns unanswered. Nevertheless, the Frankfurt Proposals illustrated the paucity of

British influence on the Continent despite the existence of subsidy treaties with all of the states in the war.[33]

Underscoring the lack of British influence, Castlereagh's September proposal for a unitary alliance received largely negative responses from the eastern powers after the British envoys finally communicated it in late November and early December 1813. Collectively, these circumstances persuaded the Cabinet of the need to send Castlereagh to the Continent with broad discretionary powers to represent British interests more forcefully and eliminate the dangerous delay inherent in managing diplomacy from London. In this regard, Liverpool's administration improved on Pitt's. Although Pitt and Grenville had consistently expressed the need of a congress with representatives from all coalition members furnished with full powers to coordinate the war, this ambition had never been realized. In part, this initiative had failed because the Continental powers proved reluctant to embrace such a measure. However, even during the Austrian court's excursion to the Flanders front, the British ministers had made no effort to send a similarly empowered emissary to coordinate with Francis at the combined army's headquarters. While such a meeting likely would not have resulted in the same degree of coordination that the allies achieved in the Sixth Coalition, it could have reduced the enormous communication delays that plagued the First Coalition.[34]

Castlereagh departed for the Continent on 28 December 1813 armed with a Cabinet memorandum that he had composed two days earlier. The memorandum outlined the policies that he would pursue throughout the remainder of the War of the Sixth Coalition and throughout the Congress of Vienna. Most notably, he insisted on a general alliance among all the coalition powers to resolve their differences and present a unified front during the war and in future negotiations with France. Castlereagh outlined five main points of British interest with regard to this alliance. First, London would insist that France be denied access to the Scheldt River and the city of Antwerp. Second, Holland would be made strong enough to protect Antwerp and the Scheldt by receiving sufficient Belgian territory. Third, the British would require the alliance to guarantee the independence of Spain and Portugal. Fourth, the Italian states should be returned to their status quo before the French Revolution with some modifications if necessary. Fifth, he desired that the general alliance continue after the war to prevent any future aggression. In a supplementary point, he would offer British acceptance of a Bonaparte on the throne of France if the peace settlement reduced the French frontiers to their pre-Revolution bounds. To secure these points, the memorandum offered that in addition to London's military and financial contributions, Britain would restore most of the colonies captured during the war. Many of Castlereagh's objectives, such as those regarding the Low Countries or the independence of Continental powers, can be attributed to a general geostrategic continuity of British interests. However, the notion of securing them through a multilateral, peacetime alliance and by trading away most colonial gains strongly reflected the influence of Pitt's prewar collective security principles.[35]

Despite quickly establishing a good relationship with Metternich, Castlereagh initially found no enthusiasm for his project among the Allies in January 1814. Unity had deteriorated in the face of success as Alexander pushed to dethrone Napoleon forcibly and rejected negotiations while Metternich advocated an armistice and a negotiated peace that left Bonaparte on the French throne. However, several factors forcefully demonstrated the need for close cooperation, thus strengthening Castlereagh's position. A series of French victories in early February shattered the tsar's hopes of a quick conquest of France. In addition, ongoing negotiations with the French at Châtillon demonstrated that Napoleon would not likely accept a negotiated peace that did not include a colonial settlement with Britain as well.[36] Finally, as the 1814 campaign became more difficult than expected, the Continental allies began to feel an increasing need for British subsidies to sustain their armies. As a result of these factors, Castlereagh succeeded in gaining Austrian, Prussian, and Russian acquiescence to a general alliance. They signed the Treaty of Chaumont on 9 March 1814, agreeing in principle to the primary points enumerated in Castlereagh's memorandum and forming the first incarnation of the Quadruple Alliance. Thus, Castlereagh succeeded where his mentor had failed in leveraging British financial and maritime power to achieve a multilateral alliance and real influence on the continent of Europe.[37]

Despite an energetic campaign from Napoleon, the Allied armies forced him to abandon Paris, and they entered the French capital on 31 March 1814. There, Talleyrand convened the remains of the French government, which deposed Napoleon and declared for Louis XVIII. The Allies secured Napoleon's abdication and exile to Elba in the Treaty of Fontainebleau on 13 April and thereafter looked toward a general peace.[38] The representatives of the four major Allies together with Talleyrand gathered in Paris to negotiate peace on 9 May. Signed on 30 May, the resulting Treaty of Paris reduced France to its territorial boundaries of 1 November 1792 with a few exceptions but at a corresponding cost of a few colonial holdings. In the treaty, Castlereagh achieved the main goals that animated Britain's struggle with revolutionary and Napoleonic France since 1793. France's territorial and diplomatic domination of western and central Europe ended, and the restored Bourbons appeared willing to accept and support the balance of power. To purchase this European settlement, Castlereagh had willingly abandoned all but three of France's colonies, much as Pitt had attempted in 1796 and 1797.[39]

The First Treaty of Paris established peace between France and the Sixth Coalition but left the remaining issues attending the dismantling of Napoleonic Europe to a future congress at Vienna. After spending the summer of 1814 engaged in festivities and preparing for the congress, delegates from all over Europe converged on Vienna in September and October 1814. Castlereagh went to the Congress of Vienna with the intention of creating a system of collective security reminiscent of Pitt's ideas in the 1780s. Having largely attained Britain's most immediate objectives in the peace with France, Castlereagh sought to use British influence at the Congress of Vienna to create a "just equilibrium" on the Continent that would restrain all aggressive powers.[40]

Like Pitt, Castlereagh found disputes over Poland among the eastern powers the greatest obstacle to a cooperative settlement. Also like Pitt, Castlereagh sought to solve the problem by integrating into the new system a strong and independent Poland as a buffer between Vienna, Berlin, and St. Petersburg. His hopes in this regard fared no better than Pitt's had in 1791. Not one of the eastern powers would cede to Poland sufficient territory to make such a scheme work, and Castlereagh recognized that the independent Kingdom of Poland that Alexander proposed would be entirely subservient to Russia. However, Castlereagh responded differently to this failure than had Pitt. While Pitt retreated from the affairs of eastern Europe entirely and refused on principle to connect Britain in any way to the partitions of Poland, Castlereagh harbored no such qualms. He accepted the necessity of compromise to secure the larger goal of collective security. In addition, Castlereagh had less reason to oppose the partition of Poland on principle as it had fought on Napoleon's side in the recent war.[41]

Castlereagh also shared Pitt's recognition that Russia posed as much danger to the European balance of power as France, if not more, and that France could become a valuable partner for resisting that threat. Castlereagh visited Talleyrand in Paris on his way to Vienna in August 1814 and established a mutual understanding with the French minister on the desirable balance of power. Correspondingly, after Talleyrand gained admittance into the inner council of the four main Allies at the Congress of Vienna, he, along with Metternich, became a strong ally for Castlereagh in the effort to resist Russian expansion. This solidarity between Britain, Austria, and France contributed to the ultimate resolution of the Polish question during the Congress of Vienna. Alexander's extensive demands for a Russian-dominated Poland became coupled with Prussian demands for the annexation of Saxony, and the two powers proved resistant to compromise on the subject. In January 1815, Castlereagh, Talleyrand, and Metternich signed a secret alliance, agreeing to resist Russo-Prussian demands for Poland and Saxony by force if necessary. This alliance convinced the Russians and Prussians to accept compromises that reduced the scope of their gains, which ended the most serious threat of a dispute between the powers. Pitt had also attempted to enlist France to oppose Russian aggression in eastern Europe in 1789 but had found his hopes frustrated by the French economic collapse and revolution.[42]

Napoleon's return from Elba to reclaim his throne on 1 March 1815 interrupted the work of the Congress of Vienna, but Castlereagh's diplomacy of the previous year enabled a quick and unified response. While the Quadruple Alliance created by the Treaty of Chaumont had been superseded by other agreements after the Peace of Paris, the Allies quickly renewed that structure to confront Napoleon. On 13 March, the Allies declared Napoleon an outlaw, and on 25 March, they signed a treaty fully recreating the Quadruple Alliance. Napoleon hoped to exploit and exacerbate Allied divisions to obtain a separate negotiated peace with at least some of the powers arrayed against him, thereby allowing him to concentrate on the remainder.[43] This strategy had served him and the revolutionary administrations before him well in the previous coalition wars. Pitt had failed, despite his best efforts, to create an alliance structure of sufficient diplomatic unity or military power to avoid succumbing to defeat in detail in the Wars of the First, Second, and Third Coalitions. In contrast, the unity that Castlereagh secured at Chaumont based on Pitt's principles ensured the failure of Napoleon's 1815 strategy.[44]

The War of the Seventh Coalition ended quickly. After mobilizing, Napoleon struck into Belgium to crush the main British and Prussian armies there before gathering fresh levies to face the larger Austrian and Russian forces on the Rhine. This campaign culminated in the Battle of Waterloo on 18 June in which close Anglo-Prussian cooperation ultimately routed the determined French assault.[45] Then, for a second time, Napoleon abdicated, and Allied armies restored the Bourbons to power. Castlereagh returned to Paris in July to make peace between France and the Allies again. In contrast to the previous year, the prominent role of the British army in directly defeating Napoleon in 1815 placed Castlereagh in a stronger position to press his views on the final peace arrangement. Still seeking to preserve a strong France to counter Russia, Castlereagh moderated the more vindictive views of the Prussians in the negotiations.[46] The Second Treaty of Paris required France to make minor border concessions on its eastern frontier, pay an indemnity, and support an army of occupation for five years. In the course of the negotiations, Castlereagh continued to strengthen British ties to the Continent, persuading the Allies to renew the Quadruple Alliance after the peace and to guarantee the Second Treaty of Paris. The sixth article of the alliance treaty stipulated that the Allies would meet at fixed intervals to address and resolve any threats to the peace of

Europe, thereby creating the Congress System. Both the peace treaty and the alliance were signed on 20 November 1815.[47]

Castlereagh's Congress System and the earlier plans of Pitt and Grenville in 1798 and 1805 are conventionally viewed as a reaction and solution to the problems created by the French Revolution. In fact, the French Revolution had merely furnished fresh examples of the defects of the predatory international system that Pitt had already been seeking to fix since 1783. As the diplomat James Harris observed in 1785, the balance of power in Europe, as outlined in the 1648 Peace of Westphalia and confirmed in the 1715 Peace of Utrecht, had ceased to provide a meaningful legitimizing framework for European diplomacy. Changes in political philosophies together with the growth of the global colonial empires of western European powers and the rise of new great powers in eastern Europe undermined the stability of the Westphalian balance. European politics had become a race among the greater powers to justify conquests of opportunity to gain advantage over each other in the name of balance. The nebulous equilibrium articulated at Utrecht thus evolved into predatory partition diplomacy. In his efforts to provide for British security in Europe, Pitt discovered a lack of consensus on what the European balance of power meant. His attempts to construct this consensus around British views evolved into a broader project to establish a new foundation for European diplomacy that ultimately proved to be beyond his reach.

In defending his stand against Russia in 1791, Pitt provided an explanation of his hopes and intents that might just as easily have described Castlereagh's efforts from 1813 to 1815: "The end of this alliance was to give by their union such strength and authority as to be able at all times to compel other powers to abandon schemes of ambition and conquest which might endanger the general tranquility. To succeed in this, it was indispensably necessary that the alliance should be kept sufficient to its object and each party be in a condition to fulfill its part to the stipulations."[48] By the end of 1815, Castlereagh could largely claim success in his efforts to realize Pitt's vision for a multilateral, cooperative diplomatic system to preserve British security through peace in Europe. That it did not last is another story.

Abbreviations

Add MS	Additional Manuscripts
ADM	Admiralty Papers
AGC	Papers of Admiral John Gell, Miscellaneous Letters
BL	British Library
Eg MS	Egerton Manuscripts
ELL	Elliot Family Papers
FO	Foreign Office
HMC	Historical Manuscripts Commission
HO	Home Office
MS	Manuscripts
NLS	National Library of Scotland
NMM	National Maritime Museum, Greenwich
NRS	National Records of Scotland
PC	Privy Council
PRO	Public Records Office Collections
TNA	National Archives of the United Kingdom
WCL	William L. Clements Library
WO	War Office

NOTES

Introduction

1. Simms, *Three Victories*.
2. For the primacy of colonial affairs, see Armitage and Braddick, *British Atlantic World*; Baugh, "Great Britain's 'Blue Water' Policy"; Baugh, "Withdrawing from Europe"; Horn, *Britain and Europe*; Jones, *Britain and the World*; McKay and Scott, *Rise of the Great Powers*; Monod, *Imperial Island*; Prest, *Albion Ascendant*; and Wilson, *Sense of the People*. For the primacy of Europe, see Conway, *Britain, Ireland, and Continental Europe*; Conway, "Continental Connections"; Harding, *Hanover and the British Empire*; Gould, *Persistence of Empire*.
3. Black, *Debating Foreign Policy in Eighteenth-Century Britain*; Black, *Natural and Necessary Enemies*; Black, *System of Ambition?*
4. Christie, *Wars and Revolutions*; Duffy, "British War Policy"; Duffy, *Soldiers, Sugar, and Seapower*; Fortescue, *History of the British Army*.
5. Blanning, *Origins of the French Revolutionary Wars*; Hall, *British Strategy in the Napoleonic War*; Nester, *Titan*.
6. Black, *British Foreign Policy*.
7. Duffy, *Younger Pitt*; Ehrman, *Years of Acclaim*; Ehrman, *Reluctant Transition*; Ehrman, *Consuming Struggle*; Hague, *William Pitt the Younger*; Turner, *Pitt the Younger*.
8. Christie, *Wars and Revolutions*, 181–234; Ehrman, *Years of Acclaim*; Ehrman, *Reluctant Transition*; Ehrman, *Consuming Struggle*; Horn, *Britain and Europe*, 22–85; Jones, *Britain and the World*, 254–80; Sherwig, *Guineas and Gunpowder*, 1–96.
9. Duffy, *Soldiers, Sugar, and Seapower*, 5.
10. Blanning, *French Revolutionary Wars*, 37–70; Blanning, *Origins of the French Revolutionary Wars*, 36–68, 131–73; Conway, *Britain, Ireland, and Continental Europe*, 71–82; McKay and Scott, *Rise of the Great Powers*, 265–89; Simms, *Three Victories*, 662–84; Ward and Gooch, *Cambridge History*, 143–264.
11. Black, *Natural and Necessary Enemies*; Horn, *Britain and Europe*, 44–70; For a critique of this paradigm, see Eagles, *Francophilia in English Society*.
12. Schroeder provides detailed explanations for the first three rules and treats the remaining four as self-explanatory. Compensations and indemnities represent opposite approaches to the same idea. In the former, states insisted on matching

any of their neighbors' gains with conquests of their own while in the latter states demanded payment from either allies or enemies for losses incurred in war. Per Schroeder, alliances functioned as contracts with precise limitations on the obligations of the contracting parties. In wars, the state initiating the war or facing a direct attack became the senior partner in the relationship, which carried the expectation that they would commit fully to the conflict. The other signatory became a junior partner merely expected to meet the obligations stipulated in the treaty of alliance. Schroeder analyzes the War of the First Coalition in the context of this model and argues that "greed, bad faith, and folly reigned among the Allies; but it is worth remarking that this was systemic." Schroeder, *Transformation of European Politics*, 5–6, 109–29.
13. Esdaile, *Napoleon's Wars*, 204–7.
14. Schroeder, *Transformation of European Politics*, 79–80.
15. Black, *British Foreign Policy*, 519–45.
16. Duffy, *Younger Pitt*, 166–96.
17. Black, *Natural and Necessary Enemies*, 1–63; Browning, *War of the Austrian Succession*, 349–78; Horn, *Britain and Europe*, 44–50; McKay and Scott, *Rise of the Great Powers*, 94–137, 171–91; Simms, *Three Victories*, 355–86.
18. Duffy, *Younger Pitt*, 174.
19. Ingram, *In Defence of British India*, 103–16; Kissinger, *World Restored*, 38; Leggiere, *Fall of Napoleon*, 55; Sherwig, "Lord Grenville's Plan," 284–93; Ward and Gooch, *Cambridge History*, 402–10; Webster, *Foreign Policy of Castlereagh*, 55.
20. Duffy, *Younger Pitt*, 174.
21. By all accounts, Pitt learned rapidly as a youth under the direction of a private tutor, excelling in the classics, literature, history, and mathematics. While studying at Cambridge from 1773 to 1776, Pitt gained from Isaac Newton's *Principia* an appreciation for careful scientific inquiry and from the works of John Locke foundational principles of his political philosophy. While he indulged a lifelong passion for reading, Pitt generally disdained contemporary writings with the notable exception of those of political economists—chiefly Adam Smith. Ehrman, *Years of Acclaim*, 6–16.
22. Duffy, *Younger Pitt*, 166–69.
23. Black, *British Foreign Policy*, 56, 62; Ehrman, *Years of Acclaim*, 536–38.
24. Barnes, *George III and William Pitt*, 27–326; Black, *George III*, 35, 262–87; Ehrman, *Years of Acclaim*, 184–87.
25. Black, *British Foreign Policy*, 54–57; Duffy, *Younger Pitt*, 49–61.
26. Jupp, *Lord Grenville*, 32; Matheson, *Life of Henry Dundas*, 83–84.
27. Auckland to Grenville, 2 February 1791, in HMC, *Dropmore*, 2:25.
28. Pitt to Grenville, 5 July 1794, in HMC, *Dropmore*, 2:595.
29. Matheson, *Life of Henry Dundas*, 80–115.
30. Matheson, *Life of Henry Dundas*, 120–21; Fry, *Dundas Despotism*, 105–10.
31. For more on Dundas and Scotland see Fry, *Dundas Despotism*. Fortescue, *British Statesmen*, 51–70; Lovat-Fraser, *Henry Dundas*, 6–67; Matheson, *Life of Henry Dundas*, 110–11.
32. Fortescue, *British Statesmen*, 77.
33. Adams, *Influence*, 2–20; Duffy, *Younger Pitt*, 49–70; Knight, *Britain Against Napoleon*, 96–101; Lovat-Fraser, *Henry Dundas*, 35–41.

34. Matheson, *Life of Henry Dundas*, 160–63.
35. Adams, *Influence*, 3–5; Duffy, *Younger Pitt*, 166–96.
36. Simms and Riotte, *Hanoverian Dimension*; Simms, *Three Victories*, 387–661.
37. Black, *America or Europe?*; Horn, *Britain and Europe*; Middleton, *Bells of Victory*; Peters, *Pitt and Popularity*; Simms, *Three Victories*, 9–386.
38. Winston Churchill, "Zurich Speech" (1946), in Klos, *Churchill on Europe*, 14.
39. HMC, *Dropmore*, 10 vols.; Malmesbury, *Diaries and Correspondence*; Auckland, *Journal and Correspondence*; Aspinall, *Later Correspondence*; Browning, *Despatches of Earl Gower*; Browning, *Political Memoranda*; Buckingham and Chandos, *Memoirs of the Court and Cabinets*; Keith, *Memoirs and Correspondence*; Minto, *Life and Letters*.
40. Bartenev, *Archiv*; Pallain, *La Mission de Talleyrand à Londres*; Spiegel, *Brieven en Negotiatien*; Vivenot, *Vertrauliche Briefe*; Vivenot, *Thugut, Clerfayt und Wurmser*; Vivenot and Zeissberg, *Quellen zur Geschichte*.
41. Ehrman, *Years of Acclaim*; Ehrman, *Reluctant Transition*; Ehrman, *Consuming Struggle*.
42. Black, *British Foreign Policy*.
43. Duffy, "British War Policy"; Duffy, *Soldiers, Sugar, and Seapower*; Duffy, "'A Particular Service'"; Duffy, "William Pitt and the Origins of the Loyalist Association Movement"; Duffy, "World-Wide-War and British Expansion"; Duffy, *Younger Pitt*.

Chapter 1

1. Black, *Parliament and Foreign Policy*, 107; Dull, *Diplomatic History*, 159; Ehrman, *Years of Acclaim*, 98–104; Ward and Gooch, *Cambridge History*, 137–40.
2. Fry, *Dundas Despotism*, 63–65; Matheson, *Life of Henry Dundas*, 123–24.
3. In one such example of Pitt's fiscal policy, he sought to rationalize Britain's internal tea trade. The existing 119 percent duty on tea encouraged smuggling and cost more to enforce than it yielded. Pitt reduced the duty to 12.5 percent, which ultimately increased compliance and thus the government's revenue. Cobbett, *Parliamentary History*, 24:1009–13; Turner, *Pitt the Younger*, 62–65; Ward and Gooch, *Cambridge History*, 147.
4. Cobbett, *Parliamentary History*, 24:1275–76.
5. After 1 February 1793, the extraordinary expenses of the war with France eliminated the government surplus. The near sacrosanct status of the sinking fund at that point and the accompanying legislation mandating its perpetuation led the government to borrow money to fuel it. Borrowing money at higher interest rates to redeem lower interest bonds naturally proved financially ineffective and earned the sinking fund the scorn of posterity. However, while the mathematical folly of perpetuating the fund in wartime is easy to see, the value to the national credit of maintaining the debt-funding plan during the war is less quantifiable and should not be lightly discarded. Turner, *Pitt the Younger*, 63–73; Cone, "Richard Price and Pitt's Sinking Fund," 243–51; Cobbett, *Parliamentary History*, 24:1009–13; Ehrman, *Years of Acclaim*, 157–87, 239–81; Rose, *National Revival*, 184; Barnes, *George III and William Pitt*, 110–11; Hunt, *Political History*, 284–86.
6. George III to Pitt, 30 March 1786, in TNA: PRO 30/8/103, fol. 188.
7. According to Dull, the allies maintained 146 ships of the line by 1782 compared with 94 British. Dull, *Diplomatic History*, 110–11. For a more thorough discussion

of the strain on the Royal Navy in the American War of Independence, see Knight, "Royal Navy's Recovery." See also, Cobbett, *Parliamentary History*, 24:1273-90; Gregory and Stevenson, *Longman Companion*, 199; Knight, *Britain against Napoleon*, 5-27; Rose, *National Revival*, 210-11; Ward, *Cambridge History*, 134-47; Webb, "Rebuilding and Repair of the Fleet," 194-209.
8. Mori, *William Pitt*, 52-59; Rose, *National Revival*, 302-4.
9. After the War of Spanish Succession (1701-14) replaced the Spanish Habsburgs with a Bourbon monarchy, the close dynastic ties between the French and Spanish Bourbons engendered friendly relations that often manifested in some form of alliance. The Franco-Spanish alliance became a fixture of European international relations in the eighteenth century with the conclusion of the first *Pacte de Famille* in 1733.
10. Catherine had first separated the Crimean Khanate from the Ottoman Empire during a period of instability in 1776. Three years later, she concluded the Convention of Aynali Kavak with the Turks, whereby the Crimea came under Russian protection but was to remain independent. McKay and Scott, *Rise of the Great Powers*, 236-37.
11. Black, *British Foreign Policy*, 61-70.
12. Fry, *Dundas Despotism*, 90-100; Matheson, *Life of Henry Dundas*, 80-100.
13. These two groups were loosely united under the nominal leadership of William Cavendish-Bentinck, Third Duke of Portland. For detailed primary documentation of this ministry and its shortcomings, see the letters published in Buckingham, *Memoirs of the Court and Cabinets*, 1:154-291; Auckland, *Journal and Correspondence*, 1:48-66; and HMC, *Dropmore*, 1:208-25.
14. Considering Shelburne's receptive attitude, Fox's views proved frustrating to the French. Fox observed on 12 August 1783, "I hear nothing can be so cried up as Shelburne is at Paris, nor so cried down as we are." He reciprocated the French animosity, predicting, "Nothing can, in my opinion, be so ridiculous as the figure France will make in this Turkish business." Fox to Ossory, 12 August and 9 September 1783, in Fox, *Memorials and Correspondence*, 2:200-201, 208.
15. Fox to Manchester, 12 September 1783, in Fox, *Memorials and Correspondence*, 2:157; McKay and Scott, *Rise of the Great Powers*, 269.
16. George III to Fox, 15 June 1783, in Fox, *Memorials and Correspondence*, 2:130.
17. Portland to Fox, 7 September 1783, in Fox, *Memorials and Correspondence*, 2:154.
18. For a discussion of Fox's brief ministry and the crisis that ended it, see Mitchell, *Charles James Fox*, 46-71.
19. Lovat-Fraser, *Henry Dundas*, 15; Matheson, *Life of Henry Dundas*, 100-110.
20. Carmarthen to George III, 27 December 1783, and George III to Carmarthen, 28 December 1783, in Aspinall, *Later Correspondence*, 1:9-10.
21. Black, *British Foreign Policy*, 74.
22. Cabinet Memoranda, in Browning, *Political Memoranda*, 101.
23. Harris to Keith, 22 December 1783, in BL: Add MS 35530, fols. 276-77.
24. Carmarthen's positive journal recordings can be found in Browning, *Political Memoranda*, 101. The more contentious correspondence in question is discussed below.
25. Carmarthen to George III, 6 July 1784, in Aspinall, *Later Correspondence*, 1:72.
26. George III to Carmarthen, 6 July 1784, in Aspinall, *Later Correspondence*, 1:72-73.

27. Pitt to Carmarthen, 10 September 1784, in BL: Eg MS 3498, fols. 54–55.
28. Carmarthen to Pitt, 9 June 1784, in BL: Eg MS 3498, fol. 36.
29. Carmarthen to Pitt, 23 June 1784, in BL: Eg MS 3498, fol. 38.
30. Pitt to Carmarthen, 24 June 1784, in BL: Eg MS 3498, fol. 40.
31. Pitt to Carmarthen, 24 June 1784.
32. Pitt to Rutland, 8 August 1785, in Pitt, *Correspondence*, 111–12.
33. Carmarthen to Pitt, 28 September 1784, BL: Eg MS 3498, fols. 56–57.
34. Black, *British Foreign Policy*, 73–75.
35. Hardman, *Louis XVI*, 95.
36. Carmarthen to Cornwallis, 2 September 1785, in Cornwallis, *Correspondence of Charles, First Marquis Cornwallis*, 1:202–4; Ehrman, *Years of Acclaim*, 469–71.
37. Carmarthen to Harris, 24 July 1786, in Malmesbury, *Diaries and Correspondence*, 2:211–12.
38. McKay and Scott, *Rise of the Great Powers*, 269; Ward and Gooch, *Cambridge History*, 1:143–44.
39. Closed to trade since the Peace of Westphalia in 1648, the Scheldt connected the once thriving commercial center of Antwerp in the Austrian Netherlands to the North Sea through Dutch territory. More than one century later, the river's closure still served Dutch interests by reducing competition from Austrian merchants. Hunt, *Political History*, 297; Ward and Gooch, *Cambridge History*, 159–61.
40. Harris to Carmarthen, 7 and 10 December 1784, in Malmesbury, *Diaries and Correspondence* 2:75–80; Atkinson, *History of Germany*, 317.
41. This project originated from the Wittelsbach claim on the Spanish throne in the late-seventeenth century. Bavarian Elector Max Emmanuel's term as lieutenant-governor and captain-general of the then Spanish Netherlands in 1691 established Belgium as the primary choice for the exchange. Austrian chancellor Wenzel Anton, Prince of Kaunitz-Rietberg, had considered the project in 1764 but did not pursue the idea. A Wittelsbach initiative to realize the exchange in 1776 had precipitated the War of Bavarian Succession, in which the Austrians abandoned the project in the face of Prussian opposition. Hochedlinger, *Austria's Wars of Emergence*, 364–70; McKay and Scott, *Rise of the Great Powers*, 229–31; Schroeder, *Transformation of European Politics*, 26–32.
42. Atkinson, *History of Germany*, 317–21; Cobban, *Ambassadors*, 48–70; Bernard, *Joseph II and Bavaria*, 202–5.
43. The quoted phrasing is from Carmarthen's stated objectives upon taking up his position as foreign secretary. Cabinet Memoranda, in Browning, *Political Memoranda*, 101.
44. Harris to Carmarthen, 21, 25, and 28 January 1785, in Malmesbury, *Diaries and Correspondence*, 2:94–100.
45. Harris to Carmarthen, 1 and 2 February 1785, in Malmesbury, *Diaries and Correspondence*, 2:101–6.
46. Malmesbury, *Diaries and Correspondence*, 2:101–6.
47. Malmesbury, 2:101–6.
48. McKay and Scott, *Rise of the Great Powers*, 1–5, 211–14.
49. Harris to Carmarthen, 1 and 2 February 1785, in Malmesbury, *Diaries and Correspondence*, 2:101–6.
50. Black, *British Foreign Policy*, 83–84.

51. Harris to Ewart, 15 March 1785, and Ewart to Harris, 4 April 1785, in Malmesbury, *Diaries and Correspondence*, 2:112–18.
52. A *Fürstenbund* referred to a "league of princes" within the Holy Roman Empire. Duke of York to George III, 28 February and 1 April 1785, in Aspinall, *Later Correspondence*, 1:132–35, 152; Atkinson, *History of Germany*, 317–21; Bernard, *Joseph II and Bavaria*, 202–5; Blanning, "George III, Hanover, and the Fürstenbund," 322; Ford, *Hanover and Prussia*, 26–28; Ward and Gooch, *Cambridge History*, 1:161–63.
53. For Catherine's attitudes toward the Holy Roman Empire, see Aretin, "Russia as a Guarantor Power"; Madariaga, *Russia*, 377–92.
54. Harris to Carmarthen, 9 August 1785, in Malmesbury, *Diaries and Correspondence*, 2:132–34.
55. Harris to Ewart, 7 August 1785, in Malmesbury, *Diaries and Correspondence*, 2:131; Hochedlinger, *Austria's Wars of Emergence*, 370–74.
56. Richmond Memorandum in TNA: PRO 30/8/332, fols. 12–26.
57. Richmond Memorandum.
58. Richmond Memorandum.
59. Richmond Memorandum.
60. Dawson, "William Pitt's Settlement," 703.
61. Cobbett, *Parliamentary History*, 26:381–514; Hunt, *Political History*, 293; Schroeder, *Transformation of European Politics*, 40; Ward and Gooch, *Cambridge History*, 1:164–70.
62. In 1786, British diplomats negotiated simultaneously, though not often successfully, for commercial treaties with eight European states. For a larger discussion of these negotiations, see Ehrman, *British Government and Commercial Negotiations*.
63. Black, *British Foreign Policy*, 93–112; Ehrman, *Acclaim*, 477–506.
64. Draft of Instructions to Eden, 26 May 1786, in TNA: PRO 30/8/333, fols. 24–31; Eden to Carmarthen, 17 April 1786 in Auckland, *Journal and Correspondence*, 1:103–5.
65. Pitt to Eden, 20 April 1786, in Auckland, *Journal and Correspondence*, 1:107–10.
66. Pitt to Carmarthen, 13 October 1785, in BL: Eg MS 3948, fols. 135–36.
67. Pitt to Eden, 19 April 1786, in Auckland, *Journal and Correspondence*, 1:105.
68. Eden to Carmarthen, 13 April 1786, in Auckland, *Journal and Correspondence*, 1:100; Eden to Pitt, 22 October 1786, in TNA: PRO 30/8/110, fols. 89–90.
69. Pitt to Eden, 19 April 1786, in Auckland, *Journal and Correspondence*, 1:106.
70. Italics are mine. Carmarthen to Eden, 25 April 1786, in Auckland, *Journal and Correspondence*, 1:112–13.
71. Cobbett, *Parliamentary History*, 26:221–24; Black, *British Foreign Policy*, 116; Hardman, *Louis XVI*, 95; Schroeder, *Transformation of European Politics*, 36.
72. Cobbett, *Parliamentary History*, 26:392–94.
73. Cobbett, 26:392–94.
74. Anderson, *Britain's Discovery*, 146.
75. Danzig and Thorn are the modern Polish cities of Gdańsk and Toruń, respectively. This book will use the older names, Danzig and Thorn, commonly used in contemporary English, French, and German correspondence. Gibson to Carmarthen, 23 February 1786, in TNA: FO 62/2, fols. 30–33.
76. Correspondence from British envoys at Warsaw often mentions the strength of the "Russian Party" in the Sejm. Charles Whitworth attributes most resistance to novel

diplomatic and political measures mooted in the Sejm to this party. Whitworth to Carmarthen, 30 September and 15 October 1788, in TNA: FO 62/2, fols. 255-67.
77. For discussion of the Patriot party and Dutch civil strife, see Schama, *Patriots and Liberators*, 64-137; Rose, *National Revival*, 306-10; Rowen, *Princes of Orange*, 205-29.
78. Black, *British Foreign Policy*, 156-67; Blanning, *Origins of the French Revolutionary Wars*, 48-49.
79. For discussion of the origins of this war, see McKay and Scott, *Rise of the Great Powers*, 234-38; Hochedlinger, *Austria's Wars of Emergence*, 378-82; and Schroeder, *Transformation of European Politics*, 19-23, 56-57.
80. Black, *British Foreign Policy*, 112-16; McKay and Scott, *Rise of the Great Powers*, 267.
81. "Considerations to be employed with ministers to prevail on them to support the Republic of Holland," 19 May 1787, in Malmesbury, *Diaries and Correspondence*, 2:302-3; Cobban, *Ambassadors*, 20-47; Schama, *Patriots and Liberators*, 64-132; Stanhope, *Mystic*, 188.
82. Malmesbury, *Diaries and Correspondence*, 2:66-78.
83. Malmesbury to Carmarthen, 1 February 1785, in Malmesbury, *Diaries and Correspondence*, 2:100.
84. Carmarthen to Harris, 14 December 1784, in Malmesbury, *Diaries and Correspondence*, 2:80.
85. Harris to Ewart, 15 March 1785, in Malmesbury, *Diaries and Correspondence*, 2:112; Schama, *Patriots and Liberators*, 106.
86. Stanhope, *Mystic*, 189.
87. Malmesbury, *Diaries and Correspondence*, 2:79-196; Cobban, *Ambassadors*, 52.
88. Harris to Ewart, 8 August 1786, in Malmesbury, *Diaries and Correspondence*, 2:218.
89. Harris to Carmarthen, 16 May 1786, in Malmesbury, *Diaries and Correspondence*, 2:196; Cobban, *Ambassadors*, 71-90; Schama, *Patriots and Liberators*, 107.
90. Harris to Carmarthen, 26 May 1786, in Malmesbury, *Diaries and Correspondence*, 2:197-200.
91. Harris to Carmarthen, 6 June, 7 July, and 8 September 1786, in Malmesbury, *Diaries and Correspondence*, 2:202-4, 208-9, 229-31.
92. Schama, *Patriots and Liberators*, 108-10.
93. Görtz, in fact, had instructions to halt and end the civil war and oppose the more bellicose maneuvers of Harris. Dalrymple to Harris and Harris to Carmarthen, 2 September 1786, in Malmesbury, *Diaries and Correspondence*, 2:224-6; Cobban, *Ambassadors*, 91-109; Schama, *Patriots and Liberators*, 124-25; Stanhope, *Mystic*, 189-90.
94. Harris to Pitt, 28 November 1786, in Malmesbury, *Diaries and Correspondence*, 2:251-53.
95. Carmarthen to Harris, and Pitt to Harris, 5 December 1786, in Malmesbury, *Diaries and Correspondence*, 253-55.
96. Carmarthen to Harris, 12 December 1786, Pitt to Harris, 26 December 1786, and Cabinet Minutes, 23 and 26 May 1787 in Malmesbury, *Diaries and Correspondence*, 262-63, 303-7; Cobban, *Ambassadors*, 110-47; Schama, *Patriots and Liberators*, 126.
97. Harris shared Spiegel's opinion that France neither could nor would fight to defend its influence in the United Provinces. He was vindicated in this when the French ambassador refused the Patriots' request for a guarantee of military

support. This refusal prompted the Patriots' request for French mediation. Harris to Carmarthen, 19, 22, and 25 June 1787, in Malmesbury, *Diaries and Correspondence*, 2:315–23.
98. Harris to Carmarthen, 29 June 1787, in Malmesbury, *Diaries and Correspondence*, 2:325–28; Cobban, *Ambassadors*, 148–51.
99. Harris to Carmarthen, 7 July 1787, in Malmesbury, *Diaries and Correspondence*, 2:332–33; Schama, *Patriots and Liberators*, 127.
100. Madariaga, *Russia*, 393–412; Stanhope, *Mystic*, 190–91.
101. Storer to Eden, 5 October 1787, in Auckland, *Journal and Correspondence*, 1:442–43.
102. During Grenville's subsequent mission to Paris, Pitt wrote in his third letter to Grenville in as many days, "Let me know what you think of all this. Even in these two days I feel no small difference in not being able to have your opinion on things as they arise." Pitt to Grenville, 23 September 1787, in HMC, *Dropmore*, 3:429.
103. Carmarthen to Ewart, 17 July 1787, in TNA: FO 64/11, fols. 128–32; Grenville to Pitt, 1 and 3 August 1787, in HMC, *Twelfth Report*, 355–57; Grenville to Pitt, 31 July and 1, 3, and 4 August 1787, in HMC, *Dropmore*, 3:408–13; Ehrman, *Years of Acclaim*, 534–38.
104. Harris to Carmarthen, 12 October 1787, in Malmesbury, *Diaries and Correspondence*, 2:396–97; Cobban, *Ambassadors*, 152–83; Dwyer, *Rise of Prussia*, 240–41; Ehrman, *Years of Acclaim*, 533–35; Schama, *Patriots and Liberators*, 128–32; Stanhope, *Mystic*, 192–94.
105. Eden had recently made some indiscreet remarks that threatened to encourage rather than avert war, so Pitt relied on Grenville again as a personal agent. Pitt to Eden, 8 and 14 September 1787, in Auckland, *Journal and Correspondence*, 1:194–96; omitted portion of Pitt's 8 September letter in HMC, *Twelfth Report*, 357.
106. "Déclaration" and "Contre-Déclaration," 27 October 1787, in Auckland, *Journal and Correspondence*, 1:255–56; Barnes, *George III and William Pitt*, 156–59; Cobban, *Ambassadors*, 184–95; Ward and Gooch, *Cambridge History*, 174; McKay and Scott, *Rise of the Great Powers*, 268.
107. Black, *British Foreign Policy*, 156–61; Ehrman, *Years of Acclaim*, 536–37.

Chapter 2

1. Hunt, *Political History*, 299–301; Schroeder, *Transformation of European Politics*, 69; Ward and Gooch, *Cambridge History*, 175.
2. "Memorandum on the Partition of Poland," 1772, in Fortescue, *Correspondence of King George the Third*, 2:428–29.
3. The Duke of Richmond addresses many of these points in his aforementioned memorandum on the Franco-Dutch alliance of 1785. Richmond to Pitt, 30 December 1785, in TNA: PRO 30/8/332, fols. 12–26; Anderson, *Britain's Discovery*, 128–42; Dull, *Diplomatic History*, 128–36.
4. William V to George III, 7 October and 25 December 1787 and 29 February 1788, in Aspinall, *Later Correspondence*, 1:340, 356, 365.
5. Thurlow to Stafford, undated (likely late October 1787 based on surrounding letters), TNA: PRO 30/29/1/15, no. 69, fols. 844–46.
6. Thurlow to Stafford, undated.
7. Thurlow to Stafford, undated.
8. The Dutch requested the return of Negapatnam, which the Dutch had ceded after the American War of Independence. The British insisted that the Dutch should

provide some territorial or commercial compensations in India as the price for this restitution. This dampened Dutch enthusiasm for a British alliance to such a degree that Harris feared the return of French influence. The separation of the European and colonial issues allowed the European treaty to succeed immediately, but the colonial and commercial treaty negotiations staggered on for four more years before the Cabinet abandoned the effort toward the end of 1791. Harris to Carmarthen, 30 October and 16 November 1787, and Carmarthen to Harris, 1 February 1788, in Malmesbury, *Diaries and Correspondence*, 2:402–4, 412–13; Ehrman, *Years of Acclaim*, 433.

9. Ewart to Carmarthen, 25 December 1787, in TNA: FO 64/12, no. 86, fol. 223; Cobban, *Ambassadors*, 196–202.
10. Ewart to Carmarthen, 27 September 1787, in TNA: FO 64/12, no. 62, fol. 75.
11. Ewart to Carmarthen, 12 October 1787, in TNA: FO 64/12, no. 67, fol. 129.
12. Carmarthen to Ewart, 2 December 1787, in TNA: FO 64/12, no. 24, fols. 197–200.
13. Thurlow to Stafford, undated, TNA: PRO 30/29/1/15, no. 69, fols. 844–46.
14. Carmarthen to Ewart, 2 December 1787, in TNA: FO 64/12, no. 25, fols. 201–4.
15. Camden to Pitt, 18 October 1787, TNA: PRO 30/8/119, fols. 134–35.
16. Ewart to Carmarthen, 20 October 1787, in TNA: FO 64/12, no. 69, fols. 143–46.
17. Carmarthen to Thurlow, 23 December 1787, in BL: Eg MS 3498, fol. 249; Carmarthen to Ewart, 26 December 1787, in TNA: FO 64/12, no. 28, fol. 231.
18. Ewart to Carmarthen, 22 December 1787, in TNA: FO 64/12, no. 86, fols. 220–21; Dwyer, *Rise of Prussia*, 241–42.
19. Carmarthen to Ewart, 2 April 1788, in TNA: FO 64/13, no. 5, fol. 105.
20. Carmarthen to Ewart, 2 April 1788.
21. Harris to Carmarthen, 2 February 1788, BL: Eg MS 3500, fol. 54.
22. Whitworth to Carmarthen, 23 January 1788, TNA: FO 62/2, no. 3, fols. 163–64.
23. Thurlow to Stafford, undated, TNA: PRO 30/29/1/15, no. 69, fols. 844–46.
24. Ewart to Carmarthen, 15 March 1788, in TNA: FO 64/13, no. 18, fol. 72.
25. Carmarthen to Ewart, 14 May 1788, in TNA: FO 64/13, no. 8, fol. 156.
26. Ewart to Carmarthen, 10 January 1788, no. 4, and Carmarthen to Ewart, 14 March 1788, no. 1, in TNA: FO 64/13, fols. 25 and 69.
27. The significance of Russia in Anglo-Prussian relations already had a long history by 1788, and, even during Pitt's ministry, the notion of making an Anglo-Prussian alliance dependent on Russian support had precedent. In Cornwallis's discussions with Frederick II in 1785, the Prussian king expressed willingness to ally with Britain if Russia would also join in a triple alliance. A year later, in expressing his overall preference for an alliance with Austria to one with Prussia, Carmarthen had written, "I never desire a connection with Prussia unless Russia, and of course Denmark, are included." Memorial on Cornwallis's conversation with Frederick II, enclosed with Ewart to Harris, 17 September 1785 and Carmarthen to Harris, 24 July 1786, in Malmesbury, *Diaries and Correspondence* 2:152, 212.
28. Ewart to Carmarthen, 31 May 1788, in TNA: FO 64/13, no. 34, fol. 168.
29. Harris to Carmarthen, 29 January 1788, in BL: Eg MS 3500, fols. 50–51.
30. Carmarthen to Ewart, 2 April 1788, in TNA: FO 64/13, no. 5, fols. 99–107.
31. Carmarthen to Ewart, 14 May 1788, in TNA: FO 64/13, no. 8, fol. 153.
32. Carmarthen to Ewart, 14 May 1788.
33. Warren Hastings had been governor general of India from 1774 to 1784, after which he returned to England. There, he was accused of several varieties of corruption

and mismanagement by Whig Members of Parliament looking for an avenue to attack the Pitt ministry. The resulting impeachment trial ran intermittently from 1788 until his acquittal in 1795. Turnbull, *Hastings*.

34. Cobbett, *Parliamentary History*, 27:1–649; Black, *Parliament and Foreign Policy*, 123.
35. Ewart to Carmarthen, 31 May 1788, in TNA: FO 64/13, no. 34, fols. 165–71.
36. George III to Princess of Orange, 6 June 1788, in Malmesbury, *Diaries and Correspondence*, 2:420–21; Clark, *Iron Kingdom*, 284–89; Dwyer, *Rise of Prussia*, 240–42; Stanhope, *Mystic*, 201.
37. Harris to Carmarthen, 15 June 1788, in Malmesbury, *Diaries and Correspondence*, 2:422–28.
38. Harris to Carmarthen, 15 June 1788.
39. Harris to Carmarthen, 15 June 1788.
40. Carmarthen to Ewart, 14 July 1788, in TNA: FO 97/323, no. 11.
41. Ewart to Carmarthen, 14 August 1788, in TNA: FO 64/14, nos. 52, 53, fols. 26–30.
42. For another account of the process of negotiating the Triple Alliance, see Browning, "Triple Alliance."
43. The fourth article of the treaty specifies that, if called by the Dutch, the British should provide at least 8,000 infantry, 2,000 cavalry, twelve ships of the line, and eight frigates. For their part, the alliance required the Dutch to answer a British call with at least 5,000 infantry, 1,000 cavalry, eight ships of the line, and eight frigates. The fifth article further allowed for both states to call for additional aid if necessary but established that the Dutch would not be required to provide more than double their normal obligation. Treaty of Defensive Alliance between Great Britain and Holland, in TNA: FO 93/46/1C.
44. The Anglo-Prussian treaty specified that both powers should provide a minimum of 16,000 infantry and 4,000 cavalry with the caveat that these supporting troops could be deployed only within the continent of Europe. As with the Anglo-Dutch treaty, this alliance also included a pledge to increase aid as necessary, but, unlike the Anglo-Dutch alliance, this treaty specified no maximum requirement for either Britain or Prussia. Provisional Defensive Alliance, in TNA: FO 93/78/2.
45. Secret Articles: Objects of Alliance, in TNA: FO 93/78/3.
46. This is seen repeatedly in Daniel Hailes's correspondence from Warsaw. TNA: FO 62/2–5; Cabinet Minute, 31 May 1788, in Aspinall, *Later Correspondence*, 1:375; Cobban, *Ambassadors*, 203–15; Feuchtwanger, *Prussia*, 87; McKay and Scott, *Rise of the Great Powers*, 269–70; Mori *William Pitt*, 59–61; Ward and Gooch, *Cambridge History*, 176–78.
47. Dwyer, *Rise of Prussia*, 242–43.
48. Anderson, *Britain's Discovery*, 143.
49. For a more thorough discussion of Gustav III's Baltic ambitions, see Barton, "Gustav III of Sweden," 13–30.
50. Pitt to Grenville, 1 September 1788, in HMC, *Dropmore*, 1:353.
51. Black, *British Foreign Policy*, 179–89; McKay and Scott, *Rise of the Great Powers*, 239–40; Mori, *William Pitt*, 63–64; Ward and Gooch, *Cambridge History*, 178–84; Schroeder, *Transformation of European Politics*, 58–70.
52. Black, *Parliament and Foreign Policy*, 117.
53. Marcum, "Semen R. Vorontsov," 146–72.

54. Black, *British Foreign Policy*, 189–203.
55. The French Revolution appears in official correspondence and parliamentary records primarily as an object of curiosity and debate but not action. In contrast, the Belgian revolt and the possible courses of action for the Triple Alliance dominated the Cabinet meeting of 30 November 1789. Browning, *Political Memoranda*, 146–47; Ward and Gooch, *Cambridge History*, 186.
56. Keith to his sister, 23 January 1790, in Keith, *Memoirs and Correspondence*, 2:248–49; Black, *British Foreign Policy*, 203–15.
57. Auckland to Keith, 19 March 1790, in Keith, *Memoirs and Correspondence* 2:267; Atkinson, *History of Germany*, 325–27; Black, *British Foreign Policy*, 206–12; Blanning, *Origins of the French Revolutionary Wars*, 52–53; Hochedlinger, *Austria's Wars of Emergence*, 388; Sybel, *French Revolution*, 1:203–5.
58. Black, *British Foreign Policy*, 216–23.
59. Fitzherbert to Leeds, 15 December 1789, in BL: Eg MS 3500, fol. 136.
60. Black, *British Foreign Policy*, 203–13, 342; Ehrman, *Reluctant Transition*, 547–48.
61. Whitworth to Leeds, 15 October and 5 November 1788, in TNA: FO 62/2, fols. 265–85.
62. Hailes to Carmarthen, 8 February 1789, in TNA: FO 62/2, no. 14, fols. 345–48.
63. Durno to Carmarthen, 23 February 1789, in TNA: FO 62/2, fols. 357–60.
64. Durno to Carmarthen, 23 February 1789.
65. Durno to Carmarthen, 23 February 1789.
66. Whitworth to Leeds, 30 September 1788, in TNA: FO 62/2, no. 27, fols. 255–56.
67. Hailes to Carmarthen, 26 March 1789, in TNA: FO 62/2, no. 20, fols. 407–8.
68. The details of this proposal remain unclear and puzzling. If trade through the ports of Samogitia was practicable, it is not clear why the Poles did not attempt to redirect their commerce with Britain through that channel instead of through Danzig and the Vistula River. If Poland's geography and infrastructure made major trade through Samogitia impracticable, it is unclear how British possession of the territory would change that reality. As there is no major river flowing through the heart of Poland to those ports comparable with the Vistula, Dniester, or Dnieper Rivers, it is most likely that trade through Samogitia was not practicable. It is probable that the abortive idea emerged from an individual unacquainted with the physical obstacles to conducting trade in that quarter. Hailes to Carmarthen, 27 March 1789, in TNA: FO 62/2, no. 21, fols. 409–11.
69. Hailes to Carmarthen, 27 March 1789; Anderson, *Britain's Discovery*, 147.
70. In one bizarre attempt to force the British to take a more aggressively pro-Polish stand in the spring of 1789, King Stanisław II offered to endorse George III's second son, Frederick, Duke of York and Albany, as a candidate to succeed him as Poland's elected monarch. York prudently rejected the offer as a measure beyond British means to defend, beyond his authority to accept, and more likely to disrupt the new alliance system than strengthen it. Hailes to Carmarthen, 14 March 1789, in TNA: FO 62/2, no. 19, fols. 405–6; Ward and Gooch, *Cambridge History*, 185.
71. Fitzherbert to Leeds, 8 December 1789, in BL: Eg MS 3500, fol. 128; Black, *British Foreign Policy*, 204–16.
72. Ewart to Carmarthen, 9 January 1788, in TNA: FO 64/13, fols. 20–23; Ewart to Pitt, April 1791, in HMC, *Dropmore*, 2:44; Ward and Gooch, *Cambridge History*, 180–85.
73. Black, *British Foreign Policy*, 279–80; Stanhope, *Mystic*, 221–34.

74. Leeds to Hailes, 8 January 1791, in TNA: FO 62/4, fols. 8–9; Pitt to Auckland, 7 March 1791, in Auckland, *Journal and Correspondence*, 2:382–83; Blanning, *Origins of the French Revolutionary Wars*, 54; Ehrman, *Reluctant Transition*, 6–7; Schroeder, *Transformation of European Politics*, 79–80.
75. Anderson, *Britain's Discovery*, 146; Black, *British Foreign Policy*, 204; Ward and Gooch, *Cambridge History*, 183.
76. Hailes to Leeds, 6 January 1790, in TNA: FO 62/3, no. 49, fols. 3–4.
77. Cobbett, *Parliamentary History*, 28:784; Ehrman, *Years of Acclaim*, 385–86.
78. Black, *British Foreign Policy*, 233–40; Norris, "Nootka Crisis," 572–76.
79. Cobbett, *Parliamentary History*, 28: 914–16; Blanning, *Origins of the French Revolutionary Wars*, 60–62; Evans, "Nootka Sound Controversy," 611–16.
80. Black, *Parliament and Foreign Policy*, 118; Ehrman, *Years of Acclaim*, 559; Norris, "Nootka Crisis," 576–80.
81. Dupont, *Archives Parlementaires*, 15:663.
82. Elliot to Pitt, 26 October 1790, in TNA: PRO 30/8/139, fols. 123–28; Black, *British Foreign Policy*, 241–52, 350; Evans, "Nootka Sound Controversy," 609–40.
83. Pitt to Stafford, 20 October 1790, in TNA: PRO 30/29/1/15, no. 97; Black, *British Foreign Policy*, 241–52.

Chapter 3

1. Schroeder, *Transformation of European Politics*, 75.
2. Keith to Leeds, 18 February 1790, in Keith, *Memoirs and Correspondence*, 253.
3. Keith to Grenville, 4 August 1791, in Keith, *Memoirs and Correspondence*, 469–72; Atkinson, *History of Germany*, 347–55; Black, *British Foreign Policy*, 257–60; Ehrman, *Years of Acclaim*, 538–71; Schroeder, *Transformation of European Politics*, 65–77; Stanhope, *Mystic*, 219–27.
4. Grenville to Auckland, 3 January 1791, in HMC, *Dropmore*, 2:1–2.
5. Blanning, *Origins of the French Revolution*, 54; Schroeder, *Transformation of European Politics*, 79–80.
6. Leeds to Ewart, 30 March 1790, in TNA: FO 64/17, nos. 8, 9; Black, *British Foreign Policy*, 274–75.
7. Pitt to Auckland, 7 March 1791, in Auckland, *Journal and Correspondence*, 2:382–83; Ehrman, *Reluctant Transition*, 6–7.
8. The correspondence from Sir Charles Whitworth at St. Petersburg from July to December 1790 is filled with the deterioration of Triple Alliance negotiations with Russia. TNA: FO 65/18.
9. Black, *British Foreign Policy*, 290–92.
10. Elgin to Leeds, 9 January 1791, in TNA: FO 7/23, no. 6, fols. 33–38.
11. Leeds to Elgin, 4 February 1791, in TNA: FO 7/23, no. 4, fols. 65–72.
12. Leeds to Hailes, 8 January 1791, in TNA: FO 62/4, no. 1, fols. 8–9; Black, *British Foreign Policy*, 293–96; Stanhope, *Mystic*, 235–36.
13. Feuchtwanger, *Prussia*, 88; Koch, *History of Prussia*, 150–51.
14. Hailes to Leeds, 14, 19, and 31 January and 22 February 1791, in TNA: FO 62/4; Lord, *Second Partition of Poland*, 169.
15. Hailes to Leeds, 2 March 1791, in TNA: FO 62/4, no. 7, fols. 63–64; Clark, *Iron Kingdom*, 289.
16. Cabinet Minute, 22 March 1791, in Aspinall, *Later Correspondence*, 1:523.

17. Black, *British Foreign Policy*, 297-99.
18. Leeds to Jackson, 27 March 1791, in TNA: FO 64/20, fols. 181-83.
19. Leeds to Jackson, 27 March 1791, in TNA: FO 64/20, no. 5, fols. 191-92.
20. Black, *British Foreign Policy*, 300.
21. Vorontsov to his brother, 26 April 1791, in Bartenev, *Archiv*, 8:20, 9:193.
22. For additional discussion of this debate, see Cunningham, "Oczakov Debate"; Marcum, "Semen R. Vorontsov," 146-82; Marcum, "Vorontsov and Pitt."
23. Draft of Leeds to Jackson, 27 March 1791, in TNA: FO 64/20, fols. 184-86.
24. Black, *Parliament and Foreign Policy*, 120.
25. Leeds's Diary, 4 April 1791, in Browning, *Political Memoranda*, 159-60.
26. Cobbett, *Parliamentary History*, 29:52.
27. Cobbett, 29:52-55.
28. Cobbett, 29:56-70; Mori, *William Pitt*, 96-97.
29. Cobbett, *Parliamentary History*, 29:71-72.
30. Cobbett, 29:71-72.
31. Cobbett, 29:73-74; Black, *British Foreign Policy*, 300-307.
32. Adams, *Influence*, 7-11; Browning, *Political Memoranda*, 148; Ehrman, *Reluctant Transition*, 21-23.
33. Malmesbury to Portland, 14 October 1791, in Malmesbury, *Diaries and Correspondence*, 2:441; Fry, *Dundas Despotism*, 151-58.
34. Auckland to Pitt, 29 January and 2 February 1791, and Auckland to Grenville, 31 December 1790 and 8 February 1791, in HMC, *Dropmore*, 2:22-23, 31.
35. Richmond to Pitt, 27 March 1791, in Stanhope, *Life of Pitt*, 2:112; Black, *British Foreign Policy*, 308.
36. Grenville to Ewart, 20 April 1791, in TNA: FO 64/21, no. 1.
37. Pitt to Ewart, 24 May 1791, in Stanhope, *Life of Pitt*, 2:117.
38. Lovat-Fraser, *Henry Dundas*, 38.
39. This is not to say that Pitt left foreign policy entirely in Grenville's hands or domestic and colonial policy in Dundas's but rather that frequency and transparency of communication between Pitt, Dundas, and Grenville was such that Pitt could trust them to carry out policies that they had all already discussed and approved together. Leeds's Diary, 31 March-10 April 1791, in Browning, *Political Memoranda*, 154-61; Buckingham to Grenville, 9, 19, 20, and 23 September 1787, in HMC, *Dropmore*, 1:281-84; Morris, *Gouverneur Morris*, 2:95; Black, *British Foreign Policy*, 314.
40. Adams, *Influence*, 13-17.
41. Whitworth to Grenville, 17 June 1791, and Fawkener to Grenville, 18 June 1781, in HMC, *Dropmore*, 2:100-103.
42. Marcum, "Semen R. Vorontsov," 204-5.
43. Grenville to Auckland, 29 July 1791, in HMC, *Dropmore*, 2:144-45.
44. Mori, *William Pitt*, 99.
45. "Substance of the Partition Treaty between the Courts in Concert" in Debrett, *Collection*, 1:1-2.
46. Paul Webb provides an excellent discussion of the complexities of the Ochakov Crisis. Webb, "Sea Power in the Ochakov Affair."
47. Barnes, *George III and William Pitt*, 235; Clark, *Iron Kingdom*, 286; Dwyer, *Rise of Prussia*, 243-44; Feuchtwanger, *Prussia*, 88-89; Lord, *Second Partition of Poland*, 170-216, Madariaga, *Russia*, 413-26.

48. Hailes to Leeds, 3 May 1791, in TNA: FO 62/4, fol. 117.
49. Grenville to Hailes, 3 May 1791, and Hailes to Grenville, 13 May 1791, in TNA: FO 62/4, fols. 148–50.
50. Hailes to Grenville, 19 May 1791, in TNA: FO 62/4, fols. 154–56.
51. Hailes to Grenville, 11 January 1792, in TNA: FO 62/5, no. 31.
52. Auckland to Morton Eden, 1 November 1791, in Auckland, *Journal and Correspondence*, 2:392; Mori, *William Pitt*, 109.
53. Auckland to Grenville, 14 March 1792, in HMC, *Dropmore*, 2:261–63; Ward and Gooch, *Cambridge History*, 222.

Chapter 4

1. Grenville to Auckland, 23 August 1791, in HMC, *Dropmore*, 2:171.
2. Hunt, *Political History*, 333–34; Rose, *Great War*, 41–44, 49; Schroeder, *Transformation of European Politics*, 94.
3. Clark, *Iron Kingdom*, 287; Hochedlinger, *Austria's Wars of Emergence*, 393–96; Mori, *William Pitt*, 97–100.
4. "Substance of the Partition Treaty between the Courts in Concert" in Debrett, *Collection*, 1:1–2.
5. Black, *British Foreign Policy*, 316, 377; Black, *Parliament and Foreign Policy*, 123.
6. George III to Grenville, 25 June 1791, in HMC, *Dropmore*, 2:107.
7. As early as December 1789, Louis XVI's youngest brother, Charles, Count of Artois, had urged Pitt to lead an international coalition to restore royal authority, even offering French colonies and the prospect of an alliance as compensation. Grenville to Keith, 19 August 1791, TNA: FO 7/27, fols. 182–83; Black, *British Foreign Policy*, 348; Black, *George III*, 288–96.
8. Grenville to Auckland, 23 August 1791, in HMC, *Dropmore*, 2:171.
9. Schroeder, *Transformation of European Politics*, 98–99.
10. Grenville to Keith, 19 September 1791, in TNA: FO 7/28.
11. Dundas to Addington, 7 August 1791, in Pellew, *Life and Correspondence*, 1:87.
12. Black, *British Foreign Policy*, 382–83.
13. Lessart to Grenville, 12 January 1792, and Talleyrand to Lessart, 2 March 1792, in Pallain, *Talleyrand*, 40–41; Hampson, *Perfidy of Albion*, 85–87; Hunt, *Political History*, 333–34; Rose, *Great War*, 41–49; Schroeder, *Transformation of European Politics*, 94; Ward and Gooch, *Cambridge History*, 212–13.
14. Grenville to Gower, 9 March 1792, in Pallain, *Talleyrand*, 149–52.
15. Grenville to George III and George III to Grenville, 28 April 1792, in HMC, *Dropmore*, 2:266–67; Black, *British Foreign Policy*, 388.
16. Grenville to Auckland, 17 January 1792, in HMC, *Dropmore*, 2:251.
17. Auckland to Grenville, 15 May 1792, in HMC, *Dropmore*, 2:269–70.
18. Grenville to Auckland, 17 January 1792, in HMC, *Dropmore*, 2:251.
19. Black, *British Foreign Policy*, 388–89.
20. Atkinson, *History of Germany*, 375–78.
21. Blanning, *French Revolutionary Wars*, 63–64; Blanning, *Origins of the French Revolutionary Wars*, 96–123; Roider, *Baron Thugut*, 94–95; McKay and Scott, *Rise of the Great Powers*, 278–79; Ross, *Quest for Victory*, 15–24.
22. Their convention became a full defensive alliance in August of 1791; Ehrman, *Reluctant Transition*, 28.

23. Auckland to Grenville, 14 March 1792, in HMC, *Dropmore*, 2:261–63; Black, *British Foreign Policy*, 389–98; McKay and Scott, *Rise of the Great Powers*, 279.
24. Barnes, *George III and William Pitt*, 224–25; Jones, *Britain and the World*, 259.
25. Grenville to Auckland, 26 August 1791, in HMC, *Dropmore*, 2:177.
26. Grenville to Chauvelin, 24 May 1792, in Debrett, *Collection*, 1:318; Black, *British Foreign Policy*, 390; Petrie to Grenville, 13 March 1792, in HMC, *Dropmore*, 259; "Réflexions pour la Négociation d'Angleterre en cas de Guerre," 30 March 1792, in Pallain, *Talleyrand*, 172–76; Ward and Gooch, *Cambridge History*, 213–14.
27. The former included groups like the Society for Constitutional Information, the London Revolution Society, and the Constitutional Club, while the latter included the London Corresponding Society, the Norwich Revolution Society, and the Manchester Constitutional Society. Mori, *William Pitt*, 78–79; Morris, *British Monarchy*, 84–85.
28. One handbill referred to the state of representative government in Britain as "a cruel insult upon the sacred rights of property, religion, and freedom." Mori, *William Pitt*, 92.
29. Ehrman, *Reluctant Transition*, 73–88; Matheson, *Life of Henry Dundas*, 153–56; Morris, *British Monarchy*, 85.
30. Black, *British Foreign Policy*, 388; Mori, *William Pitt*, 108–14.
31. Auckland to Grenville, 15 May 1792, in HMC, *Dropmore*, 2:268.
32. Nepean to P. Salter, 1 December 1792, TNA: HO 42/23, fol. 43; Grenville to George III, 1 December 1792, in Aspinall, *Later Correspondence*, 2:633; Masson, *Le Departement des Affaires Étrangères*, 237–84.
33. Cobbett, *Parliamentary History*, 29:1304–27; Mori, *William Pitt*, 112–13.
34. Sir Elliot to Lady Elliot, 14 May 1792, in Minto, *Life and Letters*, 2:23–24; Mori, *William Pitt*, 114.
35. Fry, *Dundas Despotism*, 180–90; Matheson, *Life of Henry Dundas*, 150–59.
36. The text of the proclamation is printed in full in Debrett, *Collection*, 1:222; Mori, *William Pitt*, 112–13.
37. Pitt to Portland, 9 May 1792, and Portland to Pitt, 13 May 1792, in Rose, *Pitt and Napoleon*, 249.
38. TNA: PRO 30/8/198, notebook 4, fol. 108; Mori, *William Pitt*, 92.
39. Black, *British Foreign Policy*, 393.
40. Emsley, "London 'Insurrection,'" 79.
41. Black, *British Foreign Policy*, 390–92.
42. Mori, *William Pitt*, 119.
43. In addition, the Stadtholder's second son, Prince William George Frederick of Orange, even requested to serve with the Prussian army. However, Frederick William II "refused permission for Prince Frederick of Orange to serve in the allied armies, otherwise than in his regimental rank, . . . he is therefore not to go." Auckland to Grenville, 26 June 1792, in HMC, *Dropmore*, 2:285; Grenville to Auckland, 21 July 1792, in Auckland, *Journal and Correspondence*, 2:419.
44. Auckland to Grenville, 15, 26, and 29 May and 5 June 1792, in HMC, *Dropmore*, 2:269–77.
45. Grenville to Auckland, 6 November 1792, in Auckland, *Journal and Correspondence*, 2:464; Mori, *William Pitt*, 78–107.

46. On 29 April, Marshal Jean-Baptiste Rochambeau sent three French columns into the Austrian Netherlands with General Théobald Dillon advancing from Lille on the far left, General Armand Biron marching from Quievrain in the center, and General Gilbert du Motier, Marquis de Lafayette assembling a third column on the far right at Givet. At the first sight of the Austrians, Dillon's column broke ranks, fled to Lille, and killed their commander. Lacking support, Biron began to retreat, but an attack from Austrian hussars sent his men into a rout that did not stop until they reached Valenciennes. Lafayette remained stationary. George III to Grenville, 4 May 1792, in HMC, *Dropmore*, 2:267; Fortescue, *History of the British Army*, 4:37–38.
47. Morton Eden to Grenville, 19 June 1792, in TNA: FO 64/25; Black, *British Foreign Policy*, 394.
48. Gower to Grenville, 6 July 1792, in HMC, *Dropmore*, 2:288.
49. Grenville to Gower, 13 July 1792, in HMC, *Dropmore*, 2:291.
50. Black, *British Foreign Policy*, 396.
51. "Declaration addressed by his Most Serene Highness the Reigning Duke of Brunswick-Lunenburg, commanding the Combined Armies of their Majesties the Emperor and King of Prussia, addressed to the Inhabitants of France," in Debrett, *Collection*, 1:62–65; Pitt to Grenville, 9 August 1792, in HMC, *Dropmore*, 2:299.
52. Burges to Grenville, 15 August 1792, in HMC, *Dropmore*, 2:301.
53. As early as 1790, Sir John Thomas Stanley wrote of revolutionary politics, "Passion takes the place of argument and abuse of discussion." Stanley to Auckland, in Auckland, *Journal and Correspondence*, 2:378; Blanning, *French Revolutionary Wars*, 71–72.
54. Dundas handled the recall of Gower as acting foreign secretary in Grenville's stead while the latter was on vacation. Pitt to Grenville, 17 August 1792, in HMC, *Dropmore*, 2:302; Dundas to Gower, 17 August 1792, in Debrett, *Collection*, 1:232; Matheson, *Life of Henry Dundas*, 166–67.
55. "Note in Answer to the Communication made by Earl Gower, the English Ambassador," in Debrett, *Collection*, 1:233.
56. Black, *British Foreign Policy*, 400.
57. Barnes, *George III and William Pitt*, 254.
58. Dundas to Sir James Murray, 12 September 1792, TNA: FO 26/19.
59. One such radical, Dr. William Maxwell, went so far as to make an offer to the French government to raise and equip a company of marksmen armed with rifled muskets and daggers. Maxwell ultimately placed an order for 3,000 daggers to realize this plan, which raised some alarm and brought the matter to the government's attention. TNA: HO 42/21, fol. 590 and HO 42/22, fol. 3; Barnes, *George III and William Pitt*, 254; Matheson, *Life of Henry Dundas*, 168.
60. Cobbett, *Parliamentary History*, 30:204; Goodwin, *Friends of Liberty*, 244–52.
61. The September Massacres began in response to the Prussian capture of Verdun on 20 August 1792. The fall of Verdun seemed to open the way to Paris, and a general fear of the actualization of the Brunswick Manifesto threw the Parisians into a panic. The revolutionary mob stormed prisons and churches to kill any who might betray the city to the advancing Prussian army. By the time the chaos subsided, 1,400 priests and prisoners had been killed. This atmosphere of mob violence drove many of the remaining priests and nobles to emigrate if they possessed the

NOTES TO CHAPTER 4   269

resources to do so. Browning, *Despatches of Earl Gower*, 221–35; Hibbert, *Days of the French Revolution*, 165–79.
62. Matheson, *Life of Henry Dundas*, 168; Mori, *William Pitt*, 120.
63. Goodwin, *Friends of Liberty*, 260–61.
64. Auckland to Morton Eden, 9 October 1792, in Auckland, *Journal and Correspondence*, 2:452; Clark, *Iron Kingdom*, 288; Phipps, *Armies of the First French Republic*, 1:109–32.
65. Pitt to Grenville, 16 October 1792, in HMC, *Dropmore*, 2:322; Black, *British Foreign Policy*, 406–7; Dwyer, *Rise of Prussia*, 244.
66. Phipps, *Armies of the First French Republic*, 1:141–46.
67. Burges to Auckland, 13 November 1792, in Auckland, *Journal and Correspondence*, 2:467–68.
68. Grenville to Auckland, 6 November 1792, in Auckland, *Journal and Correspondence*, 2: 464; Ehrman, *Reluctant Transition*, 206.
69. Auckland to Grenville, 9 November 1792, in HMC, *Dropmore*, 2:329.
70. "Declaration," in Debrett, *Collection*, 1:247.
71. Grenville to Auckland, 13 November 1792, in HMC, *Dropmore*, 2:332; Black, *British Foreign Policy*, 410–11.
72. Grenville to George III, 25 November 1792, in HMC, *Dropmore*, 2:339.
73. George III to Grenville, 25 November 1792, in HMC, *Dropmore*, 2:339; Black, *George III*, 296–300.
74. Pitt to Grenville, 5–12 November 1792, in HMC, *Dropmore*, 2:328.
75. Auckland to Morton Eden, 7 December 1792, in Auckland, *Journal and Correspondence*, 2:472; Grenville to Buckingham, 7 November 1792, Buckingham to Grenville, 8, 15, and 18 November 1792, Auckland to Grenville, 26 November 1792, and Grenville to Auckland, 27 November 1792, in HMC, *Dropmore*, 2:221, 326, 333, 336, 341, 344; Ehrman, *Reluctant Transition*, 213–33; Ward and Gooch, *Cambridge History*, 225.
76. Mori, *William Pitt*, 122.
77. Pitt to Dundas, November 1792, in WCL: Pitt Family Papers, box 2; Dundas to Pitt, 12 November 1792, in WCL: Viscounts Melville Papers, box 5.
78. Ehrman, *Reluctant Transition*, 206.
79. The 1648 Treaty of Münster established the Dutch right to close the Scheldt River. The Treaty of Fontainebleau had confirmed that right on 8 November 1785. Barnes, *George III and William Pitt*, 256; Jones, *Britain and the World*, 260; Rose, *Great War*, 71–72; Schama, *Patriots and Liberators*, 156; Schroeder, *Transformation of European Politics*, 113–17.
80. The full text may be found in Dupont, *Archives Parlementaires*, 53:472–74. For an English translation of the relevant text, see Blanning, *French Revolutionary Wars*, 92.
81. Grenville to Auckland, 27 November 1792, in HMC, *Dropmore*, 2:344.
82. Jones, *Britain and the World*, 260; Schroeder, *Transformation of European Politics*, 113–17.
83. Maret to Lebrun, 2 December 1792, in Debrett, *Collection*, 1:252–55.
84. Black, *British Foreign Policy*, 418–19. For a larger discussion of the development and implementation of France's revolutionary foreign policy, see Frey and Frey, "Reign of the Charlatans Is Over,"; Howe, "Charles-François Dumouriez."

85. Grenville to Auckland, 26 November 1792, in HMC, *Dropmore*, 2:341.
86. Auckland to Grenville, 26 November 1792, in HMC, *Dropmore*, 2:341.
87. These reports and rumors comprise almost the entirety of TNA: HO 42/22, 23.
88. Auckland to Morton Eden, 7 December 1792, in Auckland, *Journal and Correspondence*, 2:472–73.
89. Grenville to Buckingham, 29 November 1792, in Buckingham, *Memoirs of the Court and Cabinets*, 2:230.
90. Grenville to Buckingham, 1 December 1792, in Buckingham, *Memoirs of the Court and Cabinets*, 2:231.
91. Mori, *William Pitt*, 123–29.
92. TNA: PC 2/137, fols. 224–25.
93. Grenville to Auckland, 4 December 1792, in HMC, *Dropmore*, 2:351.
94. Grenville to Auckland, 18 December 1792, in HMC, *Dropmore*, 2:359.
95. For a more extensive discussion of Loyalism during the French Revolutionary Wars, see Colley, *Britons*, 283–310; Duffy, "William Pitt and the Origins of the Loyalist Association Movement"; Ginter, "Loyalist Association Movement"; Morris, *British Monarchy*, 143.
96. In the letter to which Grenville refers, Buckingham recommended additional mobilization to prevent mobs from gaining access to militia armories. Buckingham to Grenville, 2 December 1792, in HMC, *Dropmore*, 2:348; Grenville to Buckingham, 5 December 1792, in Buckingham, *Memoirs of the Court and Cabinets*, 2:232.
97. Cobbett, *Parliamentary History*, 30:1–80.
98. Cobbett, 29:1556–76, 30:1–80.
99. On 25 November, Grenville wrote to his brother that "the army, though I trust still steady, is too small to be depended on. We must look to individual exertions, and to the Militia." He also explained the Cabinet's plan to raise the militia "on the first appearance of tumult." Again, in a subsequent letter, the foreign secretary declared the ministry's intention to summon the militia soon because of "the total inadequacy of our military force to the necessary exertions." Grenville to Buckingham, 25 and 29 November 1792, in Buckingham, *Memoirs of the Court and Cabinets*, 2:228, 230.
100. Whig member of Parliament, Sir Gilbert Elliot, speculated on the usage of the militia as pretense to call Parliament in his journal. Minto, *Life and Letters*, 2:80. See also, Mori, "Responses to Revolution," 284–305.
101. Cobbett, *Parliamentary History*, 30:170–337.
102. Chauvelin to Grenville, 27 December 1792, in Debrett, *Collection*, 1:256–58.
103. Grenville to Chauvelin, 31 December 1792, in Debrett, *Collection*, 259–62; Ward and Gooch, *Cambridge History*, 231–33.
104. Debrett, *Collection*, 1:262–77.
105. Buckingham to Grenville, 20 January 1793, in HMC, *Dropmore*, 2:369; Cobbett, *Parliamentary History*, 30:239–70.
106. Spencer to Auckland, 18 December 1792, in Auckland, *Journal and Correspondence*, 2:474; Black, *Parliament and Foreign Policy*, 127–28.
107. Duncan to Elgin, 5 December 1792, TNA: FO 26/19; Black, *British Foreign Policy*, 423.
108. Grenville to Auckland, 4 December 1792, in HMC, *Dropmore*, 2:351–52.
109. Dupont, *Archives Parlementaires*, 55:164.
110. Cobbett, *Parliamentary History*, 30:238–337.

111. Grenville to Auckland, 18 December 1792, in HMC, *Dropmore*, 2:359.
112. Debrett, *Collection*, 1:256–77; Black, *British Foreign Policy*, 447–55.

Chapter 5

1. Aleksandrenko, *Russkie Diplomaticheskie agenty*, 250–52; Marcum, "Semen R. Vorontsov," 258–60.
2. Black, *British Foreign Policy*, 432.
3. Grenville to Whitworth, 29 December 1792, in TNA: FO 65/23, fols. 262–70.
4. Grenville to Whitworth, 29 December 1792.
5. Grenville to Whitworth, 29 December 1792; Grenville to Auckland, 29 December 1792, in HMC, *Dropmore*, 2:361; Ward and Gooch, *Cambridge History*, 229–31.
6. Grenville to Whitworth, 29 December 1792, in TNA: FO 65/23, fols. 256–71; Black, *British Foreign Policy*, 433.
7. Grenville to Straton, 29 December 1792, in TNA: FO 97/59, no. 4; Grenville to Murray, 4 January 1793, in TNA: FO 29/1; Grenville to Ostervald, 29 December 1792, in TNA: FO 63/15, no. 6; Grenville to Eden, 29 December 1792, in TNA: FO 97/324, no. 21; Grenville to Trevor, 10 January 1793, in TNA: FO 67/11, no. 1; Grenville to Jackson, 29 December 1792, in TNA: FO 72/25, no. 10.
8. Pitt's notes, in TNA: PRO 30/8/197, fol. 76; Ehrman, *Reluctant Transition*, 244–58.
9. Black, *British Foreign Policy*, 433–40.
10. Grenville to Murray, 4 January 1793, in TNA: FO 29/1.
11. This assessment from Grenville supports T. C. W. Blanning's argument that "for the history of international relations, the beginning of an upheaval of corresponding dimensions [to the French Revolution] can be located in time and space with some precision." He goes on to identify the outbreak of the Russo-Turkish war of 1787 as this point of origin—an argument with which Pitt's ministry would likely concur. The Russo-Turkish war created a new imbalance in European power politics, and much of the policies and choices of governments across Europe from then until the outbreak of a general war with France were driven by their responses to this unmitigated Russian victory. These disputes continued to dominate and disrupt wartime diplomacy, and it is worth noting that this was both anticipated and understood by the British ministers. Blanning, *Origins of the French Revolutionary Wars*, 36.
12. Finkstein, Shulenberg, and Alvensleben to Grenville, 29 December 1792, in TNA: FO 97/324.
13. Whitworth to Grenville, 18 and 22 January 1793, in TNA: FO 65/24, nos. 3, 4; Clark, *Iron Kingdom*, 289; Madariaga, *Russia*, 427–40.
14. Grenville to Murray, 4 January 1793, in TNA: FO 29/1.
15. Unaddressed note from Grenville, 12 January 1793, in TNA: FO 64/27; Black, *British Foreign Policy*, 433.
16. Grenville to Ostervald, 9 January 1793, in TNA: FO 63/16, no. 1.
17. Ostervald to Grenville, 23 January 1793, in TNA: FO 63/16, no. 15; Jackson to Grenville, 1 January 1793, in TNA: FO 72/26, no. 1; Trevor to Grenville, 30 January 1793, in TNA: FO 67/11, no. 8; Pitt's notes, in TNA: PRO 30/8/197, fol. 76; Black, *British Foreign Policy*, 433–40.
18. Duffy, "British War Policy," 4–11; Ehrman, *Reluctant Transition*, 239–41; Ward and Gooch, *Cambridge History*, 237.

19. Grenville to Murray, 6 February 1793, in TNA: FO 29/1, no. 5; Grenville to Eden, 5 February 1793, in TNA: FO 64/27, no. 5; Grenville to Auckland, 3 February 1793, in HMC, *Dropmore*, 2:377.
20. Grenville indicated that London viewed the partition of neutral Poland as more offensive to British foreign policy principles than the Belgium-Bavaria exchange, which displaced but did not partition or destroy the Bavarian Electorate. British opposition to the exchange traditionally arose from concern about replacing a strong Austrian barrier with a weak independent barrier to French incursions into the Low Countries. However, the prospect of a restored French monarchy renewing its alliance with Austria and Austria's ongoing commitment to predatory policies rendered the value of retaining Austria as the guardian of Belgium questionable for the moment. Grenville to Murray, 6 February 1793, in TNA: FO 29/1, no. 5; Grenville to Eden, 5 February 1793, in TNA: FO 64/27, no. 5.
21. Pitt on 25 April, in Debrett, *Parliamentary Register*, 35:306.
22. Grenville to Murray, 15 February 1793, in TNA: FO 29/1, no. 6; Ehrman, *Reluctant Transition*, 272.
23. Grenville to Chauvelin, 24 January 1793, in Debrett, *Collection*, 1:277.
24. Cobbett, *Parliamentary History*, 29:1556–76, 30:1–80; Black, *British Foreign Policy*, 447–55; Ehrman, *Reluctant Transition*, 233–34, 256–58.
25. Lebrun to Grenville, 1 February 1793, in TNA: FO 27/41, fols. 158–59; "Decree of War against Britain," 1 February 1793, Debrett, *Collection*, 1:111.
26. Grenville to Auckland, 18 December 1792, in HMC, *Dropmore*, 2:359.
27. Grenville to Jacobi, 29 December 1792, in TNA: FO 97/324; Eden to Grenville, 12 January 1793, in TNA: FO 64/27, no. 4.
28. Spiegel to Rhede, 24 December 1792, in Spiegel, *Brieven en Negotiatien*, 1:1; Murray to Grenville, 12 February 1793, in TNA: FO 29/1, no. 5.
29. Although Britain possessed extensive military resources, the nature of Britain's maritime empire precluded the concentration of British forces at any one point. The eighty-one infantry battalions at London's disposal remained understrength and widely dispersed. Only twenty-eight battalions were stationed on the island of Britain, and these shouldered the responsibility for home defense in case of a French invasion or rebellion, for police work to prevent rebellion, as well as for any Continental operations. At the start of the war, British regular forces available for service on the Continent numbered only 17,344 infantry and 3,730 artillerymen. The outbreak of war prompted a more concerted effort to increase the army by 25,000 men beginning on 11 February 1793. Conversely, the Royal Navy boasted approximately 18,000 seamen and 113 ships of the line in addition to smaller craft in 1792. After receiving the French declaration of war, the government further increased the naval establishment to a total of 45,000 seamen on paper in February. This considerable force far exceeded France's twenty-eight ships of the line and fifty-three frigates but could do little to make an immediate military impact on the Continental war. A State of the Amount of the Army Estimates for the Year 1793, in TNA: PRO 30/8/239, fol. 108; TNA: PRO 30/8/247, fol. 156; Fortescue, *History of the British Army*, 4:74–80, 938. Dutch military resources also offered little reason for confidence. The States-General voted to curb spending on both the army and the navy in 1791. Although the army officially numbered 43,000 men in 1792, British estimates put its real strength at 35,000. In addition, strong Dutch prejudices

against the centralization of military power limited the field army to 16,000 men while the rest remained under provincial authority. An unsigned and undated report on the state of the Dutch army among Pitt's papers offers a generally positive impression of the quality of the Dutch army, although it agrees with Meulen on the numbers involved. TNA: PRO 30/8/336, fols. 96–97; Meulen, *Ministerie van Van de Spiegel*, 220–42.
30. "Report on the Finances of France," January 1793, in TNA: PRO 30/8/334, fols. 143–63.
31. Pitt, 12 February 1793, in Debrett, *Parliamentary Register*, 34:451.
32. Dundas, in Debrett, *Parliamentary Register*, 34:477.
33. Pitt to Yarmouth, 26 July 1793, in WCL: Pitt Family Papers, box 2; Grenville to Auckland, 31 July 1793, in Auckland, *Journal and Correspondence*, 3:85; Duffy, "Particular Service."
34. Fry, *Dundas Despotism*, 209–10.
35. Duffy, "British War Policy," 8–9; Ehrman, *Reluctant Transition*, 261–63; Fortescue, *History of the British Army*, 4:74–79; Fry, *Dundas Despotism*, 190–208; Mori, *William Pitt*, 146–47.
36. Auckland to Spencer, 19 February 1793, in Auckland, *Journal and Correspondence*, 2:499–500; Auckland to Grenville, 4 March 1793, in HMC, *Dropmore*, 2:382–83. Dutch resolutions on 6 and 21 February raised the official strength of the Dutch army from 43,000 to 65,000 men. However, recruitment proceeded sluggishly, and effective Dutch strength remained substantially lower. From December 1792 to February 1793, Spiegel received repeated reports from the Dutch provincial governments complaining of inadequate defenses. Some of these reports are contained in Spiegel, *Brieven en Negotiatien*, 1:71–95. See also, Meulen, *Ministerie van Van de Spiegel*, 242.
37. Auckland to Grenville, 15 February 1793, in HMC, *Dropmore*, 2:380.
38. Schama, *Patriots and Liberators*, 153–63; Auckland to Eden, 7 December 1792, in Auckland, *Journal and Correspondence*, 2:472–73; Auckland to Grenville, 8 December 1792, 25 January and 28 February 1793, in HMC, *Dropmore*, 2:353, 374, 381; Spiegel to Rhede, 18 February 1793, in Spiegel, *Brieven en Negotiatien*, 1:96–101.
39. "Dumouriez's Manifesto to the Dutch," 17 February 1793, in Debrett, *Collection*, 1:120.
40. "Return of his Majesty's Hanoverian Forces taken into British Pay," 22 February 1793, in Debrett, *Collection*, 1:33; Gideon Duncan to Grenville, 21 February 1793, in TNA: FO 26/20; George III to Pitt, 20 February 1793, in Aspinall, *Later Correspondence*, 2:9; Grenville to Auckland, 20 February 1793, in HMC, *Dropmore*, 2:380; Calvert, *Calvert*, 20–22.
41. Ehrman, *Reluctant Transition*, 263; Fortescue, *History of the British Army*, 4:80.
42. From his post at Frankfurt, James Murray kept the Cabinet abreast of Austrian movements toward Flanders in February and March. Murray was reasonably impressed with the numbers of Austrian reinforcements but less so with their speed and leadership. Murray to Grenville, February–March, in TNA: FO 29/1; Rothenberg, *Napoleon's Great Adversaries*, 35–37.
43. Calvert, *Calvert*, 48; Fortescue, *History of the British Army*, 4:66–68.
44. "Report of Captain Crawfurd," April 1793, in HMC, *Dropmore*, 2:390; Fortescue, *History of the British Army*, 4:68.

45. George III to Pitt, 29 March 1793, in TNA: PRO 30/8/103, fol. 488.
46. George III to Grenville, 29 March 1793, in HMC, *Dropmore*, 2:387; York to George III, 31 March 1793, in Aspinall, *Later Correspondence*, 2:24; Mori, *William Pitt*, 148.
47. Pitt to Grenville, 30 March and 1 April 1793, in HMC, *Dropmore*, 2:388.
48. Duffy, "British War Policy," 17; Ehrman, *Reluctant Transition*, 264–70.
49. Auckland to Grenville, 31 March 1793, in Auckland, *Journal and Correspondence*, 3:3.
50. Grenville to Auckland, 3 April 1793, in Auckland, *Journal and Correspondence*, 3:4.
51. Vivenot and Zeissberg, *Quellen zur Geschichte*, 2:292–93; Schroeder, *Transformation of European Politics*, 105–20.
52. Thugut's Mémoire, 18 March 1793, and P. Cobenzl to Francis, 23 March 179, in Vivenot and Zeissberg, *Quellen zur Geschichte*, 2:504–16; Roider, *Baron Thugut*, 100–104.
53. Franz Metternich was the father of the more famous Prince Klemens Wenzel von Metternich.
54. Auckland to Grenville, 8 April 1793, in Auckland, *Journal and Correspondence*, 3:10; Sybel, *French Revolution*, 2:462.
55. "Proclamation of Prince the Marshal de Saxe-Coburg, General in Chief of the Armies of His Majesty the Emperor, to the French," 5 April 1793, in Debrett, *Collection*, 1:140; Sybel, *French Revolution*, 2:459–60.
56. "Proclamation of Prince the Marshal de Saxe-Coburg, General in Chief of the Armies of His Majesty the Emperor and the Empire, to the French," 9 April 1793, in Debrett, *Collection*, 1:142; Sybel, *French Revolution*, 2:463.
57. Auckland to Grenville, 9 April 1793, in Auckland, *Journal and Correspondence*, 3:12.
58. Auckland to Grenville, 9 April 1793.
59. Auckland to Grenville, 9 April 1793; Sybel, *French Revolution*, 2:463–64; Fortescue, *History of the British Army*, 4:88; Witzleben, *Coburg*, 15–80.
60. York to George III, 31 August 1793, in Aspinall, *Later Correspondence*, 2:82–84; Duffy, "Particular Service," 532; Palmer, *Twelve Who Ruled*, 88.
61. Murray to Grenville, 18 February 1793, in TNA: FO 29/1, no. 6.
62. Bentinck to Auckland, 10 April 1793, in Auckland, *Journal and Correspondence*, 3:15.
63. Auckland to Grenville, 16 April 1793, in Auckland, *Journal and Correspondence*, 3:19.
64. Grenville to Auckland, 16 April 1793, in Auckland, *Journal and Correspondence*, 3:23; Duffy, "British War Policy," 24.
65. Dundas to Murray, 16 April 1793, in Auckland, *Journal and Correspondence*, 3:23; Fortescue, *History of the British Army*, 4:89; Matheson, *Life of Henry Dundas*, 177–80.
66. They likely arrived at this decision based on the intelligence obtained from a captured resident of Dunkirk who was referenced in a letter from York to Grenville. York to Grenville, 19 April 1793, in HMC, *Dropmore*, 2:393; Fortescue, *History of the British Army*, 4:89.
67. York to George III, 19 April 1793, in Aspinall, *Later Correspondence*, 2:29; H. Calvert to J. Calvert, 16 April 1793, in Calvert, *Calvert*, 67.

68. Roider, *Baron Thugut*, 125–26.
69. Auckland to Grenville, 26 April 1793, in Auckland, *Journal and Correspondence*, 3:35; Duffy, "British War Policy," 25–26; Sherwig, *Guineas and Gunpowder*, 23–24.
70. Roider, *Baron Thugut*, 125–26.
71. Roider,, 132–36; Ehrman, *Reluctant Transition*, 271.
72. Q. Craufurd to Auckland, 29 April 1793 and Auckland to Grenville, 14 May 1793, in Auckland, *Journal and Correspondence*, 3:41, 58.
73. Auckland to Grenville and Grenville to Auckland, 23 April 1793, in Auckland, *Journal and Correspondence*, 3:31–34; Starhemberg to Thugut, 24 May 1793, in Vivenot and Zeissberg, *Quellen zur Geschichte*, 3:79; Roider, *Baron Thugut*, 135; Schroeder, *Transformation of European Politics*, 127–33.
74. Starhemberg to Thugut, 12 July 1793, in Vivenot and Zeissberg, *Quellen zur Geschichte*, 3:145–48.
75. Mercy to Thugut, 15 June 1793, and Thugut to L. Cobenzl, 16 June 1793, in Vivenot and Zeissberg, *Quellen zur Geschichte*, 3:112–13; Auckland to Grenville, 9 July 1793, in HMC, *Dropmore*, 2:404; Roider, *Baron Thugut*, 134–36; Schroeder, *Transformation of European Politics*, 134.
76. Auckland to Grenville, 9 April 1793, in TNA: FO 37/47, no. 74; Eden to Auckland, undated, and Grenville to Auckland, 31 July 1793, in Auckland, *Journal and Correspondence*, 3:68, 85; Duffy, "Particular Service," 529–37; Ehrman, *Reluctant Transition*, 273–74.
77. Dundas to Grenville, July 1793, in HMC, *Dropmore*, 2:407.
78. Eden to Auckland, undated, in Auckland, *Journal and Correspondence*, 3:68.
79. Mercy to Thugut, 17 July 1793, in Vivenot and Zeissberg, *Quellen zur Geschichte*, 3:150.
80. Auckland to Grenville, 29 April 1793, in Auckland, *Journal and Correspondence*, 3:39.
81. Convention with Sardinia in TNA: FO 94/249; Convention with Spain in TNA: FO 94/284; Convention with Naples in TNA: FO 94/271; Convention with Prussia in TNA: FO 94/183; Convention with Portugal in TNA: FO 93/77/1A.
82. Debrett, *Collection*, 1:10–19.
83. Catherine II to Vorontsov, 7 February 1793, in TNA: FO 65/24; Whitworth to Grenville, 7 February 1793, in TNA: FO 65/24, no. 9.
84. Grenville to Whitworth, 26 March 1793, in TNA: FO 65/24, no. 4.
85. Copies of the text of these treaties with the German states are reproduced in Debrett, *Collection*, 1:5, 21, 27; Whitworth to Grenville, 29 April 1793, in TNA: FO 65/24, no. 29.
86. Whitworth to Grenville, 28 June 1793, in TNA: FO 65/24, no. 58.
87. Whitworth to Grenville, 12 February 1793, in TNA: FO 65/24, no. 11; Sherwig, *Guineas and Gunpowder*, 20–23.
88. Trevor to Grenville, 2 March 1793, in TNA: FO 67/11, no. 17; Anglo-Sardinian Convention, 25 April 1793, in TNA: FO 94/249.
89. Jackson to Grenville, 25 January 1793, in TNA: FO 72/26, no. 9, fols. 76–83.
90. Grenville to Jackson, 6 February 1793, in TNA: FO 72/26, no. 3, fol. 125.
91. Grenville to St. Helens, 8 February 1793, in TNA: FO 72/26, no. 1, fols. 135–42.
92. St. Helens to Grenville, 22 and 25 March 1793, in TNA: FO 72/26, nos. 1, 2, fols. 253–70.

93. St. Helens to Grenville, 29 May 1793, in TNA: FO 72/27, no. 11, fols. 75–77.
94. St. Helens to Grenville, 29 May 1793.
95. Grenville to William Hamilton, 22 March 1793, in TNA: FO 70/6, no. 6, fols. 69–72; Grenville to Hamilton, 21 June 1793, in TNA: FO 70/6, no. 7, fols. 134–42.
96. Convention with Sicily, 12 July 1793, in TNA: FO 94/271; Ehrman, *Reluctant Transition*, 279; Baker, "Capital Ships, Commerce, and Coalition," 65–74.
97. Contingencies included Grenville forgetting to give St. Helens authority to sign the treaty he was sent to negotiate or the Neapolitan ambassador in London committing suicide on the eve of signing a treaty with Grenville. Grenville to George III, 31 May 1793, and George III to Grenville, 1 June 1793, in HMC, *Dropmore*, 2:395.
98. Why Russia did not qualify as a potential ally for Prussia in Grenville's assessment remains unclear. Perhaps he considered Russia's alliance with Austria or more recent convention with Britain as superseding any Prusso-Russian cooperation to partition Poland.
99. Yarmouth was styled Viscount Beauchamp at the start of his mission but became Earl of Yarmouth by the time of Grenville's second letter to him on 10 July. Grenville to Beauchamp, 27 June 1793, Most Secret and Confidential, in TNA: FO 29/1.
100. Yarmouth to Grenville, 17 July 1793, in TNA: FO 29/1; Convention with Prussia, 14 July 1793, in TNA: FO 93/78/4C.
101. Mori, *William Pitt*, 158.
102. Sources remain unclear on the precise number of troops from each state. Jomini puts Austrian strength across the entire front at approximately 150,000 men, and he indicates that the Prussian contingent near Mainz included at least 50,000. Fortescue identifies 20,000 men under York's command with a comparable amount from the Dutch. Pitt's notes, 28 August 1793, TNA: PRO 30/8/195, fol. 49; Duffy, "British War Policy," 81; Fortescue, *History of the British Army*, 4:221; Jomini, *Histoire critique*, 5:32–33.
103. Pitt to Murray, 19 July 1793, in TNA: PRO 30/8/102, fol. 214; Mori, *William Pitt*, 158.
104. Davies, *Wellington's Wars*, 4–6.
105. "Convention between his Majesty the Emperor and his Britannic Majesty," 30 August 1793, in Debrett, *Collection*, 1:19–20; Duffy, "British War Policy," 48–54.
106. Brown, *Impartial Journal*, 78–86; Calvert, *Calvert*, 146–67.
107. York to George III, 9 October–5 November 1793, in Aspinall, *Later Correspondence*, 2:106–17; Fortescue, *History of the British Army*, 4:147–49; Duffy, *Soldiers, Sugar, and Seapower*, 51.
108. Grenville to Robert Walpole, 27 September 1793, in TNA: FO 63/17, no. 11; Convention with Portugal, 26 September 1793, in TNA: FO 93/77/1A.
109. Grenville to Whitworth, 29 December 1792, in TNA: FO 65/23, fols. 262–70.
110. Ehrman discusses this in *Reluctant Transition*, 272–76.
111. Pitt to Yarmouth, 26 July 1793, in WCL: Pitt Family Papers, box 2.

Chapter 6

1. Tropical expeditions operated on an inverse campaigning season from European expeditions to minimize the effects of heat and disease. Duffy, *Soldiers, Sugar, and Seapower*, 41.
2. See chapter 5 for a more complete discussion of these efforts.
3. Auckland to Grenville, 17 and 18 May 1793, in Auckland, *Journal and Correspondence*, 3:60–63; Fox, 17 June 1793, in Debrett, *Parliamentary Register*, 35:652–64.

4. Quentin Craufurd to Auckland, 23 May 1793, in Auckland, *Journal and Correspondence*, 3:64–67.
5. Cobban, "Channel Isles Correspondence," 44–45; Fortescue, *History of the British Army*, 4:152–53; Matheson, *Life of Henry Dundas*, 182; Mori, *William Pitt*, 158–59.
6. Lebrun to Grenville, 2 April 1793, and Grenville to Lebrun, 18 May 1793, in TNA: FO 27/42, fols. 109–10, 114–15.
7. Grenville to Lebrun, 18 May 1793, in TNA: FO 27/42, fols. 114–15.
8. Although neither draft contains notes in the margin to indicate commentary from another source, the modifications give the appearance that Grenville adjusted the reply based on feedback from other government officials. Grenville, Pitt, and Dundas nearly always exchanged important letters with each other and with George III for commentary and proofreading. In my own opinion, the internationalist shift in tone seems to bear the mark of Pitt, and the reference to York suggests the influence of the king. Lebrun to Grenville 2 April 1793, and Grenville to Lebrun, 18 May 1793, in TNA: FO 27/42, fols. 109–10, 114–15.
9. Pitt, 25 April 1793, in Debrett, *Parliamentary Register*, 35:301–6.
10. One could argue that negotiations equally depended on British willingness to submit to revolutionary interpretations of the international order. Neither accommodation was likely in 1793. Debrett, *Parliamentary Register*, 35:301–6.
11. Pitt, 17 June 1793, in Debrett, *Parliamentary Register*, 35:672–79.
12. Pitt, 17 June 1793, in Debrett.
13. Pitt, 17 June 1793, in Debrett.
14. The fall of Federalist Marseilles to republican forces on 25 August and the subsequent massacres offered the rebels of Toulon an example of the alternative to surrendering to the coalition. Baker, "Capital Ships, Commerce, and Coalition," 100–103; Ehrman, *Reluctant Transition*, 309.
15. Pitt to Grenville, 7 September 1793, in HMC, *Dropmore*, 2:422; Fortescue, *History of the British Army*, 4:132–33; Matheson, *Life of Henry Dundas*, 187.
16. Grenville to Buckingham, 15 September 1793, in Buckingham, *Memoirs of the Court and Cabinets*, 2:241.
17. Pitt's notes, 28 August 1793, TNA: PRO 30/8/195, fol. 49; Duffy, "British War Policy," 81; Mori, *William Pitt*, 158.
18. Baker, "Capital Ships, Commerce, and Coalition," 55–71.
19. Hood to Philip Stephens, 11 August 1793, in TNA: ADM 1/391; Ehrman, *Reluctant Transition*, 305; Rose, *Lord Hood*, 14–15.
20. Henry Dundas to Henry Phipps, 8 July 1793, TNA: HO 50/455, no. 1.
21. Grenville to Dundas, 7 August 1793, in HMC, *Dropmore*, 2:411–22; Baker, "Capital Ships, Commerce, and Coalition," 111–39; Duffy, "British War Policy," 53; Matheson, *Life of Henry Dundas*, 182; Rose, *Lord Hood*, 16–17; Schroeder, *Transformation of European Politics*, 130; Sherwig, *Guineas and Gunpowder*, 24–25.
22. St. Helens to Grenville, 24 July 1793, in TNA: FO 72/27, no. 28, fols. 307–29; Ehrman, *Reluctant Transition*, 314.
23. "Hints suggested by the perusal of Lord Mulgrave's letter of the 19th August received here this morning," 27 August 1793, TNA: HO 50/455; Matheson, *Life of Henry Dundas*, 182.
24. Jupp, *Lord Grenville*, 160–61; Rose, *Lord Hood*, 17.
25. George III to Pitt, 14 September 1793, in TNA: PRO 30/8/103, fol. 506; Matheson, *Life of Henry Dundas*, 187.

26. Hood to Stephens, 7 September 1793, in TNA: ADM 1/391; Baker, "Capital Ships, Commerce, and Coalition," 106–13; Fortescue, *History of the British Army*, 4:158.
27. Rose, *Lord Hood*, 31–37.
28. Hood to Stephens, 27 September 1793, in TNA: ADM 1/391; Baker, "Capital Ships, Commerce, and Coalition," 114.
29. Ehrman, *Reluctant Transition*, 305–6; Rose, *Great War*, 151.
30. St. Helens to Grenville, 19 July 1793, in TNA: FO 72/27, no. 26, fols. 294–95.
31. Grenville to St. Helens, 9 August 1793, in TNA: FO 72/27, no. 19, fols. 394–98.
32. Grenville to St. Helens, 9 August 1793; Jupp, *Lord Grenville*, 153–55; Godoy, *Memoirs*, 1:263–65.
33. Chastenet, *Godoy*, 63.
34. The process of concluding the Anglo-Spanish convention of 25 May 1793 took nearly six months, as described in the previous chapter. Of that, negotiations took roughly one week while transmission and formalities absorbed the remaining time. Messages seemed to make the trip between the western Mediterranean and London in roughly three or four weeks, a pace too slow for Hood to defer his negotiations with the Federalists to a Cabinet decision. TNA: FO 72/25–27.
35. Hood to Stephens, 29 August 1793, in TNA: ADM 1/391, no. 114; Rose, *Lord Hood*, 31.
36. Grenville to Morton Eden, 27 September 1793, in TNA: FO 7/34, no. 11.
37. Grenville to Morton Eden, 27 September 1793.
38. Grenville to Morton Eden, 27 September 1793; Mori, "Bourbon Restoration," 706.
39. Adams, *Influence*, 22–25; Fry, *Dundas Despotism*, 155–56.
40. Draft of Instructions to Hood, Elliot, and O'Hara, October 1793, in TNA: PRO 30/8/334.
41. Cobbett, *Parliamentary History*, 30:1057–61; Baker, "Capital Ships, Commerce, and Coalition," 119.
42. Draft of Instructions to Hood, Elliot, and O'Hara, October 1793 in TNA: PRO 30/8/334.
43. Pitt to Grenville, 5 October 1793, in HMC, *Dropmore*, 2:438–39.
44. Grenville to St. Helens, 22 October, in TNA: FO 72/28, fols. 206–11.
45. Mori, "Bourbon Restoration," 713.
46. Dresnay to Dundas, 8 November 1793, in TNA: PRO 30/8/334, fols. 219–45; Dundas to Royalist Commanders, 26 October 1793, in TNA: WO 1/389, fols. 107–11.
47. Correspondence between Grenville and Harcourt from 26 October 1793, in TNA: FO 27/42, fols. 193–218; Ehrman, *Reluctant Transition*, 321–22.
48. Pitt to Elgin, 16 November 1793, in TNA: PRO 30/8/102, fols. 119–20.
49. Pitt to the Earl of Moira, 25 November 1793, in TNA: PRO 30/8/102, fols. 204–5; Matheson, *Life of Henry Dundas*, 188.
50. Pitt to Elgin, 16 November 1793, in TNA: PRO 30/8/102, fols. 119–20; Elgin to Pitt, 18 November 1793, in TNA: FO 26/22.
51. Ehrman, *Reluctant Transition*, 325.
52. Rose, *Lord Hood*, 37.
53. Thugut to Colloredo, 7 November 1793, in Vivenot, *Vertrauliche Briefe*, 1:52.
54. Duffy, "British War Policy," 68–69; Ehrman, *Reluctant Transition*, 303–9.
55. Pitt to Grenville, 17 October 1793, and Dundas to Grenville, 20 October 1793, in HMC, *Dropmore*, 2:447–48.
56. For their pledge of 5,000 men for Toulon, the Austrians produced 4,000 low-quality Hungarian troops supplemented by 1,000 Austrians to bring the total to

5,000 men. Vienna only went as far as ordering this corps to be ready to march, never actually ordering it to make for a friendly port to embark. Trevor to Elliot, 23 October 1793, no. 1, and Eden to Trevor, 26 October 1793, in NMM: ELL 100.
57. Précis of Correspondence between Hood and Admiral Don Juan Francisco de Lángara y Huarte, 20–24 November 1793, in TNA: HO 50/454; Ehrman, *Reluctant Transition*, 314–15.
58. St. Helens to Grenville, 9 October 1793, in TNA: FO 72/28.
59. Chandler, *Campaigns of Napoleon*, 15–28; Rose, *Great War*, 156–57.
60. Elliot to Dundas, 20 December 1793, in Minto, *Life and Letters*, 2:202–8; Godoy, *Memoirs*, 1:265–67; James, *Naval History*, 1:69–93.
61. Precis of Correspondence from General David Dundas to H. Dundas, December 1793, in TNA: HO 50/454; Baker, "Capital Ships, Commerce, and Coalition," 136.
62. Elliot to Dundas, 27 November 1793, in TNA: FO 20/1, no. 5; Dundas to Elliot, 23 December 1793, in TNA: FO 20/1; D. Dundas to H. Dundas, 12 December 1793, in TNA: HO 50/454.
63. Debrett, *Parliamentary Register*, 37:174–76.
64. Debrett, 37:174–76; Mori, *William Pitt*, 161–68.
65. Debrett, *Parliamentary Register*, 37:177–82.

Chapter 7

1. Mori, *William Pitt*, 161–63.
2. Grenville to Eden, 7 September 1793, in TNA: FO 7/34, no. 8; Duffy, "British War Policy," 79–80.
3. Grenville to Eden, 7 September 1793, in TNA: FO 7/34, no. 8. As noted, the Dutch acknowledged their junior position relative to the British, and the Prussians had continuously insisted on deferring all questions pertaining to the war to the Austrians as the leading partner of their alliance in the war with France. In addition, the Italian states remained secondary parties by virtue of their limited resources, and the Spanish insisted on remaining independent and aloof from negotiations involving the German powers. Thus, as they both recognized, leadership of the coalition devolved to London and Vienna, and multilateral unity required agreement between those two powers.
4. Grenville to Eden, 7 September 1793, in TNA: FO 7/34, no. 8.
5. Pitt on 25 April in Debrett, *Parliamentary Register*, 35:306.
6. Grenville to Eden, 7 September 1793, in TNA: FO 7/34, no. 8.
7. Grenville to Eden, 7 September 1793. For a more thorough description of this strategic evaluation of the Caribbean, see Duffy, *Soldiers, Sugar, and Sea Power*, 3–40, and Ehrman, *Reluctant Transition*, 350–54.
8. Grenville to Eden, 7 September 1793, in TNA: FO 7/34, no. 8.
9. Grenville to Eden, 7 September 1793.
10. St. Helens to Grenville, 25 March 1793, in TNA: FO 72/26, no. 2, fols. 260–70.
11. Grenville to Eden, 7 September 1793, in TNA: FO 7/34, no. 8.
12. Grenville to Eden, 7 September 1793.
13. Grenville to Eden, 7 September 1793; Ehrman, *Reluctant Transition*, 294–97.
14. Grenville to Eden, 7 September 1793, in TNA: FO 7/34, no 8.
15. Grenville to Eden, 7 September 1793.
16. Eden to Grenville, 25 September 1793, in TNA: FO 7/34, no. 55; Thugut to Colloredo, 4 November 1793, in Vivenot, *Vertrauliche Briefe*, 1:52.

17. Eden to Grenville, 25 September 1793; Thugut to Colloredo, 4 November 1793, in Vivenot, 1:52; Ehrman, *Reluctant Transition*, 296.
18. Eden to Grenville, 25 September 1793; Thugut to Colloredo, 5 October 1793, in Vivenot, *Vertrauliche Briefe*, 1:46–47.
19. Eden to Grenville, 25 September 1793; Thugut to Colloredo, 5 October 1793, in Vivenot, 1:46–47.
20. Eden to Grenville, 13 and 16 November 1793, in TNA: FO 7/35, nos. 67, 68.
21. Major Craufurd's Memorandum, in Aspinall, *Later Correspondence*, 2:138–41.
22. Major Craufurd's Memorandum, in Aspinall, 2:138–41.
23. Although the memorandum lacks a date, Eden's letters to Grenville put Craufurd in Vienna from 12 to 16 November 1793. Aspinall includes the memorandum between a letter from Dundas to George III on 26 December and a letter from York to George III on 31 December. Major Craufurd's Memorandum, in Aspinall, *Later Correspondence*, 2:138–41.
24. Eden to Grenville, 21 and 25 September 1793, in TNA: FO 7/34, nos. 54, 55.
25. Thugut to Colloredo, 2 January 1794, in Vivenot, *Vertrauliche Briefe*, 1:68–69, Roider, *Baron Thugut*, 148.
26. Grenville to Eden, 8 October 1793, in TNA: FO 7/34, no. 14.
27. Grenville to Eden, 14 November 1793, in TNA: FO 7/35, no. 17.
28. Grenville to Eden, 14 November 1793.
29. Grenville to Eden, 3 January 1794, in TNA: FO 7/36, no. 1.
30. Mack had resigned his post in May 1793 partially because of poor health and partially because of friction with the rest of the Austrian command. In particular, Mack and Thugut disliked each other. Grenville to Eden, 3 January 1794, in TNA: FO 7/36, no. 1; Eden to Grenville, 11 March 1794, in HMC, *Dropmore*, 2:525.
31. York to George, 4 January 1794, in Aspinall, *Later Correspondence*, 2:143.
32. Grenville to Eden, 7 January 1794, in TNA: FO 7/36, no. 3.
33. Eden to Grenville, 4 January 1794, in TNA: FO 7/36, no. 2.
34. York to George III, 22 January 1794, in Aspinall, *Later Correspondence*, 2:148.
35. Austro-Prussian forces suffered a defeat on 29 December 1793 at the Second Battle of Wissembourg. Grenville to Eden, 7 January 1794, in TNA: FO 7/36, no. 2.
36. York to George III, 2 and 4 February 1794, in Aspinall, *Later Correspondence*, 2:174–75.
37. Ehrman, *Reluctant Transition*, 329.
38. York to Dundas, 2 February 1794, and Coburg, "Considerations sur l'ouverture et les Operations de la Campagne prochaine de l'Année 1794," 4 February 1794, in TNA: WO 1/168, fols. 247–53, 259–82; Duffy, "British War Policy," 82; Ehrman, *Reluctant Transition*, 330.
39. Grenville to George III, 16 February 1794, in HMC, *Dropmore*, 2:505–6; Duffy, "British War Policy," 83.
40. York to Dundas, 2 February 1794, in TNA: WO 1/168, fols. 247–53; Duffy, "British War Policy," 81.
41. Duffy, "Particular Service" 534–35.
42. William Elliot to Grenville, 24 February 1794, in TNA: FO 37/52, no. 22.
43. Eden to Grenville, 11 March 1794, in TNA: FO 7/36, no. 18; Duffy, "British War Policy," 84; Ehrman, *Reluctant Transition*, 334.

44. Convention between George III and Frederick William II, 14 July 1793, in TNA: FO 93/78/4C; Sherwig, *Guineas and Gunpowder*, 24.
45. In the Second Partition of Poland in 1793, Prussia and Russia each took large slices of Polish territory. The Prussian portion included the cities of Danzig and Thorn and the surrounding territory. The Poles fiercely resented the partition, and resistance mounted throughout 1793, culminating in an uprising under Tadeusz Kościuszko in March 1794. See Lord, *Second Partition of Poland*.
46. Yarmouth enclosed the note in a letter to Grenville the following day. Yarmouth to Grenville, 24 September 1793, in TNA: FO 29/2, no. 9; J. B. Burges to Grenville, 30 September 1793, in HMC, *Dropmore*, 2:430–31; Lucchesini to Lehrbach, 22 September 1793, in Vivenot and Zeissberg, *Quellen zur Geschichte*, 3:190–95; Roider, *Baron Thugut*, 137–39; Sherwig, *Guineas and Gunpowder*, 27–28.
47. Pitt to Grenville, 2–10 October 1793, in HMC, *Dropmore*, 2:433–43; Sherwig, *Guineas and Gunpowder*, 28–30.
48. Grenville, "Minute of Conferences with Baron Jacobi," 7 and 8 November 1793, in TNA: FO 64/28; Frederick William II to Baron Jacobi, 10 November 1793, in TNA: FO 97/324.
49. Malmesbury had been in forced retirement since 1789 as a result of his support for Fox during the Regency Crisis. However, the ministry had reconciled with the more conservative Whigs since the start of the war, and the need for Malmesbury's talents and connections trumped stale political grudges. Ehrman, *Reluctant Transition*, 296.
50. Grenville to Malmesbury, 20 November 1793, in TNA: FO 64/31, no. 1.
51. Grenville to Malmesbury, 20 November 1793; Sherwig, *Guineas and Gunpowder*, 30–32.
52. Grenville to Buckingham, 21 November 1793, in Buckingham, *Memoirs of the Court and Cabinets*, 2:247.
53. Malmesbury to Grenville, 3 December 1793, in TNA: FO 64/31, nos. 2, 3.
54. Malmesbury to Grenville, 3 December 1793, in TNA: FO 64/31, no. 4.
55. Malmesbury to Grenville, 3 December 1793, no. 4.
56. Malmesbury to Grenville, 3 December 1793, no. 4.
57. Malmesbury to Grenville, 3 December 1793, no. 4.
58. Malmesbury to Grenville, 26 December, in TNA: FO 64/31, nos. 9, 10; Stanhope, *Mystic*, 286, 292–96.
59. Malmesbury to Grenville and Pitt, 9 January 1794, in HMC, *Dropmore*, 2:492–95.
60. Malmesbury to Grenville and Pitt, 9 January 1794, in HMC, 2:492–95; Sherwig, *Guineas and Gunpowder*, 34–36.
61. Grenville to Eden, 7 January 1794, in TNA: FO 7/36, no. 3; Mori, *William Pitt*, 164.
62. Grenville to Auckland, 16 January 1794, in Auckland, *Journal and Correspondence*, 3:169.
63. The Dutch agreed to forfeit the 12,000 troops Prussia owed them under the Triple Alliance, leaving the 20,000 owed to Britain and 20,000 more owed to Austria. For more detail on the debates and haggling over the Prussian subsidy, see Sherwig, *Guineas and Gunpowder*. Grenville to Malmesbury, 28 January 1794, in TNA: FO 64/31; Grenville to Malmesbury, 17 January 1794, in HMC, *Dropmore*, 2:496–97; Sherwig, *Guineas and Gunpowder*, 37.
64. Grenville to Eden, 18 February 1794, in TNA: FO 7/36, no. 8.

65. Grenville to Eden, 4 February 1794, in TNA: FO 7/36, no. 5.
66. Jomini identified the plan's reliance on unsecured Prussian troops as one of its chief defects. Grenville to Malmesbury, 3 February 1794, in TNA: FO 64/31; Duffy, "British War Policy," 86–87; Jomini, *Histoire critique*, 5:31.
67. Grenville to Eden, 18 February 1794, in TNA: FO 7/36, no. 7; Grenville to Malmesbury, 7 March 1794, in TNA: FO 64/32, no. 9; Mori, *William Pitt*, 165.
68. Malmesbury to Grenville, 15 March 1794, in HMC, *Dropmore*, 2:533.
69. Grenville to Malmesbury, 28 March 1794, in TNA: FO 64/33; Sherwig, *Guineas and Gunpowder*, 39–40.
70. Jomini puts the Reichsarmee at a more conservative 60,000 men. Either figure remains substantially less than 110,000. Jomini, *Histoire critique*, 5:26; Roider, *Baron Thugut*, 145–46; Wilson, *Reich to Revolution*, 338–40.
71. Duffy, "British War Policy," 88–90; Wilson, *German Armies*, 298–320.
72. York to George III, 22 March 1793, in Aspinall, *Later Correspondence*, 2:187.
73. Brown, *Impartial Journal*, 94; Colonel Sir Harry Calvert to Colonel Sir Hew Dalrymple, 25 March 1794, in Calvert, *Calvert*, 181–82.
74. Jomini, *Histoire critique*, 5:36; Fortescue, *History of the British Army*, 4:226; Sybel, *French Revolution*, 3:409.
75. Grenville to Malmesbury, 14 April 1794, in TNA: FO 64/33, no. 15; Grenville to H. Elliot, 14 March 1794, in TNA: FO 37/52, no. 18; Malmesbury to Grenville, 19 April 1794, in HMC, *Dropmore*, 2:552; Duffy, "British War Policy," 87–88.
76. Treaty of The Hague, 19 April 1794, in TNA: FO 94/183, no. 3–4; Malmesbury to Grenville, 19 April 1794, in HMC, *Dropmore*, 2:552; Malmesbury to York, 19 April 1794, in Malmesbury, *Diaries and Correspondence*, 3:93; Sherwig, *Guineas and Gunpowder*, 40–45.
77. Sherwig, *Guineas and Gunpowder*, 55–56.
78. Duffy, "British War Policy," 89–90; Fortescue, *History of the British Army*, 4:252; Sybel, *French Revolution*, 3:382–94.
79. Adolphus to George III, 31 March and 8 April 1794, in Aspinall, *Later Correspondence*, 2:190, 192; Fortescue, *History of the British Army*, 4:229.
80. Roider, *Baron Thugut*, 149.
81. Fortescue, *History of the British Army*, 4:229–30; Sybel, *French Revolution* 3:409–10.
82. Calvert to Dalrymple, 18 April 1794, in Calvert, *Calvert*, 188–91.
83. Adolphus to George III, 18 and 22 April 1794, in Aspinall, *Later Correspondence*, 2:195–97; Brown, *Impartial Journal*, 119; Calvert to Dalrymple, 22 April 1794, in Calvert, *Calvert*, 192–93; Fortescue, *History of the British Army*, 4:231–35.
84. George III to Grenville, 23 April 1794, in Aspinall, *Later Correspondence*, 2:198.
85. Auckland to Grenville, 24 April 1794, in HMC, *Dropmore*, 2:557.
86. Auckland to Grenville, 24 April 1794, in HMC, 2:557.
87. York to George III, 28 April 1794, in Aspinall, *Later Correspondence*, 2:200.
88. York to George III, 29 April and 6 May 1794, and Adolphus to George III, 5 May 1794, in Aspinall, *Later Correspondence*, 2:200–203.
89. Brown, *Impartial Journal*, 121–36; Calvert, *Calvert*, 194–207; Fortescue, *History of the British Army*, 4:235–52; Sybel, *French Revolution*, 3:411–24.
90. York to George III, 16 May 1794, in Aspinall, *Later Correspondence*, 2:206–7.
91. Coburg only committed 48,000 of his men to the battle. The French lost approximately 3,000 men, while the combined army suffered 5,500 casualties, of which York's forces bore the brunt. York to Dundas, 19 May 1794, in TNA: WO 1/169, fols.

85–95; Calvert, *Calvert*, 209–13; York, Ernest, and Adolphus to George III, 19 May 1794, in Aspinall, *Later Correspondence*, 2:209–10. Fortescue, *History of the British Army*, 4:253–69; Smith, *Data Book*, 79–80; Sybel, *French Revolution*, 3:427–35.
92. Brown, *Impartial Journal*, 141.
93. Brown,, 150–53; Calvert, *Calvert*, 221–24; Fortescue, *History of the British Army*, 4:271–73.
94. York to George III, 23 May 1794, in HMC, *Dropmore*, 2:559–60.
95. York to George III, 23 May 1794, in HMC, 2:559–60.
96. Fortescue, *History of the British Army*, 4:274–75.
97. Roider, *Baron Thugut*, 152.
98. Letter from Mrs. Harcourt, 17 June 1794, in Harcourt, *Harcourt Papers*, 5:464.
99. York to Dundas, 26 and 29 May 1794, in TNA: WO 1/169, fols. 149–60, 203–6; Sybel, *French Revolution*, 3:442–47.
100. Thugut to Mercy, 30 June 1794, in HMC, *Dropmore*, 3:513–16; Thugut to Starhemberg, 23 July 1794, in Vivenot and Zeissberg, *Quellen zur Geschichte*, 4:351; Thugut to Colloredo, 21 August 1794, in Vivenot, *Vertrauliche Briefe*, 1:126; Roider, *Baron Thugut*, 158–64.
101. Cornwallis to Dundas, 5 June 1794, and York to Dundas, 6 June 1794, in TNA: WO 1/169, fols. 305–6, 317–20; Fortescue, *History of the British Army*, 4:290–91.
102. Sybel, *French Revolution*, 3:397–400.
103. Malmesbury, who returned to London on 6 May, claimed that the ministers ignored his urgings to pay the subsidy promptly because of their preoccupation with ferreting out domestic sedition. Malmesbury to Grenville, 2 June 1794, in Malmesbury, *Diaries and Correspondence*, 3:96, 99–100; Malmesbury to Grenville, 3 June 1794, in HMC, *Dropmore*, 2:565; Sherwig, *Guineas and Gunpowder*, 46–48; Wickwire and Wickwire, *Cornwallis*, 184–85.
104. Waldeck to Thugut, 2 August 1794, in Vivenot, *Vertrauliche Briefe*, 1:389.
105. Rothenberg, *Napoleon's Great Adversaries*, 40–41.
106. Debrett, *Collection*, 2: appendix, 50–52; Sybel, *French Revolution*, 3:469.
107. For thorough discussion of the French campaign in summer and autumn 1794, see Hayworth, "Evolution or Revolution"; Fortescue, *History of the British Army*, 4:283–91; Hayworth, "Revolution in Warfare?" 103–205.
108. By the standards of this memorandum, the Allies achieved some success on the tactical level, making effective use of both cavalry and artillery at Villers-en-Cauchies and Beaumont as prescribed.
109. Duffy, "British War Policy," 95–100; Fortescue, *History of the British Army*, 4:274–75.

Chapter 8

1. Précis of Correspondence between Hood and Admiral Don Juan Francisco de Lángara y Huarte, 20–24 November 1793, in TNA: HO 50/454.
2. Elliot to Dundas, 20 December 1793, in Minto, *Life and Letters*, 202–8; Ehrman, *Reluctant Transition*, 314–15.
3. Grenville to St. Helens, 30 November 1793, in TNA: FO 72/28, no. 31, fols. 335–42; Chastenet, *Godoy*, 63; Jupp, *Lord Grenville*, 159–60.
4. St. Helens to Grenville, 14 January 1794, in TNA: FO 72/33, no. 4, fols. 71–75; Duffy, *Soldiers, Sugar, and Seapower*, 41–114.
5. Grenville to St. Helens, 30 November 1793, in TNA: FO 72/28, no. 31, fols. 335–42.

6. Godoy was known as the Duke of Alcudia at this time, but he acquired so many titles during his time in power that it is more expedient to refer to him throughout this text simply as Godoy as he is more commonly known. St. Helens to Grenville, 14 January 1794, in TNA: FO 72/33, no. 4, fols. 71–75.
7. St. Helens to Grenville, 29 May 1793, in TNA: FO 72/27, Private, fols. 135–36.
8. St. Helens to Grenville, 29 May 1793.
9. Grenville to St. Helens, 1 December 1793, in TNA: FO 72/28, no. 36, fol. 357.
10. St. Helens to Grenville, 14 January 1794, in TNA: FO 72/33, no. 4, fols. 71–75.
11. St. Helens to Grenville, 14 January 1794.
12. St. Helens to Grenville, 29 May 1793, in TNA: FO 72/27, Private, fols. 135–36; Chastenet, *Godoy*, 65; Lynch, *Bourbon Spain*, 390.
13. Elliot to Dundas, 4 February 1794, in TNA: FO 20/2, no. 13; Gregory, *Ungovernable Rock*, 15–40; Simms, *Three Victories*, 556–57.
14. Rather ambitiously, the Papal Nuncio at Madrid expressed the interest of Pope Pius VI in Corsica as compensation for the loss of Avignon. This interest received no more than passing mention from St. Helens and no mention at all from Grenville. St. Helens to Grenville, 25 March 1793, in TNA: FO 72/26, no. 2; Grenville to Francis Drake, 10 July 193, in TNA: FO 28/6, no. 1; Minto, *Life and Letters*, 2:214; Ehrman, *Reluctant Transition*, 304–5; Gregory, *Ungovernable Rock*, 40–42.
15. Hood to Admiral John Gell, 11 October 1793, in NMM: AGC 4/32.
16. St. Helens to Grenville 8 November 1793, in TNA: FO 72/28, no. 49 and Private, fols. 257–60, 274–75; Ehrman, *Reluctant Transition*, 344–47.
17. Précis of Hood to Dundas, 27 October 1793, in TNA: HO 50/454.
18. Elliot to Dundas, 20 December 1793, and Sir Elliot to Lady Elliot, 10 January 1794, in Minto, *Life and Letters*, 202–10; Elliot to Auckland, 24 December 1793, in Auckland, *Journal and Correspondence*, 3:162–64; Fortescue, *History of the British Army*, 4:179–80; Gregory, *Ungovernable Rock*, 52–56.
19. St. Helens to Grenville, 14 January 1794, in TNA: FO 72/33, no. 4, fols. 71–75.
20. Elliot reported to Dundas because operations on Corsica fell under the umbrella of Dundas's role as first home secretary and subsequently war secretary. Elliot to Dundas, from the *Victory*, 21 December 1793, in TNA: FO 20/2, no. 7.
21. Elliot to Grenville, from Milan, 11 May 1794, in TNA: FO 20/5, no. 4.
22. Francis James Jackson to Grenville, 22 October 1794, in TNA: FO 72/35, no. 54, fols. 157–59; Ehrman, *Reluctant Transition*, 345–46; Lynch, *Bourbon Spain*, 390–91.
23. Ehrman, *Reluctant Transition*, 345; Gregory, *Ungovernable Rock*, 43–64.
24. Elliot to Dundas, Livorno, 4 February 1794, in TNA: FO 20/2, no. 13.
25. Minto, *Life and Letters*, 2:211–17; Carrillo, "Corsican Kingdom"; Gregory, *Ungovernable Rock*, 55–64.
26. Elliot to Dundas, 4 February 1794, in TNA: FO 20/2, no. 13.
27. Elliot to Dundas, from Livorno, Private, 22 February 1794, in TNA: FO 20/2.
28. Elliot was neither first nor alone in harboring these ideas. Addressing a friendly overture from the pope, William Windham wrote to Pitt on 11 October 1793, "I most sincerely wish that the views which he has opened may be found capable of being realized so as not only to procure to us commercial advantages but to place us in the situation of becoming the protectors of the Italian States and (odd as the idea may seem) the supporters, within certain limits, of the Papal power." Windham to Pitt, 11 October 1793, in BL: Add MS 37844, fols. 11–12.

29. Dundas to Elliot, 31 March 1794, in TNA: FO 20/2.
30. Draft of instructions from Grenville to Elliot, March 1794, in TNA: FO 20/5, no. 1. The draft preserved in the archives lacks a specific date but is referenced as having been sent before the subsequent letter in the following footnote, therefore it must have been sent between 1 and 10 March.
31. Grenville to Elliot, 11 March 1794, in TNA: FO 20/5, no. 2; Jupp, *Lord Grenville*, 161.
32. Grenville to Elliot, 11 March 1794; Jupp, 161.
33. Trevor to Grenville, 28 January 1794, and Grenville to Trevor, 5 March 1794, in TNA: FO 67/14, nos. 7, 3; Gregory, *Ungovernable Rock*, 154.
34. Elliot to Grenville, 11 and 12 May 1794, in TNA: FO 20/5, no. 4 and Private.
35. Elliot to Grenville, Milan, 11 May 1794, in TNA: FO 20/5, no. 4; Elliot to Dundas, Milan, 12 May 1794, Private, in TNA: FO 20/2; Gregory, *Ungovernable Rock*, 157–60.
36. Elliot to Grenville, Milan, 11 May 1794, in TNA: FO 20/5, no. 4; Trevor to Grenville, 30 April and 11 May 1794, in TNA: FO 67/14, nos. 28, 32; Roider, *Baron Thugut*, 148–52.
37. Accounts of the British military and political progress in Corsica are contained in TNA: ADM 1/392, FO 20/2, and WO 1/288, 302; Fortescue, *History of the British Army*, 4:179–99; Gregory, *Ungovernable Rock*, 65–79.
38. Elliot to Grenville, 27 August 1794, in TNA: FO 20/5, no. 6.
39. During the siege of Calvi, the future hero of Trafalgar, Horatio Nelson, lost an eye on 12 July while assaulting the town. Altogether the British fired 24,000 cannon balls during the forty-day siege.
40. Elliot to Grenville, 6 May 1794, in TNA: FO 20/5; Gregory, *Ungovernable Rock*, 79–91, 155–59; Meeks, *Revolutionary Western Mediterranean*, 113–46.
41. Francis Jackson's letters to Grenville between from September to December 1794 in TNA: FO 72/35 provide commentary on the military situation in the Pyrenees. Chastenet, *Godoy*, 66; Lynch, *Bourbon Spain*, 391–94; Ross, *European Diplomatic History*, 112.
42. St. Helens to Grenville, 14 January 1794, in TNA: FO 72/33, no. 4, fols. 71–75.
43. Grenville to Jackson, 28 March 1794, in TNA: FO 72/33, no. 4, fols. 242–43; Grenville to Eden, 28 April 1794, in TNA: FO 7/36, no. 10; Eden to Grenville, 3 July 1794, Private, in TNA: FO 245/4, fols. 402–3.
44. Jackson to Grenville, 22 October 1794, in TNA: FO 72/35, no. 54, fols. 157–59; Jupp, *Lord Grenville*, 160, 176.
45. Grenville to Eden, 26 November 1794, in TNA: FO 7/39, no. 2.
46. Biro, *German Policy*, 244; Clark, *Iron Kingdom*, 292; Jupp, *Lord Grenville*, 170; Lukowski, *Partitions of Poland*, 169; Stanhope, *Mystic*, 294–97.
47. Eden to Grenville, 15 February 1794, Private, in TNA: FO 245/4, fols. 338–39.
48. Lukowski, *Partitions of Poland*, 170–71; Roider, *Baron Thugut*, 150–51.
49. Biro, *German Policy*, 1:236–42; Lukowski, *Partitions of Poland*, 172.
50. York to George III, and George III to Grenville, 23 and 25 May 1794, in HMC, *Dropmore*, 2:558–59.
51. Pitt to Grenville, 26 May 1794, in HMC, *Dropmore*, 2:558–60.
52. Ehrman, *Reluctant Transition*, 342–44; Ross, *European Diplomatic History*, 102–5.
53. Minute of Mr. Pitt in Reference to Military Operations Against France, 15 July 1794, in HMC, *Dropmore*, 2:599–600; Jupp, *Lord Grenville*, 170–71.

54. Sherwig, *Guineas and Gunpowder*, 47.
55. Cornwallis to York, 18 June 1794, in Cornwallis, *Cornwallis*, 2:248.
56. Biro, *German Policy*, 1:244–47; Jupp, *Lord Grenville*, 172.
57. Rose to Grenville, Berlin, 1 July 1794, in TNA: FO 353/18, no. 46; Eden to Grenville, 4 February 1794, in TNA: FO 245/4, no. 11, fols. 331–32; Roider, *Baron Thugut*, 140–46.
58. Paget to Grenville, 22 July 1794, in TNA: FO 353/18, no. 4.
59. Pitt to Malmesbury, 23 October 1794, in TNA: FO 97/324; Ehrman, *Reluctant Transition*, 366–67; Sherwig, *Guineas and Gunpowder*, 51–53.
60. Sherwig, *Guineas and Gunpowder*, 55–56
61. Starhemberg to Thugut, 1 April 1794, in Vivenot and Zeissberg, *Quellen zur Geschichte*, 4:175; Thugut to Mercy, 30 June 1794, in HMC, *Dropmore*, 3:513–16.
62. Roider, *Baron Thugut*, 158–64.
63. Mori, *William Pitt*, 174–98.
64. Dundas to Elliot, 11 July 1794, in NRS: GD51/1, fol. 25; Mori, *William Pitt*, 174–98.
65. Malmesbury, *Diaries and Correspondence*, 2:501–7; Minto, *Life and Letters*, 2:78–111, 157–63.
66. This shift involved some misunderstandings that nearly collapsed the whole arrangement. Portland expected to take over the Home Office, including colonial administration and direction of the war, while Pitt had intended to split the responsibilities of the Home Office, giving the title with administration of the home islands to Portland while Dundas retained control over the direction of the war and the colonies. The sticking point proved to be control over the colonies. Portland did not mind having Dundas retain responsibility for the war as a newly created war secretary, but he would not take over the Home Office unless it included the colonies. Meanwhile, Dundas had no interest in becoming war secretary unless that post included his favorite element of the Home Office (and his favorite tool for patronage), colonial administration. When Pitt insisted on giving Portland the colonies to seal the alliance, Dundas offered to resign entirely rather than take up the War Office without the colonies. Only with great difficulty and the assistance of the king did Pitt persuade Dundas to acquiesce in the new arrangement. Lovat-Fraser, *Dundas*, 59; Matheson, *Life of Henry Dundas*, 202–5.
67. This reshuffling to incorporate the Portland Whigs marked a point of transition in the continuous evolution of the structure of the British cabinet as perhaps suggested by the seeming redundancy of Dundas and Windham's positions. In simplest terms, Dundas, as war secretary, managed military policy regarding deployments and operations while Windham, as secretary at war, handled the army's administrative and organizational issues. Prior to the creation of the position of war secretary, wartime military policy had fallen under the purview of the Home Office. As Dundas had been home secretary before the rearrangement, responsibility for direction of the British war effort changed very little. On Windham's part, the responsibilities of the secretary at war remained much the same as well. However, from that post, Windham took a leading role in managing the government's dealings with the counterrevolution and generally assumed a more prominent position in contributing to government policy than had his predecessor, Sir George Yonge. Dundas to Pitt, 9 July 1794, in NRS: GD 51/1/19–40, fols. 24/1–3; Duffy, "British War Policy," 107; Matheson, *Life of Henry Dundas*, 174, 184–205; Mori, *William Pitt*, 238–44.

68. Grenville to Spencer, 19 July 1794, in TNA: FO 7/38, no. 1.
69. Grenville to Spencer, 19 July 1794.
70. Grenville to Spencer, 19 July 1794; Grenville to Spencer and T. Grenville, 25 July 1794, in TNA: FO 7/38, no. 5.
71. Grenville to Spencer and T. Grenville, 19 July 1794, in TNA: FO 7/38, no. 4.
72. Grenville to Spencer, 19 July 1794, in TNA: FO 7/38, no. 1.
73. Spencer and T. Grenville to Grenville, 12 August 1794, in TNA: FO 7/38, no. 3; T. Grenville to Grenville, 15 August 1794, in HMC, *Dropmore*, 2:618.
74. Starhemberg to Thugut, 26 August 1794, in Vivenot and Zeissberg, *Quellen zur Geschichte*, 4:403–7; Duffy, "British War Policy," 103–4; Roider, *Baron Thugut*, 164–65; Sherwig, *Guineas and Gunpowder*, 58–59.
75. Grenville to Spencer and T. Grenville, 26 August 1794, in TNA: FO 7/38, no. 4.
76. Sherwig, *Guineas and Gunpowder*, 59.
77. Grenville to Spencer and T. Grenville, 29 August 1794, in TNA: FO 7/38, no. 5.
78. Grenville to Spencer and T. Grenville, 29 August 1794; Sherwig, *Guineas and Gunpowder*, 59.
79. Minute of Mr. Pitt in Reference to Military Operations Against France, 15 July 1794, in HMC, *Dropmore*, 2:599–600; Ehrman, *Reluctant Transition*, 363–64.
80. Arguably the questions of command in Flanders and Italy differed. In the former, the numerically weaker British demanded command over the larger Austrian army, while in Italy the stronger Austrians insisted on commanding the weaker Sardinians. However, the British viewed their prospective financial support as sufficient to offset the discrepancy in physical presence. From the British perspective, the Austrians would supply an army only while the British contribution included payment for all troops involved as well as a commitment of their own forces. Vienna, naturally, viewed the matter differently. To justify his position, Thugut relied primarily on the argument that it would be politically impossible for Austria to accept a foreign commander of Austrian troops in Austrian territory (the Austrian Netherlands). The Sardinian ambassador used an identical argument to reject the Austrian demand for supreme command over Sardinian forces in Piedmont. Spencer and T. Grenville to Grenville, 15 September 1794, in TNA: FO 7/38, no. 6; Thugut to Colloredo, 14 September 1794, in Vivenot, *Vertrauliche Briefe*, 1:134; Vivenot, *Thugut, Clerfayt und Wurmser*, 604; Roider, *Baron Thugut*, 165.
81. Grenville to Spencer and T. Grenville, 14 September 1794, in TNA: FO 7/38, no. 7.
82. Spencer and T. Grenville to Grenville, 22 September and 1 October 1794, in TNA: FO 7/38, nos. 8, 9. General Ralph Abercromby, who had led a contingent of reinforcements to join York earlier in 1794, summarized the poor state of the British army concisely in a letter to Dundas in November 1794, the full text of which reads, "If we are to have another campaign, order, discipline, and confidence must be restored to this army." Abercromby to Dundas, 27 November 1794, in NLS: MS 3835, fol. 119.
83. Spencer and T. Grenville to Grenville, 7 October 1794, in TNA: FO 7/38, no. 10; Roider, *Baron Thugut*, 166; Sherwig, *Guineas and Gunpowder*, 60–61.
84. The notes on the proposal are undated and unsigned. However, the tone and handwriting strongly suggest Grenville, and it is filed between a letter of 23 October and one of 4 November. Notes on the Prussian Project delivered to Lord Malmesbury, in TNA: FO 97/324.

85. Malmesbury to Grenville, 4 November 1794, Private, in TNA: FO 97/324; Jupp, *Lord Grenville*, 173.
86. Jupp, 173; Lukowski, *Partitions of Poland*, 173–75; Stanhope, *Mystic*, 299.
87. York, Narrative of the Operations of Allied Armies, 20 November 1794, in BL: Add MS 37842.
88. Minute of Cabinet, 18 November 1794, in HMC, *Dropmore*, 2:646–47; Schama, *Patriots and Liberators*, 178–90.
89. Pitt sought York's recall because of his inexperience and poor relationship with the Prince of Orange, commander of the Dutch armies. The prime minister attributed to the former shortcoming the deterioration of discipline and confidence in the British army. Pitt to George III, 23 November 1794, in Aspinall, *Later Correspondence*, 2:271–74.
90. Much of the blame for the failure of York's attempt on Dunkirk had been attributed to a lack of naval support and therefore fell on Chatham. He similarly shared in the responsibility for the failure at Toulon. By December 1794, when Pitt made the change, the prime minister noted, "A variety of circumstances has made it impossible for [me] on full reflection not to feel (however reluctantly) that the intercourse between the Admiralty and the other departments of government cannot be satisfactorily or usefully carried on on its present footing, and that notwithstanding the objection to any change in an active department during war, some new arrangement is become indispensably necessary." Pitt to George III, 8 December 1794, in Aspinall, *Later Correspondence*, 2:278–79. For a more sympathetic treatment of John Pitt, Second Earl of Chatham, see Reiter, *Late Lord*, 24–49.
91. Grenville to Dundas, 16 September 1794, in WCL: Viscounts Melville Papers, box 8; Ehrman, *Reluctant Transition*, 373–81.
92. Windham to Dundas, 9 November 1794, in WCL: Viscounts Melville Papers, box 9.
93. Dundas to Pitt, 24 September 1794, in TNA: PRO 30/8/157.
94. Pitt to Chatham, 24 September 1794, in TNA: PRO 30/8/101, fols. 125–28; Cobban, "Channel Isles Correspondence," 47–51; Ehrman, *Reluctant Transition*, 368.
95. Pitt to Chatham, 24 September 1794, in TNA: PRO 30/8/101, fols. 125–28.
96. Moira to Dundas, 5 December 1794, in TNA: PRO 30/8/160.
97. Ehrman, *Reluctant Transition*, 368–70.
98. Pitt to George III, 18 September 1794, in Aspinall, *Later Correspondence*, 2:244.
99. Grenville to Spencer, 19 July 1794, in TNA: FO 7/38, no. 4; Ehrman, *Reluctant Transition*, 371–72.
100. Fitzgerald to Grenville, 24 September 1794, in TNA: FO 74/4.
101. Lord Grenville's Instructions to Mr. Wickham, in Wickham, *Correspondence*, 1:9–15.
102. Ehrman, *Reluctant Transition*, 372–73; Sparrow, *Secret Service*, 39–47.
103. Grenville to Eden, 26 November 1794, in TNA: FO 7/39, nos. 1, 2, 3.
104. Grenville to Eden, 26 November 1794, in TNA: FO 7/39, nos. 1, 4.
105. Grenville to Whitworth, 17 January 1794, in TNA: FO 65/26, no. 2.
106. Whitworth to Grenville, 9 May 1794, in TNA: FO 65/27, no .28; Grenville to Whitworth, 4 November 1794, in TNA: FO 65/28, no. 31; Jupp, *Lord Grenville*, 174; Sherwig, *Guineas and Gunpowder*, 69–70.
107. Grenville to Eden, 18 December 1794, in TNA: FO 7/39, no. 5.

108. Grenville to Eden, 18 December 1794; Jupp, *Lord Grenville*, 174.
109. Eden to Grenville, 18 December 1794, in TNA: FO 7/39, nos. 1–5.
110. Grenville to Eden, 13 January 1795, in TNA: FO 7/40, no. 6, fols. 23–30.
111. Grenville to Eden, 13 January 1795, in TNA: FO 7/40, nos. 7–10, fols. 23–41; Ehrman, *Reluctant Transition*, 377; Sherwig, *Guineas and Gunpowder*, 61–62
112. Roider, *Baron Thugut*, 173–74.
113. Eden to Grenville, 21 January and 14 March 1795, in TNA: FO 7/40, nos. 20, 33, fols. 44–48, 181–83; Grenville to Eden, 24 February 1795, in TNA: FO 7/40, no. 16, fols. 100–104; Duffy, "British War Policy," 147–54; Jupp, *Lord Grenville*, 179.
114. Matheson, *Life of Henry Dundas*, 190–98.

Chapter 9

1. Paget to Grenville, 20 December 1794, Private, in TNA: FO 97/324; Dwyer, "Prussian Neutrality," 355; Lukowski, *Partitions of Poland*, 175–76.
2. Atkinson, *History of Germany*, 391–95; Dwyer, "Prussian Neutrality," 355; Stanhope, *Mystic*, 302–7.
3. Biro, *German Policy*, 266–78, 314–16; Schroeder, *Transformation of European Politics*, 151–52; Sybel, *French Revolution*, 4:261–80.
4. Paget to Grenville, 30 December 1794, in TNA: FO 97/324, no. 54.
5. Paget to Grenville, 31 December 1794, in Paget, *Paget Papers*, 1:99–101.
6. Malmesbury to Grenville, 3 February 1795, in Malmesbury, *Diaries and Correspondence*, 3:232–33; Biro, *German Policy*, 326–41; Ford, *Hanover and Prussia*, 62–68; Sherwig, *Guineas and Gunpowder*, 63–64; Stanhope, *Mystic*, 307–10.
7. Aspinall, *Cabinet Council*, 217; Fry, *Dundas Despotism*, 211; Jupp, *Lord Grenville*, 180–82.
8. Pitt to Grenville, 20–28 February 1795, in HMC, *Dropmore*, 3:25–26; Ehrman, *Reluctant Transition*, 548–56.
9. Minute of Lord Grenville on the Project of a New Convention between Great Britain and Prussia, January–March 1795, in HMC, *Dropmore*, 3:26–30; Ehrman, *Reluctant Transition*, 548–49; Sherwig, *Guineas and Gunpowder*, 64–65.
10. Dundas, "Plan of Campaign," 11 February 1795, in WCL: Viscounts Melville Papers, vol. 6.
11. Minute of Lord Grenville on the Project of a New Convention between Great Britain and Prussia, January–March 1795, in HMC, *Dropmore*, 3:26–30.
12. Minute of Lord Grenville, January–March 1795, in HMC, *Dropmore*, 3:26–30.; George III to Pitt, 2 and 3 March 1795, in Aspinall, *Later Correspondence*, 2:309–10. Jupp, *Lord Grenville*, 180.
13. Sherwig, *Guineas and Gunpowder*, 65–67.
14. Correspondence of Pitt and George III, 28–29 March, in Aspinall, *Later Correspondence*, 2:323–24.
15. Correspondence of Pitt and George III, 5 and 8–9 April 1795, in Aspinall, *Later Correspondence*, 2:327, 330–31; Jupp, *Lord Grenville*, 180–82; Ross, *European Diplomatic History*, 107–9.
16. Grenville to George III, 8 April 1795, and George III to Grenville, 9 April 1795, in HMC, *Dropmore*, 3:50.
17. Biro, *German Policy*, 341–47; Ehrman, *Reluctant Transition*, 549; Sherwig, *Guineas and Gunpowder*, 67.

18. Dwyer, *Rise of Prussia*, 245; Stanhope, *Mystic*, 312.
19. Biro, *German Policy*, 265, 312; Lukowski, *Partitions of Poland*, 175–79.
20. Treaty of Peace between France and Prussia, in Debrett, *Collection*, 3(1):8–12; Biro, *German Policy*, 1:348–52; Dwyer, "Prussian Neutrality," 355–57; Ford, *Hanover and Prussia*, 69–83; Ross, *European Diplomatic History*, 111–12; Stanhope, *Mystic*, 310–12; Wilson, *German Armies*, 321–26.
21. Chastenet, *Godoy*, 66–67.
22. Hayworth, "Conquering the Natural Frontier," 257–58.
23. Biro, *German Policy*, 258–59; Ross, *European Diplomatic History*, 110; Schroeder, *Transformation of European Politics*, 151.
24. Following the Franco-Spanish Treaty of Basel, Charles IV conferred on Godoy the title, "Prince of the Peace." Treaty of Peace between the Republic of France and His Majesty the King of Spain, in Debrett, *Collection*, 3(2):27–30; Chastenet, *Godoy*, 66–68; Lynch, *Bourbon Spain*, 394–95.
25. Dwyer, "Politics of Prussian Neutrality," 356–57; Ford, *Hanover and Prussia*, 84–103.
26. Treaty between the French Republic and the Grand Duke of Tuscany, in Debrett, *Collection*, 2:19; Ross, *European Diplomatic History*, 112–13.
27. Sherwig, *Guineas and Gunpowder*, 45–54.
28. Dundas, "Plan of a Campaign, 11 February 1795, in WCL: Melville Papers, vol. 6.
29. Grenville to Wickham, 5 May 1795, in Wickham, *Correspondence*, 1:37.
30. Pitt to Chatham, 24 September 1794, in TNA: PRO 30/8/101, fols. 125–28; Ehrman, *Reluctant Transition*, 373; Sparrow, *Secret Service*, 52.
31. Wickham, *Correspondence*, 1:21–33; Ehrman, *Reluctant Transition*, 568.
32. Grenville's skepticism and persistence on the subject of Condé's army is evident in the repetition of his request for the transfer of the army in nearly every dispatch from January to April 1795, contained in TNA: FO 7/40.
33. Grenville to Eden, 17 April 1795, in TNA: FO 7/41, no. 31.
34. Grenville to Eden, 17 April 1795.
35. See the previous chapter for an explanation of these difficulties.
36. Jupp, *Lord Grenville*, 174; Lukowski, *Partitions of Poland*, 175–77; Roider, *Baron Thugut*, 170–71.
37. Accounts of the events at Den Helder remain contradictory and controversial. Most nineteenth-century French authors describe the affair as the Battle of the Texel in which a courageous charge of French cavalry supported by artillery overcame the desperate defense of the Dutch sailors in their ice-bound wooden fortresses. Their source for this appears to be Jomini, and Jomini provides no source. In contrast, Dutch sources describe a few hussars riding across the ice to negotiate an informal armistice between the two forces pending further orders. In the expectation of peace and a realignment toward the French, the remains of the Dutch government after the flight of the Stadtholder on 18 January ordered all Dutch forces to stand down and cooperate with the French on 21 January. The fleet at Den Helder received those orders the same day, making a desperate last stand two days later unlikely. Regardless of whether 23 January witnessed a dramatic French naval victory via cavalry charge or a mundane act of prudence amid political uncertainty, the day ended with the loss of the Dutch fleet as a coalition asset by virtue of the presence of French hussars on the frozen water around the ships. Jomini, *Histoire critique*, 7:171; Jonge, *Geschiedenis*, 5:192–94; Denison,

History of Cavalry, xv, 286–87; "Cabinet Minutes," in Aspinall, *Later Correspondence*, 2:300–301; Ehrman, *Reluctant Transition*, 548–50; Fortescue, *History of the British Army*, 4:295–325.

38. Whitworth to Grenville, 19 February 1795, in TNA: FO 65/29, nos. 9, 10; Defensive Alliance between Great Britain and Russia, 7(18) February 1795, in Parry, *Consolidated Treaty Series*, 52:315–26.
39. Grenville to Eden, 10 March 1795, in TNA: FO 7/40, no. 19, fols. 127–32.
40. Grenville to Whitworth, 9 March 1795, in TNA: FO 65/29, no. 4; Jupp, *Lord Grenville*, 174; Sherwig, *Guineas and Gunpowder*, 71.
41. Grenville to Eden, 24 April 1795, in TNA: FO 7/41, no. 32; Eden to Grenville, 4 and 20 May 1795, in TNA: FO 7/41, nos. 49, 57; Loan Convention with Austria, 4 May 1795, in TNA: FO 93/11/1B.
42. Defensive Alliance between Austria and Great Britain, 20 May 1795, in Parry, *Consolidated Treaty Series*, 52:399–406; Sherwig, *Guineas and Gunpowder*, 67–68.
43. Wickham to Grenville, 12 and 25 May 1795, in Wickham, *Correspondence*, 42–47, 51–54.
44. Treaty of Alliance, offensive and defensive, concluded between the Republic of France and the Republic of the Seven United Provinces, in Debrett, *Collection*, 3(1):22*–23*, 9–63; Schama, *Patriots and Liberators*, 192–210.
45. Grenville to Craufurd, 22 May 1795, in TNA: FO 29/5, no. 1.
46. Grenville to Eden, 15 May 1795, in TNA: FO 7/41, no. 34.
47. Grenville to Eden, 15 May 1795, in TNA: FO 7/41, no. 36.
48. Ehrman, *Reluctant Transition*, 584; Fortescue, *History of the British Army*, 4(1):412; Sherwig, *Guineas and Gunpowder*, 69.
49. Draft of instructions to Puisaye, 8 June 1795, in TNA: WO 1/390, fols. 217–26; Pitt to Grenville, 6 July 1795, in HMC, *Dropmore*, 3:89; Ehrman, *Reluctant Transition*, 369, 568–72.
50. Clerfayt to Francis, 20 and 24 April 1795, in Vivenot, *Thugut, Clerfayt und Wurmser*, 109–15.
51. Duffy, "British War Policy," 181–82; Roider, *Baron Thugut*, 190–92.
52. Grenville to Craufurd, 8 June 1795, Secret, and Grenville to Clerfayt, 8 June 1795, in TNA: FO 29/5.
53. Craufurd to Grenville, 16 June 1795, in TNA: FO 29/5; Craufurd to Wickham, 26 June 1795, in Wickham, *Correspondence*, 1:103–7.
54. Grenville to Artois, 19 June 1795, in TNA: FO 27/44; Louis XVIII to George III, 26 June 1795, in TNA: FO 27/45; Ehrman, *Reluctant Transition*, 581–82.
55. Pitt to Grenville, 6 July 1795, in HMC, *Dropmore*, 3:89.
56. The instructions for the various British and émigré officers involved in the expedition and Puisaye's initial reports are contained in TNA: WO 1/390, fols. 217–306.
57. Artois to Grenville, 1 July 1795, in TNA: FO 27/44.
58. Dundas to Puisaye, 23 July and 11 August 1795, in TNA: WO 1/390, fols. 323–40, 355–57; Fortescue, *History of the British Army*, 413–16.
59. Dundas to Puisaye, 23 July 1795, in TNA: WO 1/390, fols. 323–40; Draft of Instructions to Moira, 15 July 1795, in TNA: WO 1/176; Pitt to Grenville, 13 July 1795, in HMC, *Dropmore*, 3:90; York to George III and Pitt to George III, 13 July 1795, and Pitt to Moira, 19 July 1795, in Aspinall, *Later Correspondence*, 2:357–60.
60. Pitt to Artois, 15 August 1795, in TNA: FO 27/44; Ehrman, *Reluctant Transition*, 572–75.

61. Francis to Clerfayt, 30 July 1795, in Vivenot, *Thugut, Clerfayt und Wurmser*, 173–77; Roider, *Baron Thugut*, 192.
62. Grenville to Trevor, 7 July 1795, and Trevor to Grenville, 24 July 1795 in TNA: FO 67/17, nos. 10, 12.
63. Grenville to Trevor, 24 August 1795, in TNA: FO 67/18, no. 16; Jupp, *Lord Grenville*, 176–77.
64. For the deterioration of Moira's expedition, see TNA: WO 1/176, fols. 245–639; Ehrman, *Reluctant Transition*, 576–77.
65. Grenville to Macartney, 10 July 1795, Déclaration de Louis XVIII, July 1795, in TNA: FO 27/45, no. 1.
66. Atkinson, *History of Germany*, 399–400; Ehrman, *Reluctant Transition*, 582–86.
67. Eden sent the treaty to Grenville on 20 May, immediately after signing it. Grenville received it on 4 June and sent the British ratification of the treaty on 12 June. The British ratification reached Eden on 11 July, whereupon he obtained the reciprocal Austrian ratification and sent it to Grenville. This arrived on 25 July, and Grenville dispatched instructions based on the treaty then on 5 August. Eden to Grenville, 20 May and 11 July 1795, nos. 61 and 73, and Grenville to Eden, 12 June 1795, no. 37, in TNA: FO 7/41; Grenville to Eden, 5 August 1795, in TNA: FO 7/42, no. 52; Grenville to Whitworth, 5 August 1795, in TNA: FO 65/30, no. 15; Whitworth to Grenville, 25 August 1795, in TNA: FO 65/31, no. 48.
68. Whitworth to Grenville, 14 June 1795, no. 34, and Grenville to Whitworth, 23 June 1795, in TNA: FO 65/30, no. 12.
69. Interestingly, after Spain made peace with France, Grenville sent a similar (and similarly unsuccessful) request to Russia for aid in the event of an Anglo-Spanish war, proposing a secret treaty on the subject. Grenville to Whitworth, 19 September 1795, in TNA: FO 65/31.
70. Grenville to Whitworth, 5 August 1795, in TNA: FO 65/30, no. 15; Whitworth to Grenville, 28 August 1795, in TNA: FO 65/31, no. 49; Lukowski, *Partitions of Poland*, 179; Madariaga, *Russia*, 441–54.
71. Whitworth to Grenville, 29 September 1795, in TNA: FO 65/31, no. 55; Sherwig, *Guineas and Gunpowder*, 72–73; Roider, *Baron Thugut*, 196.
72. Chandler, *Campaigns of Napoleon*, 36–49.
73. Wickham, *Correspondence*, 1:161–216; Godechot, *Counter-Revolution*, 260–62.
74. Ehrman, *Reluctant Transition*, 595–98; Hochedlinger, *Austria's Wars of Emergence*, 426–27; Griffith, *Art of War of Revolutionary France*, 139–42.
75. Lukowski, *Partitions of Poland*, 177–79.
76. The most likely candidate for an additional ally appeared to be Denmark. Denmark and Sweden had been working together to promote and protect their neutral commerce, but French military successes had exacerbated differences between them. The Swedes moved increasingly toward favoring the French while the Danes preferred to favor their traditional ally, Russia, and therefore the coalition. This favor did not, however, extend to a desire to join the Triple Alliance. Whitworth to Grenville, 12 May and 30 June 1795, in TNA: FO 65/30, nos. 26, 39.

Chapter 10

1. Sherwig, *Guineas and Gunpowder*, 77–78.
2. Neely, *French Revolution*, 225–27.

3. Ehrman, *Reluctant Transition*, 589-92.
4. Matheson, *Life of Henry Dundas*, 212-14.
5. Pitt to Portland, 20 September 1795, in Rose, *Pitt and Napoleon*, 254-55.
6. Pitt to Portland, 20 September 1795.
7. "Supposing peace not to be made by this country before the next spring," Pitt, 19 September 1795, in TNA: PRO 30/8/197, fols. 3-4.
8. Grenville to Eden, 23 September 1795, in TNA: FO 7/42, no. 64, fols. 267-78.
9. Grenville to Eden, 23 September 1795; Ehrman, *Reluctant Transition*, 592-94.
10. Grenville to Eden, 9 October 1795, in TNA: FO 7/43, no. 66, fols. 14-25; Ehrman, *Reluctant Transition*, 594-95.
11. Eden to Grenville, 10 October 1795, in TNA: FO 7/43, no. 109, fols. 31-38.
12. Eden to Grenville, 10 November 1795, in TNA: FO 7/43, no. 120, fols. 117-24; Jackson to Grenville, 1 November 1795, in TNA: FO 7/43, fols. 103-7.
13. Duffy, "British War Policy," 217-18; Ehrman, *Reluctant Transition*, 598.
14. Pitt to Portland, 20 September 1795, in Rose, *Pitt and Napoleon*, 254-55; Matheson, *Life of Henry Dundas*, 216.
15. Pitt to Grenville, 3 January 1796, in HMC, *Dropmore*, 3:166; Duffy, *Soldiers, Sugar, and Seapower*, 159-266.
16. Grenville to Eden, 22 December 1795, in TNA: FO 7/43, no. 72-73, fols. 233-52.
17. Grenville to Eden, 22 December 1795; Sherwig, *Guineas and Gunpowder*, 78.
18. Whitworth to Grenville, 19 January 1796, in TNA: FO 65/33, no. 5.
19. Eden to Grenville, 22 January 1795, in TNA: FO 7/44, no. 6, fols. 20-29; Duffy, "British War Policy," 220-23.
20. Grenville to Eden, 31 January and 5 February 1796, in TNA: FO 7/44, nos. 5-9, fols. 64-105.
21. Eden to Grenville, 27 February and 2 and 5 March 1796, in TNA: FO 7/44, nos. 26-28, fols. 155-71; Ehrman, *Reluctant Transition*, 608.
22. For thorough discussion of the evolution of the natural frontiers doctrine in France, see Hayworth, "Conquering the Natural Frontier."
23. Wickham to Grenville, 28 March 1796, in TNA: FO 74/16, no. 38; Wickham, *Correspondence*, 1:269-321; Ward and Gooch, *Cambridge History*, 263-65.
24. Wickham to Grenville, 5 January, 17 March, 8 April, and 4 May 1796, in Wickham, *Correspondence*, 1:234-38, 311, 324-35, 356-58.
25. Ehrman, *Reluctant Transition*, 609-10; Mitchell, *Underground War*, 118-39.
26. The April payment was only £100,000, but the Cabinet quickly raised the agreed sum to £150,000 as the failure of the Prussian approach and peace initiative became clear. Sherwig, *Guineas and Gunpowder*, 80-81.
27. Blanning, *French Revolutionary Wars*, 150-56; Chandler, *Campaigns of Napoleon*, 53-87; Duffy, "British War Policy," 225-30; Ehrman, *Reluctant Transition*, 607-8; Gregory, *Ungovernable Rock*, 164; Rothenberg, *Art of Warfare*, 39-41.
28. Pitt to Grenville, 23 June 1796, in HMC, *Dropmore*, 3:214-15.
29. Cabinet Minute, 28 July 1796, in Aspinall, *Later Correspondence*, 2:496-97.
30. George III to Grenville, 30 July 1796, in HMC, *Dropmore*, 3:227-28; Ehrman, *Reluctant Transition*, 624-26.
31. Hammond to Grenville, 17 August 1796, in HMC, *Dropmore*, 3:235.
32. Grenville to Eden, 2 August 1796, in TNA: FO 7/46, nos. 32-33, fols. 34-39; Eden to Grenville, 13 August 1796, in TNA: FO 7/46, no. 92, fols. 69-71.

33. Duffy, "British War Policy," 232–43.
34. Blanning, *French Revolutionary Wars*, 152–53; Chandler, *Campaigns of Napoleon*, 88–98; Rothenberg, *Art of Warfare*, 40–41.
35. Thugut to Starhemberg, 10 September 1796, in HMC, *Dropmore*, 3:249; Duffy, "British War Policy," 243–47; Sherwig, *Guineas and Gunpowder*, 90.
36. Elliot to Portland, 21 and 29 September 1796, FO 20/12, nos. 122–23.
37. Jervis had replaced Admiral William Hotham in November 1795, who in turn had replaced the intractable Hood in October 1794. Gregory, *Ungovernable Rock*, 145, 64; Musteen, *Nelson's Refuge*, 15–16.
38. Western, *English Militia*, 219–24; Ehrman, *Reluctant Transition*, 611–15, 631.
39. Dundas to Admiralty Board, 28 August 1796, in TNA: WO 6/147; Duffy, *Soldiers, Sugar, and Seapower*, 267–94; Lynch, *Bourbon Spain*, 394.
40. Grenville to Eden, 3 January 1797, in TNA: FO 7/48; Clapham, *Bank of England*, 1:267–69; Ehrman, *Reluctant Transition*, 617–22, 627.
41. Negotiations with France, Grenville, 2 September 1796, in HMC, *Dropmore*, 3:239–42.
42. *Status quo ante bellum* meant using the territorial distribution prior to the war as a starting point from which to make demands based on the progress of the war. *Uti possidetis* meant using the current distribution of territorial control resulting from the war as the starting point from which to make concessions based on the notion of equivalent exchanges.
43. Negotiations with France, Grenville, 2 September 1796, in HMC, *Dropmore*, 3:239–42.
44. Ehrman, *Reluctant Transition*, 627–30.
45. Grenville to George III and George III to Grenville, 23–24 September 1796, and Malmesbury to Grenville, 14 October 1796, in HMC, *Dropmore*, 3:255–56, 259; Pitt to George III, in Aspinall, *Later Correspondence*, 2:506–7; Ehrman, *Reluctant Transition*, 636.
46. Whitworth to Grenville, 12 and 23 August and 3 September 1796, in TNA: FO 65/34, nos. 35–37.
47. British interest in retaining Corsica as a dependent kingdom had declined after 1794. After Napoleon successfully cowed the Italian mainland into submission in June, Corsica lost its value as a potential lever into Italian politics. It had also proved more of a liability than an asset as Paoli began to oppose the new British administration and Elliot struggled to navigate Corsican clan politics without his support. Grenville to Whitworth, 7 October 1796, in TNA: FO 65/34, nos. 18–20; Duffy, "British War Policy," 252–53; Gregory, *Ungovernable Rock*, 92–139.
48. Minute of Cabinet, 19 October 1796, in HMC, *Dropmore*, 3:261.
49. Rothenberg, *Napoleon's Great Adversaries*, 42–46; Sherwig, *Guineas and Gunpowder*, 83.
50. Eden to Grenville, 23 September 1796, in TNA: FO 7/46, no. 106.
51. Grenville to Malmesbury, 16 October 1796, in Malmesbury, *Diaries and Correspondence*, 3:265–66; Duffy, "British War Policy," 250–56.
52. Malmesbury to Grenville, 23 and 27 October 1796, in Malmesbury, *Diaries and Correspondence*, 3:272–83.
53. Grenville to Eden, 7 November 1796, in TNA: FO 7/47, nos. 52–53; Ehrman, *Reluctant Transition*, 645–46.

54. Chandler, *Campaigns of Napoleon*, 99–112; Rothenberg, *Napoleon's Great Adversaries*, 45–46.
55. Whitworth to Grenville, 1 and 25 December 1796, in TNA: FO 65/33, nos. 61, 68.
56. Ehrman, *Reluctant Transition*, 643–46.
57. Roider argues that Thugut proposed the measure to punish the Wittelsbachs for their failure to support the defense of the Empire. Eden to Auckland, 9 December 1796, in Auckland, *Journal and Correspondence*, 3: 367–69; Roider, *Baron Thugut*, 198–99.
58. Eden to Grenville, 26 November 1796, in TNA: FO 7/47, no. 135; Duffy, "British War Policy," 260–61.
59. Grenville to Malmesbury, 11 December 1796, in TNA: FO 27/46, nos. 11–12; Ehrman, *Reluctant Transition*, 646–47.
60. Malmesbury to Grenville, 20 December 1796, in TNA: FO 27/46, nos. 30–31; Ehrman, *Reluctant Transition*, 648–49.
61. Grenville to Eden, 10 January 1797, in TNA: FO 7/47, no. 4; Duffy, "British War Policy," 274; Ehrman, *Consuming Struggle*, 51.
62. Come, "French Threat," 179–85.
63. Malmesbury to Grenville, 20 December 1796, in HMC, *Dropmore*, 3:286–87.
64. Come, "French Threat," 179–85; Ehrman, *Reluctant Transition*, 641, 649; Emsley, *British Society*, 56–57.
65. Ahlstrom, "Captain and Chef de Brigade William Tate," 189–90; Come, "French Threat," 179–85; Ehrman, *Reluctant Transition*, 641, 649; Ehrman, *Consuming Struggle*, 5; Jones, *Last Invasion*.
66. Collectively, the financial demands of the war had reduced the Bank of England's bullion reserves from £7,000,000 in 1793 to £1,086,000 by February 1797. Sherwig, *Guineas and Gunpowder*, 86.
67. Ehrman, *Consuming Struggle*, 5.
68. George III to Pitt and Pitt to George III, 26–27 February 1797, in Aspinall, *Later Correspondence*, 2:545–47.
69. George III to Pitt and Pitt to George III, 26–27 February 1797; Ehrman, *Consuming Struggle*, 6–7.
70. George III to Pitt and Pitt to George III, 26–27 February 1797, in Aspinall, *Later Correspondence*, 2:545–47; Emsley, *British Society*, 58.
71. Ehrman, *Consuming Struggle*, 6–10.
72. George III to Pitt and Pitt to George III, 26–27 February 1797, in Aspinall, *Later Correspondence*, 2:545–47.
73. Blanning, *French Revolutionary Wars*, 174–76; Chandler, *Campaigns of Napoleon*, 113–24; Rothenberg, *Napoleon's Great Adversaries*, 46–47.
74. Vorontsov to Grenville, 9 January, 31 March, and 3 April 1797, in HMC, *Dropmore*, 3:292–93, 306, 308; Grenville to Vorontsov, 30 March 1797, in HMC, *Dropmore*, 3:306.
75. Grenville to Elgin, 2 March 1797, in HMC, *Dropmore*, 3:298; Ehrman, *Consuming Struggle*, 51–52.
76. Eden to Grenville, 8 February 1797, in TNA: FO 7/48, no. 13.
77. Eden to Grenville, 1 March 1797, in TNA: FO 7/48, no. 21; Duffy, "British War Policy," 274–76; Ehrman, *Consuming Struggle*, 50–51.
78. Grenville to Eden, 4 April 1797, in TNA: FO 7/48, no. 22.

79. Pitt to George III, 8 April 1797, in Aspinall, *Later Correspondence*, 2:559–60; Ehrman, *Consuming Struggle*, 52–53; Sherwig, *Guineas and Gunpowder*, 91.
80. Grenville to Eden, 11 April 1797, in TNA: FO 7/48, no. 23; Grenville to Eden, 11 April 1797, in TNA: FO 7/49, no. 24; Minute of Cabinet, 9 April 1797, in HMC, *Dropmore*, 3:310–11.
81. Blanning, *French Revolutionary Wars*, 177; Ehrman, *Consuming Struggle*, 54–56; Roider, *Baron Thugut*, 231–47; Rothenberg, *Napoleon's Great Adversaries*, 48.
82. Whitworth to Grenville, 3 May 1797, in TNA: FO 65/37, no. 24; Ehrman, *Consuming Struggle*, 56; Sherwig, *Guineas and Gunpowder*, 93.
83. Cabinet Minute, 22 April 1797, in Aspinall, *Later Correspondence*, 2:564–65.
84. The mutineers of the Channel Fleet demanded an increase in pay for sailors and marines, increased pensions, more and better victuals, the dismissal of abusive officers, and a royal pardon. The mutineers of the North Sea squadron demanded, in addition to the concessions made to the Channel fleet, full payment of wages in arrears, payment of an equivalent of the volunteer's bounty to men pressed into service, a more equal distribution of prize money from captured ships between officers and men, that officers ejected during the mutiny should return only with their crew's consent, and that deserters should not be punished on returning to service. Ehrman, *Consuming Struggle*, 17–28.
85. Famously, all but two of Admiral Adam Duncan's ships mutinied and joined the larger ongoing mutiny at the port, Yarmouth, after he set sail to keep watch on the Dutch fleet at the Texel. Nevertheless, Duncan obeyed his orders, keeping the Dutch contained in port by adopting an aggressive posture and frequently signaling to a supporting fleet that he did not have. He maintained this vigil for several days before a detachment from the Channel fleet arrived to reinforce him. Grenville to Vorontsov, 5 June 1797, in HMC, *Dropmore*, 3:328–29; Gill, *Naval Mutinies*, 165–91; Camperdown, *Admiral Duncan*, 95–171.
86. Coats and MacDougal, *Naval Mutinies*; Ehrman, *Consuming Struggle*, 56; Gill, *Naval Mutinies*.
87. The specific acts were the Incitement to Mutiny Act and the Certain Mutinous Crews Act, both of which became law on 6 June 1797. Pitt to George III, 2 June 1797, in Aspinall, *Later Correspondence*, 2:588; Ehrman, *Consuming Struggle*, 29.
88. York to George III, 22 May 1797, in Aspinall, *Later Correspondence*, 2:575–76; Ehrman, *Consuming Struggle*, 29–32.
89. George III to Grenville, 1 June 1797, in HMC, *Dropmore*, 3:327.
90. Pitt's memorial on the proposed negotiation, undated, in TNA: PRO 30/8/196, fols. 206–16.
91. Wickham, *Correspondence*, 2:1–68; Ehrman, *Consuming Struggle*, 57–62.
92. Ehrman, *Consuming Struggle*, 57.
93. Grenville to George III, Minute of Cabinet, George III to Pitt, and George III to Grenville, 16–17 June 1797, in HMC, *Dropmore*, 3:328–31; Baring, *Windham*, 365–68; Ehrman, *Consuming Struggle*, 57–59.
94. Adams, *Influence*, 57–60.
95. Grenville to Malmesbury, 29 June 1797, in TNA: FO 27/49, nos. 1–12; Baring, *Windham*, 368.
96. Malmesbury to Grenville, 11 July 1797, in TNA: FO 27/50, no. 4.
97. Malmesbury to Grenville, 16 July 1797, in TNA: FO 27/50, no. 9.

98. Malmesbury to Grenville, 14 August 1797, in TNA: FO 27/50, no. 22; Malmesbury to Canning, 22 August 1797, in Malmesbury, *Diaries and Correspondence*, 3:496–97; Ehrman, *Consuming Struggle*, 61–65.
99. Doyle, *French Revolution*, 325–32; Neely, *French Revolution*, 229–30.
100. Malmesbury to Pitt, 9 September 1797, and Pitt to Malmesbury, 14 September 1797, in Malmesbury, *Diaries and Correspondence*, 3:541–42, 560–61.
101. Malmesbury to Grenville, 17 September 1797, in TNA: FO 27/50, no. 37.
102. Malmesbury to Grenville, 19 September 1797, in TNA: FO 27/50, Private.
103. Malmesbury's Diary, 19 August 1797, and Malmesbury to Canning, 20 October 1797, in Malmesbury, *Diaries and Correspondence*, 3:492, 596; Pitt to Grenville, 28 August and 2 September 1797, and Pitt to George III, 6 September 1797, in HMC, *Dropmore*, 3:360, 368–69; George III to Pitt, 9 September 1797, in Rose, *Pitt and Napoleon*, 242; Ehrman, *Consuming Struggle*, 65–68; Matheson, *Life of Henry Dundas*, 228.
104. Pitt to Dundas, 25 December 1797, in WCL: Pitt Family Papers, vol. 2; Adams, *Influence*, 69.
105. Whitworth to Grenville, 8 December 1797, FO 65/38; Sherwig, *Guineas and Gunpowder*, 94.
106. Mackesy, *Statesmen at War*, 2–5
107. Mackesy, 6–9.

Conclusion

1. Auckland, 8 January 1799, in Cobbett, *Parliamentary History*, 34:202–3.
2. The familiar terminology "splendid isolation" as a descriptor for an insular British foreign policy emerged in the late-nineteenth century. Canadian MPs originally coined the phrase in reference to Britain's aversion to alliances on 16 January 1896. George Goschen borrowed the phrase for British use in February, and it thereafter gained popularity among those who viewed strong diplomatic ties to Europe as unnecessary and dangerous. Usage of the phrase to describe eighteenth-century policies is anachronistic, but it reflects an attitude of indifference toward Europe that always had its proponents throughout British history. Howard, "Splendid Isolation"; Howard, "Policy of Isolation."
3. Mori, *William Pitt*, 52–59; Rose, *National Revival*, 302–4.
4. Barnes, *George III and William Pitt*, 327–492; Ehrman, *Consuming Struggle*, 495–819; Sherwig, "Lord Grenville's Plan," 292.
5. Quoted in Webster, *British Diplomacy*, 389. Edward Ingram argues that the decisive influence on Pitt's foreign policy at this time and thus the origin of Pitt's statement of goals for the Third Coalition came from Henry Phipps, First Earl of Mulgrave, who became foreign secretary in 1805. Ingram, *In Defence of British India*, 103–16; Ingram, "Lord Mulgrave's Proposals." See also, Schneid, *Napoleon's Conquest of Europe*, 77–89.
6. Webster, *The Foreign Policy of Castlereagh*, 55; Kissinger, *World Restored*, 38.
7. Quoted in Sherwig, "Lord Grenville's Plan," 286.
8. Ingram, *In Defence of British India*, 109; Jupp, *Lord Grenville*, 212–13; Mackesy, *Statesmen at War*, 4–9; Sherwig, *Guineas and Gunpowder*, 97–115; Sherwig, "Lord Grenville's Plan," 284–93.
9. Knight, *Britain against Napoleon*, 64–5.

10. According to Aspinall, dissent within the Cabinet more often led to dropping issues entirely or a minister temporarily abstaining from the functions of office than a formal dissent. Pitt faced only four instances of a formal dissent in his twenty years as prime minister, including the two mentioned here. Aspinall, *Cabinet Council*, 217.
11. Michael Duffy addresses the question of whether British foreign policy in the 1790s reflected Pitt's or Grenville's views, challenging the predominant narrative of Grenville's ascendancy over the course of the decade. Duffy argues persuasively that Pitt consistently either reached agreement with Grenville or pressed his own views over the latter's objections. This book supports that position. While Grenville formally handled the work of the Foreign Office, the policies belonged at least equally to Pitt. Duffy, "Pitt, Grenville and the Control of British Foreign Policy," 151–77. Adams, *Influence*, 11–74; Jupp, *Lord Grenville*, 467; Mackesy, *Statesmen at War*, 4–9; Sherwig, *Guineas and Gunpowder*, 97–115; Sherwig, "Lord Grenville's Plan," 284–93.
12. Ingram, *Defence of British India*, 103–16; Kissinger, *World Restored*, 39–40; Nicolson, *Congress of Vienna*, 54–57; Webster, *Foreign Policy of Castlereagh*, 53–66.
13. Black, *British Foreign Policy*, 21–155.
14. Black, 156–255.
15. Black, 257–328; Ehrman, *Reluctant Transition*, 3–41.
16. Black, *British Foreign Policy*, 377–405; Nester, *Titan*, 67–79.
17. Ehrman, *Reluctant Transition*, 91–259; Mori, *William Pitt*, 108–42.
18. Black, *British Foreign Policy*, 406–71; Ehrman, *Reluctant Transition*, 261–383.
19. Chastenet, *Godoy*, 63; Lynch, *Bourbon Spain*, 390.
20. Duffy, "Particular Service," 529–37; Ehrman, *Reluctant Transition*, 273–74.
21. Roider, *Baron Thugut*, 137–39; Sherwig, *Guineas and Gunpowder*, 27–28.
22. Duffy, "British War Policy," 208–9; Ward and Gooch, *Cambridge History*, 236–81.
23. Ehrman, *Reluctant Transition*, 587–89.
24. Auckland, 8 January 1799, in Cobbett, *Parliamentary History*, 34:202–3.
25. Ehrman, *Consuming Struggle*, 33–68; Mackesy, *Statesmen at War*, 2–14.
26. For an explanation of Castlereagh's path to the Foreign Office, see Kissinger, *World Restored*, 29–40, and Webster, *Foreign Policy of Castlereagh*, 1–64.
27. Leggiere, *Struggle for Germany*, 1:63–65; Muir, *Defeat of Napoleon*, 220–31.
28. Leggiere, *Struggle for Germany*, 1:70–95; Nester, *Art of Diplomacy*, 308–9; Sherwig, *Guineas and Gunpowder*, 276–93; Ward and Gooch, *Cambridge History*, 392–96.
29. Castlereagh to Cathcart, 8 April 1813, in Londonderry, *Correspondence*, 355–57.
30. Leggiere, *Struggle for Germany*, 1:109; Ward and Gooch, *Cambridge History*, 399–401.
31. Leggiere, *Struggle for Germany*, 2:30–47; Nester, *Art of Diplomacy*, 310–11, 318–22; Ward and Gooch, *Cambridge History*, 402–10.
32. Kissinger, *World Restored*, 85–97; Muir, *Defeat of Napoleon*, 293–98.
33. Gates, *Napoleonic Wars*, 252–54; Leggiere, *Fall of Napoleon*, 55–62; Ward and Gooch, *Cambridge History*, 417–28.
34. Kissinger, *World Restored*, 97–106.
35. Kissinger, 104–5; Leggiere, *Fall of Napoleon*, 541–42; Nicolson, *Congress of Vienna*, 68–69.
36. Kissinger, *World Restored*, 119–27; Leggiere, *Fall of Napoleon*, 542–54.

37. Muir, *Defeat of Napoleon*, 313–21; Nicolson, *Congress of Vienna*, 80–82.
38. Nester, *Art of Diplomacy*, 339–41.
39. Nicolson, *Congress of Vienna*, 83–101; Ross, *European Diplomatic History*, 356–58.
40. Kissinger, *World Restored*, 138–43; Webster, *Foreign Policy of Castlereagh*, 325–76.
41. Nicolson, *Congress of Vienna*, 122–24.
42. Kissinger, *World Restored*, 144–74; Muir, *Defeat of Napoleon*, 334–42; Nicolson, *Congress of Vienna*, 164–81; Ross, *European Diplomatic History*, 361–64.
43. Nester, *Art of Diplomacy*, 356–58.
44. Nicolson, *Congress of Vienna*, 225–30; Muir, *Defeat of Napoleon*, 348–51.
45. Davies, *Wellington's Wars*, 214–47.
46. For an excellent discussion of the spirit of revenge among the Prussians and an account of the 1815 campaign, see both volumes of Leggiere, *Struggle for Germany*; Leggiere, *Blücher*, 405–51; Muir, *Defeat of Napoleon*, 371–73.
47. Nicolson, *Congress of Vienna*, 228–39; Ross, *European Diplomatic History*, 384–86; Simms, *Europe*, 179–80.
48. Cobbett, *Parliamentary History*, 29:71–74.

Bibliography

Archival Sources

British Library

Additional Manuscripts (Add MS)
  37842: Windham Papers. Vol. 1. Correspondence with Royal Family, 1793–1808.
  37844: Windham Papers. Vol. 3. Correspondence with the Cabinet, 1792–1807.
  35530: Hardwicke Papers. Vol. 28. Diplomatic Correspondence of Sir Robert Murray Keith.
Egerton Manuscripts (Eg MS)
  3498: Carmarthen/Leeds Papers. Correspondence of the Fifth Duke of Leeds, 1784–91. Vol. 175.
  3500: Carmarthen/Leeds Papers. Correspondence of the Fifth Duke of Leeds, 1784–88. Vol. 177.

The National Archives of the United Kingdom (TNA)

Admiralty Papers (ADM)
  1: Admiralty Department Correspondence
    391–92: Letters from Commanders-in-Chief, Mediterranean, 1793–94.
Foreign Office (FO)
  7: Austria Correspondence
    23–50: November 1790–December 1797.
  20: Corsica Correspondence
    1: Hood, Elliot, O'Hara, 01 January 1793–31 December 1793
    2: Commissioners to Toulon and Corsica, 1794.
    5: Gilbert Elliot's Italian Commission, 1794.
    12: Gilbert Elliot and Lieutenant-General De Burgh, 1796.
  26: Flanders Correspondence
    19–22: September 1792–December 1793.
  27: France Correspondence
    41–50: Diplomacy, Intelligence, and Peace Negotiations. January 1793–October 1797.
  28: Genoa Correspondence
    6: 1793.

29: Missions to Armies of German States
    1–5: January 1793–August 1795.
37: Holland Correspondence
    47–52: April 1793–June 1794.
62: Poland Correspondence
    2–5: 1786–1792.
63: Portugal Correspondence
    15–17: 1792–1793.
64: Prussia Correspondence
    11–33: January 1787–June 1794.
65: Russia Correspondence
    18–38: 1790–97.
67: Sardinia Correspondence
    11–18: January 1793–October 1795.
70: Sicily and Naples Correspondence
    6: 1793.
72: Spain Correspondence
    25–35: October 1792–December 1794.
74: Switzerland Correspondence
    4: 1794.
    16: March 1796.
93: Protocols of Treaties
    11/1B: Austrian Loan, 4 May 1794.
    46/1C: Defensive Alliance between Great Britain and Holland, 1788.
    77/1A: Treaty of Alliance between Great Britain and Portugal, 1793.
    78/2–3: Defensive Alliance with Prussia and Secret Articles, 1788.
    78/4C: Convention Regarding War with France.
94: Ratifications of Treaties
    183: Prussian Treaties, 1792–94.
    249: Treaty of Alliance with Sardinia, 1793.
    271: Treaty of Alliance with Sicily, 1793.
    284: Spanish Treaties, 1790–93.
97: Supplemental Correspondence
    59: Vienna, 1791–95.
    323–24: Prussia, 1781–95.
245: Prussia Consulate and Legation Letter Books
    4: Morton Eden, 1792–94.
353: Francis Jackson Papers
    18: Prussia, July 1792–December 1794.

Home Office (HO)
    42: Domestic Correspondence of George III
        21–23: July 1792–December 1792.
    50: Military Correspondence
        454: Precis of Mediterranean Correspondence, 1793–94.
        455: Mediterranean Military Expedition, 1793.

Privy Council (PC)
    2/137: Privy Council Register. George III, Vol. 30, May 1792–February 1793.

Public Records Office Collections (PRO)
    30/8: Chatham Papers
        101: Pitt Correspondence with Royal Family, 1783–1804.
        102: Letters to Pitt the Younger, various, undated.
        103: Letters from the King to Pitt the Younger.
        110: Auckland to Pitt, 1785–1805.
        119: Letters to Pitt, Calcharstre-Camden.
        139: Letters to Pitt, Goat-Gray.
        157: Letters to Pitt, Dundas.
        160: Letters to Pitt, Minchin-Montrose.
        195: Pitt the Younger, Notes on Foreign Affairs and Letter Books, 1785–1801.
        196–98: Pitt the Younger, miscellaneous memoranda.
        239: Army Accounts, 1779–1805.
        247: Papers relating to the Navy.
        332–34: Papers relating to France, 1784–1803.
        336: Papers relating to Holland.
    30/29/1/15: Correspondence of Second Earl Gower and First Marquis of Stafford.
War Office (WO)
    1: In-Letters and Miscellaneous Papers
        168–69: Army on the Continent, January–July 1794.
        176: Quiberon Expedition, 1795.
        288: Gibraltar, June 1794–December 1796.
        302: Corsica, 1794–97.
        389–90: Royalists in France: 1793–96.
    6/147: Secretary of State for War, Out-Letters, Admiralty, 1794–97.

National Library of Scotland (NLS)

Manuscripts (MS) 3835: Letters to Henry Dundas from Ralph Abercromby and Others, 1791–98

National Maritime Museum, Greenwich (NMM)

Miscellaneous Letters (AGC) 4/32: Papers of Admiral John Gell
Elliot Family Papers (ELL) 100: Diplomatic Correspondence, 1793–95

National Records of Scotland (NRS)

GD51/1: Melville Castle Papers, Letters and Papers on State and Public Affairs, 1752–1879

William L. Clements Library at the University of Michigan (WCL)

Pitt Family Papers
    Box 2: 1 January 1786–22 October 1795.
    Vol. 2: Letters to Henry Dundas, 1 October 1792–5 May 1805.
Viscounts Melville Papers
    Box 5: 1792.
    Box 8: May–October 1794.
    Box 9: November 1794–March 1795.
    Vol. 6: Additional Letters, 1795.

Published Primary Sources

Aspinall, Arthur, ed. *The Later Correspondence of George III*. 5 vols. Cambridge: Cambridge University Press, 1963.

Auckland, William Eden, first Baron. *The Journal and Correspondence of William Eden, Lord Auckland*. 4 vols. London: Richard Bentley, 1861.

Baring, Henry, ed. *The Diary of the Right Hon. William Windham, 1784–1810*. London: Longmans, Green, 1866.

Bartenev, Petr, ed. *Archiv kniazia Vorontsova*. 40 vols. Moscow: Tip. A. I. Mamontova, 1870–95.

Brown, Robert. *An Impartial Journal of a Detachment from the Brigade of Foot Guards*. London: John Stockdale, 1795.

Browning, Oscar, ed. *The Despatches of Earl Gower, English Ambassador at Paris from June 1790 to August 1792*. Cambridge: Cambridge University Press, 1885.

———. *The Political Memoranda of Francis Fifth Duke of Leeds*. London: Camden Society, 1884.

Buckingham and Chandos, Duke of. *Memoirs of the Court and Cabinets of George the Third*. 4 vols. London: Hurst and Blackett, 1853–55.

Calvert, Harry. *The Journals and Correspondence of General Sir Harry Calvert*. London: Hurst and Blackett, 1853.

Cobbett, William. *The Parliamentary History of England from the Earliest Period to the Year 1803*. 36 vols. London: T. C. Hansard, 1815.

Cornwallis, Charles, first Marquis. *Correspondence of Charles, First Marquis Cornwallis*. Edited by Charles Ross. 3 vols. London: John Murray, 1859.

Debrett, John. *A Collection of State Papers Relative to the War against France Now Carrying on by Great Britain and the Several Other European Powers*. 11 vols. London: John Stockdale, 1802.

———. *The Parliamentary Register: or, History of the Proceedings and Debates of the House of Commons (House of Lords)*. 45 vols. London: Debrett, 1780–96.

Dupont, Paul, ed. *Archives Parlementaires de 1787 à 1860: Recueil complet des débats législatifs et politiques des chambers françaises*. 127 vols. Paris: Librarie Administrative Paul Dupont, 1879–1913.

Fortescue, John, ed. *The Correspondence of King George the Third from 1760 to December 1783*. 6 vols. London: Macmillan, 1927.

Fox, Charles James. *Memorials and Correspondence of Charles James Fox*. Edited by Lord John Russell. 4 vols. London: Richard Bentley, 1853–57.

Godoy, Manuel de. *Memoirs of Don Manuel de Godoy, the Prince of the Peace*. Edited by J. B. D'Esmenard. 2 vols. London: Richard Bentley, 1836.

Harcourt, Edward William., ed. *The Harcourt Papers*. 14 vols. Oxford: James Parker, 1880–1905.

HMC (Historical Manuscripts Commission). *Report on the Manuscripts of J. B. Fortescue, Esq., preserved at Dropmore*. 10 vols. London: Eyre and Spottiswoode, 1892–1908.

———. *Twelfth Report, Appendix, Part IX: The Manuscripts of The Duke of Beaufort, K.G., the Earl of Donoughmore, and Others*. London: Eyre and Spottiswoode, 1891.

Keith, Robert Murray. *Memoirs and Correspondence of Sir Robert Murray Keith*. 2 vols. London: Henry Colburn, 1849.

Londonderry, Charles William Vane, Marquess of, ed. *Correspondence, Despatches, and Other Papers of Viscount Castlereagh, Second Marquess of Londonderry.* Vol. 8. London: William Shoberl, 1851.
Malmesbury, James Harris, first Earl of. *Diaries and Correspondence of James Harris, First Earl of Malmesbury.* Edited by James Harris, Third Earl of Malmesbury. 4 vols. London: Richard Bentley, 1844.
Minto, Gilbert Elliot, First Earl of. *Life and Letters of Sir Gilbert Elliot, First Earl of Minto, from 1751 to 1806.* Edited by the Countess Nina of Minto. 3 vols. London: Longmans, Green, 1874.
Morris, Gouverneur. *The Diary and Letters of Gouverneur Morris.* 2 vols. New York: Charles Scribner's Sons, 1888.
Paget, Augustus, ed. *The Paget Papers: Diplomatic and Other Correspondence of the Right Hon. Sir Arthur Paget, G.C.B.* 2 vols. London: William Heinemann, 1896.
Pallain, G. *La Mission de Talleyrand à Londres en 1792. Correspondance inédite de Talleyrand avec le Département des Affaires* Étrangères. Paris: Librarie Plon, 1889.
Pellew, G. *The Life and Correspondence of the Right Hon. Henry Addington, 1st Viscount Sidmouth.* 3 vols. London: John Murray, 1847.
Pitt, William. *Correspondence between the Rt. Hon. William Pitt and Charles Duke of Rutland.* Edited by John Duke of Rutland. London: William Blackwood and Sons, 1890.
Spiegel, Laurens Pieter van de. *Brieven en Negotiatien van Mr. L. P. Van de Spiegel, Als Raadpensionaris van Holland.* 4 vols. Amsterdam: Johannes Allart, 1803.
Vivenot, Alfred von, ed. *Thugut, Clerfayt und Wurmser.* Vienna: Wilhelm Braumüller, 1869.
———. *Vertrauliche Briefe des Freiherrn von Thugut.* 2 vols. Vienna: Wilhelm Braumüller, 1872.
Vivenot, Alfred von, and Heinrich von Zeissberg, eds. *Quellen zur Geschichte der deutschen Kaiserpolitik Oesterreichs während der Französischen Revolutionskriege, 1790–1801.* 5 vols. Vienna: Wilhelm Braumüller, 1874.
Wickham, William, ed., *The Correspondence of the Right Honourable William Wickham from the Year 1794.* 2 vols. London: Richard Bentley, 1870.

Secondary Sources

Adams, Ephraim. *The Influence of Grenville on Pitt's Foreign Policy, 1787–1798.* Washington, DC: Carnegie Institution of Washington, 1904.
Ahlstrom, John. "Captain and Chef de Brigade William Tate: South Carolina Adventurer." *South Carolina Historical Magazine* 88, no. 4 (Oct. 1987): 183–91.
Aleksandrenko, Vasiliĭ N. *Russkie Diplomaticheskie agenty v London v XVIII.* Vol. 2. Warsaw: N.p., 1897.
Anderson, Matthew S. *Britain's Discovery of Russia, 1553–1815.* New York: St. Martin's Press, 1958.
Aretin, Karl Otmar Freiherr von. "Russia as a Guarantor Power of the Imperial Constitution under Catherine II." *Journal of Modern History* 58, suppl. (December 1986): S141–S160.
Armitage, David, and Mike Braddick, eds. *The British Atlantic World.* New York: Palgrave Macmillan, 2002.
Aspinall, Arthur. *The Cabinet Council, 1783–1835.* London: British Academy, 1952.

Atkinson, Christopher T. *History of Germany, 1715–1815.* London: Methuen, 1908.
Baker, William C. "Capital Ships, Commerce, and Coalition: British Strategy in the Mediterranean Theater, 1793." MA thesis, University of North Texas, 2014.
Barker, Hannah. *Newspapers, Politics, and Public Opinion in Late Eighteenth-Century England.* Oxford: Oxford University Press, 1998.
Barnes, Donald. *George III and William Pitt, 1783–1806.* New York: Octagon Books, 1973.
Barton, H. Arnold. "Gustav III of Sweden and the East Baltic, 1771–1792." *Journal of Baltic Studies* 7, no. 16 (1976): 13–30.
Baugh, Daniel. "Great Britain's 'Blue Water' Policy, 1689–1815." *International History Review* 10 (1988): 33–58.
———. "Withdrawing from Europe: Anglo-French Maritime Geopolitics, 1750–1800." *International History Review* 20, no. 1 (March 1998): 1–32.
Bernard, Paul. *Joseph II and Bavaria: Two Eighteenth Century Attempts at German Unification.* The Hague: M. Nijhoff, 1965.
Bew, John. *Castlereagh: The Biography of a Statesman.* London: Quercus, 2011.
Biro, Sydney Seymour. *The German Policy of Revolutionary France, 1792–1797.* Cambridge, MA: Harvard University Press, 1957.
Black, Jeremy. *America or Europe? British Foreign Policy, 1739–63.* London: University College London Press, 1997.
———. *British Foreign Policy in an Age of Revolutions, 1783–1793.* Cambridge: Cambridge University Press, 1994.
———. *Debating Foreign Policy in Eighteenth-Century Britain.* Burlington, UK: Ashgate, 2011.
———. *George III: America's Last King.* New Haven, CT: Yale University Press, 2006.
———. *Natural and Necessary Enemies.* Athens: University of Georgia Press, 1986.
———. *Parliament and Foreign Policy in the Eighteenth Century.* Cambridge: Cambridge University Press, 2004.
———. *A System of Ambition? British Foreign Policy 1660–1793.* 1991. Reprint, Stroud, UK: Sutton, 2000.
Blakemore, Stephen. *Burke and the Fall of Language: The French Revolution as Linguistic Event.* Hanover, NH: University Press of New England, 1988.
———. *Intertextual War: Edmund Burke and the French Revolution in the Writings of Mary Wollstonecraft, Thomas Paine, and James Mackintosh.* Cranbury, NJ: Associated University Presses, 1997.
Blanning, Timothy C.W. *The French Revolutionary Wars, 1792–1802.* New York: Oxford University Press, 1996.
———. *The Origins of the French Revolutionary Wars.* London: Longman, 1986.
———. "'That Horrid Electorate' or 'Ma Patrie Germanique'? George III, Hanover, and the Fürstenbund of 1785." *Historical Journal* 20, no. 2 (June 1977): 311–44.
Browning, Oscar. "The Triple Alliance of 1788." *Transactions of the Royal Historical Society* 2 (1885): 77–96.
Browning, Reed. *The War of the Austrian Succession.* New York: St. Martin's Press, 1993.
Camperdown, Robert Duncan, Earl of. *Admiral Duncan.* London: Longmans, Green, 1898.
Carrillo, Elisa. "The Corsican Kingdom of George III." *Journal of Modern History* 34, no. 3 (Sept. 1962): 254–74.
Cavell, Samantha. *Midshipmen and Quarterdeck Boys in the British Navy, 1771–1831.* Woodbridge, UK: Boydell Press, 2012.

Chandler, David. *The Campaigns of Napoleon*. New York: Macmillan, 1966.
Chastenet, Jacques. *Godoy: Master of Spain, 1792–1808*. Translated by J. F. Huntington. Port Washington, NY: Kennikat Press, 1972.
Christie, Ian. *Wars and Revolutions: Britain, 1760–1815*. Cambridge, MA: Harvard University Press, 1982.
Clapham, John. *The Bank of England: A History*. Vol. 1. Cambridge: Cambridge University Press, 1966.
Clark, Christopher. *Iron Kingdom: The Rise and Downfall of Prussia, 1600–1947*. Cambridge, MA: Harvard University Press, 2006.
Coats, Ann Veronica, and Philip MacDougal, eds. *The Naval Mutinies of 1797: Unity and Perseverance*. Woodbridge, UK: Boydell Press, 2011.
Cobban, Alfred. *Ambassadors and Secret Agents: The Diplomacy of the First Earl of Malmesbury at The Hague*. London: Cape, 1954.
———. "The Beginning of the Channel Isles Correspondence, 1789–1794." *English Historical Review* 77, no. 302 (Jan. 1962): 38–52.
Colley, Linda. *Britons: Forging the Nation, 1707–1837*. 1992. Reprint, New Haven, CT: Yale University Press, 2005.
Come, Donald. "French Threat to British Shores, 1793–1798." *Military Affairs* 16, no. 4 (Winter 1952): 174–88
Cone, Carl. "Richard Price and Pitt's Sinking Fund of 1786." *Economic History Review*, n.s., 14, no. 2 (1951): 243–51
Conway, Stephen. *Britain, Ireland, and Continental Europe in the Eighteenth Century: Similarities, Connections, Identities*. Oxford: Oxford University Press, 2011.
———. "Continental Connections: Britain and Europe in the Eighteenth Century." *History* 90, no. 299 (June 2005): 353–74
Cowie, Leonard. *Hanoverian England, 1714–1837*. New York: Humanities Press, 1967.
Craig, Gordon. "Problems of Coalition Warfare: The Military Alliance against Napoleon, 1813–14." In *War, Politics, and Diplomacy: Selected Essays by Gordon Craig*. New York: Frederick A. Praeger, 1966.
Cunningham, Allan. "The Oczakov Debate." *Middle Eastern Studies* 1, no. 3 (Apr. 1965): 209–37.
Davies, Huw. *Wellington's Wars: The Making of a Military Genius*. New Haven, CT: Yale University Press, 2012.
Dawson, Frank Griffith. "William Pitt's Settlement at Black River on the Mosquito Shore: A Challenge to Spain in Central America, 1732–87." *Hispanic American Historical Review* 63, no. 4 (Nov. 1983): 677–706.
Denison, George Taylor. *A History of Cavalry from the Earliest Times: With Lessons for the Future*. Suffolk, UK: Macmillan, 1877.
Doyle, William. *The Oxford History of the French Revolution*. Oxford: Oxford University Press, 2002.
Duffy, Michael. "British War Policy: The Austrian alliance, 1793–1801." PhD diss., Oxford University, 1971.
———. "'A Particular Service': The British Government and the Dunkirk Expedition of 1793." *English Historical Review* 91, no. 360 (July 1976): 529–54.
———. "Pitt, Grenville and the Control of British Foreign Policy in the 1790s." In *Knights Errant and True Englishmen: British Foreign Policy, 1660–1800*, edited by Jeremy Black, 151–77. Edinburgh: John Donald Publishers, 1989.

———. *Soldiers, Sugar, and Seapower: The British Expeditions to the West Indies and the War against Revolutionary France*. Oxford: Oxford University Press, 1987.

———. "William Pitt and the Origins of the Loyalist Association Movement of 1792." *Historical Journal* 39, no. 4 (Dec. 1996): 943–62.

———. "World-Wide War and British Expansion, 1793–1815." In *The Oxford History of the British Empire*, vol. 2, edited by P. J. Marshall, 184–207. Oxford: Oxford University Press, 1998.

———. *The Younger Pitt*. Harlow, UK: Pearson Education, 2000.

Dull, Jonathan. *A Diplomatic History of the American Revolution*. New Haven, CT: Yale University Press, 1985.

Dwyer, Philip. "The Politics of Prussian Neutrality, 1795–1806." *German History* 12, no. 3 (1994): 351–73.

———. *The Rise of Prussia, 1700–1830*. Harlow, UK: Pearson Education, 2000.

Eagles, Robin. *Francophilia in English Society, 1748–1815*. Basingstoke, UK: Macmillan, 2000.

Ehrman, John. *The British Government and Commercial Negotiations with Europe 1783–1793*. Cambridge: Cambridge University Press, 1962.

———. *The Younger Pitt: The Consuming Struggle*. Stanford, CA: Stanford University Press, 1996.

———. *The Younger Pitt: The Reluctant Transition*. Stanford, CA: Stanford University Press, 1983.

———. *The Younger Pitt: The Years of Acclaim*. London: Constable, 1969.

Emsley, Clive. *British Society and the French Wars, 1793–1815*. London: Macmillan, 1979.

———. *Crime and Society in England, 1750–1900*. London: Longman, 1987.

———. "The London 'Insurrection' of December 1792: Fact, Fiction, or Fantasy?" *Journal of British Studies* 17, no. 2 (Spring 1978): 66–86.

Esdaile, Charles. *Napoleon's Wars: An International History, 1803–1815*. New York: Viking, 2007.

Evans, Howard. "The Nootka Sound Controversy in Anglo-French Diplomacy—1790." *Journal of Modern History* 46, no. 4 (Dec. 1974): 609–40.

Feuchtwanger, Edgar J. *Prussia: Myth and Reality*. London: Oswald Wolff, 1970.

Ford, Guy Stanton. *Hanover and Prussia, 1795–1803: A Study in Neutrality*. New York: Columbia University Press, 1903.

Fortescue, John William. *British Statesmen of the Great War, 1793–1814: The Ford Lectures for 1911*. Oxford: Clarendon, 1911.

———. *A History of the British Army*. Vol. 4. London: Macmillan, 1899–1929.

Frey, Linda, and Marsha Frey. "'The Reign of the Charlatans Is Over': The French Revolutionary Attack on Diplomatic Practice." *Journal of Modern History* 65, no. 4 (Dec. 1993): 706–44.

Fry, Michael. *The Dundas Despotism*. Edinburgh: Edinburgh University Press, 1992.

Gates, David. *The Napoleonic Wars*. London: Arnold, 1997.

Gill, Conrad. *The Naval Mutinies of 1797*. Manchester, UK: Manchester University Press, 1913.

Ginter, Donald E. "The Loyalist Association Movement of 1792–93 and British Public Opinion." *Historical Journal* 9, no. 2 (1966): 179–90.

Godechot, Jacques. *The Counter-Revolution: Doctrine and Action, 1789–1804*. Translated by Salvator Attanasio. Princeton, NJ: Princeton University Press, 1971.

Goodwin, Albert. *The Friends of Liberty: The English Democratic Movement in the Age of the French Revolution*. Cambridge, MA: Harvard University Press, 1979.
Gould, Eliga. *The Persistence of Empire: British Political Culture in the Age of the American Revolution*. Chapel Hill: University of North Carolina Press, 2000.
Gregory, Desmond. *The Ungovernable Rock: A History of the Anglo-Corsican Kingdom and Its Role in Britain's Mediterranean Strategy during the Revolutionary War (1793–1797)*. London: Associated University Presses, 1985.
Gregory, Jeremy, and John Stevenson. *The Longman Companion to Britain in the Eighteenth Century, 1688–1820*. New York: Longman, 2000.
Griffith, Paddy. *The Art of War of Revolutionary France, 1789–1802*. London: Greenhill Books, 1998.
Hague, William. *William Pitt the Younger*. New York: Alfred A. Knopf, 2005.
Hall, Christopher. *British Strategy in the Napoleonic War, 1803–15*. Manchester, UK: Manchester University Press, 1992.
Hampson, Norman. *The Perfidy of Albion: French Perceptions of England During the French Revolution*. London: Macmillan Press, 1998.
Harding, Nick. *Hanover and the British Empire, 1700–1837*. Woodbridge, UK: Boydell Press, 2007.
Hardman, John. *Louis XVI*. New Haven, CT: Yale University Press, 1993.
Hayworth, Jordan. "Conquering the Natural Frontier: French Expansion to the Rhine River during the War of the First Coalition, 1792–1797." PhD diss., University of North Texas, 2015.
———. "Evolution or Revolution on the Battlefield? The Army of the Sambre and Meuse in 1794." *War in History* 21, no. 2 (Apr. 2014): 170–92.
———. "A Revolution in Warfare? The Army of the Sambre and Meuse and the 1794 Fleurus Campaign." MA thesis, University of North Texas, 2012.
Hibbert, Christopher. *The Days of the French Revolution*. 1980. Reprint, New York: Harper Perennial, 2002.
Hochedlinger, Michael. *Austria's Wars of Emergence: War, State and Society in the Habsburg Monarchy, 1683–1797*. New York: Longman Group, 2003.
Horn, David. *Britain and Europe in the Eighteenth Century*. Oxford: Oxford University Press, 1967.
Howard, Christopher. "The Policy of Isolation." *Historical Journal* 10, no. 1 (1967): 77–88.
———. "'Splendid Isolation.'" *History* 47, no. 159 (1962): 32–41.
Howe, Patricia Chastain. "Charles-François Dumouriez and the Revolutionizing of French Foreign Affairs in 1792." *French Historical Studies* 14, no. 3 (Spring 1986): 367–90.
Hunt, William. *Political History of England, 1760–1801*. London: Longmans, Green, 1905.
Ingram, Edward. *In Defence of British India: Great Britain and the Middle East, 1775–1842*. London: Frank Cass, 1984.
———. "Lord Mulgrave's Proposals for the Reconstruction of Europe in 1804." *Historical Journal* 19, no. 2 (Jun. 1976): 511–20.
James, William. *The Naval History of Great Britain from the Declaration of War by France in 1793 to the Accession of George IV*. 6 vols. London: Richard Bentley, 1859.
Jarrett, Derek. *Pitt the Younger*. New York: Charles Scribner's Sons, 1974.
Jenks, Timothy. *Naval Engagements: Patriotism, Cultural Politics, and the Royal Navy, 1793–1815*. Oxford: Oxford University Press, 2006.

Jomini, Antoine-Henri de. *Histoire critique et militaire des guerres de la Révolution.* 15 vols. Nouvelle Édition. Brussels: J.-B. Petit, Libraire-Éditeur, 1838.
Jones, E. H. Stuart. *The Last Invasion of Britain.* Cardiff, UK: University of Wales Press, 1950.
Jones, James R. *Britain and the World, 1649–1815.* Atlantic Highlands, NJ: Humanities Press, 1980.
Jonge, Johannes Cornelius de. *Geschiedenis van het Nederlandse zeewezen.* 2nd ed. Vol. 5. Haarlem: A. C. Kruseman, 1862.
Jupp, Peter. *Lord Grenville, 1759–1834.* Oxford: Oxford University Press, 1985.
Kissinger, Henry. *A World Restored: Metternich, Castlereagh, and the Problems of Peace, 1812–22.* 1957. Reprint, Brattleboro, VT: Echo Point Books and Media, 2013.
Klos, Felix. *Churchill on Europe: The Untold Story of Churchill's European Project.* London: I. B. Tauris, 2016.
Knight, Roger. *Britain against Napoleon: The Organization of Victory, 1793–1815.* New York: Penguin, 2013.
———. "The Royal Navy's Recovery after the Early Phase of the American Revolutionary War." In *The Aftermath of Defeat: Societies, Armed Forces, and the Challenge of Recovery,* edited by George Andreopoulos and Harold Selesky, 10–25. New Haven, CT: Yale University Press, 1994.
Koch, Hannsjoachim W. *A History of Prussia.* London: Longman Group, 1978.
Leggiere, Michael. *Blücher: Scourge of Napoleon.* Norman: Oklahoma University Press, 2014.
———. *The Fall of Napoleon: The Allied Invasion of France, 1813–1814.* Vol. 1. Cambridge: Cambridge University Press, 2007.
———. *Napoleon and the Struggle for Germany: The Franco-Prussian War of 1813.* 2 vols. Cambridge: Cambridge University Press, 2015.
Lord, Robert. *Second Partition of Poland: A Study in Diplomatic History.* Cambridge, MA: Harvard University Press, 1915.
Lovat-Fraser, J. Alexander. *Henry Dundas, Viscount Melville.* Cambridge: Cambridge University Press, 1916.
Lukowski, Jerzy. *The Partitions of Poland: 1772, 1793, 1795.* London: Longman Group, 1999.
Lynch, John. *Bourbon Spain, 1700–1808.* Cambridge: Basil Blackwell, 1989.
Mackesy, Piers. *Statesmen at War: The Strategy of Overthrow, 1798–1799.* London: Longman Group, 1974.
Macleod, Emma. *A War of Ideas: British Attitudes to the Wars against Revolutionary France, 1792–1802.* Aldershot, UK: Ashgate, 1998.
Madariaga, Isabel de. *Russia in the Age of Catherine the Great.* New Haven, CT: Yale University Press, 1981.
Marcum, James. "Semen R. Vorontsov: Minister to the Court of St. James's for Catherine II, 1785–1796." PhD diss., University of North Carolina at Chapel Hill, 1970.
———. "Vorontsov and Pitt: The Russian Assessment of a British Statesman, 1785–1792." *Rocky Mountain Social Science Journal* 10, no 2 (Apr. 1973): 50–56.
Masson, Frédéric. *Le Departement des Affaires Étrangères pendant la Révolution, 1787–1804.* Paris: Paul Ollendorff, 1903.
Matheson, Cyril. *The Life of Henry Dundas, First Viscount Melville, 1742–1811.* London: Constable, 1933.

McKay, Derek, and Hamish M. Scott. *The Rise of the Great Powers, 1648–1815.* London: Longman Group, 1983.
Meeks, Joshua. *France, Britain, and the Struggle for the Revolutionary Western Mediterranean.* London: Palgrave Macmillan, 2017.
Meulen, A. J. van der. *Studies over het Ministerie van Van de Spiegel.* Leiden, Netherlands: Firma C. Kooyker, 1905.
Middleton, Richard. *The Bells of Victory: The Pitt-Newcastle Ministry and the Conduct of the Seven Years' War, 1757–1762.* New York: Cambridge University Press, 1985.
Mitchell, Harvey. *The Underground War against Revolutionary France: The Missions of William Wickham, 1794–1800.* Oxford: Oxford University Press, 1965.
Mitchell, Leslie G. *Charles James Fox.* Oxford: Oxford University Press, 1992.
Monod, Paul. *Imperial Island: A History of Britain and Its Empire, 1660–1837.* Chichester, UK: Wiley-Blackwell, 2009.
Mori, Jennifer. "The British Government and the Bourbon Restoration: The Occupation of Toulon, 1793." *Historical Journal* 40, no. 3 (Sept. 1997): 699–719.
———. "Responses to Revolution: The November Crisis of 1792." *Historical Research* 69, no. 170 (Oct. 1996): 284–305.
———. *William Pitt and the French Revolution, 1785–1795.* Edinburgh: Keele University Press, 1997.
Morris, Marilyn. *The British Monarchy and the French Revolution.* New Haven, CT: Yale University Press, 1998.
Muir, Rory. *Britain and the Defeat of Napoleon, 1807–1815.* New Haven, CT: Yale University Press, 1996.
Musteen, Jason. *Nelson's Refuge: Gibraltar in the Age of Napoleon.* Annapolis, MD: Naval Institute Press, 2011.
Neely, Sylvia. *A Concise History of the French Revolution.* New York: Rowman and Littlefield, 2008.
Nester, William. *Napoleon and the Art of Diplomacy: How War and Hubris Determined the Rise and Fall of the French Empire.* New York: Savas Beatie, 2012.
———. *Titan: The Art of British Power in the Age of Revolution and Napoleon.* Norman: University of Oklahoma Press, 2016.
Nicolson, Harold. *The Congress of Vienna: A Study in Allied Unity: 1812–1822.* 1946. Reprint, New York: Viking Press, 1961.
Norris, John. "The Policy of the British Cabinet in the Nootka Crisis." *English Historical Review* 70, no. 277 (Oct. 1955): 562–80
Palmer, Robert R. *Twelve Who Ruled: The Year of Terror in the French Revolution.* 1941. Reprint, Princeton, NJ: Princeton University Press, 1989.
Parry, Clive, ed. *Consolidated Treaty Series.* Vols. 51–52. Dobbs Ferry, NY: Oceana Publications, 1969.
Peters, Marie. *Pitt and Popularity: The Patriot Minister and London Opinion during the Seven Years' War.* Oxford: Oxford University Press, 1980.
Phipps, Ramsey Weston. *The Armies of the First French Republic and the Marshals of Napoleon I.* Vol. 1. London: Oxford University Press, 1928.
Prest, Wilfrid. *Albion Ascendant: English History, 1660–1815.* Oxford: Oxford University Press, 1998.
Reiter, Jacqueline. *The Late Lord: The Life of John Pitt 2nd Earl of Chatham.* Barnsley, UK: Pen and Sword Books, 2017.

Roberts, James. *The Counter-Revolution in France, 1787–1830*. New York: St. Martin's Press, 1990.
Rodger, Nicholas A. M. *The Command of the Ocean: A Naval History of Britain, 1649–1815*. London: HarperCollins, 1997.
———. *The Wooden World: An Anatomy of the Georgian Navy*. Annapolis, MD: Naval Institute Press, 1986.
Roider, Karl A. *Baron Thugut and Austria's Response to the French Revolution*. Princeton, NJ: Princeton University Press, 1987.
Rose, John H. *Lord Hood and the Defence of Toulon*. Cambidge: Cambridge University Press, 1922.
———. *Pitt and Napoleon: Essays and Letters*. London: G. Bell and Sons, 1912.
———. *William Pitt and the Great War*. London: G. Bell and Sons, 1911.
———. *William Pitt and the National Revival*. London: G. Bell and Sons, 1911.
Ross, Steven. *European Diplomatic History, 1789–1815: France Against Europe*. Camden City, NY: Anchor Books, 1969.
———. *The Quest for Victory: French Military Strategy, 1792–1799*. New York: Barnes, 1976.
Rothenberg, Gunther. *The Art of Warfare in the Age of Napoleon*. Bloomington, IN: Indiana University Press, 1978.
———. *Napoleon's Great Adversaries: Archduke Charles and the Austrian Army, 1792–1814*. Bloomington: Indiana University Press, 1982.
Rowen, Herbert. *The Princes of Orange: The Stadholders of the Dutch Republic*. Cambridge: Cambridge University Press, 1988.
Schama, Simon. *Patriots and Liberators: Revolution in the Netherlands, 1780–1813*. New York: Vintage Books, 1992.
Schneid, Frederick. *Napoleon's Conquest of Europe: The War of the Third Coalition*. Westport, CT: Praeger, 2005.
———, ed. *European Armies of the French Revolution, 1789–1802*. Norman: University of Oklahoma Press, 2015.
Schroeder, Paul. *The Transformation of European Politics, 1763–1848*. Oxford: Clarendon, 1994.
Sheehan, James. *German History, 1770–1866*. Oxford: Oxford University Press, 1989.
Sherwig, John. *Guineas and Gunpowder: British Foreign Aid in the Wars with France, 1793–1815*. Cambridge, MA: Harvard University Press, 1969.
———. "Lord Grenville's Plan for a Concert of Europe, 1797–99." *Journal of Modern History* 34, no. 3 (Sept. 1962): 284–93.
Simms, Brendan. *Europe: The Struggle for Supremacy from 1453 to the Present*. New York: Basic Books, 2014.
———. *Three Victories and a Defeat: The Rise and Fall of the First British Empire, 1714–1783*. New York: Basic Books, 2007.
Simms, Brendan, and Torsten Riotte. *The Hanoverian Dimension in British History, 1714–1837*. Cambridge: Cambridge University Press, 2007.
Smith, Digby. *The Greenhill Napoleonic Wars Data Book*. London: Greenhill Books, 1998.
Sorel, Albert. *L'Europe et la Révolution Francaise*. 8 vols. Paris: Librarie Plon, 1897–1904.
Sparrow, Elizabeth. *Secret Service: British Agents in France, 1792–1815*. Woodbridge, UK: Boydell Press, 1999.

Stanhope, Earl. *Life of the Right Honourable William Pitt.* 4 vols. London: John Murray, 1861–62.
Stanhope, Gilbert. *A Mystic on the Prussian Throne: Frederick William II.* London: Mills and Boon, 1912.
Sybel, Heinrich von. *History of the French Revolution.* Translated by Walter C. Perry. 4 vols. London: John Murray, 1869.
Turnbull, Patrick. *Warren Hastings.* London: New English Library, 1975.
Turner, Michael. *Pitt the Younger: A Life.* London: Hambledon and London, 2003.
Ward, Adolphus W., and George P. Gooch. *The Cambridge History of British Foreign Policy, 1783–1815.* New York: Macmillan, 1922.
Webb, Paul. "The Rebuilding and Repair of the Fleet, 1783–1793." *Bulletin of the Institute of Historical Research* 50, no. 122 (1977): 194–209.
———. "Sea Power in the Ochakov Affair of 1791." *International History Review* 2, no. 1 (Jan. 1980): 13–33.
Webster, Charles. *British Diplomacy, 1813–15.* London: G. Bell and Sons, 1921.
———. *The Foreign Policy of Castlereagh, 1812–1815: Britain and the Reconstruction of Europe.* London: G. Bell and Sons, 1931.
Western, John R. *The English Militia in the Eighteenth Century: The Story of a Political Issue, 1660–1802.* London: Routledge and Kegan Paul, 1965.
Wickwire, Franklin, and Mary Wickwire. *Cornwallis: The Imperial Years.* Chapel Hill: University of North Carolina Press, 1980.
Wilson, Kathleen. *The Sense of the People: Politics, Culture, and Imperialism in England, 1715–1785.* Cambridge: Cambridge University Press, 1995.
Wilson, Peter. *From Reich to Revolution: German History, 1558–1806.* New York: Palgrave Macmillan, 2004.
———. *German Armies: War and German Politics, 1648–1806.* London: University College London Press, 1998.
———. *The Holy Roman Empire, 1495–1806.* London: Macmillan, 1999.
Witzleben, Arwied von. *Prinz Friedrich Josias von Coburg-Saalfeld, Herzog zu Sachsen.* Vol. 2. Berlin: Decker, 1859.

Index

Abercromby, Ralph, 287
Adair, Robert, 71
Alexander I, 244, 247–48
Algiers, 25
American War of Independence, 1–3, 8–9, 13–16, 19, 26, 30, 39, 48, 58, 223, 243, 256, 260
Antwerp, 86, 103–4, 106–7, 245–46, 257
Artois, Charles, Count of, 131, 205–6, 208, 210
Asia, 10, 26, 29, 39, 237
Auckland, Baron (William Eden), 6, 11, 27, 34–35, 69, 71, 73–75, 78–79, 84–87, 89–90, 97–98, 102, 104–7, 109–10, 151, 155, 172, 238, 243
Augereau, Pierre, 236
Austria: as alliance prospect for Britain, 5, 9, 19, 21, 25–26, 30–31, 35, 38, 50–51, 62–63, 104, 114–15, 117–18, 124, 137, 140–41, 174–91, 193–94, 198–201, 239, 244, 247, 261; Austrian army, 50, 61, 77, 84, 102–3, 105, 116–17, 121, 123, 127, 131–32, 140, 142–46, 152–60, 170, 173–76, 178–83, 187–90, 195, 199, 201–2, 204–6, 208, 210–18, 221, 225, 230–31, 241, 249, 268, 273, 276, 278–79, 280, 287; as British ally, 1, 4, 23, 202–4, 209–15, 224–25, 220, 226–28, 231–35, 243, 292; domestic politics, 54, 61, 104; foreign policy, 11–12, 21–22, 48, 50, 54, 61, 104–10, 112, 115, 125, 132, 138–41, 150, 157, 162–63, 169–70, 172–74, 177, 179–80, 183, 188, 195–96, 210, 216–19, 222–23, 236, 245, 248, 257; as French ally, 15, 17, 19–24, 37, 40–41, 43, 45, 50, 59, 240, 272; as leader of Holy Roman Empire, 74, 175; as Prussian ally, 1, 71, 74–83, 85–86, 92–97, 103, 106, 113, 136, 147–49, 151, 161, 241, 279, 281; as Russian ally, 10, 16–17, 20–22, 31, 33–34, 42–44, 51, 54–56, 59–60, 67, 209, 240, 276
Austrian Netherlands, 21, 50–51, 61, 77–78, 81–82, 84, 95, 103, 105–9, 117, 139–41, 147, 150, 158, 160, 177–79, 216–17, 232, 235, 241, 257, 268, 287
Austro-Prussian Alliance (1791), 71, 74–78, 81, 85, 92, 104, 106, 136, 147, 151, 175, 199, 242, 245, 266

balance of power, 2–4, 9, 16–17, 20–24, 42–43, 47–48, 58, 60, 67, 76, 78, 84, 95, 100, 108–9, 161, 174, 217, 232, 239, 241–42, 247–48, 250
Baltic Sea, 18–19, 28, 49, 52–53, 56, 59, 62–64, 111
Bank of England, 218, 229–33, 237
Barbados, 102, 163
Barras, Paul, 236
Barthélemy, François de, 192, 196–97, 220
Basel, Switzerland, 192–93, 197–98
Battle of Arcole, 226
Battle of Beaumont, 156
Battle of Camperdown, 237
Battle of Cape St. Vincent, 230, 237

315

316 INDEX

Battle of Castiglione, 222
Battle of Fleurus, 158, 160
Battle of Handschuhsheim, 209
Battle of Hondschoote, 115
Battle of Jemappes, 84–85
Battle of Leipzig, 245
Battle of Lodi, 221
Battle of Louvain, 103
Battle of Montenotte, 221
Battle of Neerwinden, 103
Battle of Racławice, 154
Battle of the Glorious First of June, 214
Battle of the Texel, 290
Battle of Tourcoing, 156
Battle of Tournai, 156
Battle of Valmy, 84
Battle of Villers-en-Cauchies, 155
Battle of Waterloo, 249
Battle of Wissembourg (Second), 280
Bavaria, 105, 140–41, 225–27, 272
Belgian Revolution (1789), 50–51, 61, 263
Belgium-Bavaria exchange, 21, 24, 26, 75, 95, 104–6, 108–9, 138, 140, 177, 217, 221, 226–27, 257, 272
Berlin: city of, 40, 46, 64, 70, 72, 94, 148–50, 175–76, 196, 221, 239; Prussian government, 21, 24, 30, 34, 43, 45–46, 48, 50–54, 56, 58, 60–63, 75, 93, 97, 103–4, 106, 113, 139, 141, 146, 151, 155, 170, 173, 181–83, 188–90, 192–93, 195, 198–200, 209–10, 215, 219–20, 226, 231, 248
Bessarabia (territory on the northwest coast of the Black Sea), 53, 62
Black Sea, 17, 28, 52–54, 56, 62, 64–66
Bonaparte, Napoleon, 3, 133, 210, 221–22, 226, 230–32, 236, 243–49, 294
bonds, 14, 154, 176, 179, 255
Bonnecarrére, Guillaume de, 81–82
Bourbon: Family Compact, 9, 15–17, 20, 26, 59, 67, 132, 240, 256; French royal family, 23, 76, 121, 123, 127, 129–30, 132, 135, 184, 186; Spanish royal family, 164
Bremen, port of, 199, 206, 213
Brest, France, 99, 126, 214, 228, 237
Brexit, 11

British army, 19, 34, 89, 92, 99, 103–7, 114–15, 117, 121, 126, 131–32, 142, 145, 148, 155–57, 160, 162–63, 166–67, 170, 174, 177–79, 180, 182, 184–85, 187–88, 190–91, 195–96, 199, 201, 206, 210, 213, 218, 223, 226, 233, 235, 237, 249, 270, 272, 276, 282, 286–88
British government: Cabinet, 5–6, 8, 21, 25–27, 31, 34–39, 41, 44–46, 49, 51–53, 63–64, 66–70, 74–82, 84, 86–89, 92, 94–98, 100–103, 108, 111, 113–17, 120, 123–25, 127–31, 133–34, 137–38, 140, 142, 144–45, 147–48, 151–53, 155, 158, 167–68, 170, 172, 174–78, 180–81, 183–93, 195, 199–202, 204–6, 208–12, 214–15, 217–29, 231, 233–35, 239–40, 244, 246, 261, 263, 270, 273, 278, 286, 293, 298; Cabinet meetings, 221, 223, 229; referenced as London, 1, 7, 24, 30–31, 34, 43, 45, 48–49, 60, 64, 77–79, 84, 86, 92, 95–96, 100, 108–10, 115, 120–21, 126, 128, 132–34, 138–39, 141, 148, 161–64, 172, 176–79, 181, 183, 188–89, 192–93, 199–202, 204–5, 210, 214, 218, 220–21, 222, 224–26, 233, 235, 244, 246, 272, 279
British navy, 1, 6, 8–9, 13–15, 19–21, 25–26, 28, 34, 38, 57, 59, 62, 64–66, 96, 99, 112, 126, 131–32, 140, 162–63, 167, 171, 184, 201–2, 206–7, 209, 214, 222–23, 226, 228, 230–31, 233, 235, 237, 243–44, 272, 288, 296
Brittany (region of France), 114, 170, 184, 188, 202, 204–5, 210
Brunswick Manifesto, 82, 128, 268
Brussels, 84, 121, 142–43, 145, 150–51, 155, 176, 180
Bug River, 53, 62
Burges, James Bland, 84

Calonne, Charles Alexandre de, 27
Camden, Charles Pratt, Earl of, 5, 68
Campo, Marqués Bernardo del, 164, 172
Campo Formio, Treaty of, 1, 236
Cape of Good Hope, 224, 227, 232, 235
Caribbean Sea. *See* West Indies

Carmarthen, Francis Osborne, Marquess of. *See* Leeds, Francis Osborne, Duke of
Carnot, Lazare, 236
Carteaux, Jean-François, 126
Castlereagh, Robert Stewart, Viscount, 1, 4, 10, 238–39, 244–50
casus bellum, 59
casus foederis, 47, 118, 202
Catherine II, Tsarina of Russia, 16–17, 20, 24, 28, 38, 44–45, 48–49, 51–52, 57, 61–64, 66, 69, 70–72, 78, 92, 110–11, 152, 183, 187, 200, 202, 209, 214, 218–19, 225–26, 228, 256, 258
central Europe, 23, 48, 244–45, 247
Ceylon, 224, 227, 232, 235
Chambonas, Scipion-Louis-Joseph, Marquis de, 81–82
Charleroi (fortified city), 158–59
Chatham, John Pitt, Earl of, 69, 184, 288
Chaumont, Treaty of, 247, 249
Chauvelin, Bernard-François, Marquis de, 77–78, 80–84, 86, 89–92, 98, 220
Christian August, Prince of Waldeck and Pyrmont, 158, 174, 178
Churchill, Winston, 10
Clerfayt, François de Croix von, 153, 155–56, 158, 160, 180, 204–6, 210
coalition: armies, 106–9, 115–17, 121, 126–27, 132–33, 136, 138, 142, 144–45, 149–58, 160, 171, 173–74, 181, 208, 222, 247, 282, 287; various states fighting France from 1792 to 1797, 10, 92–93, 95–96, 98, 106, 110, 112–15, 118, 120–23, 126–29, 131, 133, 136–38, 140–41, 144–45, 149, 151–54, 157, 160–62, 166–67, 171–73, 175–77, 181, 183, 186, 188–91, 193–94, 197–98, 209–14, 218–19, 231, 234, 240–43, 246, 277, 279, 290, 292
Cobenzl, Johann Philipp, Count of, 104
Coburg. *See* Frederick Josias, Prince of Saxe-Coburg-Saalfeld
Cochin, India, 224, 227, 235
collective security: as alliance system, 1–4, 8, 10, 36–37, 41–43, 48, 50, 52, 58–59, 62–65, 67, 71–73, 76, 83, 92, 94, 96, 100, 150, 161, 168–69, 171, 175, 178, 181, 190, 193, 195, 219, 240–41, 243–45; as diplomatic principle, 4, 9–11, 60, 67–68, 71, 75–76, 92, 101, 109, 115, 118, 123, 135, 149, 168, 173, 192, 211–13, 224, 241–42, 247–48
colonies, 2–3, 5, 7–9, 14, 25–26, 29, 35, 39, 42, 47, 54, 57, 59, 69, 201, 214, 220, 238, 250, 253, 261, 265, 286; colonial warfare, 8, 101–2, 109, 190, 237, 243; as indemnities, 9, 109, 138, 141, 147, 163, 215, 218, 220, 223–24, 227–28, 232, 242, 245–47, 266
commander in chief, 143, 160, 181–82, 189, 204
commerce. *See* trade
compensation. *See* indemnity
Condé (fortified city), 103, 107, 179–80, 182
Condé, Louis Joseph, Prince de, 179, 185–86, 200, 202, 205, 208, 210
congress: diplomatic system, 1, 4, 10, 238, 250; proposed during War of the First Coalition, 112–13, 118, 129, 139, 145; of Vienna, 95, 243, 246, 248–49
Convention of Reichenbach (1790), 61, 150
Cornwallis, Charles, First Marquess, 20–21, 25, 158, 181–82, 204, 261
Corsica, 165–71, 178, 198, 222–23, 225–26, 284–85, 294
counterrevolution, 10, 75, 81–82, 84, 96, 100, 117, 120, 122, 126–28, 130–32, 136–37, 145, 152, 166, 172, 178, 184–91, 199–200, 205, 208, 211–12, 220, 242, 286; armies, 123, 130–31, 145, 179–81, 185–89, 200, 202, 204–5, 208, 288, 290; Federalists, 123–25, 127, 130, 134, 169, 185, 277–78; monarchists or royalists, 114–15, 121–23, 127, 129–31, 134, 163, 181, 184–86, 188–89, 191, 199, 202–6, 210–11, 213, 218, 234–36
Craufurd, Charles, 142, 160, 202, 204–5, 280
credit, 13–15, 179, 223, 255
Crimean Crisis (1783), 16–18, 256

Danzig (Gdańsk), 28–29, 53–54, 57, 63–65, 258, 263, 281

decree of fraternity (French decrees of November 1792), 86, 88, 91–92, 98, 122, 242
Delacroix, Charles-François, 226–27, 234
Denmark, 18–20, 41, 48–49, 68, 139, 214, 216, 224, 234, 261, 292
Directory (French government), 213–14, 216, 220, 224–25, 227–28, 235
Dnieper River, 28–29, 62, 263
Dniester River, 53–54, 56, 62, 263
Drake, Francis, 169
Dugommier, Jacques François, 172
Dumouriez, Charles François du Périer, 84, 86, 97–98, 102–5
Duncan, Adam, 237, 296
Dundas, Henry: as acting foreign secretary, 196, 268; as friend and political ally of Pitt, 6–8, 11, 13, 16–17, 69, 88–89, 174, 239, 265, 277; as home secretary, 70, 76, 80, 83, 86–87, 98, 100, 102, 107, 114, 125–26, 129–30, 131, 163, 166–68, 178, 280, 284; as war secretary, 184, 190, 193–95, 199–200, 218, 234–36, 286–87
Dunkirk (fortified city), 103, 106–7, 109–10, 115–16, 123, 131, 141, 163, 178, 274, 288
Durno, James, 52–53, 56
Dutch Crisis (1787), 29–40, 44–47, 58–59, 60, 68–70, 81, 198, 240

eastern Europe, 10, 14, 16, 17, 20, 23, 29, 42–45, 48, 50, 54, 56–57, 59–73, 85, 97, 108, 140, 161, 173–74, 183, 187, 191, 199, 209, 211, 217, 241–43, 248–50
East India Company, 7, 17
East Indies, 25, 39, 147, 214
economics, 4, 11, 13–15, 24, 28–29, 53, 69, 72, 90, 92, 99–100, 102, 110–11, 114–15, 117, 120, 123–24, 188, 223, 229–30, 237, 241, 243, 249, 254. *See also* trade
Eden, Morton, 107, 110, 132, 137, 139–41, 143–44, 151–52, 172–73, 186–90, 200–204, 216–17, 219–20, 222, 226–27, 232, 292
Eden Treaty (1787), 26–28, 45

Eden, William. *See* Auckland William Eden, Baron
Elgin, Thomas Bruce, Earl of, 62
Elliot, Hugh, 48–49
Elliot, Sir Gilbert, 130–31, 134, 166–71, 177–78, 222, 270, 284, 294
émigrés, 75, 77, 82–85, 87, 102, 120–21, 123, 128, 130–31, 150, 179, 185–87, 191, 199
English Channel, 25, 84, 184, 190, 228, 230, 233, 237
Ewart, Joseph, 6, 29, 31, 34–35, 39–50, 69–70, 72

family compact. *See under* Bourbon
Fawkener, William, 70–71
First Coalition, 211, 240–41, 246; War of the, 1, 3–4, 6, 8, 11, 95, 100, 196, 236, 238, 242, 254
Fishguard invasion, 228–29
Fitzherbert, Alleyne, 51, 112
Flanders. *See* Low Countries
Fox, Charles James, 5, 14, 16–19, 28, 30, 49, 65, 67, 69–71, 79, 88–90, 122, 134–35, 177, 215, 256, 281
France: as Austrian ally, 16, 19–22, 24, 38, 41, 43, 59; as counter to Russia, 42, 56, 248–49; domestic politics, 33, 50, 83, 119–24, 137, 203, 205, 208, 219, 234, 240, 243; as Dutch ally, 22, 30–34; as enemy of First Coalition, 1, 71, 74–75, 78–82, 84–86, 88–95, 97–104, 106, 108–14, 117–18, 122–25, 127–32, 134–35, 138, 140–41, 145, 147–50, 153–54, 158, 161, 163, 167, 169–70, 172–74, 177, 179, 181, 183–84, 186–94, 197–200, 202, 209, 211–17, 220–22, 224–27, 233–34, 236, 239–40, 242–43, 255, 271–72, 279, 292; as enemy of other coalitions, 239, 244–48; foreign policy, 13, 27, 37, 45, 48–49, 76–77, 165, 259, 269; French army, 81, 84, 86, 93, 99, 102–3, 105, 115, 120, 123, 125–26, 131, 133, 156, 160, 165, 167, 169, 172, 174, 179, 186, 195, 197, 201, 203, 206, 208, 210, 214, 216–17, 221, 229–30, 277, 290; French navy, 15,

18, 21, 25, 38, 123–24, 126, 132–33, 214, 228, 233, 237; as presumed rival of Britain, 3–6, 9–10, 15, 17–19, 23, 25–26, 28, 38, 46, 60, 256; as Spanish ally, 21, 41, 58, 223, 234–35; as target for conquest, 96, 115, 138–39, 149, 163, 183, 222, 241; western France as theater of operations, 114–15, 121, 131, 184, 186–87, 189, 191, 199, 206, 210
Franche-Comté, 181, 189, 200, 202, 206
Francis II, Holy Roman Emperor, 78, 82, 104, 143, 153, 155–57, 160, 169, 173–74, 217, 246
Frankfurt Proposals, 245
Frederick II, King of Prussia, 20–22, 24–25, 29, 31–32, 150, 261
Frederick Josias, Prince of Saxe-Coburg-Saalfeld, 103–5, 107, 117, 131, 144, 153–60, 174, 178, 180, 204, 282
Frederick William II, King of Prussia, 29–34, 37, 41, 44, 46–47, 50–51, 56, 64, 66, 71, 75, 82, 94, 98, 104, 113–14, 118, 147–48, 150, 152, 154, 158, 172–73, 175–76, 178, 183, 191–93, 196–97, 210, 221, 267
Frederick William, Prince of Hohenlohe-Kirchberg, 144
French Revolution, 56, 74–76, 78–80, 83–84, 89, 177, 187, 240, 246, 250
Front, Philip de Saint Martin de, 111
Fürstenbund Crisis (1785), 24–25, 38, 45, 49, 258

Gardiner, William, 73
Genoa, 125, 165, 167, 169, 171, 188
George III, King of Great Britain, 5–7, 13, 15–19, 24–25, 32–33, 35, 38–39, 46, 49–50, 69, 74–75, 77, 85, 88, 94, 96, 102–3, 106, 141–42, 144, 148, 155, 165, 168, 170, 174, 184, 193, 195, 198, 208, 221, 229, 231, 233–36, 239, 263, 277, 280
George, Prince of Wales, 49, 69
German powers, 48, 62, 74, 78–79, 82, 85, 95, 97–98, 103–4, 113, 154, 160–61, 174, 182, 195, 241, 279
Germany. *See* Holy Roman Empire

Gibraltar, 124, 127, 132, 163, 167, 198, 223
Girondins, 124, 186
Glorious Revolution, 3, 9, 79
Godoy y Álvarez de Faria, Manuel, 164–65, 171–72, 197, 284, 290
Goltz, Wilhelm Bernhard von der, 192–93
Görtz, Count Johann Eustach von, 32, 259
Gothenburg, Sweden, 18, 20
Gower, George Granville Leveson, 38, 68, 77, 79, 81–82, 85, 268
Grafton, Augustus FitzRoy, Third Duke of, 165
Grand Alliance, 3, 149–50
Grenville, Thomas, 178, 180, 182
Grenville, William Wyndham, First Baron: as a confidant of Pitt, 6–7, 66, 98, 100, 124, 149, 239, 265, 270, 277; as a diplomatic agent, 34, 70, 260; as dissenting opinion in Cabinet, 69, 184, 193–96, 234, 236, 239, 298; as foreign secretary, 8, 11, 70–78, 80–82, 84–87, 90–98, 102, 104, 107–15, 117–18, 121–22, 128–30, 132–33, 136–41, 143–48, 151–52, 158, 163–64, 166, 168, 170, 172–76, 178–82, 184, 186–90, 198–203, 206–9, 216–27, 235, 239–40, 245–46, 250, 268, 271–72, 276, 280, 292; as home secretary, 69–70; as speaker for government in House of Lords, 88–89
Grey, Charles, 163
guarantee, 10, 15, 18, 38–40, 42–43, 46–47, 61–62, 76–77, 82, 104, 108, 118, 138, 140, 147, 150, 175–76, 179–82, 187–88, 201–2, 218–19, 227, 230, 239–40, 246, 249, 259
Guilford, Frederick North, Second Earl of, 17
Gustav III, King of Sweden, 41, 43, 48–49, 61, 262

Habsburg, Archduke Charles von, 155, 178, 225–26, 230
Habsburg, Archduke Ferdinand von, 169–70

Habsburg, Archduke Joseph von, 155
Hailes, Daniel, 52–54, 56–57, 63–64, 72–73, 262
Hammond, George, 221–23, 231–32
Hanover, 5, 9, 24, 26, 49, 102, 153, 196, 198
Harcourt, William, 184
Hardenberg, Karl August von, 193, 196–97
Harris, Sir James. *See* Malmesbury, Sir James Harris
Hastings, Warren, 45, 261
Haugwitz, Christian August Heinrich Kurt von, 153–54, 158
Hertzberg, Count Ewald Friedrich von, 40, 42–47, 50, 54–56; mediation plan, 42, 54–55
Hoche, Louis Lazare, 206
Holland. *See* Netherlands
Holy Roman Empire, 17, 23–24, 48, 74, 136, 141, 175, 181, 192, 196–97, 216, 227, 239; German mercenaries, 103, 111, 126–27, 141, 147, 196, 201, 213, 219; German princes, 24, 34, 152, 221; German states, 41, 175, 179, 181, 195, 197–98, 216–18, 224, 231, 275; Germany, 22, 26, 38, 106, 174, 180–81, 185, 195–96, 198–99, 210–19, 221, 225, 228, 230–32, 243
Hood, Samuel, 123–26, 128–34, 162, 165–67, 278, 294
Howe, Richard, First Earl, 69
Hungary, 50, 54
Hyères, Bay of, 162, 166

indemnity, compensation, 3, 21, 42, 54–55, 61–62, 75, 94–96, 98, 103–4, 106, 108–10, 121–22, 125, 132, 138–39, 146–47, 174, 196, 224–25, 227, 231–32, 253, 261, 266, 284
India, 7, 29, 47, 224, 261
Ireland, 25, 85, 228
Italian league, 168–71, 173, 175, 187–88, 222–23, 284
Italy/Italian states, 96, 111, 125, 139, 141, 143, 165–71, 173, 175, 181–82, 187–89, 197–99, 202, 211–14, 216–18, 221–28, 231–32, 234, 236, 243, 246, 279, 287, 294

Jackson, Francis James, 172, 217–18, 285
Jacobin, 79, 213, 236
Jervis, John, 163, 222–23, 230, 237, 294
Joseph II, 16, 21–25, 38, 49–50, 57, 60–61
Jourdan, Jean-Baptiste, 158–59

Kaunitz-Reitberg, Franz Wenzel, 153
Keith, Robert Murray, 61
Keller, Dorotheus Ludwig Christoph von, 105
Knoblesdorff, Alexander Friedrich von, 105
Koblenz, 179
Kościuszko, 154, 188, 281

Landrecies (fortified city), 145, 155–56, 160
Lángara, Don Juan de, 133, 166
League of Armed Neutrality (1780), 38
Lebrun-Tondu, Pierre-Henri-Hélène-Marie, 82–83, 90, 121–22
Leeds, Francis Osborne, Duke of, 6, 18–22, 25–27, 29–30, 32–35, 38–45, 47, 49–52, 57–58, 61–71, 80, 92, 240, 256–57, 261, 265
Leopold II, Holy Roman Emperor, 60–63, 74–75, 77–78
liberum veto, 29, 52
Liverpool, Robert Jenkinson, Second Earl of, 244
Livorno, 162, 166
loan: for Austria, 154, 176, 179–82, 184, 188–90, 200, 202, 217–20, 222, 228, 231–32, 235; for Britain, 223; for France, 78, 82; for Sardinia, 96
London (city), 33, 52, 57, 62, 69, 80, 82, 87, 91, 96, 98, 107, 110–12, 115, 117–18, 121, 141–43, 145, 148–49, 164–65, 172, 176, 180–82, 184, 190, 209, 212, 222, 228–31, 233, 239, 246, 276, 278, 283
Louis XIV, King, 3, 21, 23, 140, 239
Louis XVI, King, 74–75, 90, 98, 165, 197, 266
Louis XVII, King, 123, 126, 128, 130, 132, 172, 197, 205
Louis XVIII, King, 205, 208, 234, 247
Low Countries, Flanders, 78, 89, 95, 103–5, 108, 111, 114–16, 120–21, 123–24,

126–27, 131–32, 136–37, 139–43, 145, 147, 150, 152–53, 157–58, 160, 162–63, 169–77, 179, 181, 184–85, 191, 195, 201, 206, 212, 246, 273, 287
Lucchesini, Girolamo, 147
Lyon, 124, 186, 199, 202, 204, 207, 210

Maastricht, 106, 158, 175
Mack (Karl Mack von Leiberich), 105, 144–47, 151–53, 155–56, 158, 160, 174, 239, 280
Madrid: city of, 30, 58, 112, 117, 163–64, 166, 172, 186; Spanish government, 58, 78, 125, 127–28, 132, 139, 162–63, 172–73, 187, 197–98, 215
Malmesbury, Sir James Harris, 6, 11, 18, 22–25, 29–35, 39, 42, 44–46, 69–70, 95, 148–54, 158, 177–78, 182–83, 193, 195, 225–28, 235–36, 240, 250, 259–61, 281, 283, 287
Maret, Hugues-Bernard, 86
Marie Antoinette, Queen, 74, 97
Marseilles, 124, 277
mediation, 1, 10, 21, 24, 33, 37, 42–43, 47–51, 54–55, 59–61, 64, 71, 76, 85–86, 92–96, 98, 111–12, 117, 120, 196–98, 212, 219–22, 224, 231–32, 241–42, 245, 260
Mediterranean Sea, 41, 43, 96, 112–13, 123–27, 130–34, 140, 160, 162–63, 165–68, 171, 198, 214, 222–23, 225–26, 230, 235, 278
Memel, 52
Mercy-Argenteau, Florimond Claude, 107–8, 110, 142–43, 150, 176–77, 180, 210
Metternich, Franz Georg Karl von, 105–6, 274
Metternich, Klemens Wenzel von, 245, 247–48
Milan, 169–70, 189, 221, 227, 232
Moira, Francis Rawdon-Hastings, Earl of, 131, 136, 185, 206, 208, 292
Möllendorff, Richard Joachim Heinrich von, 151, 158, 169, 175–76, 192
multilateral, 23, 42, 98, 110, 112, 114, 120, 132, 136, 139, 154, 174, 190–92, 198–99, 212, 223–24, 231–32, 234, 236, 243, 250, 279; alliance, 1, 3–4, 20, 76, 94, 213, 238, 244–45, 247; guarantee, 108, 240; multilateralism, 86, 137, 166, 175, 240; security system, 37, 96, 100, 118, 162
Murray, James, 61, 94, 98, 107, 114, 124–25, 136, 145, 273
mutiny, 233, 237, 296

Naples, Kingdom of, 110, 113, 117, 124–27, 131–33, 162, 167, 169, 171, 189, 198, 216, 219, 221, 226, 276
National Assembly (French), 58, 80, 165, 208
National Convention (French), 1, 83, 86, 90, 97–98, 122, 124, 197, 210, 214, 242
Nelson, Horatio, 166, 285
Netherlands, United Provinces of the: as alliance prospect for Britain, 9, 29, 30–34, 38–42, 220, 240; as British ally, 1, 4, 46–48, 50, 57–59, 61, 63, 65, 69, 73, 77–82, 84–86, 90, 92–93, 96–99, 102–5, 114–15, 118, 136, 146, 148–49, 151–52, 154, 157, 161, 176–77, 182, 193, 195, 198–99, 241–42, 245–46, 262; domestic politics, 30–32, 51, 150, 183, 202; Dutch army, 32, 81, 99, 105, 109, 145, 150, 153, 173–74, 179, 190, 195, 249, 272–73, 276, 290; Dutch navy, 15, 21, 29, 38, 59, 124, 201, 228, 233, 237, 272, 290, 296; foreign policy, 106, 109–10, 139–41, 146–47, 149, 179, 186–87, 257, 261, 269, 279, 281; as French ally, 15, 21–25, 37, 214, 216, 219, 221, 227–28, 234–35, 243, 259–60
neutrality, 1, 8, 23, 37–38, 42, 48–49, 56, 62, 74–76, 78–84, 86, 90, 92–96, 100, 102, 106, 108, 111, 113, 115, 117, 120, 122, 125, 128, 139, 189, 196, 198, 212–13, 218–19, 222, 224, 231, 234, 241–42, 272, 292
Nice (Sardinian territory), 112, 125–27, 139, 219, 224, 235
Nolcken, Gustav Adam von, 41
Nootka Sound Crisis, 57–60
North Sea, 115, 145, 230, 233, 237, 257, 296

Ochakov: Crisis, 60, 65, 70–71, 74–76, 78–80, 83, 88–90, 95, 108, 150, 177, 241, 265; fortress or district, 53–54, 56, 62, 64, 66, 69, 71
Ottoman Empire, 16–17, 20, 28–29, 42–43, 48, 51–52, 54, 56–57, 59, 61–65, 67, 75, 108, 201, 212, 214, 224, 240, 256

Paget, Arthur, 192, 196
Paine, Thomas, 83
Paoli, Filippo Antonio Pasquale, 165–67, 294
Papacy, 222, 284
Paris, France, 34, 75, 77, 79–80, 82–83, 87, 98, 103, 105, 114, 123, 129, 145, 185–86, 192, 210–11, 226, 228, 234–36, 241, 247–49, 260, 268
Parliament, 1, 5–7, 9, 15–18, 27–28, 37, 45, 49, 57–58, 60, 65–69, 74–75, 77, 80, 87–90, 97, 100, 122, 134–35, 177, 193–95, 215–16, 229–31, 233, 236–37, 241, 263, 270; House of Commons, 7, 28, 45, 65, 67, 71, 80, 88; House of Lords, 7, 45, 69, 88, 238
partition, 23, 42, 52, 56, 64, 67, 73, 75, 78, 94–95, 97, 104, 113, 115, 136, 147, 161, 164, 191, 221, 241, 243, 248, 250, 272, 276
Partitions of Poland: First, 29, 38, 54; Second, 95, 104, 108–9, 111, 118, 147, 154, 174, 183, 199, 201, 210, 242, 281; Third, 174, 183, 188, 190, 192, 196–97, 199–200, 202, 209–11, 216–17, 243
Patriot Party (Dutch political party), 29–34, 51, 81, 98, 102, 183, 202, 259–60
Paul I, Tsar of Russia, 226, 230, 233, 236
peace, 1, 4, 9–11, 19, 23, 27, 31–32, 36, 42–43, 52–53, 56, 58, 60–65, 67, 71–72, 76, 78, 81, 84–86, 92–94, 97–98, 100–103, 106, 110, 112–13, 116, 118, 120–23, 129, 132, 134–35, 137–38, 141, 154, 165, 168, 172, 174, 179, 183, 185–87, 190–94, 196, 198–99, 202, 210–28, 231–39, 242–50, 290
Peace of Amiens, 123
Peace of Basel (Prussia), 196, 198–99, 201–2, 205, 209, 212

Peace of Basel (Spain), 197–98, 206, 212, 292
Peace of Leoben, 231–34
Peace of Paris (1783), 13, 16, 235
Peace of Utrecht (1715), 23, 235, 250
Peace of Westphalia, 22–23, 95, 250, 257
Philippe d'Auvergne, Prince de Bouillon, 184
Pichegru, Jean-Charles, 154–56, 158, 209, 220
Pitt, John. *See* Chatham, John Pitt, Earl of
Pitt, William (the Elder), 2–3, 8–9
Poland: as alliance prospect for Britain, 28–29, 43, 48, 52–57, 62–65, 68, 72–73, 93, 240–41, 263; domestic politics, 51–52, 154–55; as French ally, 20, 59; as Prussian ally, 51, 60; as target for conquest, 29, 42, 64, 67, 71, 75, 78, 94–95, 97, 104–5, 108–11, 113, 118, 140–41, 143, 147, 157–58, 161, 170, 173–77, 181, 183, 187–88, 190–91, 194, 196–97, 199–200, 202, 209–12, 216–17, 241–43, 248, 272, 276, 281
Portland, William Cavendish-Bentinck, Third Duke of, 49, 177–78, 215, 256, 286
Portugal, 93, 96, 110, 113, 117–18, 197–98, 219, 234–36, 245–46
Provence, Count of, 127–28, 130–31, 187, 189, 205, 208, 210
Prussia: as alliance prospect for Britain, 5, 9, 17, 19–22, 26, 30–31, 35–36, 38–41, 45–46, 110, 113–14, 119, 139–42, 147–52, 155, 175, 177–78, 180–83, 188, 193–95, 199, 219–22, 231–32, 239, 244–47, 261, 281, 293; as Austrian ally, 1, 71, 74–78, 81–83, 85, 92–94, 96–97, 103–6, 113, 115, 118, 136, 242, 279; as British ally, 47–52, 57, 59, 61–62, 65–67, 70, 79, 92, 98–99, 240, 262; domestic politics, 29, 150; foreign policy, 24, 29–34, 37, 42–44, 53–56, 60, 63–64, 72–73, 148, 172–73, 191–92, 196–98, 201, 205, 210, 212–13, 216, 218, 224, 241, 243, 257, 276, 281; Prussian army, 33–34, 39, 56, 64, 83, 99, 105, 141, 145, 147–54,

158, 170, 173, 175–76, 179, 182, 184, 190, 193–99, 205, 219, 249, 262, 267–68, 276, 280–82; as threat, 23, 68, 95, 104, 108–9, 141, 161, 174, 179, 187, 200, 202, 209, 211, 214, 226, 248
public opinion, 9, 80, 87–89
Puisaye, Joseph-Geneviève, Comte de, 184–86, 202, 204–6
Pyrenees (theater of operations), 125–27, 162, 166, 171–72, 197, 220

Quadruple Alliance (1814), 1, 238, 247, 249
Quosdanovich, Peter Vitus von, 209
Quiberon Expedition, 202, 205–6, 213

Reeves, John, 88
reform societies, 79–81, 83, 85, 88, 90
Regency Crisis (1788), 49–50, 66, 69
Reichsarmee, 145, 152, 175, 282
Rhine: river, 84, 160, 196, 200, 202, 208, 210, 217, 220, 224–26, 231; theater of operations, 115, 132, 140, 143, 145, 152–53, 158, 170, 173, 175–76, 179, 181–82, 186–88, 202–4, 206, 208, 211, 215, 218, 221, 249
Richmond, Charles Lennox, Third Duke of, 6, 25–26, 35, 68–69, 114, 260
Russia: as alliance prospect for Britain, 5, 17–20, 22, 26, 43–44, 63, 98, 110–12, 114, 139, 184, 187–88, 190–94, 199–201, 239, 244, 261, 292; as Austrian ally, 10, 16, 31, 33, 40, 42, 50–51, 60, 67, 152, 183, 219, 240; as British ally, 202, 209–11, 214, 217, 222, 225–26, 228, 230–32, 234, 236, 243, 247; foreign policy, 11, 28–29, 52, 55, 61, 66, 71, 76, 79, 92–94, 96, 104, 154, 190, 192, 220–21, 224, 256, 281, 292; Russian army, 26, 52, 111, 154, 183, 187–89, 202, 209, 214, 218–19, 225–26, 231, 249; Russian navy, 26, 38, 64, 201, 223, 230, 233; as threat, 1, 5, 9, 16, 21, 23, 38, 41, 45, 48, 53–54, 56, 59, 62, 64–65, 68–69, 72, 78, 95, 108–9, 157, 174, 196, 241, 248–50, 264, 271
Russo-Turkish War (1787), 33, 37, 42–43, 45, 47, 54, 60, 69, 95, 241, 271

Samogitia, 53, 263
Sardinia (Kingdom of Piedmont-Sardinia): as alliance prospect for Britain, 43, 84, 96, 110–13, 118, 198; as coalition member, 124, 167, 179, 197, 216, 219, 221, 224, 235; as prospective member of Italian league, 139, 169–71; relations with Austria, 141, 170, 181, 189, 287; Sardinian army, 111–12, 125–26, 132, 162, 189, 202, 206, 211, 214, 217, 221, 287
Savoy, 84, 112, 139, 206–7, 219, 224, 235
Saxony, 24, 248
Scheldt River, 21–22, 24, 31, 86, 97, 156, 158, 246, 257, 269
Scotland, 7, 11, 80, 86–87, 254
Second Coalition, 4, 239, 249
Second Hundred Years War, 3, 9
Sejm, 29, 52, 54, 64, 72, 258–59
Selim III, Sultan of the Ottoman Empire, 71
September Massacres, 82–83, 85, 268
Seven Years War, 2, 8, 15, 21, 40
Shelburne, William Petty, Second Earl of, 4, 16–17, 256
sinking fund, 14–15, 255
Sixth Coalition, 4, 239, 243–46, 248
Smith, Adam, 7, 13, 254
southern Europe, 187, 189, 198, 213, 219
Spain: as alliance prospect for Britain, 5, 41, 43, 49, 62, 93, 96, 110, 112, 117–18, 187, 231, 278; as coalition member, 124–25, 130, 132, 134, 139, 163, 167–69, 172–73, 175, 191, 198–99, 214, 243; foreign policy, 26, 78, 113, 128, 132, 171, 187, 197, 212–13, 216, 220, 279; as French ally, 9, 13, 15, 21, 25, 37, 221–25, 227, 234–35, 245, 256; as rival to Britain, 4, 57–59, 133, 163–66, 242–43, 292; Spanish army, 125–27, 132, 165–66, 171; Spanish navy, 15, 21, 38, 123–24, 128, 133, 162, 166, 172, 228, 230, 233, 237
Spencer, George, 178–80, 182, 184, 186
Spiegel, Laurens Pieter van de, 32, 39, 81, 105, 149–50, 259, 273
Spielmann, Anton, 104

Stadion, Johann Philipp, Graf von, 107–8, 115
Stadtholder, 29–33, 47, 79, 105, 150, 179, 183, 214, 220, 267, 290
Stafford, Granville Leveson-Gower, First Marquess of, 38, 68–69
Stanisław II, King, 72, 263
Starhemberg, Ludwig Joseph Maximilian von, 105, 107, 115, 154, 180, 184, 232
status quo ante bellum, 1, 8–10, 24, 28, 37, 42, 48, 50, 54–56, 58, 61–62, 64–67, 69, 72, 75–76, 85, 92, 95–97, 108–9, 139, 175, 219, 224, 227, 238, 240–41, 246, 294
St. Domingue, 163–64
St. Helens, Alleyne Fitzherbert, First Baron, 112–13, 127–28, 139, 163–66, 172, 276, 284
subsidy, 50, 96, 112, 147, 151–54, 158, 169, 173, 175–76, 180–83, 187, 191–96, 202, 209, 218, 239, 246, 281, 283
Sweden, 18, 20, 41, 43, 48, 51, 54, 56–57, 59, 61, 68, 76, 139, 212, 214, 216, 224, 234, 240, 292
Switzerland, 126, 139, 141, 145, 185–86, 189, 220, 234
Sydney, First Viscount (Thomas Townshend), 69

Talleyrand-Périgord, Charles Maurice de, 76, 78, 247–48
taxation, 14, 154, 230
Thermidorian Reaction, 186, 192, 197, 213, 236
Third Coalition, 4, 238, 249, 297
Thirty Years War, 23
Thorn (Toruń), 29, 54, 57, 63, 258, 281
Thugut, Baron Johann Amadeus Franz von, 104–5, 107–10, 125, 132, 140–44, 146–47, 152, 154–55, 157–58, 163, 173–77, 179–83, 185, 187–90, 200, 202, 204, 206, 208, 211, 217–20, 222–23, 225–27, 231–32, 287, 295
Thurlow, Edward Thurlow, First Baron, 5, 35, 38–40, 43, 49, 67–69
Tobago, 78, 82, 102, 163
Tory, 2, 8–9, 243

Toulon, 114, 123–34, 136–37, 145, 160, 162–66, 168–69, 171, 175, 178, 184–86, 198, 214, 235, 277–78, 288
trade, 1, 5, 8–9, 13–14, 18, 21, 25–30, 37–39, 42–43, 45, 47, 52–57, 62–65, 68, 76, 82, 89, 100–101, 110–13, 117, 120–21, 123–25, 136, 138–40, 167, 169, 171, 196, 212, 219, 225, 231, 240, 243, 255, 257–58, 261, 263, 284, 292
Trevor, John, 111, 169–70
Triple Alliance (1788), 37–38, 40, 47–54, 56–64, 66–67, 69, 71–73, 75, 78–79, 81, 85, 92, 94, 98, 110, 118, 147–49, 151, 161, 181, 193, 195, 198–99, 210, 240–41, 261–64, 281
Triple Alliance (1795), 191, 202, 209–12, 214, 216–17, 226, 236, 243, 292
Turkey. *See* Ottoman Empire
Tuscany, Grand Duchy of, 167, 171, 188, 198, 216, 222

United Provinces. *See* Netherlands
uti possidetis, 224, 294

Valenciennes (fortified city), 114, 153, 155, 179–80, 182, 268
Vendée, 121, 123–24, 130–32, 134, 136, 145, 184–85
Vendémiaire uprising, 210–11, 213, 220
Verbal Note of Merle, 104, 106
Vergennes, Charles Gravier, Comte de, 16, 27
Vienna: Austrian government, 22, 38, 59, 61, 63, 75, 77, 93, 97, 103–10, 113, 115–16, 125, 127, 131, 137–41, 144, 147, 170, 176, 178–79, 181, 187–89, 192, 194, 198–200, 204–5, 210–11, 215, 216, 218–22, 224, 226, 230–32, 241, 243, 248, 279, 287; city, 54, 62, 94, 129, 142–43, 155, 157, 172–73, 180, 182, 190, 209, 217, 225, 231, 248, 280;
Vistula River, 28–29, 53–54, 63, 263

War of the Spanish Succession, 23, 256
Warsaw: city, 72–73, 94, 154, 183, 188, 258, 262; Grand Duchy of, 245; Polish government, 29, 52–53, 55–56, 63

West Indies: territories, 18, 163, 227, 235; theater of operations, 3, 25, 102, 114, 120, 124, 126–27, 132, 136, 162–63, 214–15, 218, 220, 223, 237
western Europe, 3, 16, 20, 23, 29, 43, 50, 57, 108, 187, 214, 243, 247, 250
Whig Party, 2, 5, 7, 9, 49, 57, 66, 71, 81, 90, 177, 215, 262, 270, 281; Foxites, 14, 16, 79, 177; Portland Whigs, 80, 177–78, 184, 190, 234, 286
Whitworth, Charles, 52, 73, 95, 111, 188, 200–202, 209, 218, 225, 258, 264
Wickham, William, 185–86, 188, 199–200, 202, 210, 220, 234
Wilhelmina, Princess of Orange, 31–33, 46, 149
William Frederick, Hereditary Prince of Orange, 103, 105–6, 153, 155, 267, 288
William V, Prince of Orange, 29, 31–32, 34, 38–39, 79, 105, 149, 195, 201, 214, 220
Windham, William, 177–78, 184–85, 284, 286
Wittelsbach, 21, 227, 257, 295
Wurmser, Dagobert Sigmund von, 206, 209–11

Yarmouth, Francis Seymour-Conway, Earl of, 113–14, 118, 147, 276, 281
York, Frederick, Duke of, 102–3, 105, 107, 114–15, 117, 123, 127, 131, 142, 144–45, 153, 155–58, 160, 174, 177–80, 182, 184–85, 195, 206, 263, 276–77, 282, 287–88
Yriarte, Don Domingo d', 197

www.ingramcontent.com/pod-product-compliance
Lightning Source LLC
Chambersburg PA
CBHW020942230426
43666CB00005B/123